Flying off Course

The airline industry presents an enigma. High growth rates in recent decades have produced only marginal profitability. This book sets out to explain, in clear and simple terms, why this should be so. It provides a unique insight into the economics and marketing of international airlines.

Flying off Course has established itself over the years as the indispensable guide to the inner workings of this exciting industry. This enlarged fourth edition, largely re-written and completely updated, takes into account the sweeping changes which have affected airlines in recent years. It includes much new material on many key topics such as airline costs, 'open skies', air cargo economics, charters and new trends in airline pricing.

It also contains two exciting new chapters on the economics of the low-cost no-frills carriers and on the future prospects of the industry.

The book provides a practical insight into key aspects of airline operations, planning and marketing within the conceptual framework of economics. It is given added force by the author's hands-on former experiences as a Chairman and CEO of Olympic Airways and as a non-executive Director of South African Airways.

Rigas Doganis is a Consultant to airlines and governments, and is a non-executive director of easyJet and Hyderabad Airport. He is the author of *The Airline Business* and *The Airport Business*, also published by Routledge.

Flying off Course

Airline economics
and marketing

Fourth edition

Rigas Doganis

Routledge
Taylor & Francis Group

LONDON AND NEW YORK

First published 1985
by HarperCollins Academic
Second edition 1991
Third edition 2002
Fourth edition 2010
by Routledge
2 Park Square, Milton Park, Abingdon, Oxon OX14 4RN

Simultaneously published in the USA and Canada
by Routledge
270 Madison Avenue, New York, NY 10016

Routledge is an imprint of the Taylor & Francis Group,
an informa business

© 1985, 1991, 2002, 2010 Rigas Doganis

Typeset in Bembo by Keyword Group Ltd.
Printed and bound in Great Britain by the MPG Books Group

British Library Cataloguing in Publication Data
A catalogue record for this book is available from the British Library

Library of Congress Cataloging in Publication Data
Doganis, Rigas.
  Flying off course : airline economics and marketing /
  Rigas Doganis. – 4th ed.
  p. cm.
  Includes bibliographical references and index.
1. Aeronautics, Commercial. 2. Aeronautics, Commercial–Marketing.
3. Airlines. 4. Airlines–Marketing. I. Title.
HE9780.D64 2009
387.7'1–dc22   2009023298

ISBN 10: 0-415-44736-4 (hbk)
ISBN 10: 0-415-44737-2 (pbk)
ISBN 10: 0-203-86399-2 (ebk)

ISBN 13: 978-0-415-44736-2 (hbk)
ISBN 13: 978-0-415-44737-9 (pbk)
ISBN 13: 978-0-203-86399-2 (ebk)

Contents

Figures

Tables

Acknowledgements

The international airline industry is complex, dynamic and subject to rapid change and innovation. What is more, as a result of progressive liberalisation and deregulation, it has become inherently unstable. To understand the industry's economic and operational features one must be close to its pulse beat. In this I have been fortunate. I have been able to work both within the airline industry itself and as an academic and consultant in air transport.

In February 1995 I was lucky enough to be suddenly parachuted into Athens to be Chairman and Chief Executive of Olympic Airways, the Greek national airline. Olympic had been losing money heavily. My task was to implement a restructuring plan and turn the company round. Fourteen months later my Greek colleagues and I were able to announce that Olympic had produced its first profit for 18 years. Managing a state-owned airline was a roller coaster ride which can best be described as 'long period of crisis management interspersed by short periods of catastrophe management'.

After Olympic I spent four years in the early 2000s as a non-executive director of South African Airways, another state-owned airline, which manifested several of the same problems as Olympic. In December 2005, I became a non-executive director of easyJet, one of Europe's leading low-cost airlines. My experiences of these three airlines has enlivened and enriched my understanding of the airline business. I have learnt a great deal from colleagues and executives at Olympic, SAA and easyJet.

Over the last 30 years I have also been closely involved in the industry's problems and aspirations as a professor, researcher and consultant in air transport. I have taught many in-house air transport seminars or led executive workshops for airlines such as Aer Lingus, Cyprus Airways, Emirates, LOT, Malaysia Airlines, Royal Jordanian, SAS, Thai International, Vietnam Airlines and most notably Singapore Airlines, where I ran management short courses for twenty years. These seminars and workshops provided an open forum for frank discussions of airline trends and problems, where established truths were constantly challenged. In the process I learnt much about the airline industry. I am indebted to the countless participants from these and many other airlines who helped me gain a deeper insight into their industry. For the same reasons, I would also like to thank the numerous postgraduate students in Air Transport at the Universities of Westminster and Cranfield, many of whom now hold key positions in aviation.

In the many years of my involvement with air transport there have been so many who have influenced my thoughts that it is difficult to mention them all. But I would like to single out my former colleagues at the Department of Air Transport at Cranfield University, Dr Fariba Alamdari (now at Boeing), Professor Peter Morrell and Ian Stockman; John Balfour of Clyde and Co., Beaumont and Son; Paul Clark, formerly

Managing Director of the Air Business Academy in Toulouse; Dr Nigel Dennis from the University of Westminster; and Dr Conor Whelan, Andy Hofton, Andrew Lobbenberg, Tim Coombs and Chris Tarry. The numerous discussions I have had with them on a variety of air transport topics during the last five years have contributed significantly to the current edition. I am also indebted to Andy Hofton, Dr Conor Whelan and Alexia Doganis for helping with several of the graphs and to Airbus Industrie, who provided some key diagrams for Chapter 5.

Abbreviations

ACMI	Aircraft, crew, maintenance and insurance (type of aircraft operating lease)
AEA	Association of European Airlines
APEX	advance purchase fare
ATB	automated ticket and boarding pass
ATK	Available tonne-kilometre
BAA	British Airports Authority
CAA	Civil Aviation Authority
CAB	(US) Civil Aeronautics Board
CASK	Cost per available seat-kilometre or CASM cost per seat-mile
CRM	customer relationship management
DOC	direct operating cost
EASA	European Aviation Safety Agency
EC	European Community
ECAC	European Civil Aviation Conference
EDI	electronic data interchange
EEA	European Economic Area
EU	European Union
FAA	(US) Federal Aviation Administration
FFP	Frequent Flyer Programme
GDP	gross domestic product
GDS	global distribution system
GNP	gross national product
GTX	group promotional fare
HHI	Herfindahl-Hirschman index
IATA	International Air Transport Association
ICAO	International Civil Aviation Organisation
IFE	in-flight entertainment
IOC	indirect operating costs
IT	information technology
ITC	inclusive tour charter
ITX	individual inclusive tour fare
JAA	Joint Airworthiness Authority
JAL	Japan Airlines
JARs	Joint Airworthiness Requirements
JIT	just in time
LCCs	low-cost carriers

MAS   Malaysian Airline System
MTOW   maximum take-off weight
OPEC   Organisation of Petroleum-exporting Countries
PAL   Philippine Airlines
RASK   Revenue per available seat-kilometre or RASM – revenue per seat-mile
RPK   revenue passenger-kilometre
SAS   Scandinavian Airlines System
SIA   Singapore International Airlines
SITC   Standard International Trade Classification
td   time-definite cargo
TWA   Trans World Airlines
ULD   unit load device
UPS   United Parcel Service
VFR   visiting friends or relatives

N.B.: ATK and RPK are referred to in the Glossary and these abbreviations are already shown there.

Introduction

In 2008 the airline industry was once again in crisis. During the first half of the year fuel prices escalated to the highest levels ever seen and airline costs sky-rocketed. Airline losses began to mount. Numerous airlines had collapsed by mid-2008, including ATA, Maxjet and Aloha in the United States, Sterling, Futura and XL in Europe and Oasis in Hong Kong. Then, after August, the fuel prices dropped rapidly, but for many airlines this only helped marginally. When fuel prices had been rising early in the year, such airlines had bought a large part of their 2008, 2009 or even 2010 future fuel requirements at fixed but high 2008 prices, in the expectation that they would continue to rise. As a result, they were locked in, continuing to pay inflated prices for fuel even after fuel prices had plummeted.

Worse was to come. The worldwide financial and banking crisis which gathered pace during the second half of 2008 led to an economic downturn in many key economies and a recession in some. Trade flows were hit. In the last quarter of 2008 and early 2009 air freight volumes collapsed by about a quarter and passenger demand also fell sharply, particularly from high-fare business travellers. The international Air Transport Association (IATA), which late in 2007 had been predicting profits for the airline industry as a whole for 2008, eventually acknowledged that losses for the year would be of the order of US$8.5 billion.

The 2000s were not a happy decade for the airline industry. Between 2000 and 2006, while many individual airlines continued to operate profitably, most made losses in some of these years. The United States airlines posted huge losses during this period. The airline industry as a whole took seven years to recover fully from the economic downturn in 2000, the attack on the twin towers in New York in September 2001, the Iraq war in March 2003 and the SARS epidemic which followed. These were external shocks. They resulted in the airline industry as a whole making substantial losses in the years 2000 to 2005, breaking even in 2006 and posting the first industry-wide profit of US$12 billion in 2007. Then came the crisis of 2008, which continued into 2009.

The 2000s were a difficult decade for airlines but the industry's failure to generate adequate profits sooner was due not only to the external shocks but also in part to internally inflicted wounds. Liberalisation and the increased opportunities for competition led to overcapacity in many markets and induced airline managements to cut fares and tariffs even when costs were rising. But it was the airlines themselves who had created the overcapacity in the first place, either by over-rapid expansion or by failing to cut back capacity in markets where they were no longer competitive. By late 2008, the airline industry appeared once more to be flying off course.

During the last 50 years the airline industry has undergone an expansion unrivalled by any other form of public transport. Its rate of technological change has been exceptional. This has resulted in falling costs and fares which have stimulated a very rapid growth in demand for its services – a seemingly insatiable demand. In addition, for the first half of this period scheduled airlines enjoyed considerable protection from both internal and external competition. Any other industry faced with such high growth of demand for its products, especially while cushioned from competition, would be heady with the thought of present and future profits. But not the airline industry: it is an exception to the rule. High growth has for the most part spelt low profits. Increased demand has not resulted in long-term financial success. While some airlines have consistently managed to stay well in the black, the industry as a whole has been only marginally profitable.

There is no simple explanation to the apparent contradiction between the industry's rapid growth and its marginal profitability during recent decades. But for the individual airline financial success depends on matching supply and demand in a way which is both efficient and profitable. This is the underlying theme and focus of the book. While airline managements have considerable control over the supply of air services, they have relatively little control over the demand. They can influence demand but cannot control it. Hence the matching process is not an easy one. To help in understanding the process the present book provides a practical insight into key aspects of airline operations, planning and marketing within the conceptual framework of economics.

The book works through the issues logically. Any understanding of the economics of the industry must start with the regulatory framework which circumscribes and constrains airlines' freedom of action. On many international air routes a traditional and highly regulated market environment still persists, though such routes are declining in number (Chapter 2). Elsewhere the economic regulation of air transport has been progressively relaxed as a result of pressure from the United States, the European Union and several other states (Chapter 3). Thus regulated and so-called 'open skies' markets co-exist side by side. In order successfully to match the supply of air services with the demand it is essential to understand both airline costs and the factors that affect them (Chapters 4 and 5) and the nature of the demand. While the book is concerned primarily with traditional or network airlines, one cannot ignore the fastest growing sector, that of the low-cost, no-frills airlines. The low-cost model needs to be assessed (Chapter 6). There is an older low-cost model, that of the charter or non-scheduled airline. Its particular characteristics and advantages also require special attention (Chapter 7). Understanding demand is the first step in the marketing process (Chapter 8). A thorough appreciation of demand must also be used to develop traffic and other forecasts, since every activity within an airline ultimately stems from a forecast (Chapter 9). Supply and demand are brought together in a number of ways, but most crucially through effective product planning (Chapter 10). Price is a key element of the airline product or service. Alternative airline pricing policies and strategies need careful consideration, especially as low-cost airlines have introduced new pricing concepts (Chapter 11).

While the book focuses primarily on passenger services, the importance and role of air freight should not be forgotten. For several airlines it is crucially important both in output and revenue terms. Freight requires special attention since many of its economic and operational characteristics are different (Chapter 12). But the book begins with the theme of this introduction. It examines the underlying trends in the airline industry, including its rapid technological change, the high growth rates and the marginal profitability (Chapter 1).

The book is concerned primarily with international air transport which accounts worldwide for about two thirds of the industry's output. Only for the airlines of a few large countries such as the USA, the Soviet Union, Brazil and China are domestic operations of greater significance than international, though most of their major domestic airlines also operate internationally. In most countries the larger airlines are primarily concerned with international air services while several of them operate only internationally. Nevertheless, the economic analysis which follows is in many respects equally relevant to domestic air transport.

Since the third edition of this book appeared, the international airline industry has undergone considerable change. Further liberalisation of international regulations, the privatisation of many government-owned airlines, globalisation and the growing impact of electronic commerce are among the many developments that have led to new operating practices and management concepts. This fourth edition sets out to reflect the impact of these changes on airline economics and operations. It has been largely rewritten and entirely updated. A separate book entitled *The Airline Business* explores several of the key issues mentioned here at much greater depth. These include airline alliances, labour costs, the economics of low-cost, no-frills airlines, airline privatisation and survival strategies (Doganis, 2006).

There is no magic wand to ensure success within the international airline industry. This book attempts to flesh out the economic and operational issues which must be understood in order to match supply and demand. Only when this has been done can there be some measure of success in this most dynamic of industries. So come, fly with me.

1 Characteristics and trends in airline operations

> At Continental, our biggest focus is not to worry that much about revenue per available seat-mile or cost per available seat-mile; it is to worry about the margin. We target a 10 per cent operating margin.
>
> (Larry Kellner, Chief Financial Officer, Continental Airlines, 2000)

1.1 The paradox

The airline industry presents a paradox. For the last 50 years it has been characterised by continued and rapid growth in demand for its services. Yet it has remained only marginally profitable.

Inevitably growth was much faster in the 1950s and 1960s when aviation was a new industry than it is today when it is reaching maturity. But growth rates are still impressive. In the 1970s the annual growth in world passenger traffic was close to 10 per cent. This meant that passenger demand, and the airlines with it, doubled in size every seven years or so. In the following decade growth declined to around 6 per cent annually and during the 1990s growth was down slightly at around 5.2 per cent on average each year. The more turbulent early years of the new millennium saw a drop in traffic in 2001 with little growth in the next two years. This was compensated for by a 13 per cent jump in 2004 followed by lower but reasonable growth rates in 2004 to 2008. Over the eight-year period after 2000, annual traffic growth, passenger plus freight, averaged a little below 4.0 per cent. These figures suggest a long-term decline in the rate of growth of air transport. But in absolute terms, because of the much higher base a 4.0 per cent jump in recent years represents a much greater surge in demand than a 10 per cent annual growth 30 years ago. Most recent long-term forecasts for the next 20 years indicate growth at just above or below the 5 per cent mark.

The airline industry appears to be both cyclical and strongly influenced by external factors. This inevitably means that growth rates can fluctuate wildly from year to year. Nevertheless the underlying trend has been one of consistently good growth in demand but at a declining rate. Most industries or businesses faced with continued and high growth of demand for their products or services would be basking in substantial profits. Not so the airlines. This is the paradox.

The financial performance of the world's airlines taken as a whole has been very marginal, even in the years when the industry was highly regulated and largely protected from internal competition. The traditional measure of profitability, namely the rate of return on assets employed, cannot be applied easily to the airline industry as a whole. This is because of the difficulty of estimating real asset values for airlines with varied depreciation

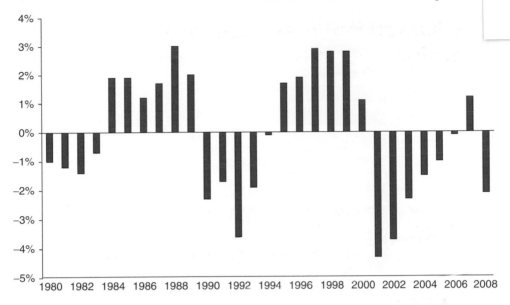

Figure 1.1 Annual net profit or loss as percentage of total revenue of ICAO member airlines, 1980–2008.

policies, using varying proportions of leased equipment and often receiving direct or indirect government subsidy in a variety of forms. An alternative measure of profitability commonly used among airlines is the operating ratio, which is the annual operating profit or loss or the net profit or loss, after tax, expressed as a percentage of the total annual revenue. This is calculated annually for the world's airlines by the International Civil Aviation Organisation (ICAO). The net operating ratio is shown diagrammatically in Figure 1.1. This shows the net profit after payment of interest and any other non-operating items.

The cyclical nature of the airline industry's financial performance is clearly evident. Four to five years of poor or bad performance are generally followed by an upturn and five or six years of improving results. However, even in the good years profit margins are low. The profits after interest and tax rarely achieve even 2 per cent of revenues. These are of course global figures and mask the fact that some airlines such as Singapore Airlines, Cathay Pacific or British Airways have frequently produced much better profit margins. Nevertheless, such low average profit margins are poor for a dynamic and high growth industry.

More surprisingly, airlines are the worst performing of any of the individual sectors in the air transportation chain. This is clearly evident from a study carried out for IATA aiming to establish the ROIC (return on invested capital) for different sectors in the aviation supply chain (Figure 1.2). This also shows that the 5 per cent return on capital earned by the world's airlines in the years 1996 to 2004 was below the cost of capital, which for most airlines would have been around 7.5 per cent. The period covered by the study included some relatively good years in 1996 to 2000 at the peak of a cycle and some very bad years after 2001. These other suppliers of aviation goods and services would also have been affected by the cyclical downturn, too. Yet they still out-performed the airlines by a big margin. It is worth noting that among sectors with the highest return on

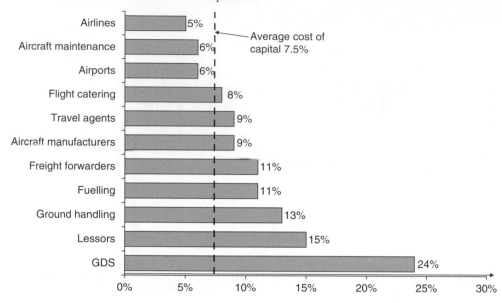

Figure 1.2 Average rate of return on invested capital in Aviation Supply Chain (1996–2004). Source: Value Chain Profitability. IATA Economics Briefing No. 04, Geneva, 2006.

capital are several, such as global distribution systems (GDS) or aircraft leasing, which are dominated by a small number of major suppliers. Two major lessors, GECAS and ILFC, controlled around 45 per cent of the market during this period while four GDS suppliers dominated that sector. This is in marked contrast to the airline sector where no group has market dominance except in restricted geographical areas.

1.2   The essence of airline planning

There is no simple explanation of the apparent contradiction between the airline industry's rapid long-term growth and its cyclical and marginal profitability. But for the individual airline overcoming this contradiction means matching supply and demand for its services in a way which is both efficient and profitable. This is the essence of airline management and planning. It is about matching the supply of air services, which management can largely control, with the demand for such services over which management has much less influence.

To be successful in this an airline can be a low-cost operator or a high-cost operator. What determines profitability is the airline's ability to generate unit revenues which are higher than its unit costs. An airline, within any regulatory constraints, can itself determine the supply of services it offers in the various markets it serves. In turn, the way it organises these services and manages the inputs required to supply them impacts directly on its costs. Though external factors, such as the cost of oil, also affect certain costs, an airline has considerable control over its overall cost levels. But cost efficiency and low unit costs are no guarantee of profit if an airline is unable to generate even the low unit revenues necessary to cover such costs.

From a review of a sample of various airlines' costs and revenues in 2007, which was a good year for most airlines, it is immediately apparent that unit costs vary enormously

Table 1.1 Operating results selected airlines, financial year 2007

	Operating cost per ATK (US cents)	Operating revenue per ATK (US cents)	Operating profit/loss before interest/tax/exceptionals (US$ millions)
	1	2	3
SIA	30.6	35.1	+1,088
PIA	40.0	37.1	−90
Malaysia	40.3	42.2	+181
Air India (2006)	51.3	44.8	−271
American	56.8	58.6	+702
South African	62.4	59.8	−136
British Airways	63.0	70.7	+1,720
Air Portugal	70.3	73.5	+114
Austrian Group	85.2	86.6	+49
Czech Airlines	91.6	93.0	+15
SAS	109.9	115.6	+290
Alitalia	111.6	104.9	−427

Source: Compiled by author using ICAO data.

(Column 1, Table 1.1). The highest cost airlines at the bottom of the table, SAS and Alitalia, had unit costs that were two to three times as high as the low-cost carriers in the top half. Did this mean that they were merely inefficient high-cost carriers? Not necessarily. As will become apparent in the course of this book, their high costs were and still are a function of the nature of their operations and the externally determined costs of their inputs rather than a result of poor management. Such factors also explain in part the very low costs of Singapore Airlines (SIA), Pakistan (PIA) or Malaysia Airlines.

To assess how successful airlines are in matching supply, which they largely control, with demand which they can influence but do not control, one must examine their unit revenues (Column 2). Since revenues per available tonne-km are a function of average fares or cargo tariffs and *load factors* achieved, they are a good measure of an airline's success in dealing with the demand side. If unit revenues of the sample airlines are higher than their unit costs then the airlines are profitable. If not they are making operating losses (Column 3). Clearly Table 1.1 indicates that low costs are not a guarantee of financial success though they should make it easier. Thus, PIA, one of the lowest-cost airlines, fails to generate even the low level of unit revenues needed to cover its costs and ends up with a loss. Surprisingly two of the airlines with very high unit costs, SAS and Czech Airlines, were able, through their product and marketing strategy, to generate high yields and produce profits. They were successful in the matching process. Of the other high-cost airlines, Alitalia failed dismally in trying to do this and incurred huge losses in 2007, as it had done for several years.

Among the airlines with fairly average unit costs ranging between 50 and 70 cents per ATK, South African Airways stands out. Its unit revenues were below its unit costs and it, too, lost money in 2007, a good year for most airlines.

Airlines can be low-cost and very unprofitable or high-cost and financially sound. Unit costs or unit revenues are not critical in themselves. For airline executives the key to financial success is to ensure that unit revenues exceed unit costs. This is precisely what

Larry Kellner, Executive Vice President and Chief Financial Officer of Continental Airlines, meant in October 2000 when he stated:

> You've got to manage both sides of the equation, the revenue side and the costs side. At Continental, our biggest focus is not to worry that much about revenue per available seat mile or cost per available seat mile; it's to worry about the margin.
>
> (Kellner 2000)

Airlines that fail to focus on the margin end up 'flying off course'. If they do this repeatedly without taking corrective action they are likely to enter a spiral of increasing losses that leads ultimately to collapse – unless they have backers or governments prepared to bail them out.

The difficulties faced by airline executives in trying to match supply and demand have been compounded by the fact that the airline industry is very dynamic and subject to structural instability. Two factors above all have contributed to this: the rapid technological change, which is characteristic of air transport, and the liberalisation of economic and market access regulations during the 1980s and 1990s. The latter are discussed in the following chapters. Technology has been a key driver of the airline industry's economic fortunes and merits closer attention.

1.3   Rapid technological change

In the last 50 years technological innovation in air transport has far outstripped that in any other transport mode. The only comparable innovations in other transport sectors have been the emergence of the super-tankers in shipping and the development of high-speed trains, though the impact of the latter is still limited geographically. Innovation in aviation has centred on the development of the jet engine for civil use, first in a turbo propeller form and later as a pure jet. Successive developments in the jet engine have consistently improved its efficiency and propulsive power. The emergence of larger and more powerful engines in association with improvements in airframe design and in control systems has resulted over the last 30 years or so in successive and significant improvements in aircraft speed and size. Higher speeds and larger aircraft have in turn produced significant jumps in aircraft hourly productivity. (This is calculated by multiplying the maximum payload an aircraft can carry by its average hourly block speed, i.e. the distance it can fly in an hour.) In turn higher hourly productivity meant lower costs per seat.

While technological innovation has focused on improving aircraft speeds, range or size, it has had a major impact on the costs of airline operations. An appreciation of technological developments and their impact is crucial in understanding airline economics.

Even in the era of the piston engine dramatic improvements were made so that the hourly productivity of the Super Constellation was seven times greater than that of the Douglas DC-3 (Table 1.2). The early turbo-prop aircraft also significantly improved productivity. Though the Viscount's productivity was less than that of the Super Constellation, as a DC-3 replacement the Viscount's productivity was four times as great. Likewise, the Britannias were a significant improvement on the Super Constellations they were meant to replace.

The arrival of the turbo-jet engine had a twofold impact. In the 1960s the turbo-jets led to a dramatic increase in speeds, while the size of the aircraft did not increase appreciably. In the later 1960s and early 1970s there was no appreciable increase in speeds, because

Table 1.2 Impact of technological advance on aircraft productivity

Aircraft type	Year of entry into service	Mean cruise speed (km/h)	Maximum payload* (tonnes)	Typical passenger payload	Hourly productivity** (000t-km/h)
Piston					
DC–3	1936	282	2.7	21	0.5
Lockheed 1049 Super Constellation	1952	499	1.0	47–94	3.8
Turbo-prop					
Viscount 700	1953	523	5.9	40–53	2.2
Britannia 310	1956	571	15.6	52–133	6.2
Turbo-jet – short-haul					
Caravelle VI R	1959	816	8.3	52–94	4.7
Airbus A300	1974	891	31.8	245	19.8
Airbus A320	1988	834	20.4	179	11.9
Turbo-jet – long-haul					
Boeing 720 B	1960	883	18.7	115–49	11.6
Douglas DC-8-63	1968	935	30.6	259	20.0
Boeing 747–100	1969	908	49.5	430	31.5
Boeing 747–300	1983	908	68.6	420	43.6
Boeing 777–200	1995	869	55.1	305	33.5
Airbus A380	2007	882	85.0	555	52.5
Concorde	1976	2,236	12.7	110	19.3

Source: Compiled by author.

Notes

  * Later versions or developments of these aircraft may have had different maximum payload or passenger payloads.
  ** Calculated on the basis of an average block speed assumed to be about 70 per cent of the cruise speed. This is likely to be an under-estimate for aircraft on medium- or long-haul sectors.

existing speeds were approaching the sound barrier, but there was a significant increase in the size of aircraft, particularly with the introduction of wide-body fuselages. The earlier increases in speeds combined with these significant jumps in aircraft size together produced major improvements in aircraft productivity so that while the Boeing 720B in 1960 was producing 11,600 tonne-km per flying hour, only ten years later the hourly productivity of the Boeing 747, the first so-called 'jumbo', was three times as great. The Airbus A-300 introduced in 1974 was the first short-haul wide-body aircraft. Its productivity was about twice as high as that of the narrow-body, short-haul aircraft then in service.

The next major technological breakthrough was the production of civil aircraft flying faster than the speed of sound. But in economic terms it was a failure. The Anglo-French Concorde which entered service in 1976 flew more than twice as fast as its predecessors yet was able to do this only through a very significant reduction in size. Because of this penalty, supersonic aircraft had a lower hourly productivity than their competitors on long-haul routes. This meant high costs per seat or seat-km and very high fares. It was this factor which made their commercial viability so problematic, even on over-water routes where there were no noise constraints. In practice this aircraft was only operated by British Airways and Air France, very much as a public relations exercise and only after some of the capital debts arising from its purchase were written off. Eventually in the early 2000s both airlines grounded their Concordes to cut their losses. The last Concorde scheduled flight landed at London Heathrow on 24 October 2003.

From the mid-1970s onwards the rate of technological innovation slackened. Attention switched from the long-haul end of the aircraft market to the development of more efficient wide-bodied medium-haul aircraft such as the Boeing 767 and the Airbus A-310. Developments here were based essentially on existing engine and air-frame technology, though there were major developments in avionics, in the use of lighter composite materials in air-frame construction and in other areas. At the same time, the trend towards larger aircraft flying at the same speed continued. An example is the Airbus A-320 introduced in 1988 which, with up to 180 seats, was significantly larger than the 100- to 130-seater aircraft it was intended to replace. Thus important gains in hourly productivity have continued to be made as airlines switch to larger newer aircraft types.

During the 1990s there were two important developments. First was the introduction of extended range versions of the newer twin-engined jets such as the Boeing 767–200 EQ offering 200 to 250 seats. These allowed more direct non-stop flights on thinner long-haul routes that could not support the large traditional long-haul aircraft such as the Boeing 747 with 400 seats or more. This trend towards medium-sized aircraft for long-haul services led to the introduction of the Airbus A340 in 1993 and the Boeing 777 in 1995. The second important development, one which technologically was perhaps more significant, was the development of small, efficient and light jet engines that could be used to power smaller passenger aircraft. Such aircraft had hitherto been dependent on turbo-propeller engines. But they were noisy and aircraft speeds were low. The 50-seater Canadair Regional Jet (CRJ) which first entered service in November 1992 and the Embraer ERJ 145, also with 50 seats, which launched services in 1997 revolutionised regional air services. They offered faster and more comfortable jet travel on thinner short-haul routes previously the preserve of turbo-prop aircraft. They were followed in the early 2000s by larger versions such as the CRJ 900 with 86 seats and the 98-seater Embraer 190.

While technological improvements in all areas of both engines and airframes have continued, in the early years of the new millennium the focus was on two developments, both of which were to have a significant economic impact. The first was the increasing use of lighter composite materials in airframes. By reducing the weight of the aircraft, such composites, if used extensively, would reduce fuel consumption and consequently operating costs. This was critically important after fuel prices trebled in the period 2004–6 and continued rising to a peak in 2008. Reducing fuel burnt per aircraft kilometre was also critically important in view of growing concern about the impact of aircraft emissions on the environment. Leading in the adoption of this new technology has been the mid-sized Boeing 787 Dreamliner, in which as much as 50 per cent of the primary structure, including the fuselage and wings, is made of composite materials. It was due to come into service in 2008, but was delayed, probably till 2010. Boeing claimed that the extensive use of lighter composites plus improved engines would result in a reduction of up to 25 per cent in fuel consumption per passenger carried, compared to existing aircraft types. The Airbus A350, similar in size and entering service later, would also have a high composite component.

The second development was the move to make a quantum jump in aircraft size, spearheaded by the Airbus A380, which first entered service with Singapore Airlines in October 2007. With a maximum take-off weight of around 40 per cent greater than that of a Boeing 747–400, it can carry up to 550–600 passengers in a three-class cabin or up to 800 in an all economy configuration. This major increase in size marked another jump in hourly productivity (Table 1.2).

1.4 The economic impact of new technology

These developments described so briefly above, which were matched by equally rapid innovations in other areas of aviation technology in the air and on the ground, were due primarily to the increasing efficiency of the jet engine. For a given level of propulsive thrust successive engines were able to carry a larger payload and to carry it faster as well. This, combined with other economies arising from the greater size of aircraft, resulted in ever-decreasing costs per capacity tonne-kilometre (see Chapter 5, Section 5.5 for the impact of size and speed on unit costs). Herein lies the significance of the technological improvements in aviation and of the increase in aircraft productivity which they made possible. They enabled airlines to cut their unit costs rapidly in the 1950s and 1960s when advances in size and speed were most marked and then steadily, though less rapidly, in subsequent decades.

Between 1960 and 1970 unit costs per available tonne-km were halved in constant value terms.

During the 1970s airline unit costs expressed in current values began to rise rapidly as a result of world inflation. They rose particularly sharply following the fuel crises of 1973 and 1978. The airlines tried to counteract the upwards pressure on costs by the accelerated introduction of more modern and usually larger jet aircraft and by more effective cost control. Because of the oil crisis of 1978 unit costs in 1980 were very high. But during the 1980s the price of fuel began to decline in real terms, falling particularly sharply in 1986. It then fluctuated around this low 1986 level. Helped by both the switch to larger aircraft and the fall in the real price of fuel, airline costs again declined in constant value terms during the early 1980s but stabilised in the second half of the decade.

In the 1990s the steady decline in unit costs continued. But during this decade it was driven less by improvements in aircraft technology and more by the steady fall in the real price of aviation fuel, at least until 1999, and by the strenuous efforts made by airlines, especially in the early years of the decade, to drive down their costs. Cost reduction was necessary both to climb out of the disastrous downturn in the airline industry's fortunes between 1990 and 1994 and because of the increased price competition as more and more international markets were liberalised. In constant value terms, unit costs fell by about one third between 1990 and 2000.

In the early years of the new millennium the collapse in yields in many markets and rising losses increased pressure on airlines to reduce costs. The focus was on reducing staff numbers, in order to reduce wage costs, and on reducing distribution costs by switching to direct airline internet sales, cutting or eliminating agents' commission where possible and introducing electronic ticketing. In the USA several major airlines filed for Chapter 11 bankruptcy protection. This enabled them to cut staff levels dramatically, by up to one third, while also cutting average salaries by around 30 per cent. The US majors also renegotiated leasing and other contracts. Non-fuel costs dropped. The trebling of the fuel price between 2002 and 2006 (see Table 1.3) reinforced the need to cut all other costs. For the airline industry as a whole, reductions in non-fuel costs more or less balanced the increasing cost of fuel. As a result, airline costs were more or less stable in real terms in the period 2000 to 2006. But when fuel prices doubled between 2007 and mid-2008, airline total unit operating costs shot up.

The technological developments in aviation, while they were beneficial in their impact on operating costs and in improving safety, also created problems. The increasing size and capacity of aircraft and the speed with which new, larger aircraft were introduced, often in reaction to competition from other airlines, created a strong downward pressure on load factors. This resulted primarily from two factors. First because airlines have always been reluctant to reduce frequencies on a route, since they felt high frequencies provided an important competitive advantage. So there was a large increase in seats to sell as they switched from smaller to larger aircraft but flew the same frequencies. Second, and more importantly, airlines rushed to order aircraft in the peak of the cycles, because profits and load factors were high, but too frequently the extra new capacity was delivered 2–4 years later, when there was a cyclical downturn and demand growth rates were well below those anticipated when the orders were placed. Too often, to fill the new larger aircraft, fares were reduced.

The technical innovations also posed the problem of financing the new capital investments which they made necessary. Whereas a 189-seater Boeing 727–200 cost the airlines $8–9 million in 1974, ten years later, in 1984, the same airlines were having to pay around $45 million for a 265-seater Airbus A310 with spares to replace their 727s. (Note: throughout this book all references to dollars are US dollars unless otherwise specified.) By 1990 the price for the same aircraft was up to $60 million. Since airlines normally acquired several aircraft at a time to replace existing aircraft and/or to support their expansion, the capital costs were enormous. In 1990 Singapore Airlines ordered 50 aircraft costing $8.6 billion for delivery between 1994 and 1999. In November 2000 Qantas announced an order for 31 aircraft, 13 Airbus A330–200s, 6 longer-range Boeing 747–400s and 12 Airbus A380s. These were to cost $4.9 billion. Such figures are indicative of the escalating capital investment necessary for any large domestic or international airline.

Various developments eased the problem of raising capital on this scale. The aircraft manufacturers themselves, in their eagerness to sell more aircraft, became increasingly involved with facilitating finance for their customers, either through the commercial banks in their own country or through special export trade banks, such as the United States Export-Import Bank. Manufacturers vied with each other in trying to get better financing arrangements for their client. The terms of such purchase loans became an increasingly important factor for airlines in making a choice between aircraft. The banks, too, helped. With the ability to use aircraft that are very mobile assets as collateral, bankers were very innovative in developing a variety of financial instruments and packages to facilitate airlines in acquiring aircraft (see Morrell, 2007).

In the 1970s consortia of banks emerged which purchased aircraft and then leased them to the airlines. The consortia enjoyed tax concessions and also retained ownership of the aircraft which was a valuable security at a time when the resale value of aircraft was high. During the 1980s these bank consortia were overtaken by the rapid growth of aircraft leasing companies. By 2006 the two largest of these, GECAS (with 986 aircraft) and the International Lease Finance Corporation (1,323 aircraft), controlled just over 50 per cent by value of the world's leased aircraft fleet. It was also estimated that over 25 per cent of the world's commercial airliners were being operated under various leasing arrangements. As the leasing companies ordered large numbers of aircraft in advance, many airlines found they could only acquire aircraft by leasing from such companies. By 2008 most large airlines operated a mix of leased and owned aircraft.

Even when the industry as a whole was doing badly or a particular airline's results were poor, the manufacturers' need to sell inevitably ensured that finance would be forthcoming. But for the airlines this was a mixed blessing. It pushed them to invest when they should have been holding back. As a result during periods of capacity expansion as in the early 1980s and in the mid-1990s, too many international airlines became heavily over-indebted. In other words, the ratio of their debts to their equity capital became much too high. They were under-capitalised. When it is easy to lease-in aircraft or to borrow money for aircraft purchase, then it is inevitable that growth and expansion is financed through loans or leases rather than through injections of equity capital. This was especially true of many loss-making government-owned airlines (see Doganis, 2006 for analysis of state-owned airlines). When traffic or revenue failed to reach the forecast levels, airlines were no longer able to service these huge debts or lease payments. As a consequence, during each downturn in the airline industry's economic cycle, many airlines have collapsed because they could no longer meet their interest and debt repayments or their lease payments. In many cases they have been bailed out by government financial aid. New start-ups face this problem all the time. It is easy to acquire aircraft in order to launch services – much more difficult to keep paying the lease payments or capital costs when traffic levels are less than anticipated.

This pattern was repeated in the mid-2000s. Improved profitability and a surging traffic demand in 2006 and 2007 led to a boom in aircraft orders in those two years. For instance, by early 2007 both Boeing and Airbus production lines for short-haul single-aisle aircraft were sold out till 2011 or so. Such aircraft for earlier use could only be obtained from leasing companies and at high lease rates. The aircraft ordered in 2006–7 would be delivered in 2009–10 and later. Unfortunately, the financial crisis that gathered pace during 2008 triggered a worldwide economic slow-down and a collapse in air traffic growth. By 2009 the airline industry found itself in yet another cyclical downturn, just as new aircraft deliveries were due to reach a peak. Most airlines around the world scuttled around trying to defer or cancel deliveries.

1.5   Declining yields

The reasons for the relatively rapid overall growth rate, which is so characteristic of air transport, are not difficult to find. The falling level of operating costs, previously described, enabled airlines to offer tariffs that were lower in real terms. The impact of lower costs on fares was reinforced by the growing liberalisation of international air transport during the 1980s and 1990s. Liberalisation had a double impact. Increased and open competition created further pressures to reduce costs while liberalisation also led to the gradual removal of tariff controls, thereby facilitating price competition.

Prior to 1980, the yield or average fare charged per passenger kilometre declined rapidly in real terms, that is in relation to the cost of other goods and services. This decline occurred at a time when the per capita incomes in the developed countries of the world were increasing at a rate of 8 per cent per annum while discretionary incomes were growing at an even faster rate. As a consequence the demand for non-business air travel rose rapidly. During the same period a boom in world trade generated an increase in both business travel and in the demand for air freight facilities. The fall in the real cost of freight charges was even more marked than the decline in the real value of passenger fares.

It was not until 1980 and the two or three years that followed that economic recession affecting many developed countries began seriously to undermine demand and annual growth rates declined appreciably. They did so even though real air fares fell rapidly as a result both of over-capacity and the gradual liberalisation in some international markets and the US domestic market.

The major economic downturn in the early 1990s pushed most airlines into several years of losses or sharply lower profits (Figure 1.1). Inevitably attempts were made to stem or even, where possible, to reverse the decline in average yields. But any success was short-lived. Yields in real terms continued to decline. European and US airlines' real yields dropped 25–35 per cent between 1991 and 2006–7 in different markets (Figure 1.3). In the mid-1990s real yields declined most rapidly on long-haul international flights while US domestic and intra-European yields fell more slowly. This pattern was mirrored in other regions of the world.

The most marked collapse in average yields came in the period after 2001 when a cyclical downturn in demand was made much worse by the terrorist attacks in the US in September 2001, the Gulf War in 2003 and the later SARS and avian flu epidemics. For a time demand growth rates collapsed in several markets, especially in the US. Airlines frantically cut fares to stimulate demand. Matters were made worse by growing over-capacity in long-haul routes and the impact of low-cost carriers on shorter routes in the USA, Europe and Australia. But from 2005 onward yields in some international markets rose as world economic and business travel boomed. That is until the collapse of both in mid-2009. Then the downward trend in airline yields re-asserted itself.

Despite short-term fluctuations, airline managements have to live with a stark reality: there will continue to be a strong downward pressure on real average yields especially on competitive international routes and markets attacked by low-cost airlines. It is clear that falling average yields destabilise the process of matching supply and demand profitably. Falling yields can be offset, where possible, by further reductions in unit cost levels. When this is not possible then airlines must push up their load factors to compensate for the fact that they are receiving less per passenger or per tonne carried. It is when airlines lose control of this dynamic process of matching yields, unit revenues and load factors that they start making losses.

1.6   A cyclical industry

It was pointed out earlier that the airline industry is marginal in terms of its profitability and is also very cyclical. This is evident from Figure 1.1 above. Each complete cycle is about eight to ten years in duration. While Figure 1.1 shows the cycles since 1980, this cyclical pattern was manifest in the earlier decades, too. An examination of the recent cycles shows why the industry is inherently unstable.

After several good years in the late 1970s the international airlines once again entered a *period of deep crisis from 1979 to 1983*. They were in the anomalous position of enjoying the highest load factors for more than 20 years, while facing increasing losses. The second oil shock, in 1978, resulted in dramatic increases in fuel prices. By 1980 fuel costs represented nearly one third of total operating costs. High costs, combined with stagnating demand and falling yields, generated losses. The high load factors were themselves symptomatic of the crisis for they resulted from the industry's attempt to compensate for the down-ward pressure on fares and freight tariffs. They did not compensate enough. In 1980 the world's airlines as a whole made an operating loss before paying interest for the first time since 1961. Further operating losses occurred in 1981 and 1982. Several airlines went bankrupt in this period, including Braniff in the United States and Laker Airways in the UK, while many others accumulated large debts or had to be financially supported by their national governments. It was not till 1984 that results began to improve.

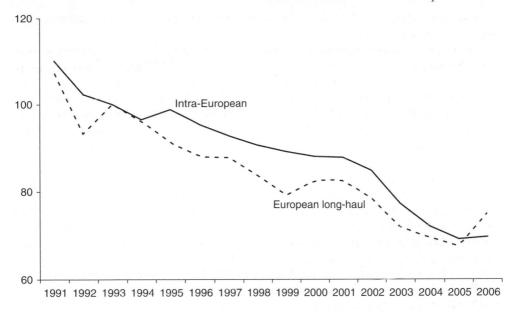

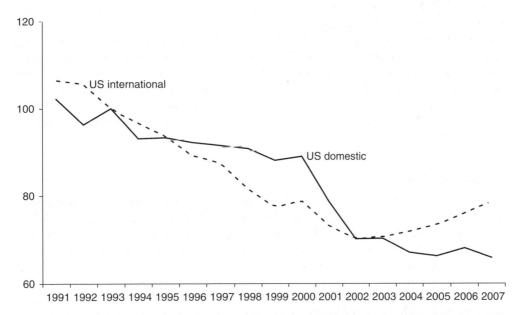

Figure 1.3 Trends in unit revenues, US and European network airlines, 1991–2007. Yields in real values adjusted for inflation and exchange rate changes. 1993 indexed at 100.
Source: Compiled using ATA and AEA (2008) data.

While all airlines were under pressure during this period, many continued to operate profitably, either by achieving higher than average load factors or by reducing their costs in real terms or both. This was the case with several of the new third world airlines that were able to benefit from their low labour costs and from the high growth rates in the markets in which they operated. Singapore International Airlines (SIA), for example, was very profitable throughout this period.

The *second half of the 1980s* saw a dramatic turn-around in the airline industry's fortunes, though overall profitability remained marginal. While airline chief executives around the world gladly took credit for this turnaround, in reality it was due primarily to two external factors, a significant fall in the real price of aviation fuel and a surge in demand as the world's economies improved. Airlines that had been making losses for years suddenly found themselves in profit, especially in 1987 and 1988. The underlying financial position, however, was still very weak because the industry as a whole and many individual airlines now found themselves with huge debt burdens. These arose from the need to cover their accumulated losses during the lean years of the early 1980s and to finance the new orders they were placing as traffic growth accelerated. Huge interest payments were needed to finance these debt burdens.

The late 1980s did have one poor year in 1986 when the Chernobyl nuclear disaster, the American bombing of Libya and increased terrorism in Europe and the Middle East led to a sharp fall in United States travel to Europe. This adversely affected the financial results of many US and European carriers especially those with substantial North Atlantic operations.

While the years 1987 to 1989 were highly profitable, *the period 1990–1993* saw another cyclical downturn. The airline industry faced the worst crisis it had ever known. The crisis started early in 1990 as fuel prices began to rise in real terms while a worsening economic climate in several countries, notably the USA and Britain, began to depress demand in certain markets. The Iraqi invasion of Kuwait on 2 August 1990 and the short war that followed in January 1991 deepened the crisis for many airlines. Eastern Airlines in the US and Air Europe in Britain collapsed early in 1991 while Pan American and several smaller airlines such as Midway in the United States and TEA in Belgium had gone by the end of the year. The end of the first Gulf War early in 1991 did not lead to any improvement in airline fortunes. In many markets, such as the North Atlantic, liberalisation and insufficient traffic growth was resulting in over-capacity and falling yields as airlines fought for market share. Financial results in 1992 were worse than in 1991 and 1993 was little better. Of the world top 20 airlines, only British Airways, Cathay Pacific, SIA and Swissair made an overall surplus in each of the three years 1991 to 1993. But some of the losses were huge. In 1992 Continental and Northwest each posted net losses after tax of over $1 billion while in the following year, Air France lost on average $4 million every day.

Many airlines required massive injections of capital to survive through the early 1990s. The state-owned airlines within the European Union received over $10 billion in 'state aid' approved by the European Commission plus a further $1.3 billion not categorised as 'state aid (Doganis, 2006). But many privatised airlines also received capital injections.

The period 1995 to 1998 was again one of improving profitability. After 1994, as the cost-cutting measures launched earlier began to have an impact and as demand growth began to pick up, many airlines returned to profit. While for the industry as a whole 1997 and 1998 were the most profitable years ever, many Asian carriers hit by the melt-down in several East Asian economies posted much reduced profits or even losses. Cathay Pacific, historically one of the industry's most profitable airlines, made its first ever loss in 1998. In 1999 a few airlines, including British Airways and US Air, also posted markedly lower profits. These were the first warning signs of an impending downturn.

As 2000 progressed many airline chairmen issued profit warnings. What were the causes of so much concern? Several factors were undermining profits. First, overcapacity in many markets, especially on international routes as airlines and alliances fought for market share, was pushing down average yields. This trend was exacerbated in Europe and the United States by the pricing strategies of low-cost, no-frills carriers, which were forcing network airlines to cut their own domestic and short-haul fares. While yields were going down costs were starting to climb in real terms. During 1999 the OPEC countries had imposed production quotas so as to push up the price of oil. Aviation fuel prices hit a high of US cents 104 per gallon in September–October 2000. This was more than double the September 1998 price, though they did fall back to around US cents 75 per gallon for much of 2001. Airlines which had not hedged their future fuel purchases were badly hit. The strengthening of the US dollar against many currencies, including the euro, made matters worse, since a significant proportion of airline costs such as fuel, insurance or aircraft lease payments are usually fixed in US dollars. Finally, many of the collective wage agreements that had been signed in the mid-1990s began to unwind in early 2000 and 2001. New agreements coming at the end of several years of profit inevitably resulted in significant wage increases despite the deteriorating situation. An example was the trend-setting agreement in September 2000 between United Airlines and its pilots which granted the latter an average 30 per cent wage rise. Similar agreements in the US and in Europe once again began to push up wage costs after years of restraint.

As a result of all these factors, the top seven US airlines announced marked reductions in net profits for the year 2000 while US Air posted a $269 million loss and TWA filed for bankruptcy protection. The only airline to buck the trend was the low-cost carrier Southwest Airlines. Its net profits actually rose by over $100 million in 2000. Several European carriers also announced falling profits or losses for 2000. These included Swissair ($1.7 billion loss), Sabena ($278 million) and Alitalia ($240 million).

By early 2001 the danger signals were evident. Once more the world's airlines appeared to be 'flying off course' and failing to adequately match supply and demand. Attempts to push up load factors or yields to compensate for rising costs were only partially effective. In fact the slowing down in major economies, notably those of Japan and the United States, which began in the second half of 2000, adversely affected both passenger and freight demand. Far from rising, both traffic levels and average yields were going down in many markets.

In August 2001 the airline industry appeared to be on the verge of a major cyclical downturn. Then the fateful terrorist attacks in the United States on 11 September 2001 turned crisis into catastrophe for many of the world's airlines. This was not only because of its immediate impact in terms of a huge drop in demand for travel and increased insurance and security costs, but more especially because 11 September ensured that the economic recession in the US, in Japan and elsewhere would be deeper and longer-lasting. As a result, the industry's cyclical collapse which began in 2000 turned out to be deeper and longer-lasting than any of the previous downturns.

In the few weeks preceding September 11th 2001 and in the two months following several airlines went to the wall. In Australia, Ansett closed down, while its parent company Air New Zealand had to be rescued by its government. In Europe, Swissair and Sabena were declared bankrupt, as were some smaller European airlines which had been part of the Swissair group. In North America, Canada's second largest airline, Canada 3000, stopped flying at the beginning of November 2001. These were the first casualties of the cyclical crisis. Others followed, too.

As in previous decades the cyclical downturn which started in 2000 was made much worse by successive external shocks. The attack on the twin towers in New York in September 2001 was the first of these. It was followed by the launch of the Iraq War in March 2003 and the SARS epidemic in East Asia. All of these shocks adversely impacted

Table 1.3 Fuel price escalation deepens in 2001–8 downturn

Average price for:	Fuel price (cents/US gal)	Change to year ago %
Year 2002	67.9	
Year 2003	81.1	+19
Year 2004	116.1	+43
Year 2005	167.7	+45
Year 2006	194.8	+16
Year 2007	213.7	+10
2008 June	394.6	+91
December	140.6	−32

Source: *Airline Business*.

on demand for travel. Traffic growth rates collapsed in the years 2001 to 2003. Then oil prices, which had stabilised in 2001–2, suddenly rose up to unprecedented levels as demand for oil in the fast-expanding economies of China and India outstripped supply. Fuel prices in 2004 were almost double the 2002 level and by 2006 they had almost trebled (Table 1.3). Over-capacity in long-haul markets, as demand growth slowed down, together with expansion of low-cost carriers in Europe, South-East Asia and elsewhere, combined to further erode average fares and yields. This was happening at a time when escalating fuel prices were pushing up costs.

The net result of the cyclical downturn plus the external shocks was that *in the period 2000 to 2006* the airline industry faced the longest and deepest crisis in its history. During the previous downturn in 1990 to 1993 member airlines of IATA (the International Air Transport Association) collectively lost $15 billion. This figure rises to $26 billion if one includes $11 billion of government aid given to European airlines to see them through the crisis. But in the five years 2000 to 2005, the collective loss was $29.5 billion, which effectively rises to $37.4 billion after inclusion of $8 billion aid given to US carriers by the Federal government in 2002–3.

The US airlines suffered most during this period. The collapse in demand following the attacks of September 2001 which led to falling yields plus the escalating fuel prices in 2004–6 meant that the nine largest US airlines posted losses in most of the years between 2001 and 2005. Some losses were huge. For instance, United Airlines lost close to or over $3 billion each year in 2001, 2002 and again in 2003. Four of the US majors, United, US Airways, Delta and Northwest, were under Chapter 11 bankruptcy protection for some of the period. Southwest, the low-cost carrier, was the only one of the larger US airlines consistently to post profits in all years. It was not till 2006 that results overall showed a significant improvement, though United and Delta still made a net loss.

In other parts of the world, notably Europe and Asia, airline results were more mixed in the period up to 2006. Most of the larger airlines, such as Lufthansa, British Airways, Korean Airlines or Japan Airlines, lost money in one or two years and then returned to profit. A few were consistently unprofitable and were unable to salvage their financial situation. These included Swiss Airlines, until it was bought by Lufthansa, and Alitalia. But as in the USA, the two largest low-cost carriers in Europe, Ryanair and easyJet, continued to generate profits throughout these difficult years.

Results improved in 2006 and 2007. In 2006 the world airline industry at last produced an overall profit of around $0.5 billion. The operating environment was improving. The best year for a long time proved to be 2007, in fact since 1999. Fuel prices were only marginally higher than in 2006 (Table 1.3), but traffic continued to grow strongly and airlines' cost-cutting measures began to pay off especially among US carriers. The ten largest US airlines were in profit after years of losses and bankruptcies.

Unlike previous cycles, the good times did not last long. A cataclysmic year was 2008. Airlines were hit thrice: first, by soaring fuel prices in the first half of the year when they almost doubled (Table 1.3); second, by having to continue to pay inflated prices for fuel in the latter part of the year when fuel prices fell, because many airlines were locked into fuel hedges bought when fuel prices were soaring (for example, Cathay Pacific lost $90.7 million because of fuel hedges in the second half of 2008; SIA lost $225 in the last quarter of 2008, while United Airlines and Air France-KLM both lost $370m); and finally, the plummeting of the financial and banking business triggered by the collapse of Lehman Brothers' bank in September 2008 led to slowing traffic growth rates in the latter part of the year and collapsing yields in many markets. The top ten US airlines saw their net income collapse from a profit of $4.3 billion in 2007 to a loss of $19.4 billion in 2008. Only Southwest once again stood out as the sole profit-maker.

By early 2009 most airlines were reporting traffic down by 5 to 10 per cent compared to a year earlier. In air freight markets, especially those from the exporting economies of Asia, volumes were down 20 per cent or more. For airline executives uncertainty reigned. The airline industry was entering yet another cyclical downturn. But this time it followed a very short period of profitability. And, no-one knew how long the downturn would last.

1.7 International focus shifts to East Asia

The high though declining growth rates for air traffic mentioned earlier mark the fact that growth has been very uneven. Wide variations between different parts of the world and between different airlines have been evident. This is particularly true of international air traffic. For the last 25 years or so the airlines of Asia and the Pacific have grown much more rapidly than airlines in other parts of the world and at annual rates that are well above the world average. This is true both of passenger traffic and of cargo.

Much of this growth has been generated by traffic to, from and between the countries of East Asia and Australasia. The explanations are not difficult to find. For more than 20 years, till the East Asian economic crisis of late 1997 and 1998, Japan and the tiger economies of South East Asia were developing much more rapidly than the traditional economies of Europe and North America. Their export-oriented economies generated considerable business travel while rising per capita incomes stimulated leisure and personal travel. At the same time, many of their manufactured exports were high-value goods well suited to carriage by air. Countries such as Thailand, Singapore and Indonesia were also rapidly developing their tourism infrastructure and thereby attracting growing numbers of tourists both from within and outside the region. In the 2000s the key driver for very rapid growth in air travel and air freight became China, as its export-led economy boomed. Even after the economic downturn that began in 2008, China's GDP was expected to grow at 6 per cent per annum or more.

It should also not be forgotten that most of the countries and many of the major cities of East Asia are separated by large expanses of water. In many cases there is no alternative

Table 1.4 Regional distribution of international scheduled traffic

Airline by region of registration	Share of total international tonne-km carried			
	1973 %	*1988 %*	*1997 %*	*2007 %*
Asia and Pacific	14.1	29.0	32.6	31.9
North America	27.5	21.5	19.8	17.4
Middle East	4.0	4.9	4.3	8.2
Latin America and Caribbean	6.3	5.7	5.0	3.6
Europe	44.3	35.5	35.8	36.0
Africa	3.8	3.4	2.5	2.8
World	100.0	100.0	100.0	100.0

Source: Compiled using ICAO data.

to air travel. Even when surface travel is possible, as between Kuala Lumpur and Bangkok, the infrastructure is poor and journey times are too slow. The 1970s and 1980s also saw the rapid expansion of new Asian airlines originally state-owned such as Singapore Airlines (SIA), Malaysia Airlines (MAS), Thai International, Garuda and Cathay Pacific, Eva Airways and Asiana. Most of these were not initially IATA members and were able to bypass IATA rules on service standards and traffic. Offering superior in-flight service and aggressive marketing, they both stimulated demand and captured a growing share of it.

As a consequence of above average traffic growth in East Asia and the dynamic expansion of Asian airlines, there has been a dramatic restructuring of the world's international airline industry away from the traditional United States and European international airlines and in favour of the East Asian/Pacific airlines (Table 1.4). Whereas in 1973 the Asian and Pacific region airlines carried only 14 per cent of the world's international scheduled traffic by the late 1990s their share was up to almost one third. By 2007 it had dropped slightly as a result of the very rapid growth of low-cost carriers in Europe after 1997. Conversely, the once-dominant US and European airlines have lost market share. In 1973 airlines from these latter two regions carried three quarters of the world's international traffic. By 2007 their joint share was down to 55 per cent and North American airlines as a group had dropped from second to third place. Long-term forecasts of international air traffic all indicate that growth on routes to/from and within Asia, and especially on routes to and within China, will continue to outstrip growth elsewhere during the next decade. The Asian carriers will be well placed to benefit from this.

The data in Table 1.4 excludes domestic traffic and thus ignores the US domestic market which is by far the largest single market in the world. If domestic traffic is included, the US airlines are pre-eminent, generating around one third of the world's total traffic (measured in tonne-kms).

While traffic growth rates in Europe and North America have generally been lower than those in Asian markets, some European or US airlines have grown in size more rapidly than their Asian counterparts through a process of acquisitions and mergers. For example, Air France's purchase of KLM in 2003, Lufthansa's acquisition of Swiss, Austrian airlines and SN Brussels in the mid-late 2000s, Delta's takeover of Northwest in late 2008 have created very large global players. Except domestically within China, consolidation in Asia has been very limited, largely because of the ownership barriers within the

Table 1.5 Distribution of traffic and revenue on scheduled services of world's airlines, 2007

	Tonne kms performed in 2007			Revenue split 2007
	International % 1	Domestic % 2	All services % 3	All services % 4
Passenger	63.9	84.4	70.5	87.4
Freight	35.3	14.9	28.7	12.0
Mail	0.8	0.7	0.8	0.6
Total	100.0	100.0	100.0	100.0

Source: Compiled by author using ICAO data.

bilateral air services agreements (see Section 3.7 in Chapter 3). As a result, individual Asian carriers have moved down in the rankings in terms of traffic volumes.

In contrast to the airlines of Asia/Pacific, the airlines of Africa and Latin America have not increased their market share during the last three decades. With one or two notable exceptions, such as Lan Airlines and South African Airways, their international airlines are generally medium-sized or often financially weak. On the other hand, though few in number, Middle East airlines, led initially by Emirates and more recently by Qatar Airways and Etihad, have increased their share of the global market.

1.8   A passenger and freight business

It is generally assumed that airlines are primarily concerned with carrying passengers and that freight and mail traffic are relatively unimportant both in terms of output and of revenue. This is far from being the truth. In 2007 nearly 30 per cent of the world's scheduled airline output was concerned with the carriage of freight and mail, though mail itself is tiny (Table 1.5). Passenger traffic accounted for the rest. On international routes, where distances are greater and air transport becomes more competitive, freight comes into its own, generating slightly over a third (35.3 per cent) of the world's tonne-kms. Moreover, this share has tended to increase. Conversely, freight's share is very much lower on domestic air services. This is because surface transport, road and rail, is generally more competitive in domestic freight markets.

These global figures hide considerable variations between airlines. A few large international airlines, such as Federal Express and UPS in the USA or Cargolux, are exclusively concerned with the carriage of freight. They are the exceptions. Most airlines are combination carriers, that is they transport both freight and passengers on their international services. But their degree of involvement in the carriage of freight varies enormously (Table 1.6). At the bottom of this table are airlines such as Lan Airlines of Chile, Korean Airlines, Cathay Pacific or SIA, for whom air freight represents about half or even well over half of their total international production in terms of revenue tonne-kilometres, that is traffic carried. These airlines invariably bolster their cargo capacity by operating fleets of all-cargo freighters.

They are clearly quite different airlines from those at the top end of the table, such as Aeromexico, Egyptair, Air India or Iberia, for whom freight and mail together account for less than 20 per cent of their total international traffic. Interestingly the US major carriers, American, United and Delta, tend to be at the lower end of the scale generating

Table 1.6 Traffic mix on international scheduled passenger and all cargo services in 2007

	Distribution revenue tonne-kms carried			
	Passenger %	Mail %	Freight %	Total %
Aeromexico	87	*	13	100
Egyptair	87	*	13	100
Air India	84	1	15	100
Delta	82	1	17	100
Iberia	78	1	21	100
American	75	2	23	100
United	74	3	23	100
Qantas	70	3	27	100
South African Airways	68	*	32	100
British Airways	68	1	31	100
Air France	63	1	36	100
Emirates	61	*	39	100
IATA Airlines' average	**60**	**1**	**39**	**100**
Lufthansa	58	1	41	100
Malaysian	57	*	43	100
All Nippon Airways	55	2	43	100
JAL	54	2	44	100
SIA	52	*	48	100
China Eastern	50	*	50	100
Cathay	46	1	53	100
Lan Airlines	41	*	54	100
Korean	33	1	66	100

Source: Compiled by author from IATA Statistics.

Note
* = 0.5% or less.

only around a quarter of their business from freight. This is largely because they have lost much of the US international and, for that matter, most of the domestic, freight market to the integrators; that is the all-cargo door-to-door carriers such as Federal Express, UPS and DHL (see Chapter 12), or to foreign airlines such as Korean or Lufthansa.

It is significant that while freight accounts for well over a quarter (29.5 per cent) of total airline production it generates only about one-eighth (12.0 per cent) of total operating revenue (Table 1.5). This means that the average revenue per tonne-kilometre of freight and, incidentally, of mail, must be very much lower than the average revenue or yield generated by passenger tonne-kilometres. Despite this, freight revenues make an important contribution to many airlines' overall profitability (Chapter 12 below).

Over the airline industry as a whole, the carriage of freight is a significant factor, both in terms of the amount of productive resources absorbed by it and in terms of its contribution to overall revenues. For an individual airline the split of its activities between passengers and freight clearly affects both its marketing policy and the structure of its revenues. As Tables 1.5 and 1.6 show, the importance of mail as a revenue is very limited and declining. Inevitably, much of the discussion which follows, except in Chapter 12, concentrates on the passenger aspects of both supply and demand. However, this should not mask the significance of air freight for the international airline industry as a whole.

When comparing airlines' performance one must take account of the degree to which and the way in which they are involved in air freight. This impacts many aspects of their operations, and their labour productivity, as well as their cost and revenue performance.

1.9   The nature of the airline product

As far as passenger services are concerned, there are several contrasting aspects to the airline product. On the one hand, the air journey is seen not as an end in itself, but as part of a business trip, a two-week or two-day leisure trip, or of a weekend visit to see relatives. The air journey is a part of a variety of other products or services. A number of important considerations flow from this. The demand for passenger air services is a derived demand. It is dependent on the demand for these other activities. This means that to forecast the demand for air services one needs ideally to forecast the demand for all these other types of expenditure. It also means that there has been strong pressure on the airlines to expand vertically into other areas of the travel industry, such as hotels, travel agencies, car hire or tour organisers, in order to gain greater control over the total travel product. There is also a direct effect on airline marketing techniques in the sense that these are frequently oriented towards selling and promoting the total product, whether it be a business or holiday trip or a weekend excursion, rather than selling a particular airline. In newspaper and television advertisements many airlines try to interest the reader or viewer in a particular destination or a particular type of trip, and only as an afterthought, almost, do they suggest the airline which might be used.

On the other hand, airlines have to face the realisation that one airline seat is very much like another and that there is from the passenger's viewpoint little difference between one jet aircraft and another. Equally, for the shipper or freight forwarder the major decision will be whether to ship by air or surface and having taken the decision to use air he may have difficulty in perceiving any significant difference between one airline and the next serving a particular route with similar frequencies. Thus, while air journeys may be only one part of a variety of heterogeneous products or services with different market structures, the air service part of these various products is itself fairly homogeneous. One airline seat is very much like another and one freight hold is no different from the next. Even when airlines wish to differentiate their products, competitive and economic forces and the fact that they are flying similar or identical aircraft have meant that they often end up offering very similar products.

The consequences of the homogeneous nature of the airline product are twofold. First, in competitive markets, it pushes airlines into making costly efforts to try to differentiate their services and products from those of their competitors. They do this by being first to introduce new aircraft types, by increasing their frequency of service, by spending more on in-flight catering or on ground services and by advertising. Moreover, much of the advertising is aimed at trying to convince passenger or freight agent that the product they offer is appreciably better than that of their competitors because of the friendliness of the hostesses or the culinary expertise of their chefs, or because of other claims, all of which are dubious and difficult to assess. Because of the difficulties of substantiating many claims related to service quality, airlines very frequently resort to competing on price, which is tangible and tariff differences are demonstrable. This is the strategy most clearly adopted by the low-cost airlines. Second, the homogeneous nature of the airline product makes the emergence of entirely new airlines or the incursion of new airlines on existing routes relatively easy.

This dichotomy between the heterogeneity of the various products, of which the air service is only a part, and the homogeneity of the air services themselves is a constant constraint in airline planning, a constraint which often results in apparently contradictory decisions and actions by airline managements.

2 Traditional bilateralism – the impact of economic regulation

> The Chicago Convention and its technical standards are not the issue. The bilateral system is the problem. The so-called freedoms of the air are really restrictions on our business . . .
>
> (Giovanni Bisignani, Director-General IATA, June 2008)

2.1 Two regulatory regimes

Airline managers are not free agents. It has been argued earlier that airline planning and management is the process of matching the supply or provision of air services, which airline managers can largely control, with the demand for such services which they can influence but not control. It is not as simple as that. Traditionally the airline industry has been one of the most highly regulated of industries. As a result, the actions of airline managers are circumscribed by a host of national, bilateral or international rules and regulations. These are both economic and non-economic in character and may well place severe limitations on airlines' freedom of action. An examination of the scope and impact of such regulations is crucial for an understanding of the economics of international air transport.

In the period 1919 to 1949 a framework of international regulation evolved in response to the technological, economic and political developments in air transport. It was uniform and, broadly speaking, worldwide in its application. For the next three decades till the late 1970s this international regulatory framework remained largely unchanged. It was supported by three pillars, the bilateral air services agreements, inter-airline pooling agreements and the tariffs and pricing agreements negotiated through the International Air Transport Association (IATA). Taken together, these three elements created a highly regulated operating environment unlike that of any other international industry – an environment, moreover, that stifled innovation and change. But a review of United States international aviation policy in 1979 inaugurated two decades of gradual liberalisation of the economic regulations affecting international air services. This process of liberalisation became more rapid after the mid-1980s when it was adopted by key European countries and eventually by the European Union. It reached a peak with the March 2007 'open skies' agreement between the European Union and the USA.

As a result, by 2009–10 there were, broadly speaking, two different regulatory regimes in the world. On the one hand many major routes to and from the United States, those between the member states of the European Union and some routes between a few European states or the United States and some Asian countries, such as Singapore, were operated under what might be termed 'open skies' regimes. On the other, international air services in many parts of the world were and still are operated within the traditional regulatory structure. In practice it is not a simple twofold division. There are gradations in each of the regulatory regimes. Some traditional bilateral agreements are very restrictive while others are much more open and allow more effective competition. Equally in some liberalised markets, such as that within the European Union, economic deregulation has removed most of the constraints on inter-airline competition, whereas in others some vestiges of traditional regulation survive.

It is also the case that most states have a mixture of bilateral air agreements with some being more or less liberal while others may be restrictive. Member states of the European Union provide a good example. One finds that most European states, whose airlines operate in an open, deregulated market on services within Europe, have some very restrictive bilateral air services agreements with non-European states which are protective of their own airlines.

The present chapter examines the traditional and restrictive regulatory framework and explores the arguments for and against liberalisation. The following chapter deals with the spread of liberalisation and the 'open skies' regimes that have emerged progressively in some key markets since the early 1980s. But first, one should also bear in mind that airlines must also satisfy a host of technical and safety regulations.

2.2   Non-economic technical and safety regulations

The advanced level of aviation technology, the need to ensure passenger safety despite the rapidity of technological innovation and the international nature of much of the airline industry have all created pressure for the introduction of more complex and more wide-ranging external controls and regulations than are found in most industries. These are broadly of two kinds. First, there are those which are economic in nature and are concerned with regulating the business and commercial aspects of air transport. Second, there is a whole host of technical standards and regulations whose prime objective is to achieve very high levels of safety in airline operations. Such regulations cover every aspect of airline activity and, broadly speaking, they fall into one of the following categories:

(i)   Regulations which deal with the airworthiness of the aircraft not only in terms of its design and production standards but also in terms of its performance under different operating conditions such as when there is an engine failure during take-off.

(ii)   Regulations covering the timing, nature and supervision of maintenance and overhaul work and the training and qualifications of the engineers who carry out such work.

(iii) Regulations governing the numbers of flight and cabin crew, their training and licensing, their duties and functions on board and their work-loads and schedules.

(iv)   Detailed regulations covering both the way in which aircraft are operated, that is aspects such as flight preparation and in-flight procedures, and also the operation of the airlines themselves. In all countries, air transport operators must be licensed by the relevant civil aviation authority and must satisfy certain criteria and operating standards.

(v)   Finally, there is a complex profusion of regulations and recommended standards dealing with aviation infrastructure, such as airports, meteorological services, en-route navigational facilities, and so on.

Many of the technical and safety requirements are general, that is not specific to a particular aircraft type, and are promulgated as regulations of the civil aviation directorates or the relevant transport ministries of each country. In the United States they are known as Federal Aviation Regulations, while in the United Kingdom such regulations appear in the Air Navigation Order (CAA, 2000c).

In Europe, the various national regulations are being progressively superseded by European-wide standards, the so-called Joint Airworthiness Requirements (JARs). The latter were agreed through and promulgated by the Joint Airworthiness Authority (JAA), which was made up of 42 member states, though by early 2007 only 34 were full members and 8 were candidate members. Working through technical committees composed of experts in each particular field, the JAA promulgated requirements, known as JARs, related to specific areas such as aircraft maintenance or pilot licensing. JARs were not mandatory. But most of the European states in fact incorporated the key JARs into their own regulations. The next logical step was the establishment by the European Union of a European Aviation Safety Agency (EASA), with mandatory powers. This became operational in 2003 with the aim of developing common safety and environmental rules. By 2008 EASA had taken over many of the functions of the Joint Airworthiness Authority.

While technical and airworthiness regulations may vary in particular detail from one country to another, they are generally based on a whole series of 'International Standards and Recommended Practices' promulgated by the International Civil Aviation Organisation (ICAO) as 16 annexes to the 'Convention on International Civil Aviation'. This is the so-called Chicago Convention signed in 1944. For instance, Annex 8 deals with the 'Airworthiness of Aircraft' and Annex 1 with 'Personnel Licensing'. These are constantly revised and updated. As a result there tends to be considerable uniformity in the technical regulations for air transport in most member states of ICAO. Operational and safety requirements specific to an aircraft type are contained in its flight manual. But the operational constraints and practices recommended in the flight manuals conform to the more general regulations mentioned above and are approved by the relevant national airworthiness authorities. Among other requirements, the flight manual will impose payload limitations on an aircraft at airports with high temperatures or inadequate runway length. In this and numerous other ways airworthiness and other technical regulations have direct economic repercussions on airlines.

While international technical and safety regulations have been adopted by virtually all countries they are not always fully and adequately implemented. This may occur, for instance, if the civil aviation authorities in a country do not have the expertise, the staffing or the financial resources to effectively monitor whether their national airlines are carrying out the required maintenance procedures and checks on their aircraft or whether pilot training is adequate. During the 1990s there was growing concern about the airworthiness and safety standards of aircraft registered in certain countries. As a reaction, in 1996 the International Civil Aviation Organisation (ICAO) began a voluntary programme of audits of individual states' capabilities to oversee the effective application of safety requirements. This culminated in a mandatory programme of audits of all states (ICAO, 1999). But, in advance of effective action by the ICAO, the US Federal Aviation Administration (FAA) had launched its own 'safety oversight' procedures whereby the FAA itself inspects and monitors the degree to which airworthiness and other safety-related regulations are adequately implemented in certain countries where concerns have been raised. The FAA has carried out inspections in well over 100 countries. If the airworthiness standards are deemed inadequate, those states are identified as falling into Category 2. If that happens, then aircraft from such countries can no longer fly into the United States. In 1999–2000 a number of states in Central America fell into this category. Their scheduled international airlines had to abandon flights to the US. Alternatively, their airlines may be prevented from increasing existing frequencies to the USA and have been required to abandon code-sharing agreements with US carriers. In 1996 in Europe a JAA and ECAC (European Civil Aviation Conference) joint programme for 'Safety Assessment of Foreign Aircraft' (SAFA) was launched. This differs from the FAA approach in that it is based on ramp inspections of aircraft landing at European airports. But the ultimate sanction is the same: to ban an airline's aircraft from flying to Europe. Each year several are black-listed and not allowed to enter European markets. The threat of such sanctions imposed by major destination countries are a strong incentive on civil aviation authorities of countries with aspiring international airlines to ensure that airworthiness regulations and standards are met. In parallel, IATA airlines have to submit to IATA's Operational Safety Audit (IOSA), which assesses an airline's operational management and control systems. Only airlines that have met the IOSA requirements can now join IATA.

These various technical standards and safety procedures undoubtedly constrain airline managers and, at the same time, impose cost penalties on airline operations. But such external controls are inevitable if high safety standards are to be maintained, and significantly all airlines are equally affected by them. No major international airline can enjoy a competitive advantage by operating to airworthiness standards below the generally acceptable level. The implementation of ICAO standards and the safety oversight procedures together ensure that, unlike the shipping sector, there are very few 'flags of convenience' in air transport, that is, states that allow airlines to circumvent national or international safety or manning regulations as a way of reducing costs. Those few airlines that do bend the rules tend sooner or later to find themselves banned from flying to the major markets.

In addition to the various technical and safety regulations and rules, international air transport is circumscribed by a multitude of national, bilateral and multilateral regulations and agreements whose objective is the economic and, sometimes, political regulation and control of the industry. Such economic controls, unlike the technical standards outlined above, do not affect all airlines equally, since they vary from market to market, and therein lies their importance.

2.3   The growth of economic regulation

When the Paris Convention, signed in 1919, accepted that states have sovereign rights in the air space above their territory, direct government intervention in air transport became inevitable. A country's air space became one of its valuable natural resources. As a result, the free-trade *laissez-faire* approach towards air transport of the early years of aviation was gradually replaced by an incomplete pattern of bilateral agreements between countries having airlines and the countries to or through which those airlines wished to fly. But the restrictive character of 'bilateralism' was soon apparent. Even before the Second World War was over, 52 member states met in Chicago in 1944 to consider some form of multinational agreement in three critical aspects of international transport:

(i)   the exchange of air traffic rights, or 'freedoms of the air' (see Appendix);
(ii) the control of fares and freight tariffs;
(iii) the control of flight frequencies and capacity.

From an economist's viewpoint these three aspects together effectively determine the nature of any industry, for they regulate the entry of firms into each market (through traffic rights), the degree of pricing freedom and the nature of controls on the level of production, if any. If there is a maximum exchange or traffic rights, which means open market access, combined with little or no control of tariffs or frequencies and capacity offered, then a market could be considered to be very competitive, provided, of course, there were no other barriers to market entry. If on the other hand traffic rights, tariffs and frequencies are all tightly regulated then such markets will be uncompetitive or even monopolistic.

At Chicago there were two conflicting approaches. The United States, whose civil aviation industry was going to emerge from the Second World War largely unscathed and much larger and better equipped than anyone else's, wanted no control of tariffs or capacity and the maximum exchange of traffic rights, including fifth freedom rights. This 'open skies' policy was supported by states such as the Netherlands or Sweden whose airlines would have to depend on carrying traffic between other countries because their home base was so small. On the other hand, the United Kingdom and most European countries were more protectionist, understandably so since their civil airlines had been decimated in the war. They supported tight controls on tariffs and capacity and the limitation of the so-called fifth freedom traffic rights (see Appendix for definition of traffic rights). These two conflicting views could not be reconciled. No multilateral agreement was reached on the three key issues of traffic rights, tariff control and capacity.

The participants at Chicago did manage to agree on the mutual exchange of the first two freedoms – the right to over-fly another state while on an agreed service and the right to land in each other's country. This was done through the International Air Services Transit Agreement signed in December 1944 and to which many more states have subsequently adhered. But no agreement was reached on the exchange of the commercial traffic rights. These are the third and fourth freedoms, which allow for the mutual exchange of traffic rights between two countries, enabling their respective airlines to carry passengers and freight between them. There is also the fifth freedom, which is the right granted by country A to an airline(s) from country B to carry traffic between A and countries other than B (see Appendix).

The most significant result of the Chicago Conference was the signing of the Convention on International Civil Aviation, known subsequently as the Chicago Convention. This provided the framework for the orderly and safe development of international air transport. It did this through its various articles and the annexes (mentioned earlier), which deal with every aspect of the operation of aircraft and air services both in the air and on the ground. The Convention also set up the International Civil Aviation Organisation (ICAO), an inter-governmental United Nations agency which provided the forum for further discussion of key aviation issues and the basis for the worldwide coordination of technical and operational standards and practices. ICAO also provided crucial technical assistance to many countries, especially newly independent states in Africa and Asia, helping them to establish airport and air navigation facilities and to organise other aspects of civil aviation infrastructure.

A further attempt at a multilateral agreement on traffic rights, pricing and capacity was made at the Geneva Conference of 1947, but this also failed. In time, government and airlines together found a way of circumventing the failures of Chicago and Geneva. The exchange of traffic rights became a matter for *bilateral air services agreement* between states; the control of capacities and frequencies became a matter for *inter-airline agreements*, and sometimes for bilateral state agreements; and tariffs came to be regulated by the *International Air Transport Association (IATA)*. As a result, a framework for the international regulation of air transport emerged based on these three separate but interlinked pillars.

2.4   Bilateral air services agreements

From the mid–1940s onwards, each country negotiated a series of bilateral air services agreements (known as 'bilaterals'), with other states aimed at regulating the operation of air transport services between them. The prime purpose of such bilaterals has been the control of market access (points to be served and traffic rights) and of market entry, by determining which airlines could be designated to use the traffic rights granted. Some bilaterals also control the flight frequencies or the capacity that can be offered by each airline on the routes between the two countries. Such bilateral agreements, and there are over 1,500 of them still today, became and, in most of the world, remain the fundamental core of the regulatory regime. This is so even when the bilaterals have been renegotiated and have become very liberal or 'open skies' agreements. Air service agreements have three distinct parts.

First, there is *the bilateral itself.* This consists of a number of articles covering a variety of administrative provisions to facilitate the operation of air services. These include articles dealing with exemption from customs duties on imports of aircraft parts, with airport charges, with the setting up of sales offices or the transfer abroad of an airline's sales revenues and so on. Of greater significance are the articles dealing with the economic provisions of the agreement. The key articles are those dealing with the regulation of tariffs and those on capacity. Most of the traditional bilaterals specify that passenger fares and cargo tariffs should be agreed by the designated airlines, due regard being paid to all relevant factors, including cost of operation, and a reasonable profit. But in the early years airlines were encouraged to use the tariff fixing machinery of IATA to reach agreement on fares. Most bilaterals included words such as

> The tariffs . . . shall if possible be agreed by the designated airlines concerned of both Contracting Parties . . . and such agreement shall, wherever possible, be reached by the use of the procedures of the International Air Transport Association for the working out of tariffs.
>
> (UK–Singapore Air Services Agreement 1971)

However, both governments were required to approve such fares and tariffs. In other words, ultimate control of tariffs rested with governments, though in practice the vast majority of governments automatically approved the IATA agreed fares. On capacity, some traditional bilaterals require very strict control and sharing of capacity by the airlines of the two countries while others have minimal control.

Another economic issue to be resolved is the number of airlines which will be designated to operate between the two signatory states. In most bilaterals only 'single designation' was envisaged, that is one airline from each state. Most states, in any case, only had one airline. However, a few bilaterals, especially those with the United States, did allow for 'double' or 'multiple designation'. Irrespective of the number of airlines to be designated, all had to be *'substantially owned and effectively controlled'* by nationals of the 'designating state'. This nationality rule found in virtually all the traditional bilaterals has proved the biggest obstacle to the normalisation of the international airline industry.

The second part of the bilateral is the annex containing the '*Schedule or Routes*'. It is here that the traffic rights granted to each of the two states are made explicit. The schedule specifies the routes to be operated by the 'designated' airline(s) of each state. Airlines are never mentioned by name. It is up to each state to designate its airline or airlines subsequently. The points (towns) to be served by each designated airline are listed or, less usually, a general right might be granted such as from 'points in the United Kingdom' without specifying the points. The routes or points granted to the designated airline of one state are not necessarily the reverse image of those granted to the airline of the other state signing the bilateral. If a town or country is not specifically listed in the route schedule a designated airline cannot operate services to it unless the bilateral is amended.

The schedule will also indicate whether the designated airlines have been granted rights to pick up traffic in other countries or from airports lying between or beyond the two signatory states. These are the fifth freedom rights. But they cannot be used unless the third countries involved also agree. Thus the current USA–Singapore bilateral grants the Singapore designated airline fifth freedom rights between London and New York as an extension of its services between Singapore and London. The London–New York rights cannot be exercised until the UK Government agrees to this in its own air services agreement with Singapore, which hitherto it has been loath to do.

The final part of the bilateral may consist of one or more '*Memoranda of Understanding*' or 'Exchange of Notes'. These are agreements, often confidential, that amplify or subsequently modify particular aspects of the basic air services agreement. Bilaterals are government to government trade agreements. Once negotiated and signed their validity is indefinite until they are renegotiated. Even then the basic articles and structure tend to remain unchanged and modifications are made through a 'Memorandum' or an 'Exchange of Notes'. If a state wishes to terminate an agreement it must give 12 months' notice. This is sometimes done when the other state is unwilling to open negotiations or refuses to accept any of the modifications being discussed.

Underlying all bilateral agreements from the early days has been the concept of reciprocity, of an equal and fair exchange of rights between countries very different in size and with airlines of varied strengths. This has traditionally been enshrined in an article containing the words '*There shall be fair and equal opportunity for the airlines of both Contracting Parties to operate the agreed service on the specified routes between their respective territories.*'

Many of the traditional type of bilateral agreements reflect protectionist attitudes. They insist on prior agreement on the capacity to be provided on the route and also specify that the agreed capacity should be shared equally by the designated carriers of the two states, normally only one from each state. In the past some went even further and specified that services must be operated in 'pool' by the airline concerned. At the same time few if any fifth freedom rights are granted.

Slightly more liberal but still traditional bilaterals are frequently referred to as being Bermuda-type agreements, after the air services agreement signed in 1946 between the United Kingdom and the United States in Bermuda. They differ from the protectionist or 'predetermination' type of agreements described above in two respects. First, fifth freedom rights are more widely available. Second, there is no control of frequency or capacity on the routes between the two countries concerned.

The other significant clause of the Bermuda Agreement was that on tariffs. While both governments maintained their ultimate right to approve or disapprove the tariffs proposed by the airlines, they agreed that where possible such tariffs should be arrived at using the procedures of the International Air Transport Association. For the United States this was a major compromise. It agreed to approve tariffs fixed by an association of producers, the international airlines, even though such price-fixing was illegal under United States domestic anti-trust legislation. In essence, IATA tariff decisions were exempted from the provisions of such legislation. As pointed out earlier, the tariffs article of most bilaterals included wording to the effect that tariff agreements should '*where possible be reached by the use of the procedures of the International Air Transport Association*'. Even states such as Singapore or Malaysia, whose national airlines did not become members of IATA until 1990, agreed in their bilaterals to approve where possible tariffs agreed through IATA. Thus approval for the IATA tariffs procedures was enshrined in most bilateral agreements. It was this that gave the IATA tariffs machinery such force until liberalisation set in after 1978.

Bermuda-type agreements became widespread, but the effect was not as liberal as their terms might suggest. This is because they did not preclude inter-airline pooling agreements which effectively restricted capacity competition. Nor do they preclude subsequent capacity restrictions imposed arbitrarily by governments to prevent foreign designated carriers from introducing a new aircraft type or to limit increases in frequencies.

2.5   Purchasing traffic rights

The traditional air services agreements are essentially restrictive. They prevent airlines from operating to points or on routes which they may wish to enter, even if it makes economic sense for them to do so, because they do not enjoy particular traffic rights. If their government is unable or unwilling to renegotiate the relevant bilaterals to obtain the additional rights then airlines have only one option left. They can try to purchase such rights by paying royalties or 'revenue compensation' to the airlines whose rights they wish to share.

Such royalty payments have been most common when airlines have wanted to pick up fifth freedom rights on medium or long-haul multi-sector services, but are much less common today.

Surprisingly, in some cases, airlines have been forced into making royalty agreements to cover the carriage of the 'sixth'-freedom traffic. The concept of sixth freedom has rarely appeared in any bilateral agreement, though the expression has been widely used for many years. It involves the carriage of traffic between two points, between which an airline does not have fifth-freedom rights, by the use of two sets of third and fourth freedom rights. For instance, Malaysia Airlines can carry traffic between London and Kuala Lumpur using their UK third and fourth freedom traffic rights. It can then carry those passengers on to Australia using the third and fourth freedom rights, granted under the Australia–Malaysia bilateral. Malaysia Airlines is effectively carrying traffic on a sector UK to Australia for which it does not formally have traffic rights. Up to the mid-1980s attempts were made to limit such sixth freedom through traffic between London and Australia or on other routes by the imposition of various controls such as the need to make stopovers of several days in Kuala Lumpur or other intermediate points. In fact for many years up to 1985 Malaysia Airlines paid a royalty to British Airways of around $50 for each sixth freedom passenger it carried on this route. Thai International was also paying British Airways for doing the same via Bangkok. KLM in Europe and SIA, Thai International, and Malaysia Airlines in South East Asia, as well as several Middle East airlines such as Emirates, were so successful in generating sixth freedom traffic that the various regulatory controls were slowly eroded and are now widely ignored.

Today, the generation of sixth freedom traffic is common and widespread. Liberalisation, the expansion of 'hubbing' and the growth of global alliances, whose members share flight codes, has made it very difficult to exact royalties for sixth freedom passengers.

A less common phenomenon was the payment of royalties for third and fourth freedom traffic. This occurred when one of the two designated carriers on a route has decided not to operate that particular route. It could then argue that the other country's designated carrier would carry all the traffic including that which would have been carried by the airline which is not operating. The non-operating airline would want to be compensated for giving up its traffic share and may be able to push the other carrier into a royalty agreement. Under a 1988 agreement between Malev, the Hungarian airline, and Olympic Airways the former paid the latter a royalty for all passengers carried on any scheduled flights between the two countries over and above the four flights weekly frequencies originally agreed, because Olympic did not operate any services to Hungary at all. Malev paid $13.00 for each such passenger on its Budapest–Athens flight and $11.00 for such additional passengers on Budapest–Salonica. This revenue compensation agreement was terminated in April 1999.

Where royalty payments enable airlines to buy traffic rights that they do not have under the terms of existing bilateral agreements, they may improve the viability of certain routes. But if the airlines are forced to pay royalties for third and fourth freedom traffic, whose rights they already have under the bilaterals, then the result is merely to push up costs. In the past, royalty payments have been an integral part of the bilateral traffic rights system. But as liberalisation has spread during the last 20 years or so, such payments have become much rarer.

2.6   Inter-airline pooling agreements

Prior to liberalisation, the vast majority of international sectors had only two major carriers, the designated airlines of the two countries involved. This is still the case today on many routes, especially short haul international routes and long-haul routes to/from Asia, Africa and Latin America. As in many duopolistic situations, there is a strong incentive for formal or informal agreements between the duopolists to share out the market. In the years up to the early 1990s such agreements generally took the form of revenue-sharing pools or, less frequently, revenue and cost-sharing pools. Where one of the two airlines in a duopolistic market was much weaker or smaller, then pooling was a way of guaranteeing its share of capacity and revenue when faced with a much stronger or well-established rival. When the two carriers were of similar strength, then pooling helped push up load factors by removing frequency competition and avoiding over-capacity. It also helped to reduce costs and rationalise schedules. Without a pooling agreement both competing airlines tended to bunch their departures at peak periods of demand. If all revenue is shared then airlines do not mind operating some flights at less attractive times. Pool partners can plan their schedules so as to offer a good range of departure times throughout the day. This benefits the passengers and stimulates demand.

Pooling agreements were forbidden on routes to or from the United States by that country's anti-trust legislation. But they became very widespread in Europe, where until the early 1990s, 75 per cent to 80 per cent of intra-European passenger-kms were operated on pooled services. They were also common in South East Asia and to a lesser extent in other parts of the world. Agreements can cover a single route or sector or more normally, all the routes on which the two signatory airlines operate between their two countries.

In general, airline pools cover third and fourth freedom traffics. While most pool agreements involve two airlines, three or four airline pools were not uncommon, especially in South East Asia. Though it is often known that airlines are operating in pool, the terms of any pooling agreement are closely guarded commercial secrets.

In some instances where the traffic is not considered to be adequate for two-airline operation, there may be a *revenue/cost pool*. This means that one airline alone operates the service on behalf of the airlines in the pool, but costs and revenues are shared between them on a pre-arranged basis. Some airlines have extended the concept of the revenue/cost pool, which has been seen essentially as a solution for thin routes, into agreements covering routes which can support two carriers. In such wider cost-sharing pools *both* airlines operate on one or more routes between their countries and all their costs and revenues are shared on the basis of an agreed formula. The flight numbers often carry the code of both airlines. Malaysia Airlines is one airline which has pursued such pools, which it calls 'joint ventures', as a matter of policy. Its agreements have until recently included one with Thai International, covering air services between Thailand and Malaysia.

The most widespread pooling agreements have been those involving *revenue-sharing*. In these all revenue on a route or sector is shared by the participating airlines in proportion to the capacity, that is the agreed number of seats, they each offer on the route or routes involved.

The next key item is to agree the revenue to be shared. This is based on an agreed pool accounting unit. This is the notional fare or revenue which each airline earns from one passenger on each pool sector. The number of revenue passengers carried on each sector by an airline is multiplied by the pool accounting unit for that sector to produce the revenue which that airline has to put into the pool. It is this notional revenue which is pooled, not the actual revenue collected. Such a system is less open to cheating because each airline need not know its pool partner's actual revenue, only the number of passengers carried, which is easy to verify. The pool accounting unit is normally related to the average revenue per passenger in the preceding period. There may be a single pool unit irrespective of class or there may be two or three separate unit values applicable to passengers in different classes.

In practice most pools have had a limit to the revenue that could be transferred from one airline to the other. This transfer limit could be expressed as a percentage of the total pooled revenue, or as a percentage of the donor's or the recipient's revenue. Alternatively the transfer limit might be an agreed maximum sum of money. Once limits on revenue transfers are imposed, particularly if they are very low, then competition begins to creep back, for the more passengers a pool carrier can carry the more revenue it can keep. But there is still no competition in terms of frequencies or capacities which are agreed in advance.

The effect of all pooling agreements, once entered into, has been to reduce the freedom of action of the airlines involved and to reduce or even blunt any competitive tendencies. This is particularly so if the transfer limit on pooled revenue is relatively high. Then there is little incentive for pool partners to compete since they are assured of half or close to half of the total revenue, whatever their relative market performance. Another feature of pooling agreements which is anti-competitive is that they require the pool partners to agree jointly on the capacity and frequencies offered. This enables them to push up load factors and tariffs and avoids frequency competition. The joint impact of the bilateral air services agreements with that of inter-airline agreements, where they exist, has been to restrict the routes on which airlines can operate and to determine the capacity shares of the two designated carriers in these markets.

It is precisely because they were deemed to be restrictive and anti-competitive collusive agreements between supplies of air services that pooling agreements were never permitted on routes to and from the United States. This was also the reason why in its December 1987 decisions on air transport liberalisation, the so-called 'First Package', the European Council of Ministers deemed that pooling agreements would be illegal unless granted specific exemptions by the European Commission. Temporary exemptions were subsequently granted for pooling agreements on intra-European Union routes. Nevertheless, during the early 1990s European Union airlines gradually unwound their pooling agreements. Today, pooling agreements can generally be found only among some Asian, Middle Eastern and African airlines.

A key question arises, however. Pooling agreements have disappeared from most major international routes, especially those involving European airlines. But have they merely been replaced by code-sharing, block space or other inter-airline commercial arrangements, whose prime objective is the same – namely, to co-ordinate schedules, avoid capacity or frequency competition and thereby push up load factors and, hopefully, tariffs and yields? After all, most airline alliances involve agreement on some or all of these issues.

2.7   The role of IATA

The International Air Transport Association (IATA) was founded in Havana in 1945, as a successor to the pre-war association which had been largely European. Its primary purpose was to represent the interests of airlines and to act as a counter-weight to ICAO, which was an inter-governmental agency primarily concerned with government interests in aviation. Through its various committees and sub-committees, which bring together airline experts for a few days each year, IATA has been able to coordinate and standardise virtually every aspect of international airline operation. Thus the Financial Committee has harmonised methods of rendering, verifying and settling accounts between airlines while the Traffic Committee has standardised aircraft containers and other unit load devices as well as many other aspects of passenger or cargo handling. IATA produces invaluable statistics, surveys and research reports covering many areas of airline activity. IATA also represents the airlines in negotiations with airport authorities, governments or ICAO on matters as diverse as airport charges or anti-hijacking measures. IATA works both as a forum for inter-airline discussion and resolution of key issues and as a pressure group representing the interests of international airlines.

One of IATA's most important functions is to operate the Clearing House for inter-airline debts arising from interline traffic, that is the carriage by one airline of passengers (or freight) holding tickets issued by other airlines. The sums involved are enormous. In the year 2007 the 201 IATA and 82 non-IATA airlines using the Clearing House, together with 97 airlines of a United States-based clearing house and 60 or so other participants, submitted inter-airline claims amounting to $44 billion. The Clearing House settles inter-airline accounts in both dollars and sterling by offsetting members' counter claims against each other. In 2007, 73 per cent of all claims could be offset without the need for any cash transaction. The Clearing House speeds up and simplifies the process of clearing inter-airline debts and substantially reduces the cost. Airlines that do not use the Clearing House must negotiate individually with each airline whose ticket stubs they might hold. This is slow and laborious. It may involve long delays before debts are cleared as well as additional bank charges. IATA also operates a 'Billing and Settlement Plan' (BSP) that simplified the selling, reporting and remitting procedures at IATA-accredited travel agents. There is a similar system for settling accounts between cargo agents and airlines (Cargo Accounts Settlement Systems – CASS).

IATA has made and continues to make a vital contribution in establishing common standards and recommended practices for the selling and distribution of air services. This is crucial, given the vast number of very different airlines involved in international operations and the large number of different countries each of those airlines may be flying to. It is IATA which has made it possible for a passenger to buy a round-the-world ticket from United Airlines in Chicago involving travel on several different airlines and for the passenger to have his ticket accepted for the sector from, say, Port Moresby (in Papua New Guinea) to Hong Kong by an airline he may have never heard of.

Historically, IATA's most important function has been to set airline fares and cargo rates. Up to 1979 the process for establishing fares was rather rigid (IATA, 1974). It involved the so-called Traffic Conferences; one covering North and South America, the second covering Europe, the Middle East and Africa, and the third the Pacific region and Australasia. Airlines operating in or through these areas belonged to the relevant conference. The conferences, meeting in secret and usually about 4–6 months in advance, established the tariff structure which would be operative for a specified period, usually of one year. The conferences also agreed on fares between the conference regions. About 200,000 separate passenger fares and over 100,000 cargo rates were negotiated together with complex conditions of in-flight service associated with each fare, such as seat pitch, number of meals to be served, whether they were hot or cold, charges for headphones and so on. Since such detailed service conditions had to be strictly applied by IATA member airlines there was little scope for competition in service standards or fares. The proposed tariff packages had to be agreed unanimously. In other words, any airline, no matter how small, could veto the proposed tariffs and force further renegotiation. The tariffs process was lengthy and time-consuming. While in the early years unanimity was usually reached fairly quickly, by the early 1970s unanimity became increasingly difficult to achieve.

From the airlines' point of view the Traffic Conference system had clear advantages: it produced a coherent and worldwide structure of interrelated passenger fares and cargo rates, together with tariff-related rules and regulations. The Traffic Conferences were also instrumental in developing standard documents and contracts of air carriage – tickets, waybills, baggage checks, and so on.

IATA tariffs were accepted worldwide because in so many bilateral air services agreements governments had explicitly agreed that they would approve fares negotiated through the IATA process. This was the case even with some governments whose airlines were not IATA members. Non-IATA airlines needed to adopt IATA fares in order to get their tickets accepted by IATA carriers. To give added force to its tariff agreements, IATA had compliance inspectors checking that member airlines were not illegally discounting on the IATA tariffs. If caught selling tickets or cargo space at discounted rates, IATA airlines faced heavy financial penalties.

Since IATA airlines were not allowed to deviate from the IATA tariffs, no price competition was possible. There can be little doubt that IATA was effectively a suppliers' cartel, whose object was to maximise its members' profits by mutually fixing the prices at which they sold their services. But there were some safeguards, which aimed at preventing the airlines' cartel from abusing its power. One was the *de facto* ban on any kind of agreement on capacity so as to make it difficult for the airlines to extract monopoly profits by fixing both fares and output at the appropriate levels. In practice, on many routes capacity was controlled either through the bilaterals or through airline agreements such as revenue pools or later on by code-sharing agreements.

But if IATA was a cartel it was failing to achieve the prime objective of any cartel, namely high profits for its members. Our earlier analysis has shown an industry characterised by poor financial results (Section 1.1 and Figure 1.1 in Chapter 1). Nevertheless, the travelling public and consumer groups remained unconvinced of the benefits of the IATA tariff machinery. During the 1970s pressure began to build up on governments in Europe and North America to allow greater pricing freedom.

At the same time IATA tariffs procedures began to prove too rigid and inflexible to deal with two new developments. The first of these was the growth in the 1960s and 1970s of non-scheduled or charter air services offering much cheaper fares. Attempts by IATA and many governments to stem their growth had failed. As a result, charter airlines were making serious inroads into scheduled markets in Europe and on the North Atlantic. The second development was the expansion in the 1970s of new dynamic airlines belonging to smaller states in the developing world, especially in South East Asia. Airlines such as Thai international, SIA and Korean began to make an impact on regional and long-haul markets. As non-IATA carriers they captured market share either by offering much higher levels of in-flight service than was permitted under IATA's 'conditions of service' or, less frequently, through greater flexibility in their tariffs.

Faced with these external competitive pressures, IATA was forced to change. The aim of new rules introduced in 1979 was to allow greater flexibility in tariff setting and offer greater freedom to airlines to opt out of the agreed tariffs. At the same time the secretive and confidential Traffic Conferences of earlier days were replaced by the much more open and public Tariff Coordinating Conferences.

Perhaps the most radical change was that after 1978 airlines could join IATA as a trade association without participating in the Passenger or Cargo Tariff Coordinating Conferences. A major breakthrough occurred in July 1990 when four Asian airlines, SIA, Cathay Pacific, Malaysia Airlines and Royal Brunei, joined as trade association members for the first time. Many others followed. Also, trade association members were no longer obliged to implement IATA tariffs. IATA's more open structure and its role in pursuing airline interests on many issues, such as airport charges or infrastructure, made it increasingly attractive to airlines that had previously stayed aloof.

By the start of the new millennium IATA's role in the setting of passenger and cargo tariffs was seriously diminished. The IATA tariffs provided a guide to fare levels. But in reality, the market environment had changed drastically on many major international routes. In long-haul markets competition had increased as a result both of the development of more effective hubs and the growth of global alliances. In many short-haul markets, the rapid expansion of low-cost carriers had totally undermined attempts to control fare levels. By 2007 fares in many markets were determined by competitive pressures rather than IATA tariff setting. At the same time the regulatory authorities were increasingly concerned about the anti-competitive character of IATA tariff processes.

The European Union adopted a Regulation in September 2006 which ended the block exemption from competition law which had been previously granted to IATA fare conferences. The exemption for intra-European passenger services ended on 31 December 2006, on trans-Atlantic services on 30 June 2007 and on all other routes from Europe as from 1 November 2007. Exemptions were also withdrawn for cargo conferences (OJ, 2006). The US Department of Transportation followed suit with a March 2007 decision withdrawing the exemption from US anti-trust laws previously granted to IATA tariff conferences in the trans-Atlantic and US–Australia markets. According to its final order the Department believes that '*Pricing discussions among competitors . . . at the IATA Tariff conferences are inherently anti-competitive and likely to increase the fares paid . . .*' (DoT, 2007).

Once again IATA was forced to adapt to a changing political environment. For air markets from and within regions of the world, notably Asia, Africa, South America, where governments want controlled and IATA-agreed tariffs, regional tariff conferences continue to meet to fix tariffs. But for regions where governments are opposed to the tariff conferences, IATA has developed a mechanism for airlines to agree fares electronically without face-to-face meetings. These are the so-called 'e-fares'. Airlines are free to apply them or not. But the value of 'e-fares' is that they provide the basis for calculating the 'flex-fare', which is the notional fare used to allocate revenue between airlines when a passenger buying one end-to-end ticket travels on two or more airlines. The 'flex-fare' is based on a weighted average of the highest 'e-fares' filed by each airline on a particular sector and for a particular cabin class to which is added an agreed premium. While the importance of IATA fares has been greatly reduced, the widespread adoption of IATA tariffs on international air routes in the past means that there is today some uniformity in the structure of air fares.

2.8   Limited regulation of non-scheduled air services

Unlike scheduled rights, non-scheduled traffic rights were traditionally not regulated by bilateral air services agreements. At the time of the 1944 Chicago Convention non-scheduled air services were not expected to be of any significance, and a more liberal attitude was therefore adopted. Whereas, under Article 6 of the Convention, scheduled air services specifically required 'special permission or other authorisation' from the destination countries, Article 5 left authorisation for non-scheduled services at the discretion of individual states (ICAO, 1980).

In practice most countries have insisted on giving prior authorisation to incoming non-scheduled flights, but attitudes towards authorisation have varied significantly. Some countries, such as India, have been restrictionist in their approach and have refused to authorise charter flights unless they are operated by their own national carrier or unless it can be shown that no scheduled traffic will be diverted. Others may insist, before authorising an incoming charter, that one of their own airlines should be allowed to tender for the charter contract. In contrast, many other countries, particularly tourist destinations such as Spain, Morocco or Tunisia, have followed a more liberal policy and have readily authorised non-scheduled services.

In 1956, the member states of the European Civil Aviation Conference (ECAC) agreed to mutually waive the requirement for any prior authorisation from the destination country for a wide range of non-scheduled flights (HMSO, 1956). This agreement greatly facilitated the development of charter services, particularly inclusive tour charters, within Europe. It was subsequently superseded by the various liberalisation measures agreed within the European Union during the 1990s.

While access to many non-scheduled markets was relatively open even from the early days, most countries, especially those with new airlines emerging, brought non-scheduled operations within some form of national regulatory control. Such regulation was aimed at clearly delineating the area and scope of non-scheduled operations so as to protect scheduled airlines, while giving non-scheduled operators considerable freedom of action within their defined area.

In the United States, under a 1962 law, supplemental carriers, as US charter airlines were then called, were restricted exclusively to non-scheduled operations and certified by the Civil Aeronautics Board (CAB) to operate in designated geographical areas. In 1968 the Inclusive Tour Charter Bill empowered the CAB to authorise the operation of inclusive tour charters (ITCs). An inclusive tour is a holiday package where a single charge includes travel, hotel accommodation and possibly local ground transport, visits, and so on. IT charters were developed in parallel with 'affinity' group charters operated by both supplemental carriers and scheduled airlines. Similarly, the European airlines meanwhile had based their own non-scheduled operations on developing inclusive tour charters (ITCs) though several were operating affinity charters to the US or Canada.

As charter flights grew in the 1960s and 1970s IATA and many governments, under pressure from IATA, and to protect their own scheduled airlines, imposed arbitrary and often restrictive regulations on charter services. But as the tide of public opinion in many European countries and in North America swung strongly in favour of cheap charter flights governments were forced to gradually dismantle the various domestic controls on charters. This process was given added impetus by the moves in the United States after 1978 to deregulate both domestic and international air transport. In particular, the United States set out to remove all price and other controls on charters while at the same time making the granting of non-scheduled traffic rights explicit within bilateral air services agreements.

The gradual liberalisation of non-scheduled services and the dismantling of often arbitrary regulations led to a rapid growth in charter traffic. By 1977, nearly one third of passengers flying across the Atlantic were on inclusive tour or affinity group charters. This was the peak year. Then in 1978 the long-haul charter market collapsed. This was a direct result of deregulation of fares and entry on many North Atlantic scheduled routes. Several new entrant and lower cost airlines, such as Laker Airways, began operating scheduled services. Competitive pressure pushed both new and existing scheduled carriers to offer fares which were charter competitive. With little price advantage to offer, charter airlines found their traffic shrinking rapidly. Today charters account for well below 5 per cent of North Atlantic passenger traffic. However, in other areas, especially in European holiday markets, charter operations continued to grow rapidly, normally outstripping the growth rates of scheduled carriers, until they were undermined by the emergence of low-cost airlines after 1996. (See Chapter 7 for more on charter economics.)

Generally speaking, non-scheduled operations have been subject to two different regulatory regimes. While in many parts of the world, such as the European-Mediterranean market or that of the North Atlantic, they have traditionally been subject to less regulatory controls than scheduled carriers, at least until the 1990s, in some states there has been a virtual ban on allowing incoming or even outgoing charter flights, except in exceptional circumstances. But here too the need to encourage tourism arrivals is leading to a gradual relaxation of the regulatory constraints.

2.9   Operational constraints imposed by the traditional regulatory framework

The traditional three-pronged structure of international regulation based on the bilaterals, the inter-airline agreements and IATA has constrained the freedom of action of individual scheduled airlines in a number of ways.

First, their markets have often been restricted. Airlines could not enter any market at will, but have been dependent on government action and support; first in making bilateral agreements to open up air routes and obtain the necessary traffic rights and, second, in negotiating the points which should be served on these routes. This is not always straightforward, particularly if an existing bilateral has to be renegotiated. The other country may refuse to negotiate or may want to exact a high price for accepting changes to routes or traffic rights granted under the existing bilateral. In practice, to obtain fifth freedom rights some airlines have had to pay royalties to other carriers. Some have even had to pay royalties to exercise third and fourth freedom rights granted to them under air services agreements.

Second, the level of output of each airline has not been entirely at its own discretion. Its production may have been limited through bilateral agreements on capacity control or on equal sharing of capacity, or through any inter-airline agreements on revenue sharing with the consequent control of capacity. An airline wishing to increase its capacity and output on routes where there was some form of bilateral or inter-airline capacity control has often found that the other airline in the duopoly may be unable or unwilling to increase its own capacity, and therefore may veto the expansion plans. Thus competing in terms of frequencies became virtually impossible. Limitations on increasing frequencies have been widespread but have not existed in all markets. For instance, on many routes to or from the United States there was little effective capacity control even before deregulation.

Finally, airlines' pricing freedom has also been limited. This is partly because, until liberalisation in the 1980s, most tariffs have traditionally been set by the IATA Tariffs Conferences in which the influence of any individual airline was limited and partly because governments must ultimately approve all tariffs. Even non-IATA airlines have frequently been required by governments to apply IATA tariffs on most of their international routes. Prior to international liberalisation, pricing freedom only existed in markets where either there was widespread discounting of IATA tariffs or in markets where, with the connivance of governments, the IATA tariffs had been abandoned. Under traditional bilateralism, airline managers have not been as free as they might have wished to choose and set their own tariffs.

From 1978 onwards many international air transport markets have been progressively liberalised. This is the topic of the next chapter. Where this has happened, many of the constraints imposed on airlines, which have been summarised here, have been relaxed or removed altogether. However, there are many point-to-point markets, such as inter-African and many Asian routes, which are still operated under more traditional bilateral regulatory regimes. This means that market access or points to be served, as well as capacity and frequencies offered, are tightly controlled in many markets. But on pricing there is more variability since attempts to prevent price competition in many bilateral markets have largely collapsed.

In practice most airlines have to operate their services under two different regulatory regimes. On many of their routes they will be constrained by having to operate within the limitations of traditional bilaterals while on some other routes they may be operating in an 'open skies' regime. Singapore Airlines (SIA) is a case in point. It has 'open skies' bilateral agreements with the United States, Brunei and New Zealand and fairly open agreements with some European states such as Germany. But SIA operates the majority of its services to other Asian countries, to points in the Middle East, Africa or Eastern Europe, with the constraints arising from the traditional bilateral regime. Even the

United States, which has pursued 'open skies' bilaterals so vigorously, still had a very large number of bilaterals in 2007 that had not been liberalised. But, as one can see in the following chapter, even 'open skies' regimes do not allow airline managers unlimited freedom of action. Whatever the regulatory regime, whether restrictive or 'open', airlines are still constrained in what they can do to a greater or lesser extent. Airline planning and economics can only be understood in the context of this mixed regulatory environment.

3 Liberalisation – open markets, open skies and beyond

> International aviation is in a period of extraordinary change . . . The inexorable economic forces that are creating a global economy won't bypass civil aviation.
>
> (John Byerly, US Deputy Asst. Secretary of State for Transportation,
> April 2007)

3.1 The case for and against regulation

In the period up to the late 1970s economists had justified the tight regulation of both international and domestic air services on several grounds. In the United States the Civil Aeronautics Act of 1938 had been introduced to regulate and control competition between US domestic carriers because the unregulated competition which had prevailed up to then had led to chaotic economic conditions, little security for investors and low safety margins. During the early years of civil aviation the American view was that, while domestic air transport is not a natural monopoly, regulation was required because 'unregulated competitive market forces may have adverse consequences for the public at large' (Richmond, 1971). The same philosophy had been widely adopted to justify the regulation of international air transport as well. It was argued that, whereas there were strong oligopolistic tendencies in air transport, absence of any regulation of market entry would inevitably lead to wasteful competition. This is because the industry has a non-differentiated product and a relative ease of entry. At the same time economies of scale are not very marked, so small new entrant airlines would not have a cost disadvantage when operating against much larger incumbents. On the other hand, new entrants into a particular market would try to establish themselves by undercutting existing fares, and a price war would result with adverse consequences for all participants.

The second economic argument favouring regulation was based on the concept that air transport is a public utility, or at least a quasi-public utility. It was argued that the external benefits arising from civil aviation were such that the industry needed to be regulated in order to ensure that any benefits were not jeopardised. These benefits were assumed to be not only economic but also strategic, social and political. The public utility nature of air transport has, rightly or wrongly, been considered so important that initially most countries, except the United States, concentrated on developing one major scheduled operator, usually with direct government participation. The same carrier often operated domestic services and acted as the designated foreign carrier. It was a natural extension of this point of view to believe that free and unregulated competition on international air routes would endanger national interests because it might adversely affect that national state-owned airline.

A third argument supporting regulation of international air transport was linked to the rapid development of non-scheduled air traffic in the 1960s and early 1970s. It was argued that where states wished to have scheduled services providing regular and readily available capacity with the minimum of special conditions for the public at large, some form of protection against the encroachment of lower-cost charter operators was required. This was particularly so where the scheduled traffic was relatively thin, for even a small loss of traffic might jeopardise the continuation of scheduled operations.

During the 1960s, economists in the United States and elsewhere began to question these benefits of regulation and argued the advantages of freer competition in air transport. The then existing international regulations, described previously, limited pricing freedom and product differentiation, restricted capacity growth and excluded new entrants. If these regulations were relaxed, a more competitive environment would provide considerable benefits to the consumer in lower fares, innovatory pricing and greater product differentiation. Lower tariffs would push airlines to re-examine their costs and would force them to improve their efficiency and productivity. Lower costs would facilitate further reductions in tariffs. Some inefficient airlines might be forced out of particular markets. But it was argued that the economics of the airline industry did not justify the fear that freer competition would lead to economic instability. The capacity of most large international airlines to fight tariff wars on a limited number of routes at a time, combined with a strong sense of self preservation, would prevent the established carriers from going too far in a price war because of the dangers of getting 'locked-in'. In other words, they would avoid successive fare reductions which would ultimately leave each airline with much the same share of the market but with very low and possibly unprofitable fare levels. Fear of new entrants would almost certainly push down fares to a level where only normal profits were being secured. Excess profits in any markets would attract new entrants until profits dropped to normal levels.

At a more general level many economists argued there was little reason to believe that the airline industry was so different from other industrial and service sectors that both suppliers, that is the airlines, and consumers needed special protection. Surely the normal anti-monopoly regulations would be enough to safeguard consumer interests. Since entry by new airlines was assumed to be easy, there was no need to protect incumbent carriers. If through bad management they collapsed, others would step in.

3.2   Mounting pressures for liberalisation

Whatever the economic arguments, political and consumer pressures for liberalisation of the tight regulatory regimes was building up. Consumers in the United States and Europe could not understand why various rules were needed to prevent them from having free access to much cheaper charter flights or cheaper and unrestricted fares on scheduled services. Then in 1978, the newly-elected President Carter, who had made support for consumers a key part of his election platform, signed the Airline Deregulation Act into law on 24 October. This set off a chain of events which over the next 30 years were to transform international air transport from a protected and highly regulated industry into one which is more truly open and competitive. Changes were slow at first but then gathered pace.

The Act provided for the complete elimination of the Civil Aeronautics Board by 1985, bringing an end virtually to all controls over US *domestic* route licensing and fares. Other aspects of the Board's responsibilities would be taken over by other branches of the Federal government. The significance of US domestic deregulation which was so rapid and total, was that the pressures for change inevitably spilled over to international air transport.

In Europe there were similar winds of change. In the United Kingdom the Civil Aviation Authority became increasingly liberal in its licensing decisions from 1975 onwards. The European Parliament in Strasbourg and the European Commission in Brussels all began to discuss various aspects of deregulation within Europe. But it was not until 1983 that the first European Directive, for the deregulation of inter-regional air services between member states of the European Community, was approved (CEC, 1983). This Directive, a watered down version of earlier proposals, had little impact, but it did mark the first step towards liberalisation on a European Union–wide basis. It should be borne in mind that whereas domestic deregulation in the United States was implemented very quickly and almost overnight, in Europe the process was more gradual. It moved slowly from limited liberalisation in the mid-1980s to a more fully deregulated intra-European Union market ten years later.

In international aviation the United States had acquiesced for more than 30years in the traditional pattern of tight regulation described earlier. Then late in 1977 US international aviation policy began to change dramatically. Far from accepting the existing regulatory framework, the United States suddenly appeared to be hell bent on deregulation, on reducing existing regulatory controls to a minimum. It was supported in this by several other governments, especially those of the Netherlands and Singapore, but it was the United States that was the prime generator of change.

Following public hearings, a statement on 'International Air Transport Negotiations' was signed by President Carter on 21 August 1978 (Presidential Documents, 1978). This stated that the United States' aim was '*to provide greatest possible benefit to travellers and shippers*' and that '*maximum consumer benefits can best be achieved through the preservation and extension of competition between airlines in a fair market place*'. Through the renegotiation of existing bilateral agreements the US aims were first, to create greater opportunities for innovative and competitive pricing, second, to eliminate restrictions on capacity frequencies and traffic rights, third, to eliminate restrictions on charters, fourth, to allow multiple designation of US airlines (i.e. to allow more than one airline to use negotiated traffic rights) and finally, to liberalise cargo rules.

The United States set out to achieve greater competition in a series of crucial bilateral negotiations which took place in the period 1977 to 1985. The major objective of US policy was generalised liberalisation. This made sense given the free enterprise and competitive aviation environment in the United States. But in most of the countries with which the United States was negotiating there was only one airline or only one large scheduled airline, which was usually state-owned and was the 'chosen instrument' of each country's aviation policy. As a result the United States faced a mixed response from other countries when renegotiating key bilaterals.

Nevertheless, the reversal of US international aviation policy in 1978 inaugurated the first steps towards liberalisation. The period 1978 to 1991 is best described as the 'open market' phase, when international markets were opened up to increased competition, but many constraints on airline operating freedom still remained. This was followed after 1991 by the 'open skies' phase during which most but not all remaining constraints were removed in many US bilaterals and most clearly within Europe.

3.3   Open market phase of liberalisation: 1978–91

3.3.1   *Renegotiation of US bilaterals*

From 1978 onwards, picking off a country at a time, the United States began renegotiating its bilateral air services agreements. Because of the importance and size of the US international market, most countries wanted to serve more gateway cities in the United States. Increased access to the US market was the carrot used by American negotiators to obtain most of the policy objectives outlined above. The key bilaterals that were renegotiated were those across the Pacific with states in East Asia and those with certain European states. On these long-haul routes from the United States a more liberalised regulatory regime was progressively introduced. By the mid-1980s similar concepts were being introduced in markets outside the United States through the renegotiation and revision of bilateral air services agreements by other states.

It was the revised United States–Netherlands air services agreement, signed in March 1978, which was to set the trend for subsequent US 'open market' bilaterals. Both sides set out to reduce the role of the government in matters of capacity, frequency, tariffs and in the setting of market conditions. The key innovations of the agreement can be summarised as follows:

(a) Multiple designation accepted (i.e. more than one airline from each state).
(b) US airlines given unlimited authority from any points in USA via intermediate points to Amsterdam and points beyond with full traffic rights (i.e. fifth freedom rights).
(c) Dutch airlines given only five points in the United States (i.e. Dutch were only given limited number of US gateways).
(d) No restrictions on the frequencies or capacities offered by airlines of each state.
(e) No restrictions on 'sixth' freedom traffic (see Appendix).
(f) Unlimited charter rights between any points in either territory (charter rights included in a bilateral for the first time).
(g) Country of origin rules for scheduled tariffs (i.e. each government to set its own rules for tariffs originating in its own country). Subsequent bilaterals introduced double disapproval for tariffs (i.e. only disapproval by both governments can block a fare proposed by an airline).

Not wishing to see their own traffic diverted via Amsterdam, Belgium and Germany concluded bilaterals with the United States at the end of 1978 which were very similar to the earlier US–Netherlands agreement. There were variations but the pattern was set. Other countries in the European area were under pressure to follow suit in their own negotiations with the United States. One or two of the larger European aviation powers, notably the French and the Italians, held out against the trend towards deregulation, though they too had to compromise on some issues.

Liberalisation through bilateral renegotiation was also being pursued by the United States in other international markets. The most important after the North Atlantic for American airlines was perhaps the North and mid-Pacific market. Here the United States negotiated several key bilaterals between 1978 and 1980 with Singapore, Thailand, Korea and the Philippines. These bilaterals follow the same pattern as those in Europe. As it did with the Netherlands agreement mentioned above, the United States offered these countries a handful of gateway points in the United States, usually less than five, in exchange for most if not all of the US objectives previously outlined. US moves towards deregulation inevitably impacted on other countries, such as Canada and the United Kingdom, and induced them to be more liberal in their own aviation policies.

3.3.2   *Focus switches to Europe*

In Europe, consumer pressures for liberalisation of air transport built up throughout the 1980s. They were reinforced by the mounting pressure both from within the European Parliament and from the Commission of the European Communities for major changes to the structure of regulations affecting air services between the member states of the Common Market. But it was not till the mid-1980s that the first significant breakthroughs were achieved. Changes in the regulatory environment were introduced in two ways, first, bilaterally through the renegotiation of air services agreements between pairs of countries; second, multilaterally, through actions initiated by the European Commission in Brussels or the European Court of Justice.

The more liberal and free market attitudes towards air transport prevailing in the United Kingdom pushed it to renegotiate most of its key European bilaterals in the period from 1984 to 1993. The first major breakthrough was in June 1984 when a new air services agreement was negotiated with the Netherlands, another country set on liberalisation. This agreement, together with further modification in 1985, effectively deregulated air services between the two countries. Free entry of new carriers, access by designated airlines to any point in either country, no capacity controls and a 'double disapproval' regime for fares were the key features introduced. These features, some of which were first introduced in the revised United States bilaterals discussed earlier, represented a clear break with the traditional and more protectionist European bilaterals which had prevailed till then.

The UK–Netherlands agreement set the pattern for the renegotiation of European bilaterals.

While the United Kingdom set the pace, other European states also began to renegotiate their bilaterals in this period. Though they did not usually adopt all the features of the UK–Netherlands agreement in one go, the aim of such negotiations was usually to introduce gradual liberalisation.

The European Commission's Directorate General of Transport espoused liberalisation early on and had been trying to push various proposals through the Council of Ministers since 1975. Initially its only very limited success was the July 1983 Council Directive on Inter-Regional Air Services (CEC, 1983). This set the precedent for action on air transport at European Community level. More significant was the so-called 'December 1987 Package' of measures, agreed at that time by the European Council of Transport Ministers. This was the first step towards liberalisation of air transport within the Community as a whole. It introduced a more liberal fares regime including the concept of fare zones. These allowed airlines some pricing flexibility within agreed upper and lower limits, the so-called fare zones. It abandoned the previous practice of equal sharing of capacity by airlines of each state and facilitated the entry of new airlines by opening up market access (CEC, 1987a).

The 1987 'package' was important because it explicitly acknowledged that the competition articles of the Treaty of Rome applied to air transport (CEC, 1987b). In turn this meant that many of the inter-airline agreements then in existence, such as those dealing with capacity planning, revenue pooling or pricing, would be anti-competitive and therefore illegal unless specific exemptions were granted. Block exemptions were published by the European Commission in August 1988. But these block exemptions were granted, at that time and subsequently, only if certain demanding conditions were met (CEC, 1988). One consequence was that revenue pooling agreements between European airlines (see Section 2.6 in Chapter 2) were progressively abandoned. In June 1990 the Council of Ministers agreed the details of a new second liberalisation package. This made only marginal improvements to the 1987 package. The more significant steps towards liberalisation in Europe in the 1980s came about through the renegotiation of bilateral air services agreements, rather than through action at European Community level.

3.3.3   Liberalisation spreads

Outside Europe and North America a number of other countries also began to move cautiously towards reducing controls on their air transport industries. In Japan, JAL's effective monopoly of international air services was broken when from 1986 onwards domestic carriers All Nippon Airways or Japan Air Systems were designated as the second Japanese carriers on a number of key international routes. In several South East Asian countries new airlines were allowed to emerge to operate both domestic and international air services often in direct competition with the established national carrier. In South Korea, for instance, Asiana Airlines was formed in February 1988 and launched domestic services at the end of that year and regional services to Tokyo, Bangkok and Hong Kong in 1990. The emergence of Eva Air in Taiwan and Dragonair in Hong Kong were other examples. In Australia in 1987, a new government aviation policy re-affirmed Qantas's continued role as the country's sole designated international carrier but announced a complete deregulation of domestic air services from October 1990. This meant that the government would withdraw from regulating domestic fares or capacity. The previous policy of limiting domestic trunk operations to only two carriers, Ansett and Australian, was also abandoned, though Qantas would still be precluded from operating purely domestic services.

In the East Asian–Pacific region such attempts at liberalisation were often localised, haphazard and uncoordinated as between neighbouring countries. Their impact was fairly limited. On most routes, single designation continued to prevail (except on routes to Japan); third and fourth freedom capacities and frequencies were still regulated and many services were covered by revenue pooling agreements. On tariffs there was more flexibility. In many countries governments, aviation authorities and airlines turned a blind eye to illegal discounting of government approved IATA fares. In this way *de facto* liberalisation of tariffs was introduced on many international routes.

3.3.4   The new rules of the game

In the process of renegotiating many of its key bilaterals between 1977 and 1985 the United States introduced some new concepts into international regulation which significantly changed the rules of the game as airlines were concerned, offering them greater freedom of action. In the second half of the 1980s these were incorporated into the revised bilaterals negotiated by some European states which in some respects went even further than the US bilaterals. These are summarised in Table 3.1. (For more details see Doganis, 2006.)

Table 3.1 Key features of traditional and post-1978 'open market' bilaterals

	Traditional bilaterals	*New 'open market' bilaterals*
Market access	Only to points specified	Open access – airlines can fly between any two points*
	Limited fifth freedoms granted – more in US bilaterals	Extensive fifth freedom rights granted in US bilaterals but still very limited in intra-European bilaterals
	Charter rights not included	Unlimited charter rights granted (in Europe granted earlier under 1956 ECAC agreement)
Designation	Single – some multiple in US bilaterals (e.g. in US–UK agreement)	Multiple
	Airlines must be 'substantially owned and effectively controlled' by nationals of designating state	
Capacity	Capacity agreed or shared 50:50	No frequency or capacity controls
	No capacity/frequency controls in liberal bilaterals, but subject to review	
Tariffs	Double approval by both governments required	Double disapproval (i.e. only *both* governments can block)
	To be agreed using IATA procedures	Country of origin rules (in some US bilaterals)

Note

* While US 'open market' bilaterals gave US airlines rights from any point in USA, foreign airlines restricted to a handful of named points in USA.

A significant change was the opening up of market access. Whereas under the traditional bilaterals the number of points to be served in each country was strictly limited, under the 'open market' bilaterals, *access was opened up to several new points*. The US bilaterals were, however, somewhat unbalanced in this respect. While US airlines were granted the right to fly from any point in the USA to specified points in the other country, the other country's airlines could only fly to/from a larger but still limited number of points in the USA. Revised bilaterals between European states and states outside Europe also limited the points to be served. The intra-European bilaterals, however, were generally more liberal in allowing flights *between any points* by carriers from either state. On the other hand, the US bilaterals granted more *extensive fifth freedom rights* than did the European ones. All the new bilaterals also tended to allow *unlimited charter rights* though some permitted governments to establish their own regulations for charters originating in their own state, so called 'country of origin' rules.

On traffic rights the other significant development was the adoption of *unlimited or multiple designation*. This is the right of each party to a bilateral to designate as many airlines as it wishes to operate its own agreed routes. Some earlier bilaterals, such as the 1946 UK–USA agreement, had accepted double or multiple designation but they were the minority. In addition, many of the new US bilaterals included *break of gauge* rights.

This is the right to change from a larger to a smaller aircraft in the other country's territory on a through service that is going beyond the other country, usually, but not necessarily, with fifth freedom rights. In order to use its break of gauge rights an airline would need to station smaller aircraft at the airport where the change of gauge took place.

The major change introduced in terms of capacity was to *remove limits on the frequencies or seat capacity* offered by airlines on the routes they operated. Most earlier bilaterals had imposed some attempts to balance or control capacity and the previous European bilaterals had mostly required a 50:50 sharing of capacity by the airlines of each state.

On pricing the new concept introduced in the 'open market' bilaterals was that of *double disapproval*. Under traditional air services agreements tariffs could not become operative unless approved by both governments. However, under a double disapproval regime, a tariff can only be blocked if *both* governments reject it. In agreeing to double disapproval governments gave up their veto powers on tariffs. This was a major step in freeing up airline pricing.

These new rules of the game, wherever applied, represented a significant shift towards a more liberalised and competitive environment for international airlines. But the spread of 'open market' bilaterals was somewhat haphazard and geographically rather patchy. By the early 1990s, the most liberalised markets for scheduled air transport were those to and from the United States and Canada. On the North Atlantic routes, for instance, capacity or frequency constraints had largely disappeared and entry of new carriers was, in theory, easy because of multiple designation. The number of US gateway points had more or less doubled and on many routes US carriers could add new gateway points almost at will, though European carriers did not have the same freedom. The tightly regulated tariffs agreed through the IATA mechanism had been replaced by a more flexible system of fare zones, with airlines free to pitch their fares anywhere within the relevant agreed zones for each fare type. Attempts to control and standardise in-flight service had been abandoned. On the trans-Pacific routes the situation was similar in many respects but not so liberal. There was probably greater pricing freedom than on the North Atlantic since the agreed fares were widely discounted.

Within Europe the situation was very mixed. The most liberalised markets were those between the UK and the Netherlands and UK to Ireland. At the other extreme the Austria–Greece scheduled market or air services to Eastern Europe were still tightly regulated by capacity controls, revenue-pooling agreements and enforcement of IATA tariffs.

Elsewhere in the world real liberalisation had not processed very far by 1991. On long-haul routes from Europe to central and South East Asia and Australasia there was some pricing freedom through widespread discounting of IATA and government-approved fares to which many governments turned a blind eye. The same was true of air services within South East Asia and the Pacific region. On the other hand, traffic rights and capacities were strictly regulated and revenue-pooling agreements were widespread. In Africa, South America, the Middle East and Western Asia deregulation had had even less impact and the traditional regulatory framework remained largely intact.

3.4   The United States pushes for 'open skies': 1992 onwards

Though the regulatory environment appeared patchy and mixed, the trend to further liberalisation and eventually to deregulation could not be reversed or even stemmed. On the contrary, the need for further liberalisation became increasingly apparent as a result of several developments.

First, there was a growing body of expert opinion that the airline industry should be normalised; that is, it should be allowed to operate as any other major international industry. This view gained ground during the 1980s both among aviation specialists and government officials in several key countries.

A second and perhaps stronger argument against bilateralism was that even when countries signed the more liberal open market bilaterals, the market opportunities opened up tended to be those considered acceptable by the least liberal of the two countries.

The third factor pushing towards further liberalisation was that the airline industry had matured during the previous decade. As a result of the liberalisation that had already taken place during the 1980s the industry had undergone structural changes, which made it progressively more difficult for airlines to operate within the confines of a restrictive bilateral system. Such structural changes included:

- A growing concentration within the US airline industry as the smaller post-1978 new entrant carriers collapsed or were taken over by the more successful majors. At the same time one saw the emergence of the US domestic majors, such as American or United Airlines, as big players in international markets.
- Outside the United States, marketing benefits of very-large-scale operations was being achieved through airline mergers within the same country, and by minority share purchases or strong marketing alliances with airlines in other countries (Doganis, 2006). Here too there was growing market concentration and the need to search for new markets.
- Finally, airline ownership outside the United States was changing. In many parts of the world there was a growing view that governments should not be running commercial businesses. This view, combined with fiscal pressures to reduce government exposure, was pushing many governments to privatise their airlines, in part or fully. The UK Government set the trend here with the successful privatisation of British Airways in 1987. Privatised airlines would be expected to stand on their own without regulatory protection.

These structural changes created a critical need for successful airlines, whether private or state-owned, to be able to operate more easily outside the narrow confines of their own national markets, while freed from the remaining constraints imposed by bilateralism.

Again the initial motor for change was the United States. Following the 'open market' liberalisation, the unresponsive traditional US airlines such as Pan Am and TWA were progressively replaced by the powerful and very large domestic majors such as American, Delta and United. These carriers benefited from having huge domestic networks to feed their international services and enjoyed great marketing power from their sheer size. They could outsell the competition on selected routes by high frequencies and innovative pricing made possible by lower unit costs. But many of the existing bilaterals, even if of the 'open market' type, still limited their scope and freedom of action. American, United, Delta among others pushed for further liberalisation. They felt that in a fully liberalised open skies environment they would do better than their foreign competitors because of the traffic feed that they would obtain from their huge domestic US networks and from their sheer size. The US State Department and the Department of Transportation also felt that open skies would benefit both American consumers and their airlines. At the same time, developments within the European Community, later to become the European Union, were also pushing inexorably towards open skies.

In the case of the United States bilaterals, the first key breakthrough came in 1992 in negotiations with the Netherlands, whose Government and airline, KLM, were also keen to adopt open skies. KLM had done well under the earlier 1978 'open market' agreement with the United States and by the mid-1980s its market share on the US–Amsterdam routes was over 80 per cent. Much of this traffic was travelling to other points in Europe through KLM's well-operated hub at Amsterdam's Schiphol airport. KLM was anxious to reinforce its position while its government felt that as a small country the Netherlands had much to gain from further liberalisation of international air services, especially if it was the first in Europe to do so.

In September 1992 the Dutch and United States Governments signed what was effectively the first 'open skies' agreement and inaugurated a new phase of international deregulation. In brief the new features of this bilateral, which had not been included in the earlier 1978 'open market' bilateral, were as follows:

- open route access – airlines from either country can fly to any point in the other with full traffic rights;
- unlimited fifth freedom rights;
- no tariff controls (except if tariffs too high or too low);
- airlines free to code-share or make other commercial agreements;
- break of gauge permitted.

These new features represented a further and significant easing of the regulatory environment. Open and free market access, together with no pricing controls when added to the absence of capacity restrictions and multiple designation, already granted in the earlier 'open market' bilateral, meant that one had moved from a liberalised regime to one that appeared to be deregulated. But not quite. As discussed later the open skies agreements still left some regulatory issues unresolved. Nevertheless, they represented a major step forward.

After the US–Netherlands agreement there was a lull, due in part to the fact that the fortunes of the airline industry deteriorated dramatically in the period 1990 to 1993. Spurred on by the findings of the 1993 'National Commission to Ensure a Strong Competitive Airline Industry', the Clinton Administration saw the urgent need to create open aviation markets with unrestricted access for the airlines concerned and with greater freedom for airlines to develop types of services required by the market place. These twin objectives were to be achieved primarily by entering into 'open skies' aviation agreements initially with like-minded states and later with other less liberal states. (For more details on the development of US aviation policy see Doganis, 2006.) But for those countries not willing to advance market liberalisation the threat of US counter-measures was explicit. In particular, foreign airlines should not expect code-sharing arrangements with US airlines to be approved and be given anti-trust immunity if their states did not agree to 'open skies' bilaterals.

Shortly after the 1992 'open skies' agreement with the United States, KLM applied for and obtained anti-trust immunity from the US authorities to enable it to exploit more fully the potential benefits from its partnership with Northwest. Immunity provided KLM-Northwest with considerable freedom jointly to plan their code-shares, schedules and pricing policy on routes from the USA to Amsterdam and beyond.

European airlines negotiating commercial alliances with US carriers appreciated the potential benefits which anti-trust immunity could provide. The US government grabbed the opportunity. In the 1980s it had offered access to more US gateway points in order

Table 3.2 US 'open market' and post-1991 'open skies' air services agreements

	1978–91 'open market' bilaterals	*Post-1991 'open skies' bilaterals*
Market access	Named number of points in each state – more limited for non-US carriers	Unlimited
	Generally unlimited fifth freedom	Unlimited fifth freedom
	Domestic cabotage not allowed	
	Seventh freedom not granted	
	Open charter access	
Designation	Multiple	
	Substantial ownership and effective control by nationals of designating state	
Capacity	No frequency or capacity control	
Tariffs	Double disapproval or country of origin rules	Free pricing
Code sharing	Not part of bilateral	Code-sharing permitted*

Note

* Co-operative arrangements, e.g. code-sharing, blocked-space, or leasing, allowed between airlines of signatory states or with airline(s) of third states if they permit reciprocal arrangements.

to persuade countries to sign up to 'open market' bilaterals. Now it offered an even more enticing exchange – anti-trust immunity for alliance partners in return for agreement on new 'open skies' bilaterals.

By mid-2007 over 60 new 'open skies' agreements had been signed by the United States with most of its major aviation partners except the United Kingdom and Japan which were the two largest markets for US carriers. All these agreements, such as the one with Singapore signed in 1997, were very similar to the US–Netherlands agreement detailed above. Some countries, such as Italy, reluctant to jump to a full 'open skies' agreement in one step – often to protect their own airlines – signed phased bilaterals. In these the full 'open skies' features were introduced gradually over a two-year period.

Open skies policies have also been adopted and actively pursued by a few other states. New Zealand, which signed an open skies bilateral with the United States, had secured similar deals with Singapore, Malaysia, Brunei, the UAE and Chile by the end of 1999. This was in addition to the Single Aviation Market pact concluded earlier with Australia. The latter country pursued its own open skies agreements and signed the first one with the UAE. This represented a major policy shift. Australia was prepared to offer not only all the key features of US-style open skies agreements but was also willing to consider granting Seventh Freedom rights for stand-alone air services between Australia and a third country on a case-by-case basis. Domestic cabotage, however, was not negotiable. On the other hand in a new aviation policy, Australia relaxed its ownership rules to allow foreign interests or airlines to own up to 100 per cent of Australian domestic airlines. This made it possible for Ansett Australia to become majority owned by Air New Zealand.

The 'open skies' agreements, generally very similar to the US–Netherlands agreement described earlier, were a significant improvement on the 'open market' agreements they replaced in several respects, most notably in relation to market access and tariff regulation (Table 3.2). They opened route access to any point in either country whereas the earlier bilaterals had tended to limit the number of points that could be served by foreign carriers in the United States. Also mutual fifth freedom rights were granted without restraint compared to the more limited fifth freedom in earlier bilaterals. On tariffs, double disapproval or the country of origin rule were replaced by a clear decision that governments should not meddle in tariffs except *in extremis* to prevent discriminatory practices, to protect consumers from unreasonably high or restrictive prices or to protect airlines from artificially low fares due to government subsidies or support.

A further innovation was the inclusion of an article dealing specifically with inter-airline commercial agreements such as code-sharing (this is when airlines add their partner's code to their own flight number) and block space or leasing agreements. This was critically important. Close-knit commercial agreements, which went further than simple code-sharing on routes between the two countries, risked falling foul of US anti-trust legislation unless an open skies agreement had been signed.

3.5   Creating the European Common Aviation Area

In parallel to the United States, Europe was also moving towards open skies but the approach was structurally quite different. The US strategy was essentially bilateral. The implementation of open skies was being promoted by one country through a series of bilateral air services agreements. In contrast to this, the development of a single open aviation market in Europe was to be achieved through a comprehensive multilateral agreement by the member states of the European Union. This multilateral approach to opening up the skies enabled the Europeans to go further in pursuit of deregulation than was possible under US bilateralism.

Within the European Union (previously known as the European Community) the push towards multilateral liberalisation of air transport among the Member States was driven by two complementary lines of approach. The Directorate General for Transport espoused airline liberalisation early and had been trying from about 1975 to push various proposals through the Council of Ministers. The second driver for change was the Directorate General for Competition, which was trying to ensure that competition between producers and service providers within the Union was not distorted by uncompetitive practices imposed by governments or introduced by the industries themselves. The twin objectives of air transport liberalisation and fair and open competition were only achieved in stages. In the late 1980s, the first two packages of liberalisation measures, described earlier, did not go very far but they did set the trend and identify the direction of Community aviation policy. The major breakthrough was achieved through the so-called 'Third Package' of aviation measures, which came into force on 1 January 1993.

The Third Package consists of three inter-linked regulations which have effectively created an 'open skies' regime for air services within the European Union. First, there is *open market access*. Airlines from member states can operate with full traffic rights between any two points within the EU and without capacity restrictions even on intra-EU routes entirely outside their own country (CEC, 1992b). Governments may only impose restrictions on environmental, infrastructure capacity, regional development or public service grounds, but any restrictions would have to be justified. Second, there are *no price controls*.

Airlines have complete freedom to determine their fares and cargo tariffs but there are some limited safeguards to prevent predatory or excessive pricing (CEC, 1992c). Finally, the third Regulation *harmonises the criteria* for granting of operating licences and air operators' certificates by EU member states (CEC, 1992a). Apart from technical and financial criteria which have to be met, the airline must be majority owned and controlled by any of the Member States or their nationals or companies. But they do not need to be nationals or companies of the state in which the airline is registered. In addition, henceforward, all regulations applied equally to scheduled and charter services with no distinction being drawn between them.

The Third Package went further than the US-style 'open skies' bilaterals in two important respects. First, it was a multilateral agreement to open up the skies covering not just pairs of states but a whole region, which by 2009 had grown to twenty-seven Member States of the European Union (EU) plus Norway, Iceland and Switzerland, as well as some Balkan states that have all adopted the package of measures in phases without joining the EU. Second, whereas the open skies bilaterals did not change the nationality rule at all, the Third Package for the first time explicitly allowed cross-border majority ownership. It gave the right to EU nationals or companies from any Member State to set up and operate an airline in any other EU Member State or to buy such an airline. In the 1990s this enabled British Airways to own and manage Deutsche BA in Germany, though it was later sold. However, this so-called right of establishment was restrictive in one important sense. While Deutsche BA could operate freely within the area of the European Union it could not, as a British-owned airline, operate international services from Munich to, say, Moscow, because the Germany–Russia air services agreement contained the traditional article regarding substantial ownership and effective control by nationals of the designating state.

On 1 November 2008, a new Regulation (No. 1008/2008) came into force which consolidated and updated the earlier three Regulations, which comprised the 'Third Package'. It introduced several minor changes. On ownership and control of EU airlines it requires that '*Member States and/or nationals of Member States own more than 50 per cent of the undertaking and effectively control it . . .*' Financial fitness tests for operator licences were tightened. The Regulation also introduced important new rules on air fares to ensure non-discrimination and greater transparency. For example, the final ticket price must be indicated at all times, including on adverts and websites, and must include all unavoidable charges and fees.

In parallel with the liberalisation of air transport regulations, the European Commission felt that greater freedom for airlines had to be accompanied by the effective application and implementation to air transport of the European Union's so-called 'competition rules'. These were designed to prevent monopolistic practices or behaviour which was anti-competitive or which distorted competition to the detriment of consumers. The competition rules cover three broad areas, namely cartels and restrictive agreements, monopolies and mergers and state aid or subsidies to producers. The basic principles on competition were originally laid down in articles 81 to 90 of the Treaty of Rome and the separate Council Regulation on Mergers of 1989 (Regulation No. 4056/89).

The European Commission has used Articles 84 and 85, which relate to transitional measures, to take action on air transport between the EU and third countries and in particular on the alliances between European airlines and major US carriers. In its decisions in the late 1990s on both the proposed American Airlines–British Airways alliance, which did not progress and the Lufthansa–SAS–United alliance, the Commission required the partners to give up substantial numbers of runway slots at their European hubs to competitors so as to ensure effective competition.

The subsidisation of airlines by central or local government clearly distorts competition. So Articles 88 and 89 of the Treaty of Rome specifically prohibit 'state aid' of any kind. Yet during the 1980s and early 1990s most of Europe's numerous state-owned airlines were being heavily subsidised by their governments. To overcome this contradiction, the European Commission in a series of decisions between 1991 and 1997 approved major injections of state aid to a number of airlines but with strict conditions whose purpose was to ensure their transformation into profitable enterprises. The state aid had to be used for financial and operational restructuring of the airline through debt repayment, early retirement of staff and so on (Doganis, 2006, pp 245–55). Moreover, the state aid was approved on the basis of a 'one time, last time' principle. In other words, no further requests for approval of additional state aid would be considered. With the exception of the authorised state aid schemes no direct or indirect subsidisation of any kind by governments or their airlines is now permitted within the European Union. For example, governments can no longer guarantee airline borrowings or offer reduced airport charges to their owned airlines. But governments can offer support for the operation of air services to meet social service needs but in a manner which is transparent.

But it appears that in emergencies state aid may be authorised to deal with unexpected crises! For example, the Commission allowed the Belgian Government to give an emergency loan to the Belgian airline Sabena in 2001 as it was on the verge of collapse. This was subsequently transferred to its subsidiary, DAT, enabling it to be relaunched as SN Brussels Airlines, in 2002, the successor to Sabena. The Commission also approved emergency state aid to Cyprus Airways early in 2005, which was in the form of a government-backed loan.

A key element of the competition rules is the EU's Regulation on Mergers first agreed in 1989 and subsequently modified in 1997 (Regulation 1310/97). Any mergers or acquisitions which exceed the stated threshold in terms of turnover must be first notified to the Commission. It will only give its approval if the transaction does not lead to the strengthening or creation of a dominant position. To ensure that this does not happen the Commission may impose demanding conditions, as it did in February 2004 when approving the Air France–KLM merger. It ruled that, since the merger would eliminate or significantly reduce competition on 14 routes both airlines served, they would have to surrender 47 pairs of airport slots on the affected routes (O.J. No. C60, 9 March 2004). The Commission has subsequently attached conditions when approving other acquisitions or mergers, such as Lufthansa's purchase of Swiss Airlines in 2006 or its take-over of SN Brussels Airlines in 2008.

There is an extra-territorial dimension to the EU competition rules. This was evident in October 1999 when the Commission, using the cumbersome Article 85 of the EC Treaty, launched an investigation into the proposed merger of Air Canada and the Canadian Airlines on the grounds that it would reduce competition on services between London and Canada. However, its powers regarding air services to/from non-EU states were limited and unclear. But on 1 May 2004 a new EU Regulation (Regulation EC411/2004) came into force which granted the Commission the ability to apply the key competition articles 81 and 82 to air services between the Community and third countries.

In addition to its decisions arising directly out of the application of the competition rules, the European Commission, acting through the Council of Ministers and the

European Parliament, has passed various Directives, Regulations or Codes of Conduct both to ensure greater competition in areas where competition was previously limited and to ensure that competition is not distorted through unfair practices. Both the code of conduct for slot allocation at airports (Council Regulation 95/93, amended 2009/0042 COD) and the Directive on ground handling services (Council Directive 96/97) were both aimed at ensuring greater competition. More recently the Airport Charges Directive in March 2009 aimed to ensure a level playing field for airlines at different airports (Directive 2009/12/EC). On the other hand, the Code of Conduct for computer reservation systems was aimed at avoiding unfair practices (Council Regulations 3089/93 and 323/99). Such Directives and Regulations were in addition to the numerous measures introduced to protect consumers directly (e.g. Regulation No. 261/2004 on passenger compensation rights) or to ensure safety of aircraft and so on.

If the aim of transport deregulation and open skies is to encourage much greater competition, then competition rules appear to be necessary to ensure that the increased competition is effective and is not undermined by anti-competitive practices or the abuse of dominant market positions, hence the parallel but contradictory development in the European Union of an intra-European open skies regime and a raft of new competition rules.

The 'Third Package' and the various EU Directives, Regulations and Codes of Practice have created a truly 'open skies' regime for air transport within the European Common Aviation Area. By 2008 this covered not only the 27 EU member states but several other European countries, such as Norway and Iceland, which had adopted these various measures into their own regulations without joining the European Union.

3.6   Clouds in the 'open skies'

By the early years of the new millennium, the pursuit of 'open skies' bilaterals by the United States and the creation of 'open skies' within the European Common Aviation Area had gone much of the way towards normalising the economic and regulatory framework for international and domestic air transport in certain major markets. But the process of normalisation was not universal. While air transport was largely deregulated for services within and between the countries of the European Union, most of the bilaterals between EU states and countries outside the EU, except those with the USA and Canada and possibly Singapore, were of the traditional type. Equally while the United States had over 60 'open skies' bilaterals virtually all the bilaterals between non-European states, with only a few exceptions, were again of the traditional kind. Many were and still are very restrictive. Thus 'open skies' co-existed side by side with skies that are relatively closed and protected.

More worrying was the fact that, even within those markets that claimed to be operating under 'open skies' regimes, many clouds were visible. While much more liberal and open than anything that preceded them, the 'open skies' agreements still contain certain restrictive features. To start with, not all traffic rights are freely exchanged. Two types of services in particular are still excluded in virtually all cases (Table 3.2 above). The first is the right of an airline to carry domestic traffic between two airports within the territory of the other signatory country to the bilateral agreement. This would normally be on an extension of international flights within that country. This is referred to as domestic cabotage. The second right which has not yet been given away is the 'seventh freedom'. This is the right to carry passengers between points in two foreign countries by an airline operating entirely outside its home country. Perhaps the most glaring anomaly is the continued restriction on foreign ownership of airlines. Airlines still have to be 'substantially owned and effectively controlled' by their own nationals even though minority ownership by foreign individuals or companies may be permitted. In the United States the position is still that only up to 25 per cent of foreign ownership of its airlines may be allowed, despite the recommendation of the 1993 National Commission to go to 49 per cent. (For more detailed discussion of the nationality rule see Doganis, 2006, pp 54–9.)

In other respects, too, the new open skies bilaterals were not as open as one might imagine. In fact they continued to be blatantly protective of US carriers in several respects. Under the so-called 'Fly America' policy, officials or others travelling on behalf of the US Government were required to fly on US airlines or flights operated by foreign airlines but with a US carrier code share. International airmail contracts by the US Post Office were also effectively limited to US carriers even though the latter can bid for UK or other mail contracts. Also, while US airlines could not lease in foreign aircraft and crews, they could offer their own aircraft on wet leases to foreign carriers. For instance most of Atlas Air's 40 or so Boeing 747 freighters are wet leased to European and Asian carriers. Finally, cargo generated as a result of US Government contracts also had to 'Fly America'.

In view of all this, it is hardly surprising that the European Commission has always been very critical of the 'open skies' agreements signed by several Member States with the United States. First, the Commission felt that by giving away extensive fifth freedom rights to United States airlines on routes that were essentially 'domestic' routes between Member States within the European Union, signatory states were granting rights that were no longer at their discretion because they affected trade within the single European market. Second, the open skies bilaterals dealt with issues that in recent years had come within the competence of the Commission. As a result, the Commission believed that individual states had no powers to negotiate in these areas. Third, by making separate agreements with the United States, such countries were undermining the negotiating strength of the Commission to obtain greater concessions from the United States in any future bloc negotiations.

Furthermore, both the Commission and many European airlines had long felt that 'open skies' bilaterals created an asymmetry and an imbalance of opportunities. While US carriers could fly from any airport in the United States to a wide range of airports in the EU, European airlines could only operate to the United States from their own country. Consequently they could not exploit fully the whole EU market of 360 million passengers (or about 440 million following enlargement in 2004) to compete more effectively with their transatlantic competitors. In addition, US carriers obtained, and in many cases have used, extensive fifth freedom rights between European points which had now become essentially domestic sectors within the European Common Aviation Area. Yet European airlines could not enjoy the equivalent rights to serve domestic city pairs in the United States.

Because of such concerns the European Commission launched a case in the autumn of 1998 against eight Member States in the European Court of Justice, arguing that the 'open skies' agreements they had signed with the United States contravened EU regulations and should be suspended. It was the Court's judgments on this case handed down on 5 November 2002 that were to drive the next phase of liberalisation.

3.7   European Court changes the rules

The cases on which the European Court of Justice (ECJ) issued a series of parallel judgments in November 2002 hinged on two different legal issues. The first, related to the claim by the Commission that it alone had exclusive competence to negotiate bilateral air services agreements. On this issue, the Court found that EU Member States did have the right to negotiate bilateral air services agreements with the USA, or for that matter any other non-EU state, and that this was not the exclusive preserve of the European Commission. But states could not negotiate on matters which EU legislation had previously established as being within the competence of the Commission. These include fares within the EU, Computer Reservation Systems, and allocation of airport slots.

The second legal issue was related to the nationality rule. Here, the Court agreed with the Commission that traditional nationality clauses in bilateral air services agreements infringed Article 43 of the European Community Treaty. This article requires each EU state to allow nationals or companies of any other state to establish and operate businesses within that state. Yet for air transport services the traditional ownership and nationality clause is clearly very restrictive. For instance, under the then existing open skies bilateral between Germany and the United States the German government could only designate airline(s) that were 'substantially owned and effectively controlled' by German nationals. Only German airlines could use the traffic rights granted by the bilateral. In effect the ECJ was saying that this restriction was illegal because it discriminated on the grounds of nationality. To conform with Article 43 any EU airline should have the opportunity to be designated to fly on routes between Germany and the USA. This would in effect mean that airlines owned by nationals or companies from any one of the then 25 EU states could in principle have access to routes from, say, Germany to the USA.

While the November 2002 ECJ judgments referred specifically to bilateral agreements with the USA, it was clear that all other bilateral agreements between EU Member States and third countries faced the same legal problems. First, many include articles dealing with issues on which only the Commission has the legal competence to enter into international agreements. Second, they all contain nationality articles which infringe the right of establishment under Article 43 of the Treaty of Rome. Thus the ECJ decision meant that not only would bilaterals with the USA have to be modified but so would hundreds of bilaterals between each of the 25 EU states and third countries around the world. A daunting task. Moreover, a task that had to be addressed urgently because the Court's decision created considerable uncertainty both for EU airlines and for airlines flying into EU countries.

In June 2003, the European Council of Transport Ministers adopted two decisions to tackle the complex task of renegotiating so many bilaterals. The first measure was to give the Commission a mandate to negotiate with the United States to fully liberalise air transport within and between the EU and the USA. The aim of this mandate was to move from 'open skies' to 'clear skies'. This had been a European objective for some time.

The second measure was another mandate to the Commission to negotiate so-called 'horizontal agreements' with third countries in order to correct the legal problems in existing bilaterals with EU states which had been highlighted by the European Court's judgments. In order to avoid a very large number of separate renegotiations by individual Member States with numerous third countries, this horizontal mandate empowered the European Commission to open negotiations with individual third countries in order to replace certain provisions in all their existing bilaterals with EU states by a single Community agreement bringing all these separate air services agreements into line with EU laws. This would mean, for instance, replacing existing nationality clauses by an article in which third countries would accept designation by EU states of any carrier owned by

EU nationals. Such 'horizontal' agreements would also ensure that provisions on safety, air fares within the EU, on fifth freedom flights or on customs and taxes were in conformity with European Community laws.

It is important to emphasise that any agreements between the EU and third countries under the 'horizontal' mandate would amend the nationality clauses but not replace the existing bilateral air services agreements. Nor would they change the provisions concerning traffic rights in the bilaterals. But they would permit all EU airlines to apply on a non-discriminatory basis to operate on routes between any EU country and third countries. This sounds simple enough, if there are no capacity or frequency restrictions in the air services agreements. But if in practice there are capacity or frequency limitations embedded in the existing bilateral, as is the case, for example, between the UK and China, then it is no longer so simple. If British Airways and Virgin are operating all the agreed frequencies to India how can another EU airline access the UK–China market? Do BA and Virgin have a historic right to these frequencies they already operate? If additional frequencies are granted, how will they be allocated between any EU airlines that may want to use them to compete directly with British airlines already serving China? The Commission subsequently published a Regulation (No. 847/2004) on the negotiation and implementation of air service agreements between Member States and third countries. This recommended the establishment of a transparent process for allocating traffic rights and frequencies between competing carriers. It was left to individual states to adopt this Regulation into their own laws.

Even before the Commission began to implement its various negotiating mandates the longer-term implications of the ECJ judgments became starkly clear. In September 2003 Air France and KLM announced a proposed merger of the two airlines, which was realised in April 2004 following approval by the Commission's Competition Directorate and acceptance by the two airlines of the Commission's conditions. This marked the start of the long-awaited consolidation of the European flag carriers. The ECJ judgments, by relaxing the strict definition of 'nationality', have opened the door for cross-border mergers and acquisitions. Lufthansa was one of the first through this open door, purchasing the ailing Swiss Airlines in 2006, SN Brussels in 2008 and the British Bmi in 2009.

The European Court of Justice, in its decisions of November 2002, has totally undermined the traditional very narrow concept of nationality. As individual Member States progressively renegotiate their own bilaterals or as the Commission negotiates horizontal agreements with more and more third countries, international routes from the European Union to such countries will be opened up to any EU carrier. Already by early 2009 the European Commission had concluded such agreements with over 30 states including Australia, New Zealand, Malaysia, the UAE and Chile. In time, other regions and other countries will also begin to liberalise their own nationality rates and designation criteria.

The significance of the November 2002 European judgment is that it set this process of change in motion and made further liberalisation inevitable. Over the next five to ten years the international airline industry will be progressively normalised and will begin to operate more and more like any other global industry or service sector. A key breakthrough came in March 2007 when, after nearly four years of stop and start negotiations, the European Union and the United States agreed to set up what was the first step towards the creation of a single transatlantic common aviation area.

3.8   Towards a trans–Atlantic common aviation area?

The negotiating mandate granted to the European Commission in June 2003 at last gave the Commission the authority to push for liberalisation with the United States in all areas. The Commission wanted to go much further than an 'open skies' type of agreement. It wished to pursue liberalisation in other areas such as ownership and the right of establishment, domestic cabotage, seventh freedom and so on. The US Government, however, was more hesitant. For the USA there were internal political difficulties in moving beyond 'open skies'. First, under US law, at least 75 per cent of the voting stock of a US airline must be owned or controlled by US citizens and the Chief Executive and two thirds of the board of directors must also be citizens. In order to open up ownership and domestic cabotage, the law would need to be changed. But it would be extremely difficult to get such a change through both houses of Congress, especially since labour unions would object. Second, airlines are seen as a component of national security and the Department of Defense depends on US-owned carriers for transportation needs, at times of war or other crises, through the Civil Reserve Air Fleet (CRAF) programme. The Department was seriously concerned that aircraft belonging to a foreign-owned US airline might not be readily available in emergencies to join the CRAF. Third, the 'Fly America' policy ensured that the US Government's air transport needs for passengers and cargo take place on US airlines or their code-share partners. This too might require legislative action. Finally, there was considerable concern among labour unions that permitting airline ownership by foreign citizens or opening up domestic cabotage to foreign carriers would result in job losses to foreign workers. This concern deepened following the airline crisis and downturn in the period 2000 to 2003, which led to reductions of about one third in staff numbers among most US carriers.

Inevitably, given these reservations the negotiations which took place periodically in the period 2003 to 2006 repeatedly stalled as each side accused the other of intransigence. Then in March 2007, the European Council of Ministers of Transport decided that a limited first phase agreement was better than no agreement. This agreement, which was due to come into force a year later on 30 March 2008 replaced all the existing bilateral air services agreements between EU states and the USA. Clearly it did not meet all the objectives of the European negotiators.

Its key provision was to open up all traffic rights between the US and EU member states to any US or Community airlines. The latter can fly from any point within the EU and not just their own country to any point in the USA. The US airlines can do likewise. All airlines have fifth freedom traffic rights on behind, intermediate and beyond points on their services to or from the USA or Europe. There is no control of frequencies or capacity or of tariffs. The USA accepts designation on any route of any 'Community airline' whose substantial ownership and effective control are vested in a Member State of the EU and whose principal place of business is within the EU (Official Journal of the European Communities, 25 February 2007).

In essence, the USA agreed to this wider definition of nationality. But it did not agree to granting Community carriers domestic cabotage rights in the US nor to relaxing the strict ownership and control rules for US airlines which would have allowed European companies to gain control of US airlines or to establish their own subsidiaries in the USA. However, franchising and branding agreements between US and European airlines would be permitted.

It is because of these shortcomings that a provision was included for negotiations to re-start 60 days after the agreement would come into force in March 2008 with the aim of examining further liberalisation of traffic rights, foreign investment opportunities (i.e. ownership), environmental issues and wet-leasing of aircraft in order to conclude a second-stage agreement. If after 18 months no such agreement has been reached, either side has the right to give 12 months' notice of suspension of the 2007 first-stage agreement. This is a tough requirement put in by the European negotiators to force the Americans to move towards real clear skies. In reality it is difficult to envision suspension since European airlines would be hard hit. Despite pessimism on the European side about American willingness to move to a second-stage agreement, the 2007-message from the then US chief negotiator, John Byerly (Deputy Assistant Secretary of State for Transportation), was more hopeful: '*It would be mistaken for our European friends and, more important, tragic for American stakeholders, to view the agreement as all that our country would want to achieve*' (speaking at Washington Aviation Club, April 2007).

Despite any shortcoming the 2007 EU–US agreement represents a major breakthrough in two respects: first in relaxing the very strict definition of 'nationality' used in traditional bilaterals; second, in creating a vast 'open skies' market between most of Europe and the USA. The effects would be a wider range of point-to-point services across the Atlantic with new carriers on new routes, lower fares and increased opportunities for mergers and consolidation between European airlines. British Airways, Air France and Lufthansa quickly announced that in 2008 they would launch new transatlantic services from European cities outside their own countries. The rocketing fuel prices of 2008 slowed down their plans, as did collapsing demand at the end of 2008 and early 2009. Nevertheless BA, through its subsidiary Open Skies Airlines, was operating from both Paris and Amsterdam to New York.

In June 2008, US–EU negotiations re-started, aiming at a second-stage agreement. There was no quick breakthrough. The key outstanding issues for the European negotiators were the right of European companies or individuals to set up or acquire US airlines, in other words abandoning the strict nationality rule, and domestic cabotage, that is, the right of European carriers to operate on domestic sectors in the USA with full traffic rights. There were several secondary issues too. But the worsening economic climate for airlines as 2008 turned into 2009, combined with a new Democratic President and Congress in the United States, dimmed the prospects for an early second-stage agreement on the crucial issues.

But there was a breakthrough elsewhere on the North Atlantic. Early in May 2009 the European Union and Canada announced the signing of an 'open skies' agreement similar to that between the EU and the USA but going even further in some respects. Notably, it would allow European investors to acquire up to 49 per cent of Canadian carriers. In the longer term full ownership rights were envisaged. The creation of a single open European–North American aviation market moved a step nearer.

3.9 Liberalisation spreading worldwide

In other parts of the world, too, air transport liberalisation has been accelerating both bilaterally and multilaterally in recent years. First, many governments that had previously followed a protectionist aviation policy began to appreciate the benefits of a more open competitive aviation environment to both their airline sector and to their tourism industry. India is a good example. It liberalised domestic air services and as a result several new low-cost airlines, such as Indigo, Spice jet, Air India Express, were launched in 2005–6 as well as other new entrants such as Kingfisher. Internationally, India has renegotiated several bilaterals opening up new points to be served in India and increasing frequencies.

For instance, on routes between India and the United Kingdom following a revised bilateral in 2005 weekly frequencies by airlines of each country were increased from 19 each week to 81 a week and Jet Airways and Bmi entered this market for the first time. China, like India, also began opening up its bilaterals in the mid-2000s. For example, in June 2007 the earlier 2004 air services agreement with the United States was amended to allow more frequencies and three new US carriers.

Second, one has seen several plurilateral regional agreements aimed at furthering liberalisation. In May 2001 five Pacific states, the United States, Brunei, Chile, New Zealand and Singapore, later joined by Peru (for a time only), Samoa, Tonga and Mongolia entered into a multilateral 'open skies' agreement. This was notable in that it allowed these states to designate, on services to the other signatory states, airlines that are not owned by their own nationals. But such airlines must be incorporated in and have their principal place of business in the territory of the designating state. The United States, which brokered this agreement, known as the 'Multilateral Agreement on the Liberalisation of International Air Transport' (MALIAT), hoped that other states would accede to it. In this way its geographical impact could be widened. By signing up, countries would readily gain access to several markets in one agreement without having to negotiate with several countries individually. They would also broaden their potential sources of inward investment. But new signatories have been few and insignificant.

Other multilateral agreements have attempted to move in the same direction. For instance, in November 2004 the Association of South East Asian Nations (ASEAN) announced plans for the phased establishment of a regional open skies area between the ten member states. The aim was the gradual liberalisation of passenger and cargo rights by 2015. Air services between their capital cities were due to be freed of all restrictions by December 2008.

Earlier, meeting in November 1999 in the Ivory Coast, African states adopted a new policy framework, the so-called Yammoussoukro II agreement, for the liberalisation of the continent's air transport industry. The agreement aimed to liberalise market access by the year 2002 in order to create a single African aviation market. It was far-reaching. Though ratified by many states, in practice Yammoussoukro II had failed to be effectively implemented by early 2009 and was being by-passed by smaller regional initiatives within Africa.

There is little doubt that the trend towards liberalisation of international air services accelerated in the early and mid-2000s in many parts of the world, not just Europe and the United States. As the airline industry entered a new cyclical downturn in 2009, the key question was whether such a downturn, if long-lasting, would dampen or accelerate further liberalisation.

3.10   The significance of the regulatory environment

It is perhaps surprising that a book on airline economics starts with two chapters which appear legal in character and deal with the international regulation of air transport. The reasons for this are clear. Airlines, especially those operating internationally, are constrained in where they can fly to and how they operate by a complex web of domestic, bilateral and international rules and regulations which are both technical and economic in character.

To make matters worse, the regulatory regime, as we have seen, varies from country to country and market to market. Within the European Common Aviation Area, airlines have the most freedom to operate as they deem commercially attractive while the major constraint appears to be airport or ATC capacity shortage. Across the North Atlantic, the same European airlines can fly between any points in Europe and the USA with whatever flight frequency they wish and offering fares of their choice. But they cannot buy a US airline or set up a subsidiary in the United States or operate domestic services there. On routes to many Asian or African countries a European airline may not be able to fly at all, because another European airline has already been designated for that route. If it can get designated it may only be allowed a very limited number of weekly frequencies and may have to share capacity (i.e. the number of seats offered) with the foreign carrier on the route.

Despite the liberalisation which has taken place, the European example illustrates the difficulties faced by managers of international airlines. In other parts of the world the constraints faced by airline executives may be even worse. On each route, what managers can or cannot do is circumscribed by the regulatory regime prevailing on that route. An appreciation of the regulatory environment is fundamental for an understanding both of airline economics and of the reasons why airline operating and marketing decisions sometimes appear to be irrational or even contradictory.

4 The structure of airline costs

4.1 The need for costing

The airline industry is dynamic, fast–changing and subject to sudden and unexpected variations in the cost of many of its inputs. This is why a clear understanding of the costs of supplying airline services is essential to many decisions taken by airline managers. But there are many ways of looking at costs. The way that an airline's costs are broken down and categorised will depend on the purpose for which they are being used. In airline planning, cost information is generally needed to meet four key requirements. First, airlines need an overall breakdown of their total expenditure into different cost categories as a general management and accounting tool. They require a general breakdown of costs to show cost trends over time, to measure the cost efficiency of particular functional areas such as flight operations or maintenance, and ultimately to enable them to produce their annual accounts and their operating and non–operating profit or loss. Second, airlines require very detailed cost information by flight and route in order to make operating decisions such as whether to add more frequencies on a sector or reduce them, or whether to operate that route at all. Third, cost identification is crucial in the development of pricing policies and pricing decisions, for both passengers and cargo. Finally, an assessment of costs is essential in any evaluation of investments, whether in new aircraft or in new routes or services.

No single cost categorisation is capable of satisfying all of these management requirements simultaneously. A cost breakdown developed for general management and accounting purposes may be useless as a guide to pricing strategy and may be of little help in making operating decisions. As a result, most airlines break down their costs in two or more different ways depending on the purpose for which the cost analysis is required.

While the approach to cost categorisation used by each airline is strongly influenced by accounting practices in its home country, it has also been influenced by the cost classification adopted early on by the International Civil Aviation Organisation (ICAO). The governments of the member states of ICAO have been required to provide ICAO each year with financial data about their airlines on a standard form. These data provide the basis for ICAO's annual *Digest of Statistics, Series F, Financial Data*, which contains the balance sheets and profit and loss statements for all the ICAO member airlines, though in practice each year data for several airlines are missing. The need to provide ICAO with a particular breakdown of costs and the ability once this is done to compare one's costs on a fairly straightforward basis with other airlines have over time induced many airlines to adopt a cost classification similar to that of the ICAO. The ICAO cost classification was in any case based fairly closely on prevailing cost practices in the United States and among several European airlines. Thus worldwide throughout the airline industry, there tends to be a fairly standard and traditional approach to the categorisation of costs for general management use.

4.2 The traditional approach to airline costs

It is normal practice to divide airline accounts into operating and non-operating categories. The aim is to identify and separate out as non-operating items all those costs and revenues not directly associated with the operation of an airline's own air services. Following ICAO and US practice, most airlines have adopted this approach which identifies as *non-operating* the following five items:

1 The gains or losses arising from the retirement of property or equipment, both aeronautical and non-aeronautical. Such gains or losses arise when there is a difference between the depreciated book value of a particular item and the value that is realised when that item is retired or sold off.

2 Interest paid on loans, as well as any interest received from bank or other deposits. It is considered that bank interest paid or received has little to do with the business of flying. For some costing purposes, however, such as aircraft evaluation, some airlines would include interest paid on aircraft-related loans as an operating cost.

3 All profits or losses arising from an airline's affiliated companies, some of which may themselves be directly involved in air transport. In some cases this item may be of some importance in the overall financial performance of an airline. Early in 2009 British Airways, for example, had 18 majority-owned subsidiaries and minority investments in at least four other aviation companies, including three airlines (Iberia, with a 13.15 per cent shareholding, Comair Ltd in South Africa, and Flybe in the UK), and in the UK's National Air Traffic Services.

4 An assortment of other items which do not fall into the previous three categories, such as losses or gains arising from foreign exchange transactions or from sales of shares or securities. In recent years airlines have from time to time made large losses or profits as a result of sudden marked fluctuations in exchange rates. These are clearly a non-operating item.

5 The final item includes any direct or indirect government subsidies or taxes on profit or other corporate taxes. In the case of some airlines, subsidies have at times been very substantial. Thus, in the mid-1990s Air France, like several other state-owned airlines in Europe, received massive injections of state funds to enable it to reduce its debts and restructure its operations (see Doganis, 2006). Subsidies have also been paid periodically to most government-owned airlines outside Europe. Such subsidies should appear as non-operating items. Similarly, profit taxes or other corporate taxes would also be categorised as non-operating.

For some airlines non-operating items may have a major impact on their financial results. Singapore Airlines (SIA) provides a dramatic example. In the financial year 2006–7 SIA produced an overall net profit before tax of $1,456 million. Of this, a little less than half $717 million or 49.2 per cent was from airline operations (Table 4.1). The remainder (50.8 per cent) came from non-operating items. Nearly 30 per cent of the profits came from surpluses generated by selling assets – aircraft (10.4 per cent of profits), the HQ building (9.6 per cent) and its investment in a leasing company (8.7 per cent). There was also an exceptional tax write back in that year of $157 million following a change in the tax rate. In the following financial year 2007–8, there were no large exceptional items and the surplus on sale of aircraft and engines was substantially less. As a result, non-operating items accounted for only 17 per cent of SIA's pre-tax profits. The SIA case amply illustrates why it is essential to separate out non-operating items so as to get a true assessment of how well the core business, which is flying aircraft, is doing.

Table 4.1 The impact of non-operating items on financial results – the SIA case in 2006–7

	Sources of Singapore Airlines group profits FY 2006–7	
	US$ millions	*Share of profits %*
A: Non-operating		
1 Surplus on sale of aircraft/engines	152	10.4
2 Dividends from investments	25	1.7
3 Share of profit from subsidiaries/joint ventures	87	6.0
4 Other non-operating	50	3.4
5 Exceptional items:		
(i) Surplus on sale of SIA building	142	9.6
(ii) Surplus on sale of investment in leasing co. (SALE)	126	8.7
(iii) Tax write back after tax rate cut	157	10.8
Total non-operating	739	50.8
B: Airline operations	717	49.2
C: Total profit before tax	1,456	100.0

Source: Compiled by author from SIA, 2007 (using US$ = S$1.57).

Non-operating items are not necessarily profits or surpluses as in SIA's case. They may well be losses or costs. Most airlines normally pay out a great deal more in interest charges on their loans than they receive from their own cash deposits at the bank. This is particularly so of state-owned airlines whose development has been financed by a succession of loans rather than through injection of equity capital. But even many privatised airlines face large interest payments on their debts, which may not be off-set by interest they may earn on their cash in hand.

The nature of each airline's non-operating costs and revenues is probably unique, in that many non-operating items are influenced by circumstances which are very particular to each airline. As a result inter-airline comparisons of net profits or total costs including non-operating costs are of little value.

In fact, in years when their profits decline, many airlines 'massage' their non-operating costs or revenues to improve their bottom line results. For instance, it is common for hard-pressed airlines to sell some of their aircraft and then lease them back. This generates a substantial cash inflow which appears as a positive non-operating item which may offset any operating losses. Because of such anomalies and complexities it is better when assessing an airline's costs or revenues to leave non-operating items aside and to focus on its operating costs or revenues. These are the best descriptors of its performance as an airline.

On the operating side, airline accounts are divided into *operating revenue* and *operating costs*. The latter can be further subdivided into direct operating and indirect operating costs. But direct and indirect have a different meaning in the airline industry from that in normal accounting usage.

In theory, the distinction between these two cost categories is fairly clear. *Direct operating costs* should include all those costs which are associated with and dependent on the type of aircraft being operated and which would change if the aircraft type were changed. Broadly speaking, such costs should include all flying expenses (such as flight crew salaries, fuel and oil), all maintenance and overhaul costs and all aircraft depreciation costs. *Indirect operating costs* are all those costs which will remain unaffected by a change of aircraft

Table 4.2 Traditional categorisation of airline operating costs

---

DIRECT OPERATING COSTS (DOC)

1 Flight operations
   - Flight crew salaries and expenses
   - Fuel and oil
   - Airport and en-route charges*
   - Aircraft insurance
   - Rental/lease of flight equipment/crews**
2 Maintenance and overhaul
   - Engineering staff costs
   - Spare parts consumed
   - Maintenance administration (could be IOC)
3 Depreciation and amortisation
   - Flight equipment
   - Ground equipment and property (could be IOC)
   - Extra depreciation (in excess of historic cost depreciation)
   - Amortisation of development costs and crew training

INDIRECT OPERATING COSTS (IOC)

4 Station and ground expenses
   - Ground staff
   - Buildings, equipment, transport
   - Handling fees paid to others
5 Passenger services
   - Cabin crew salaries and expenses (could be DOC)
   - Other passenger service costs
   - Passenger insurance
6 Ticketing, sales and promotion
   - General and administration
7 Other operating costs

Notes
 * ICAO classifies airport and en-route charges as an indirect operating cost under 'Station and ground expenses'.
 ** The US practice is to classify rentals under 'Depreciation'.

type because they are not directly dependent on aircraft operations. They include areas of expenditure which are passenger related rather than aircraft related (such as passenger service costs, costs of ticketing and sales, and station and ground costs) as well as general administrative costs. In practice, however, the distinction between direct and indirect operating costs is not always clear-cut. Certain cost items, such as maintenance administration or costs of cabin staff, are categorised as direct costs by some airlines and as indirect costs by others. The main categories of airline operating costs are shown in Table 4.2. The cost categories shown are those currently accepted and used, with some modification, by most international airlines around the world. They are broadly based on the cost categorisation traditionally used by the International Civil Aviation Organisation.

4.3 Direct operating costs

4.3.1 *Cost of flight operations*

This is undoubtedly the largest single element of operating costs which is aircraft dependent. It includes, in the first place, all costs associated with *flight crew*. Such costs cover not only direct salaries and travelling and stopover expenses but also allowances, pensions, insurance and any other social welfare payments. While most jet aircraft have two-man cockpit crews, their salaries normally depend on the type of aircraft being flown. For safety reasons, pilots and co-pilots are licensed to fly only one aircraft type during any period of time. As a general rule the larger the aircraft the higher the salaries paid. So pilot costs are aircraft-specific. However, cockpit commonality in some aircraft types such as the Airbus 319 and Airbus 320 are allowing airlines to use pilots who are common-rated to fly two aircraft types. Flight crew costs can be directly calculated on a route-by-route basis or, more usually, they are expressed as an hourly cost per aircraft type. In the latter case the total flight crew costs for a particular route or service can be calculated by multiplying the hourly flight crew costs of the aircraft being operated on that route by the block time for the route (see Glossary for definition of block time).

The second major cost element of flight operations is *fuel*. Again, it is very aircraft-specific. Fuel consumption varies by aircraft type depending on the number and the size or thrust of the engines and the type and age of those engines. During operations, actual fuel consumption varies considerably from route to route in relation to the sector lengths, the aircraft weight, wind conditions, the cruise altitude, and so on. Thus an hourly fuel cost tends to be even more of an approximation than an hourly flight crew costs, and it is normal to consider fuel consumption on a route-by-route basis. In addition to aviation fuel, aircraft also use up *oil*, though the oil consumption is negligible, as is the cost. Fuel includes any fuel throughput charges levied by some airport authorities on the volume of fuel uplifted, the fuel handling charges paid to fuel suppliers for the loading of fuel and any relevant fuel taxes or duties levied by governments, though these are not usual.

Another significant element of flight operation costs is made up of *airport and en route charges*. Airlines have to pay airport authorities for the use of the runway and terminal facilities. Airport charges normally have two elements: a landing fee related to the weight of the aircraft, usually its maximum take-off weight, and a passenger charge levied on the number of departing passengers boarded at that airport (occasionally it may be calculated on the number of disembarked passengers). Clearly both the landing fee and, indirectly, the total passenger charge are related to the type of aircraft operated. Some Third World airports do not charge the airlines for the number of passengers embarked but collect a fee directly from each passenger on departure. This slows down passenger check-in. It is contrary to the recommendations of the International Civil Aviation Organisation which wants passenger-related charges to be paid by the airlines and included in the price of the ticket (for details on airport charging practice see Doganis, 1992). When passengers pay an airport charge directly to the airport authority on departure, this cost does not appear as an airline cost. At most airports a free parking period of 2–6 hours is covered by the basic aircraft landing fee. If an aircraft stays at an airport beyond this free time period, it will have to pay additional aircraft parking or hangarage fees. These are relatively small compared with the basic landing and passenger charges.

Airlines must also pay en-route navigation charges to cover the cost of en route navigation services and aids that their aircraft use while flying and during landing and take-off. The actual level of the en-route navigation charge is related to the weight of the aircraft and the distance flown over a country's airspace. As a result, both airport charges, where they are not passenger related, and navigation services charges will vary with the type of aircraft used and are therefore considered as a direct operating cost. On the other hand, the total passenger-related charges do not vary directly with aircraft type. This may partly explain why ICAO insists on treating landing and en-route charges as an indirect cost, though few airlines follow this lead. Since landing and en-route charges vary by individual airport and country, they must be separately calculated for each flight or route.

A relatively small cost in flight operations is that of the *insurance of the flight equipment*. The insurance premium paid by an airline for each aircraft is calculated as a percentage of the full purchase price. The annual premium may be between 1.5 per cent and 3 per cent depending on the airline, the number of aircraft it has insured, and the geographical areas in which its aircraft operate. If the airline wants full war risk cover, if it wants to be covered against terrorist action or if it is operating in or through an area where there is armed conflict, an additional premium of up to 2 per cent may need to be paid. The annual premium, which is fixed, can be converted into an hourly insurance cost by dividing it by the projected aircraft utilisation, that is, by the total number of block hours that each aircraft is expected to fly during the year.

Many airlines may, in addition, have to meet *rental or lease charges* for the hiring or leasing of aircraft from other airlines or leasing companies. Lease charges are usually considered as part of flight operation costs. Several of the small national airlines were originally launched on the basis of leased aircraft, though over the last 20 years, leases have become widespread even among larger airlines. They are broadly of two kinds: operating leases which are generally for five years or less with ownership resting with the lessor, and financial leases in which after 10 or more years aircraft ownership is transferred to the airline (for details of leasing arrangements see Morrell, 2007). In such cases, rental or lease charges are high, pushing up that airline's total flight operations costs to abnormally high levels. This is because the rental charges for leased aircraft effectively cover both the depreciation and the interest charges paid by the owners of the aircraft. Conversely, airlines heavily dependent on leased equipment tend to have very low depreciation charges, since they pay for depreciation indirectly through the rental charge.

It is because rentals include a large element of depreciation that the American practice is to categorise lease rental charges under the heading of depreciation rather than to treat them as a cost of flight operations. Many non-US airlines also follow this approach. Lease costs and depreciation taken together can be considered as aircraft ownership costs. Many airlines also include interest paid on loans for aircraft as a cost of aircraft ownership.

Lastly, there may be some costs related to flight operations which do not fall into any of the above categories. Such additional costs may include costs of *flight crew training* or of *route development*. However, if training costs are amortised over two or three years then they are grouped together with depreciation.

4.3.2 Maintenance and overhaul costs

Total maintenance costs cover a whole series of separate costs, related to different aspects of maintenance and overhaul, which ideally ought to be treated separately. In practice there are so many joint costs in the separate maintenance areas that it is difficult, if not impossible, for many airlines to break down total maintenance costs into separate cost categories. While the ICAO groups all maintenance and overhaul expenditure into a single undivided cost item, the UK's Civil Aviation Authority in its own airline statistics splits maintenance into two categories, fixed and variable. The latter are those costs which are dependent on the amount of flying done.

Maintenance costs cover not only routine maintenance and maintenance checks carried out between flights or overnight but also the more extensive periodic overhauls and major checks. They encompass two major cost areas, first, the very extensive use of labour and the expenses related to all grades of staff involved directly or indirectly in maintenance work. Where possible, costs of maintenance staff at outstations should be separated out from station costs and included under maintenance. Second, there is a major cost associated with the consumption of spare parts. Most parts of each engine and airframe have a usable life which is measured in terms of block hours or numbers of flight-cycles, that is, landings and take-offs. Once its certified life has expired, each part must be removed and checked or replaced. Hence the consumption of spare parts is high and costly. The costs of workshops, maintenance hangars and offices are also included. Finally, if an airline is subcontracting out any of the maintenance done on its own aircraft, then the charges it pays for any such work should be allocated to the maintenance and overhaul category.

In the United States, the Department of Transportation requires airlines to split their flight equipment maintenance costs into three categories: direct maintenance on the airframe; direct maintenance on the engines; and a maintenance burden. The maintenance burden is essentially the administrative and overhead costs associated with the maintenance function which cannot be attributed directly to a particular airframe or engine but are allocated on a fairly arbitrary basis. US airlines are obliged to furnish the federal government with these three categories of maintenance costs separately for each aircraft type that they operate. These data are published and provide an excellent basis for the comparison of maintenance costs between airlines and also between different aircraft types and engines.

Outside the United States, airlines also try to apportion their maintenance costs between different aircraft types, but there is no standard way of doing this, so inter-airline comparisons would not be valid even if such data were publicly available. Individual airlines, having estimated the total maintenance costs for one particular aircraft type, may then convert these costs into an hourly maintenance cost by dividing them by the total number of block hours flown by all the aircraft of that particular type operated by the airline.

4.3.3 Depreciation and amortisation

Depreciation of flight equipment is the third component of direct operating cost since it is very much aircraft dependent. Airlines tend to use straight-line depreciation over a given number of years with a residual value of 0–15 per cent. The residual value is the predicated or assumed resale value of the aircraft at the end of the depreciation period. Up to the mid-1970s, depreciation periods were generally 12 years or less. The introduction of wide-bodied jets led to a lengthening of the depreciation period, first, because the capital cost of such aircraft was very much higher than that of the previous generation of aircraft; second, because air transport technology appeared to have reached a plateau. It became much more difficult than it had been previously to predict that further developments in technology might adversely affect and shorten the economic life of the wide-bodied jets. Their economic life was dependent on the strength and technical life of their various components and was unlikely to be affected by any new leaps forward in aircraft technology which might make them obsolescent. In response to these two factors, airlines throughout the world tended to lengthen the depreciation period of their large, wide-bodied jets and of new generation single-aisle aircraft to 14–16 years with a residual value of around 10 per cent. For smaller short-haul aircraft, especially if they were turbo-props, the depreciation periods were generally shorter. During the crisis years of 2001 to 2003 many airlines lengthened their depreciation periods to 18–20 years as a way of reducing their annual costs. Low-cost carriers have done the same. Using 25 or even 30 years with 10 or 15 per cent residual value is not uncommon, especially among US airlines, which were hardest hit by the downturn after 2001.

The purpose of depreciation is twofold. First it aims to spread the cost of an aircraft over the useful life of that aircraft. If the full cost of a new aircraft was all debited in the year in which the aircraft was bought it would seriously inflate costs and undermine profits in that year, especially if a fleet of aircraft was bought. Instead, only a proportion of an aircraft's full cost is charged against revenues each year. The depreciation policy chosen determines how much that proportion should be. By covering its depreciation costs an airline ensures that it is also meeting the costs of owning its aircraft assets. Second, depreciation allows money out of each year's revenues, equivalent to the depreciation charge, to be put into a general reserve fund. These monies, together with any retained profits, can, in theory, be used to pay back the loans with which the aircraft were bought together with any accrued interest. If the aircraft have been bought fully or in part with the airline's own cash, then the accumulated depreciation reserve can be used to fund the new aircraft when the current aircraft are replaced.

The annual depreciation charge or cost of a particular aircraft in an airline's fleet depends on the depreciation period adopted and the residual value assumed. An airline which had bought several Boeing 747–400 aircraft in, say, the early 2000s might have paid $170 million for each aircraft and, say, another $30 million per aircraft for a spares holding, making a total cost of $200 million per aircraft. Assuming it depreciated each aircraft over 20 years to a 10 per cent residual value, then the annual depreciation charge would be $9.0 million:

Annual depreciation

$$= \frac{\text{Price of aircraft and spares (\$200m) less residual value (10 per cent)}}{\text{Depreciation period (20 years)}}$$

$$= \frac{\$200m - \$20m}{20} = \frac{\$180}{20} - \$9.0m$$

If an airline chooses a shorter depreciation period, then the annual depreciation cost will rise. Thus Singapore Airlines (SIA) has, in recent years, been depreciating its aircraft over 15 years with a 10 per cent residual value. On this basis, the annual depreciation cost of any Boeing 747–400 aircraft purchased by SIA in 2000 would rise from $9.0 million to $12.0 million. The immediate effect would be to increase annual operating costs by pushing up the annual depreciation costs for each aircraft.

So why would SIA or any other airline choose a faster depreciation policy if the effect is to push up operating costs? If an airline wants a young fleet and renews its fleet every three to five years then the faster depreciation is compensated for by higher non-operating profits when its young aircraft are sold. This is because it will be selling the aircraft at prices above their book value in the company's accounts.

For example, using a more traditional depreciation period of 20 years for a new Boeing 747–400 as described above, this aircraft at the end of four years would have a book value in the airline's asset registry of $164 million ($200m − 4 × $9.00m). For airlines, such as SIA, depreciating faster at $12.0m per year, the book value of its aircraft at the end of the fourth year is $152m ($200m − 4 × $12.0m). All other things being equal, a four-year-old aircraft will have a market price which reflects both market conditions at the time but also the more widely-used depreciation policy, namely the longer one. So, during settled market conditions, a four-year-old aircraft, plus its bank of spares, will be valued at around $160–70m. If the airline, wishing to renew its fleet, sells its aircraft, which it values in its own books at $152m, when prevailing second-hand prices are much higher, it will make a profit. If it sells, say at $165m, it will have made a profit on the sale of assets of $13.0m ($165.0 less the $152.0m book value). Higher depreciation costs in the short term are counter-balanced by high profits on aircraft sales four or five years later. This strategy is reinforced if there are significant tax allowances, which reduce an airline's tax liability when it undertakes new investments. This is the case in Singapore. SIA has historically used a short depreciation period resulting in relatively higher unit depreciation charges. But conversely it has been consistently making substantial non-operating profits from selling relatively new aircraft (item 1, Table 4.1).

Once the depreciation policy has been determined, the annual depreciation cost for each aircraft becomes a fixed cost. But the hourly cost is dependent on the hours of flying that an aircraft undertakes each year. The hourly depreciation cost of each aircraft in any one year can be established by dividing its fixed annual depreciation cost by the aircraft's annual utilisation, that is, the number of block hours flown in that year. Thus, if the Boeing 747–400 aircraft in the above example flew 2,800 block hours in a year, which is how long Saudi Arabian Airlines flew their 747–400s in 2007, its hourly depreciation cost would be $3,215 ($9.0m divided by 2,800 hours). If the annual utilisation could be pushed up to 5,250 hours, which is what Cathay Pacific managed in 2007, then the hourly cost would be cut to $1,715 ($9.0m divided by 5,250). It would be 47 per cent lower. This is why pushing up the daily and annual utilisation of an airline's aircraft as much as possible is so crucial.

The more an aircraft flies each day and year the lower is the depreciation cost per block hour. It is evident that any changes in the depreciation period, in the residual value or in the annual utilisation will all affect the hourly depreciation cost.

A major issue for airline accountants in recent years has been whether to use the historic purchase price of the aircraft as the basis for calculating its annual depreciation cost or the current cost of replacing that asset which may be substantially higher, especially for aircraft that are more than five or six years old. Current or replacement cost depreciation would result in substantially higher annual depreciation charges and few airlines have adopted this. Some airlines, however, have adopted a policy of charging extra depreciation in good years when profits are high. This enables them to put more money aside for fleet replacement.

It is ICAO practice to include depreciation of ground property and equipment as a further item of direct operating costs. This practice is questionable in that such depreciation charges are not directly related to the operation of aircraft and, except where they relate to ground equipment which is specific and unique to a particular aircraft type, they will remain unaffected if an airline changes its fleet.

Many airlines amortise the costs of flight crew training as well as any developmental and pre-operating costs related to the development of new routes of the introduction of new aircraft. In essence this means that such costs, instead of being charged in total to the year in which they occur, are spread out over a number of years. Such amortisation costs are grouped together with depreciation.

4.4 Indirect operating costs

4.4.1 *Station and ground expenses*

Station and ground expenses are all those costs incurred in providing an airline's services at an airport other than the cost of landing fees and other airport charges. Such costs include the salaries and expenses of all airline staff located at the airport and engaged in the handling and servicing of aircraft, passengers or freight. These should include all costs associated with an airline's lounges for Business or First class passengers. In addition there will be the costs of ground handling equipment, of ground transport, of buildings and offices and associated facilities such as computers, telephones, and so on. There will also be a cost arising from the maintenance and insurance of each station's buildings and equipment. Rents may have to be paid for some of the properties used, as well as charges for electricity, heating and so on. Clearly, by far the largest expenditure on station and ground staff and facilities inevitably occurs at an airline's home base.

At some airports, especially the smaller ones it serves, an airline may decide to contract out some or all of its check-in and handling needs. Handling fees charged by third parties should appear as a station expense. Since the crisis period in 2001–4 there has been a strong tendency for legacy network airlines to outsource more and more of their handling, away from their major bases, to specialist ground handling companies, as a way of reducing such costs. European low-cost carriers have done this as an integral part of their business model. An airline may contract out of all of its handling including passenger check-in, baggage and freight handling and loading, aircraft cleaning and so on, or only some of these activities. It may pay a global fee irrespective of the aircraft type actually used. However, if the fees paid for handling to be provided by a handling agent or another airline vary with the size or type of aircraft being used then such handling charges may legitimately be considered a direct operating cost.

Some light aircraft maintenance may be done at an airline's out-stations and the costs arising from such maintenance work should ideally be included as a direct operating cost under the 'maintenance and overhaul' category. But maintenance expenditures are frequently difficult to disentangle from other station costs and are in many cases left as part of station and ground costs.

4.4.2   Costs of passenger services

The largest single element of costs arising from passenger services is the pay, allowances and other expenses directly related to aircraft cabin staff and other passenger service personnel. Such expenses would include hotel and other costs associated with overnight stops as well as the training costs of cabin staff, where these are not amortised. Unlike pilots, cabin crew are licensed to work on any aircraft type within an airline's fleet. They are not restricted to one or two types only. Hence cabin crew costs are assumed to be independent of the type of aircraft being used. On the other hand, as the number and grading of cabin staff may vary by aircraft type, some airlines consider cabin staff costs as an element of flight operations costs; that is, as a direct operating cost.

A second group of passenger service costs are those directly related to the passengers. They include the costs of in-flight catering, the costs of accommodation provided for transit passengers, the costs of meals and other facilities provided on the ground for the comfort of passengers, and expenses incurred or compensation paid as a result of delayed or cancelled flights.

Lastly, premiums paid by the airline for passenger liability insurance and passenger accident insurance should also be included. These are a fixed annual charge based on an airline's total number of passengers or passenger-kilometres produced in the previous year. The premium rate will depend on each airline's safety record, on the regions it operates within or to and on the type of insurance cover it requires.

4.4.3   *Ticketing, sales and promotion costs*

Such costs include all expenditure, pay, allowances, and so on, related to staff engaged in reservations ticketing, sales and promotion activities as well as all office and accommodation costs arising through these activities. The costs of retail ticket offices or shops, whether at home or abroad, would be included, as well as the costs of telephone call centres, of the computerised reservations systems and the operation of the airline's internet website. Problems of cost allocation arise. It is frequently difficult, especially at foreign stations, to decide whether particular expenses should be categorised as station and ground expenses or as ticketing, sales and promotion. For instance, where should an airline allocate the costs of ticketing staff manning a ticket desk at a foreign airport who may also get involved in assisting with the ground handling of passengers? The same difficulty arises with the costs of an airline's 'country manager' in a foreign country, who may have overall responsibility for sales as well as the handling of passengers at the airport.

A significant cost item within this area is that of commissions or fees paid to travel agencies for ticket sales. Commissions are also paid to credit card companies for sales paid for using cards as well as to the global distribution systems for all reservations made on their worldwide computer systems. Finally all promotional expenditure including the costs of all advertising and of any other form of promotion, such as familiarisation visits by journalists or travel agents, also fall under this heading.

4.4.4   *General and administrative costs*

General and administrative costs are normally a relatively small element of an airline's total operating costs. This is because, where overhead costs can be related directly to a particular function or activity within an airline (such as maintenance or sales), then they should be allocated to that activity. Thus, strictly speaking, general and administrative costs should include only those cost elements which are truly general to the airline or which cannot readily be allocated to a particular activity. Inter-airline comparison of these general costs is of little value, since airlines follow different accounting practices. While some airlines try to allocate their central costs to different cost centres as much as possible, other airlines do not do so either as a matter of policy or because their accounting procedures are not sophisticated enough to enable them to do so.

Where airlines cannot legitimately include a particular expense under one of the cost categories discussed above, they may include it as a separate item under '*Other operating expenses*'. If the sums shown under this heading for a particular airline are large, this is usually an indication of poor cost control and/or inadequate accounting procedures.

4.5   Trends in airline costs

The trends since 1994 in the distribution of total operating costs between the various cost elements discussed can be seen in Table 4.3. It is apparent that for the world's scheduled airlines as a whole over half of total operating costs now arise from direct costs. The rest are indirect costs. The trend in recent years has been for direct operating costs to become increasingly important. In 1994 they represented just under half (49 per cent) of total operating costs. Thirteen years later, by 2007, their share had risen to around 61.9 per cent and rose further in 2008. Two factors explain this trend. First, rising fuel prices after 2002 have increased the relative importance of fuel as the largest direct cost. In 1994, fuel represented only 11 per cent of total costs. Thirteen years later it was 25.4 per cent. Second,

Table 4.3 Trends in structure of costs – scheduled airlines ICAO member states, 1994–2007

		1994 %	2000 %	2007 %
A	DIRECT OPERATING COSTS (DOC)			
	1 Flight operations – total	32.8	38.0	46.5
	Flight crew (including training)	(8.0)	(8.6)	(7.5)
	Fuel and oil	(11.4)	(14.4)	(25.4)
	Airport and en-route charges	(7.1)	(7.0)	(6.6)
	Aircraft rental, insurance, etc.	(6.4)	(8.1)	(7.0)
	2 Maintenance	10.0	10.6	10.3
	3 Depreciation – aircraft	6.1	5.5	5.1
	Total DOC	49.0	54.1	61.9
B	INDIRECT OPERATING COSTS (IOC)			
	4 Station/ground expenses*	12.0	11.3	10.5
	5 Passenger services (including cabin crew)	10.8	10.0	8.7
	6 Ticketing, sales, promotion	15.8	12.7	8.5
	7 Admin and other costs	12.4	11.8	10.4
	Total IOC	51.0	45.8	38.1
C	TOTAL OPERATING COSTS (TOC)	100	100	100

Source: Compiled by author from ICAO: Series F financial data.

Note
* includes depreciation of property and ground equipment.

a major indirect cost, namely that of ticketing and sales, has become less significant as airlines have switched increasingly to online sales, cut back their sales staff and outlets and reduced or eliminated commissions to agents (item 6, Table 4.3). This revolution in selling has brought down sales and marketing costs from 15.8 per cent of total costs in 1994 to 8.5 per cent in 2006. They are continuing to decline.

The most significant factor affecting both the overall level and the structure of unit costs during the last two decades has been the variation in the price of aviation fuel. After two major hikes in the price of oil in 1973 and 1978–9 fuel prices stabilised and then began to decline slowly in dollar terms in the latter part of 1982. This steady decline continued till 1986 when a more dramatic price fall occurred. This large drop in the fuel price was a major factor in the improved financial performance of many airlines in the period 1987–9 (see Figure 1.1).

As the real price of fuel declined after 1982 so did its share of total costs, so that by 1994 this was down to 11 per cent. This helped the airlines achieve record profits in 1997 and 1998. But after 2003, the war in Iraq, the booming demand for oil from China and India combined with production quotas imposed by OPEC members led to a rapid escalation of oil prices. The oil price per barrel tripled in US dollar terms between 2002 and mid-2006. Aviation fuel prices followed. The average cost of aviation fuel also tripled from an average of 67.9 US cents per US gallon to a peak of 195 cents in 2006 (Table 1.3). The fuel price stabilised at first in 2007 and then started to climb again. It reached a new peak of almost $4 in June–July 2008 and then declined sharply to around $1.40 by the end of that year. But many airlines which had bought fuel hedges when prices were rising were still paying well above the market price in 2009. As a result, for many airlines in 2009 fuel still represented around 25 per cent or more of their total costs despite the drop in price.

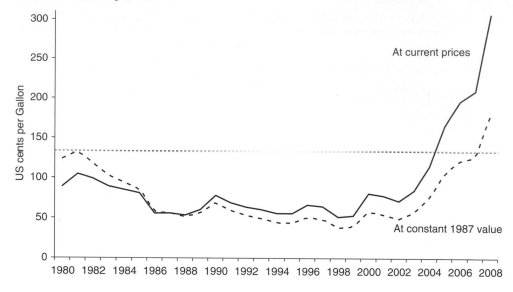

Figure 4.1 Average fuel price in current and constant 1987 US cents: 1980–2008. Annual average
fuel prices paid by US airlines.
Source: Compiled using data from *Airline Monitor* (2009).

The long-term trend in fuel prices paid by US airlines can be seen Figure 4.1. This
also mirrors the worldwide trend. Between 1986 and 2003 average fuel prices fluctuated
but within manageable limits. But the dramatic escalation in prices, both in current and
constant values, after 2003 and especially in 2007–8 is clearly apparent. It was a major
contributor to the airline industry's losses in 2008.

Surprisingly, the two other elements of direct operating costs – maintenance costs and
depreciation – were not as adversely affected by the general inflation of costs during the
last 20 years. Both these cost elements, but particularly depreciation, were helped by the
more widespread use of wide-bodied jets since the 1980s, which were technically more
proficient and had lower maintenance requirements. At the same time, their annual productivity was such that, despite their high purchase price, their unit cost of depreciation
was actually lower in real terms than that of the aircraft they were replacing. As a result,
the share of both maintenance and depreciation in total costs has been fairly stable.

However, the depreciation figure in Table 4.3 does not cover the full cost of aircraft
ownership because during the last 20 years a growing proportion of aircraft are leased
rather than purchased. This explains why in Table 4.3, rental and insurance of flight
equipment (together with other similar items) have increased slightly as a proportion of
total costs between 1994 and 2007. In fact, aircraft ownership costs, that is lease payments, depreciation and aircraft insurance, if taken together, totalled around 12–13 per cent
of total costs in 2007.

While the view that direct costs in general are around 60 per cent of total costs is a
useful generalisation, it hides the fact that there are differences between airlines in their
cost structures. A number of factors, such as average sector length, nature of traffic or
region of operation, etc., may cause variations in airline cost composition. But for most
airlines direct operating costs are generally between 55 and 70 per cent of total operating

Table 4.4 Contrasting cost structure of long- and short-haul airlines, financial year 2007

Average sector length	Composition of costs	
	Bmi (British Midland) 760 kms %	Virgin Atlantic 7,270 kms %
A: *DIRECT COSTS*		
1 Flight operations		
Flight crew	7.3	4.5
Fuel	20.6	27.6
Airport and en-route	20.7	7.1
Insurance	0.7	0.2
2 Maintenance	11.2	8.7
3 Depreciation/lease, rentals	10.4	12.4
TOTAL DIRECT	70.9	60.5
B: *INDIRECT COSTS*		
4 Station and ground costs	10.2	5.4
5 Passenger services* (inc. cabin crew costs)	6.1	13.6
6 Ticketing, sales and promotion	8.4	7.9
7 Admin and other costs	4.3	12.6
TOTAL INDIRECT	29.1	39.5
C: TOTAL OPERATING COSTS	100.0%	100.0%

Source: Compiled using CAA (2009a).

Note
* Bmi's financial year to end December 2007, Virgin's to end February 2008.

costs. Today, direct operating costs tend to be highest, as a proportion of total costs, for short-haul and low-cost carriers.

The very different cost structures of short- and long-haul operations are very apparent when contrasting the cost structure of Bmi-British Midland with that of Virgin Atlantic in the financial year 2007 (Table 4.4). For Bmi, direct operating costs represent 70.5 per cent of total costs and for Virgin 60.5 per cent. The contrast in other aspects of their cost structure is quite stark. Bmi operates very short average sector lengths, only 760 kms in 2007, compared to Virgin, whose average sector is 7,270 km, which is almost ten times as long. As a result Bmi has high airport landing and passenger fees and station costs because landings are so frequent, whereas for Virgin they occur only after many hours of flying. Consequently for Bmi, airport and en-route charges represent one fifth of total operating costs, or 20.7 per cent, while station and ground costs are a further 10.2 per cent. For Virgin, on the other hand, these costs represent only 7.1 and 5.4 per cent respectively.

For Virgin, its very long-haul flights mean that the two most significant costs are fuel, 27.6 per cent (compared to Bmi where it is only 20.6), and passenger services which are 13.6 per cent. Fuel costs are a higher proportion for Virgin and other long-haul operations in part because airport, en-route and station expenses occur less frequently. It also means that long-haul flights are more affected by rising fuel prices.

Passenger service costs are high for Virgin because of the need to provide adequate and expensive catering on long flights, with two or three classes of cabin, while cabin crew costs are higher because of the need to night stop crews for up to three nights at long-haul destinations. Conversely, short-haul airlines increasingly try to minimise spend on in-flight catering and try to avoid night stopping their crews. Bmi, like other legacy airlines, has been reducing its passenger service costs in response to competition from low-cost carriers and some of its short-haul services were operated by its low-cost subsidiary Bmibaby.

4.6   The concept of escapability

The traditional classification of costs described above is essentially a functional one. Costs are allocated to particular functional areas within the airline, such as flight operations or maintenance, and are then grouped together in one of two categories, as either direct or indirect operating costs. This cost breakdown is of considerable value for accounting and general management purposes. This is particularly so where the organisational structure within an airline corresponds fairly closely to the same functional areas as may be used for costing purposes – in other words, where an airline has a flight operations division, an engineering (maintenance) division, a sales division, and so on. A functional classification of costs is useful for monitoring an airline's performance over time and also for inter-airline comparisons. Costs can be broken down relatively easily to produce disaggregate costs within a particular functional area. For instance, one could analyse separately labour costs in the maintenance area as opposed to the labour costs in station and ground operations.

In addition, the broad division into direct and indirect costs is especially useful when dealing with aircraft evaluation. The indirect costs of a particular network or operation can be assumed to remain constant, since they are unaffected by the type of aircraft used. An evaluation of a new aircraft type or a comparison between several aircraft for a particular network can then be based purely on an assessment of the direct operating costs. This simplifies the process of evaluation.

The great advantage of the traditional approach to cost classification is its simplicity and the fact that in allocating costs by functional area it avoids many of the problems associated with trying to allocate joint or common costs. For instance, station and ground costs common to a number of different services are grouped together and are not allocated to particular flights or services. However, the simplicity of this cost classification is also its major drawback. It is of only limited use for an economic evaluation of particular services or routes; or for pricing decisions; or for showing how costs may vary with changes in the pattern of operations on a particular route.

To aid decision-making in these and other related areas the concept of 'escapability' of costs needs to be introduced. The degree of escapability is determined by the time period required before a particular cost can be avoided. Clearly some costs may be immediately escapable, as a result of a particular management decision, while others may not be avoidable except in the very long run. The concept of escapability involves a temporal dimension. Different costs will require different periods before they can be avoided, but ultimately all costs are escapable. There is also a technical dimension to the concept, in that the degree of escapability also varies with the size and nature of the airline service or activity being considered. Thus, if all services on a particular route were to be cut, the nature of the escapable costs would be different from if only the flight on a particular day of the week was cancelled on this same route. The first course of action might involve not only a saving of flight operation costs but also the closure of a complete station or a reduction in the number of crews or even the number of aircraft in the fleet. Cancellation of only one flight a week may involve a reduction in some flight operation costs but little else. This is because many costs are joint or common costs and will go on being incurred to support the remaining flights even if one flight a week is cancelled. The interaction of the temporal and technical aspects of escapability must be constantly borne in mind by airline managers.

Airlines vary in the way they introduce the concept of escapability into their costing procedures. The most usual way is by adopting the traditional accounting distinction of fixed and variable costs. Airlines do this by taking those elements of cost generally accepted as being direct operating costs, together with some of the indirect costs, and further subdividing them into 'fixed' and 'variable' costs. There are several ways in which this can be done because of the temporal and technical considerations outlined above. The larger and more sophisticated airlines may use one breakdown of costs for, say, pricing decisions and a different one for evaluating the profitability of particular services or routes. One possible approach is discussed below.

4.6.1   Variable and fixed direct operating costs

Variable or flying costs are costs which are directly escapable in the short run. They are those costs which would be avoided if a flight or a series of flights was cancelled. They are immediately escapable costs, such as fuel, flight crew overtime and other crew expenses arising in flying particular services, landing charges, the costs of passenger meals, and so on. These are fairly self-evident. Less self-evident are the engineering or maintenance costs which should be classified as variable. Certain maintenance checks of different parts of the aircraft, involving both labour costs and the replacement of spare parts, are scheduled to take place after so many hours of flying or after a prescribed number of flight cycles. (A flight cycle is one take-off and landing.) Undercarriage maintenance, for example, is related to the number of flight cycles. Since a large part of direct maintenance is related to the amount of flying or the flight cycles, cancelling a service will immediately reduce both the hours flown and the flight cycles and will save some engineering expenditure, notably on the consumption of spare parts, and some labour costs.

Fixed or standing costs are those direct operating costs which in the short run do not vary with particular flights or even a series of flights. They are costs, such as annual depreciation or lease charges, which in the short or medium term are not escapable. They are certainly not escapable within one scheduling period. That is to say, having planned its schedules for a particular programme period and adjusted its aircraft numbers, staff and maintenance requirements to meet that particular schedules programme, an airline cannot easily cut back its schedules and services, because of public reaction and its own obligations towards the public, until the next schedules programme is introduced. New schedules would normally be introduced twice a year. If the airline decided to cut back its frequencies when the next schedules programme was introduced, it could possibly reduce its fleet by selling some aircraft and it could reduce its staff numbers and cut its maintenance and other overheads. Fixed or standing DOCs may be escapable but only after a year or two, depending on how quickly the airline could actually change its schedules and cut back on aircraft, staff, and so on. Thus most staff costs for pilots, cabin crew or maintenance engineers are fixed in the short term but staff travel expenses or pilots' bonuses related to flying activity would be a variable cost.

While most *indirect operating costs* are fixed costs in that they do not depend in the short term on the amount of flying undertaken, others are more directly dependent on the operation of particular flights. This is particularly true of some passenger service costs such as in-flight catering and hotel expenses and some elements of cabin crew costs. Fees paid to handling agents or other airlines for ground handling of aircraft, passengers or freight can be avoided if a flight is not operated. Some advertising and promotional costs may also be escapable in the short run. Airlines breaking down their costs according to their escapability take some or all of the above expenses previously categorised as indirect costs and redefine them as fixed or variable direct operating costs. This leaves within the indirect cost category costs which are not dependent on the operation of particular services or routes. They are fixed in the short term.

One possible threefold division of costs based on the concept of escapability is shown in Table 4.5. All direct operating costs, as categorised earlier in Table 4.2, have now been divided into fixed or variable. In addition, a number of expenses previously categorised as indirect operating costs in Table 4.2 are here re-classified as direct costs. These include all cabin crew costs, handling fees paid to others and the costs of in-flight catering and passenger hotels. But they are further sub-divided into fixed and variable direct costs. Handling and passenger service costs are now deemed to be variable costs, as are some cabin crew costs, as they depend on the amount of flying undertaken. On the other hand, most cabin crew costs, including basic annual salaries, are now considered to be fixed direct costs.

The concept of cost escapability has been applied to British Airways, whose cost structure is fairly typical for a major international airline with a well-developed short, medium and long-haul network. Using published operating cost data for the financial year April 2007 to March 2008, it proved possible to break down British Airways' costs in the way suggested earlier. This breakdown is shown in greater detail in Figure 4.2. It is clear that in 2007–8 over half of BA's total operating costs or 52.8 per cent were immediately escapable. About a quarter of costs, 25.6 per cent, were fixed direct operating costs and a further quarter, 21.6 per cent, were indirect operating costs. In the early 2000s, when fuel prices were lower, generally accounting for around 10–12 per cent of total costs, then BA's variable costs were also lower, around 40 per cent. The fuel price has a major impact on the significance of variable costs.

It was the very high fuel prices in late 2007 and early 2008 that pushed BA's variable direct costs to more than half its total costs. The same would have been the case with other airlines.

Variable direct operating costs are related to an airline's activity level, that is, the amount of flying it actually does. When variable costs are as high a proportion as indicated in the British Airways example, there are important implications for operations planning and for pricing. It means that revenue losses can be reduced significantly in the short term by cancelling a flight or a series of flights – if low load factors and/or low yields generate revenues which fail to cover the very significant variable costs. In other words, revenues should at least cover variable costs. If not, that flight or service is haemorrhaging money. The risks of this happening are greatest when the price of fuel is high, since this increases the relative proportion of variable costs.

Variable direct costs are those that are immediately escapable. In the medium term, that is, within a period of a year or so, many *fixed direct operating costs* previously considered fixed start to become variable. Such costs are essentially related to the size of the fleet. If the fleet size is reduced many fixed costs can be reduced too. Aircraft can be sold, cutting depreciation costs, flight and cabin crew numbers can be run down or staff redeployed, and engineering staff facilities can be reduced in size.

Indirect operating costs tend to be related primarily to the number of routes being operated, the quality of services offered and the nature of the sales and distribution systems built up to support the network. Advertising and promotion costs are also influenced by

Table 4.5 Cost structure based on fixed and variable direct operating costs

Variable direct operating costs	Fixed/standing direct operating costs	Indirect operating costs
1 Fuel costs: • Fuel • Oil consumed	7 Aircraft standing charges: • Depreciation of lease rentals • Aircraft insurance	11 Station and ground expenses
2 Variable flight crew costs:* • Flight crew subsistence and bonuses	8 Annual flight crew costs:* • Fixed salaries and other expenses unrelated to amount of flying done • Flight crew administration	12 Passenger services: • Passenger service staff • Passenger insurance
3 Variable cabin crew costs: • Cabin crew subsistence and bonuses	9 Annual cabin crew costs: • Fixed salaries and other expenses unrelated to amount of flying done • Cabin crew administration	13 Ticketing, sales and promotion
4 Direct engineering costs: • Related to number of flight cycles • Aircraft utilisation	10 Engineering overheads: • Fixed engineering staff costs unrelated to number of flying hours • Maintenance administration and other overheads	14 General and administrative
5 Airport and en-route charges: • Landing fees and other airport charges • En-route navigation charges		
6 Passenger service costs:* • Passenger meals/hotel expenses • Handling fees paid to others		

Note

* These items previously categorised as 'Indirect' (Table 4.2).

	%
Aircraft standing charges	11.5
Flight crew salaries/training	5.4
Cabin crew salaries	4.9
Fixed engineering	3.2
Passenger insurance	0.6
	25.6

	%
Station	7.1
Ticketing, sales, promotion	6.0
General and admin.	6.1
Depreciation ground equipment	2.1
Cargo specific	0.3
	21.6

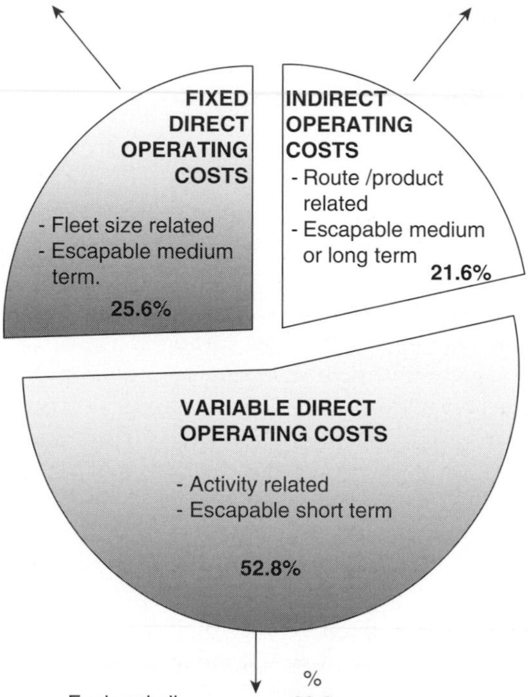

FIXED DIRECT OPERATING COSTS

- Fleet size related
- Escapable medium term.

25.6%

INDIRECT OPERATING COSTS

- Route /product related
- Escapable medium or long term

21.6%

VARIABLE DIRECT OPERATING COSTS

- Activity related
- Escapable short term

52.8%

	%
Fuel and oil	28.2
Flight/cabin crew	4.4
Direct engineering	4.8
Airport and en-route	7.1
Handling and parking	3.2
Passenger services	4.8
Cargo specific	0.4
	52.8

Figure 4.2 British Airways' costs in terms of escapability, 2007–8.

the route structure. The number of routes operated can be cut back in the medium term and over a longer period the whole network can be modified. Thus even some indirect operating costs are escapable in the medium term and most are escapable in the longer term. In short, elements of both fixed direct costs and indirect costs are escapable in the medium term.

What is perhaps more significant and often forgotten is that as much as 90 per cent of total costs can be varied in the medium term, that is after a year or so, either by discontinuing all operations or by a partial withdrawal of certain operations. Airlines can disinvest or dramatically cut their operations more easily than most forms of public transport because they do not have fixed investments in navigational aids, runways or terminals, though there may be some exceptions, as in North America where airlines may own and operate their own terminals. But while disinvestment may be relatively easy it may also be costly if it involves redundancy payments to laid-off staff, financial penalties for early termination of aircraft leases and so on. Disinvestment is easier if the industry as a whole is doing well. Aircraft can be easily sold or leased out and staff more readily redeployed. But it is usually during industry downturns that airlines want to cut back their production. Reducing the fleet in such times becomes very difficult since no-one is keen to acquire new capacity or staff.

4.7   Allocation of costs for operating decisions

In order to be able to use the concept of cost escapability in making operating decisions – such as whether to reduce or increase frequencies on a route or whether to open up an entirely new route – the various fixed and variable costs need to be allocated to individual flights or routes. Broadly speaking, the approach adopted by various airlines is similar, though there may be differences in the details.

Allocating *variable direct operating costs* is fairly straightforward since nearly all of them are specific to individual flights. Fuel costs, variable flight and cabin crew costs, airport and en-route charges and passenger service costs (as defined in Table 4.5) depend directly on the type and size of the aircraft used and the route over which it is being flown. They are clearly very specific and can be easily measured. The exceptions are the variable engineering or maintenance costs. Here some averaging out is required.

Some direct maintenance work and checks are related to the amount of flying that an aircraft undertakes, while other checks depend on the number of flight cycles. Maintenance on those parts of the aircraft which are most under pressure on landing or departure, such as the undercarriage or the flaps, is clearly related to the flight cycles undertaken. For each aircraft type an airline will normally work out an average cost of maintenance per block hour and a separate average cost per flight cycle. The variable maintenance cost of an individual flight can then be calculated on the basis of the number of block hours and flight cycles required for that flight.

An airline's *fixed direct operating costs* are normally converted into a cost per block hour for each aircraft type within its fleet. They can then be allocated to each flight or route on the basis of the aircraft type(s) being used and the block times for the sector or route. The first element of fixed direct operating costs is aircraft standing costs, that is, depreciation and any rentals for leased aircraft plus aircraft insurance. Such costs are aircraft type specific since they depend on the purchase price or lease rate of the aircraft. They are a fixed annual cost, based on the number of aircraft of a particular type, which when divided by the annual utilisation of these aircraft produces a depreciation and insurance cost per block hour (see Section 4.3 above). If aircraft are leased there is normally an annual leasing cost made up of 12 equal monthly payments. These are fixed annual costs independent of how much flying is undertaken. Therefore, the hourly lease cost, as with depreciation, depends on the amount of hours flown in each year. In addition airlines may have to pay a separate hourly charge per block hour into a 'maintenance reserve'. This is a fixed hourly charge. The total annual amount paid is dependent on the amount of flying undertaken. Its purpose is to build up a cash reserve for major and costly overhauls known as D checks, which normally occur every four to six years. Though ultimately needed for major maintenance checks, the hourly maintenance reserve charge is often included under rentals.

It is relatively easy to identify and allocate the fixed annual flight crew costs, since each aircraft type has its own dedicated complement of pilots and co-pilots. In many cases, if there are several aircraft of a particular type, that fleet will have its own administrative managers as well. Some flight crew overheads, however, will not be aircraft type specific and will need to be allocated on some basis between the different aircraft types, usually the number of aircraft or annual utilisation. The total annual fixed flight crew cost for a fleet of aircraft of a particular type can then be divided by the total annual utilisation (that is, block hours) flown by all the aircraft in that fleet to arrive at a flight crew cost per block hour for that aircraft type.

A similar approach is adopted with other fixed elements of direct operating costs. In the case of cabin crew, problems of allocating fixed annual costs between aircraft types arise because, unlike flight crew, cabin crew can work on different aircraft types at any time. Nevertheless, the annual cabin crew costs can be apportioned to different aircraft types on the basis of the number and seniority of the cabin crew they use and the sectors they fly on. Some fixed maintenance costs will be aircraft type specific; others will be common costs that need to be allocated between aircraft types, usually on the basis of maintenance man hours required for different aircraft. Thus, for each aircraft type, airlines can estimate an hourly flight crew and cabin crew cost and an hourly maintenance cost to cover the fixed element of such costs. Some airlines take this process a step further and calculate different hourly crew and maintenance costs for different types of routes. For instance, some carriers use a higher hourly flight crew cost for a given aircraft type when it is flying on short sectors than when it is used on longer sectors.Since all the fixed direct costs discussed above are allocated to specific aircraft types, some airlines refer to them as 'fleet' costs, associated with operating a fleet of aircraft of a particular type.

When one turns to *indirect operating costs*, difficult problems of allocation arise since by definition such costs are independent of the type of aircraft being operated. Some indirect costs may be route specific and may be escapable in the medium term if a whole route operation is closed down. If an airline operates a single route to another country, the sales and advertising costs in that country as well as the station and ground costs at the airport served can be readily identified as a cost specific to that route. But most indirect costs are fixed joint and common costs that cannot be easily allocated to individual flights or routes except on some arbitrary basis. Most station costs, passenger insurance expenses and the costs of ticketing, sales and promotion as well as overhead administrative costs will normally be allocated to particular services or routes on the basis of some output measure such as the revenue tonne-kilometres or revenue generated. Each approach has its advantages and drawbacks. Using a traffic measure, such as the revenue tonne-kilometres generated on each route, may penalise long-haul routes where tonne-kilometres generated are high but revenues per kilometre are low because fares, like costs, taper with distance. Allocating indirect costs on the basis of the revenue earned on each route or flight may appear more equitable, but not so favourable to shorter routes where fares per kilometre are high. More than one allocative method may be used. Sales, ticketing and passenger service costs may be divided between flights on the basis of passenger-kilometres produced, while cargo-specific costs may be apportioned using freight tonne-kilometres carried.

Using an allocative methodology such as that outlined above, but adapted to its own particular requirements and accounting procedures, an airline can allocate costs to individual flights or routes. Such costs would be made up of four elements:

A   All *variable direct operating costs*. These are flight specific and can be calculated per flight or aggregated to arrive at the total variable DOC, i.e. covering all flights for a particular route. (Such costs are likely to be in the range of 45–60 per cent of total operating costs if fuel prices are at the high 2007 levels and will also be influenced by the sector distance.)

B   Those *indirect operating costs which are route-specific* such as advertising in the destination country or region or station costs. Such costs can, if necessary, be broken down further and allocated to individual flights on that route (generally 5–10 per cent of total operating costs).

C   *The fixed direct operating costs* which are joint costs and are normally allocated to each flight or route on the basis of the block hours flown as shown earlier (ranging between 15 and 25 per cent of total costs).

D   Those *indirect operating costs which are not route-specific* and which have been allocated to each flight or route on the basis of some output or revenue measure (15–20 per cent of total costs).

By comparing these costs with the revenues generated, airline planners are in a position to make decisions as to the number of frequencies that should operate on a route or whether the route should be operated at all.

Some airlines and analysts assess flights or routes in terms of their contribution to overhead or fixed costs. This is called contribution analysis. In other words, a particular flight or route is expected at least to cover its variable flight or route specific costs (items A and B above) out of the revenues it generates. In other words it must cover its escapable costs. If it does not do so at present and is unlikely to do so in the near future then its continued operation must be in doubt. Revenues in excess of the route or flight specific costs are deemed to make a *contribution* to fixed direct costs and to non-specific indirect costs (items C and D above). Ideally, revenues should cover all of these additional costs too. Even if they do not, the key issue is the level of contribution that revenue generated by a particular route makes to such costs. Discontinuing flights will not save any of these fixed direct and indirect costs in the short term. Thus some contribution to meeting these costs is better than none. In the medium and longer term fixed direct operating costs can be cut by reducing fleet size, while indirect costs can be reduced by abandoning routes or downsizing the network and level of operations.

If there are many routes which cover their variable and specific costs but make only marginal contributions to overheads, that is, fixed direct and indirect costs, then an airline is haemorrhaging. It would be wise in the medium term to cut out those routes which make only minimal contribution and have little prospect of improving and to downsize both the fleet and the operations. Unfortunately airline managers are generally reluctant to take such corrective action, even when it becomes obvious, except at times of real crisis. But few airline executives have the nerve to cut services quickly when market conditions begin to worsen.

This is in part because seats are sold on flights up to 9 or 12 months in advance and airlines are loath to upset customers. It is also because airline executives are invariably optimistic. In the second half of 2008, when a major downturn in travel demand was becoming apparent, many airlines did cut their 2008–9 winter and summer 2009 capacities, but not enough. Capacity cuts did not match drops in demand and seat factors went down.

5 Determinants of airline costs

Being able to control costs is the only way to survive as an airline.
(Sir Michael Bishop, British Midland – Bmi, August 2009)

5.1 Management control of costs

The theme of this book is that airline planning and management is about the process of profitably matching supply, which within certain constraints an airline can very largely control, with demand, which it can influence but cannot control. Low unit costs in themselves do not ensure efficiency or guarantee profitability if an airline fails to generate sufficiently high revenues. Nevertheless, controlling and, if possible, reducing costs is a key management objective. As both domestic and international markets have become more liberalised, competition and especially price competition has intensified. In virtually all markets average yields per passenger-km have tended over time to drift downward in real terms. This has reinforced pressures to reduce unit costs. But to what degree can airline managements influence and reduce their unit costs? Or, are such costs very largely externally determined by factors and developments beyond management control?

It is clearly evident that among international airlines unit costs vary widely. The accompanying Table 5.1 shows the unit costs for the five or six largest international passenger carriers in each of three regions of the world. Together these 19 airlines carried over half (around 55 per cent) of the world's international tonne-kms in 2007. The unit costs per available tonne-km are for their total operations, that is international and domestic. (Subsequent tables also refer to these airlines except where data is unavailable.) The table amply illustrates both the wide range in cost levels between airlines and the existence of marked regional variations. High-cost airlines such as SAS, Japan Airlines, KLM or Continental have unit costs more than twice as high as Singapore Airlines (SIA) or Cathay Pacific at the bottom of the table. In the case of SAS unit costs were nearly four times as high. East Asia is the region that clearly stands out as having the lowest-cost airlines, though it also encompasses one or two high-cost operators, notably the Japanese airlines Japan Airlines and All Nippon Airways. As a group, the European carriers appear to have the highest unit costs, but among the largest Europeans, British Airways enjoys the lowest unit costs.

In order to gain an insight into the causes of such a wide diversity of unit costs between airlines one needs to assess the determinants of operating costs paying particular attention to the degree to which they can be influenced by management.

The numerous factors which affect airline operating costs can be grouped into three broad categories according to the degree to which they are under management control

Table 5.1 Unit operating cost of major international airlines, financial year 2007

Rank	North American		European		East Asia	
	US cents per available tonne-kilometre					
1			SAS	109.9		
2					Japan Airlines	90.1
3			KLM	89.3		
4	Continental	79.9				
5			Iberia	72.5		
6			Air France	70.5		
7			Lufthansa	70.2		
8					All Nippon	68.5
9	Delta	63.3				
10			British Airways	63.0		
11	Air Canada	57.7				
12	United	57.5				
13	American	56.8				
14					China Southern	55.8
15	Northwest	55.2				
16					Thai Airways	46.9
17					Malaysia	40.3
18					Cathay Pacific	33.6
19					SIA	30.6

Source: Compiled using ICAO (2009) data.

(Table 5.2). First, one can identify a number of external economic inputs over whose prices airlines have little control. Such input prices include the prevailing fuel prices, airport and en-route navigation charges and certain distribution costs. An airline has to accept these as more or less given and can only marginally mitigate their impact through negotiations with service providers or fuel suppliers.

Second, there are three major determinants of costs over which airlines have some-what greater but still limited control. These are labour costs, the type of aircraft used and the pattern of operations for which the aircraft are used. While the latter two of these might seem to be entirely at the discretion of airline management, in practice manage-ments' hands are tied to some extent by factors beyond their control. The geographical location of an airline's home base, the bilateral air services agreements signed by its gov-ernment, the traffic density on its routes and other such factors will strongly influence the type of aircraft required and the network operated. Management does not have an entirely free hand to do as it wishes. This is particularly so of national airlines in countries with only one flag carrier, especially if it is majority owned by its own government.

The third category of cost determinants is that over which management has a high level of control or even total control. Marketing, product planning and financial policy fall into this category, as does corporate strategy. In the final analysis one must also con-sider the quality of management and its efficiency as a cost determinant. It is crucial because management determines the degree to which the impact of the other factors mentioned above, whether favourable or unfavourable, can be modified to the benefit of the airline concerned.

The analysis in this chapter of the effect of different variables on costs is qualitative rather than quantitative. Some earlier studies have used various forms of multivariate analysis to establish the influence of a range of independent variables (for instance airline

Table 5.2 Factors affecting airline operating costs

	Degree of management control		
Externally determined input costs	LITTLE		
Cost of labour		SOME	
Type/characteristics of aircraft used		SOME	
Route structure/network characteristics		SOME	
Airline marketing and product policy			HIGH
Airline financial policy			HIGH
Corporate strategy			HIGH
Quality of management			HIGH

size, pilot wage levels or stage length) on a dependent variable such as unit costs or labour productivity. For instance, Pearson used a multivariate approach in a comparative assessment of European airlines in the mid-1970s (Pearson, 1977). In theory multivariate analysis should be able to establish the relative impact of the various independent variables on the unit costs of the airlines concerned. Certainly Pearson in his work was able to produce high coefficients of determination suggesting that a high proportion of the variations in the dependent variable could be explained by variations in the independent variables. Subsequent work by the UK's Civil Aviation Authority questioned the value of multivariate analysis (CAA, 1977, Appendix B). The CAA carried out its own multivariate analysis of European airline performance. For instance, it examined labour productivity as a dependent variable. Using different independent variables than Pearson but comparable ones, it was able to produce equally high coefficients of determination. But one or two airlines that were labour-efficient when analysed by Pearson were inefficient in their use of labour when assessed by the CAA model. Such discrepancies occurred in other areas too. Two models using the same technique and broadly comparable sets of explanatory variables should have produced consistent results. The fact that they did not raises serious doubts about the validity of multivariate analysis for comparative studies of international airlines.

It has subsequently been argued by some economists that studies such as those mentioned above are essentially inductive. They can correlate events rather than establish cause and effect between them. This is an added shortcoming of such an approach. The alternative might be to develop a deductive approach which by using selected measures of total factor productivity allows comparisons between airlines in different countries by adjusting for differences in factor prices, network characteristics, aircraft size and so on (see for example Tae Hoon Oum and Chunyan Yu, 1995). This is an interesting and potentially valuable approach, but it is mathematically complex. While a good descriptor of an airline's overall productivity, total factor productivity is of more limited value as a management tool which can pinpoint where corrective action is needed. In order to provide a better conceptual understanding of the determinants of airline costs, a more qualitative approach would appear to be preferable to both the above techniques and has been adopted in the analysis which follows.

5.2   The influence of demand on costs

Before assessing the factors which directly impact on the costs of supplying airline services, it is important to appreciate that demand too impacts on unit costs. It is generally understood and accepted that airline costs have a direct impact on the demand for air services since they influence the prices at which those services are sold. Costs also reflect service quality and other product features. What is frequently forgotten, however, is that costs are not entirely independent of demand. They are themselves influenced by demand. There is a two-way relationship between supply (costs) and demand. Each affects the other. There are two aspects of demand, in particular, which impact on costs, namely route traffic density and sector length.

The traffic density on a route and the sector length(s) on that route will influence the size and type of aircraft chosen for that route. Aircraft type, and more especially the size of the aircraft, is a key determinant of unit costs. Route traffic density also influences the frequencies which are needed and will thereby affect the annual utilisation, that is the number of hours flown by each aircraft. The higher the utilisation, the lower the costs. Traffic density also affects the level of station costs per passenger or per tonne of cargo. Since station costs do not go up in proportion to the traffic handled then more traffic going through a station means lower costs per unit of traffic. These relationships will become clearer in the following sections. There is one other aspect of demand which impacts on costs and that is the variations in demand over time. Marked seasonal peaks create a need for extra capacity in terms of aircraft, crew, ticketing and sales staff, catering facilities and so on which may be grossly under utilised in off-peak periods. Carrying that extra capacity during the off-peak is costly. From a cost point of view airlines are better off if they are trying to satisfy a pattern of demand that is more or less constant throughout the year (Section 8.6).

In a truly open and competitive environment airlines would be free to choose their own markets in terms of the length of routes and traffic densities that they wish to serve. This may be the case among United States domestic airlines and to a more limited extent among European low-cost airlines or other airlines operating entirely within the European Union. But the vast majority of international airlines do not have a free hand with regard to the demand that they set out to satisfy. The routes they serve and the density of demand on those routes are largely determined by the interplay of geographical, political, economic and social factors outside the airlines' control. The starting point for any international airline is its home base. The geographical location of the home base, together with the level of business and tourist interaction between the home country and other nations, will influence the potential sector lengths and traffic densities that can be fruitfully operated. Australia and Malta represent the two extremes. A major international airline based in Australia must operate a long-haul network with some very long sectors because of Australia's geographical isolation and the long distances to key markets. Conversely the national airline of Malta, as a result of the island's location on the southern periphery of Europe and its small size, is predetermined to be a short-haul airline with only a relatively small number of rather thin routes.

Where an airline is a country's only international airline, which is frequently the case, it may also be under political pressure to operate some routes which it would otherwise ignore. Conversely, where there are several international carriers, as in the United Kingdom or the United States, these may have much more choice as to the routes they can serve. For example, the UK's Virgin Atlantic has, as its corporate mission, focused purely on long-haul intercontinental services and, unlike other major European airlines, operates no short, intra-European routes.

Though constrained by some of the above factors airlines do have some ability to influence the patterns of demand on the routes they serve or wish to serve. First, they can as a matter of policy concentrate on the denser traffic sectors. Second, they can try to increase the total traffic on their routes through their marketing policy and their promotional activity. Third, they can try to improve their own traffic density by increasing their market share when they have competitors on the route. Many airlines place considerable marketing effort into increasing their market share on their major routes. Greater market share is seen as a key objective, not merely because it increases their revenues but also because it can help in reducing costs.

5.3   Externally determined input costs

The costs of a number of key airline inputs or factors of production are determined by external economic variables and are largely outside the control of individual airline managements. Since the external variables vary between countries and regions the factor input costs of different airlines may also vary significantly. While airlines can try to reduce the prices of their inputs, in the case of some key inputs they can only do so to a limited extent. They have to accept the general level of these input prices as given and they have only limited scope to negotiate downwards from that given level. Another feature of these input prices is that they are subject to sudden and often marked fluctuations. Adjusting to sudden changes in the price of fuel or in the level of charges at a particular airport is a common headache among airline managers.

5.3.1   Price of aviation fuel

As shown in the previous chapter, fuel for many airlines in 2006 and 2007 represented a quarter or more of total costs. For most airlines, it is frequently the largest single input cost. Unfortunately, however, it is a cost over which airline managers have little control. The prevailing worldwide price of aviation fuel is directly linked to the price of oil and moves up and down in response to changes in global oil prices, which are themselves determined by the interplay of the global demand for and supply of crude oil.

At the local level, however, there may be very significant variations in the price of aviation fuel and, consequently, on its impact on airline costs. A number of factors influence the fuel price at individual airports. The prices of crude oil and of refinery costs are broadly similar worldwide. But distribution and handling costs vary considerably. While oil refineries are widely scattered around the world only a relatively small number refine jet fuel. The supply of fuel to some airports may involve lengthy and costly transportation especially if the airport is well away from a seaport. Transportation costs also rise if the total volume of fuel supplied to an airport is small. Handling costs at airports vary in relation to the facilities used and the volume of fuel uplifted. Governments may influence the price of jet fuel in two ways. They may impose import duties or some other kind of tax, though most governments do neither of these things to fuel supplied for international flights. Some governments may also try to control or fix the price of fuel as a matter of government policy. For example, in India domestic airlines have had to pay both an excise duty on aviation fuel and a local state sales tax which together might add as much as 40 per cent of the basic fuel price. It was not until 2005–6 that these duties began to be reduced.

While jet fuel prices move up and down in response to changes in crude oil prices, there are quite marked regional variations in jet fuel prices as a result of the above factor (Table 5.3). In August 2008, when fuel prices were at an all-time high, they tended to be

Table 5.3 Average jet fuel prices by region: mid–August 2008

Region	Average jet fuel price US cents per US gallon
Latin and Central America	364.1
Europe and CIS	327.0
North America	319.4
Asia and Oceania	319.0
Middle East and Africa	314.0
World average	323.0

highest in Latin America and lowest in the Middle East and Africa. But within each region there are wide variations in fuel prices between individual airports. For example, African airlines seem particularly disadvantaged by the very high fuel prices at many African airports south of the Sahara. Inland locations, long distances from oil refineries producing aviation fuel and relatively small volumes of fuel uplift seem to be the root cause of high fuel prices at airports such as Dakar or Nairobi, which may be as much as a third higher than those at some airports in North America or Europe. In Europe jet fuel costs more at airports such as Budapest which are inland and well away from major seaports.

The interplay of crude oil prices and oil company refining and transportation costs, as well as their pricing strategies, broadly determine the posted fuel prices at airports around the world. In addition to the basic fuel price, airlines will normally also pay a handling or so-called 'into plane' charge. This may vary markedly between airports.

The posted price is the price that an airline without regular scheduled services might have to pay. In practice few airlines pay the posted price. Regular users of an airport will negotiate their own contract price with the fuel suppliers. This will be at a discount on the posted price, the level of the discount depending on the total tonnage of fuel that an airline expects to uplift during the contract period. This in turn will depend on the number of daily departures an airline operates from that particular airport, the size of the aircraft being used and the sector distances over which they will be flying. Clearly an airline is likely to pay the lowest price at its own home base airport as it will be by far the biggest user of fuel.

The discount will also be influenced by the number of fuel suppliers. If there is only one oil company providing fuel, the scope for pushing down the price is clearly limited. At most airports around the world there are generally only a few aviation fuel suppliers. In the United States, on the other hand, the existence of a large number of small refineries and of common carrier pipelines open to use by any company has resulted in very large numbers of companies competing for fuel supply contracts. This creates a strong downwards pressure on jet fuel prices.

While the prices negotiated in individual fuel contracts are confidential there are prevailing discount levels at each airport depending on an airline's total fuel uplift. Each airline has a fairly good idea what other airlines are paying. Thus airlines each operating twice daily long-haul departures from London's Heathrow airport with Boeing 747 aircraft will all end up paying very similar prices. The exact price will depend on the negotiating skill of each airline's fuel buyer. The latter might try to get a better price by negotiating with one fuel company for the supply of fuel at several airports.

But ultimately it is the prevailing market price at each airport and the accepted discount levels that will determine the fuel prices at any airport. The airline fuel buyer who is a good negotiator may shave one or two or even more tenths of a US cent off the price per gallon, but he can do little more. Fuel prices are largely externally determined by prevailing market conditions at each airport.

It is also clear that the level of fuel prices paid by airlines varies markedly between airports – even between airports in the same region – and this impacts directly on their operating costs. Air India flying out of Delhi faces the problem that fuel at its main base, where its fuel uplift is greatest, is relatively expensive, in part because of various taxes imposed on aviation fuel. Even though as the largest buyer it will be paying less than the average price, the high fuel price at its home base will inevitably push up its operating costs. On the other hand Singapore Airlines or Malaysia Airlines undoubtedly benefit from very low fuel prices at their home airport.

Airlines can try to mitigate the impact of high fuel prices at certain airports by reducing their fuel uplift at those airports to the minimum necessary. Instead, captains may be instructed to tanker as much fuel as possible at airports where fuel prices are low. Such a policy, however, needs careful monitoring since extra fuel will be burnt during the flight to carry the additional fuel loaded. This is because fuel consumption rises as the total weight of the aircraft increases.

An added problem for airlines is that oil companies insist on escalation clauses in fuel supply contracts. These allow the fuel price to move up or down in response to changes in the price of crude oil. However, airlines can hedge against future increases in fuel prices by buying fuel forward for future delivery at fixed prices.

Delta Air Lines provides an interesting example of how airlines were *hedging* against increases in fuel costs during 1999 and 2000 when prices were rising sharply. Delta hedged by taking out so-called call options on heating oil because its prices closely track those of jet fuel. Call options give the airline the right but not the obligation to buy heating oil at set prices on given future dates. The airline paid a premium for this right. If actual prices on the date set were below the agreed set prices, the airline could walk away but lose the premium. If market prices were above the set price plus the premium, the airline could buy heating at the previously agreed and set price and resell at the market price making a profit. Such profits could then be used to offset any higher prices for aviation fuel. In the 15 months to September 2000 Delta had paid around $100 million in premiums on call options but had netted a surplus of $600 million from hedging (*International Herald Tribune*, 23 October 2000). But to reduce the risks of hedging, Delta normally would only take out call options to cover around half of its fuel needs.

As fuel prices began rising in 2003 and more especially in 2004 airlines turned increasingly to hedging to mitigate the impact. But as fuel prices became more volatile while rising rapidly, airlines were forced to hedge by buying some of their future fuel needs at fixed prices rather than use options as Delta had done. The most successful in doing this was Southwest Airlines in the USA, which in 2005 had hedged 85 per cent of its fuel needs at $26 per barrel and in 2006 65 per cent at $32, when fuel prices were running at twice that level or higher. But hedging can also go wrong: Singapore Airlines, for example, made a loss of $167 million on its hedges in the financial year 2005, but generated a gain of $94m the following year, 2006–7 (SIA, 2007). In early to mid-2008, when jet fuel prices were sky-rocketing, many airlines bought hedges at very high prices, anticipating further increases. When, in the autumn of that year, the fuel price collapsed, airlines with hedged fuel found themselves paying well above the market price. For instance, in the final quarter of 2008, Air France-KLM made a loss of $370m from fuel hedges, SIA lost $225m and United Airlines $370m (*Airline Business*, March 2009). Many continued to be hit in this way well into 2009.

More complex methods of hedging such as the use of 'collars', whereby one tries to limit the future fuel price paid within an agreed range, have also emerged (see Morrell, 2007).

The differential impact of fluctuating exchange rates may also adversely affect some airlines since fuel prices in most parts of the world are quoted in United States dollars. If the dollar exchange rate of a particular currency drops rapidly then the cost of fuel in that country in terms of its own currency will rise equally rapidly. This will hit hardest the country's own national airline, most of whose earnings are in local currency, thereby pushing up its fuel costs. As with fuel, many airlines also hedge against currency movements, especially in relation to their own currency vis-à-vis the US dollar. This is because, apart from fuel, aircraft leases and loan repayments are often in US dollars too.

Fuel prices are largely externally determined, yet for most airlines in 2008 fuel costs represented between 20 and 30 per cent of total operating costs, though at times of low oil prices, fuel costs may fall to 12–15 per cent. While unable to influence the basic price of fuel except marginally, airlines can lower their fuel costs by trying to reduce their fuel consumption. A number of options are open to them. They can try and reduce the weight of their various aircraft by using lighter equipment in the cabin, and less paint on the outside of their aircraft. They can also reduce weight by avoiding unnecessary 'tankering', that is carrying more fuel than is required to meet safety minima on a particular sector. Then they can save fuel by reducing the aircraft cruising speed. A 3 to 4 per cent reduction in the cruising speed of a jet aircraft on a sector of one hour or more may reduce fuel consumption by 6 to 7 per cent at the cost of a few minutes' extra flying. Computerised flight planning can also help. By choosing slower rates of climb or descent and higher cruise altitudes, where available, airlines may be able further to reduce the fuel consumed. But ultimately the biggest savings come from switching to newer, more fuel-efficient aircraft, especially where one can replace four-engined jets by aircraft having fewer and more advanced engines.

5.3.2 *User charges*

For the world's airlines as a whole user charges, that is, airport charges and en-route facility charges, account for 6 to 7 per cent of their total costs (Table 4.3 in Chapter 4). But this is an average global figure. For those international airlines operating relatively short sectors, where landings occur more frequently, the impact of user charges is much greater. Thus, in 2007 Bmi, British Midland, primarily a short-haul airline, found that airport and en-route navigation charges together represented 20.7 per cent of its total costs (Table 4.4 above). For Virgin Atlantic, a long-haul carrier, the figure drops to around 7 per cent, as it does for British Airways, which has a more mixed network. For United States carriers airport and en-route charges are low, generally 2 to 4 per cent of total costs, because such facilities are funded differently in the USA.

User charges, like fuel prices, are largely externally determined. But unlike fuel, user charges give little room for manoeuvre. While the airlines as a whole acting through IATA may try to hold down increases in landing fees or en-route charges in a particular country, an individual airline has no scope for negotiating better rates for itself. All are in the same boat. This is because under Article 15 of the 1944 Chicago Convention all airlines are to be treated equally. There should be no discrimination. In practice, some airports may offer reduced charges for 2 or 3 years to airlines opening new routes. But such reductions are in theory open to all operators of new services. In recent years, low-cost airlines in Europe have been able, at a few airports, to negotiate lower or special charges on the grounds that they are using cheaper or poorer facilities or because they had an economic developmental impact on poorly developed regions to whose airports they were flying.

The level of *airport charges* will depend partly on the costs at the airports and partly on whether the airport authority or the government is trying to fully recover those costs or even make a profit. As a result, landing and passenger-related charges vary enormously between different airports. It is evident from Figure 5.1 that in 2008 British Airways, operating an intercontinental Boeing 747–400 flight from London-Heathrow, had to pay around $4,300 when landing and taking off at Delhi. But on returning to London the airport charges, excluding government passenger taxes, would have been around $12,000 or three times as high. Clearly airlines based in high-cost airports such as Kansai, Dallas or Vienna face a significant cost disadvantage since a high proportion of their landings will be at their high-cost base airport. On the other hand, Emirates or Air India benefit from being based at low-cost airports.

Airport charges consist of two major elements: a landing fee based on the weight of the aircraft and a passenger charge levied on a per passenger basis (Figure 5.1). In the United States, a passenger-related charge known as the Passenger Facility Fee was introduced in 1991. In addition to the two basic charges, there may be further charges for the use of air bridges, for aircraft parking beyond a short free period, for use of terminal air navigation services, or for security, and so on. At many airports, the balance of charging in the last 20 years has moved towards generating more revenue from the passenger fee rather than the aircraft-related charges (Figure 5.1).

ICAO recommends that the passenger charges should be levied on the airlines and their cost recouped through the ticket. Most European and some Third World airports do this. Elsewhere the fee is collected directly from passengers on departure and therefore does not appear as an airline cost. Airlines based in or operating through airports where passenger charges are levied directly on passengers enjoy a cost advantage. This is reinforced if the aircraft landing fee is also low.

The position in the United States is unique. Landing fees and passenger charges are generally very low. On the other hand at most airports major airlines run and may even build their own terminals, which clearly increases their costs. Elsewhere in the world it is very unusual for airlines to operate their own passenger terminals, though they may have their own cargo complexes.

Unlike most other countries, the United States government has for many years levied a variety of taxes on passengers at its airports. These include an international passenger tax, plus separate charges for agricultural inspection and for immigration and customs facilities. The latter three charges are included under passenger-related charges in Figure 5.1 and explain why these are so high at US airports. In the 1990s a number of governments elsewhere also began to introduce fiscal taxes on passengers purely to raise government tax revenues since the funds raised are not to be used for airport investments. This happened first in the United Kingdom, Norway, Greece and Denmark. Several governments have subsequently followed suit and more are expected to follow. These were in addition to the normal charges levied by the airport authorities. As they are

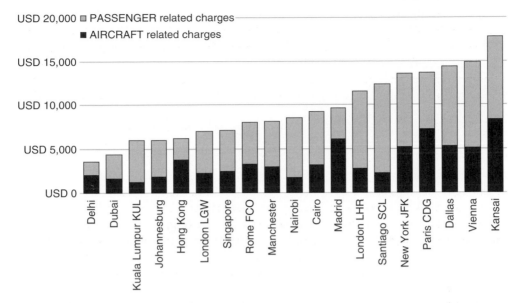

Figure 5.1 Airport charges for a Boeing 747 400, December 2008 (US dollars).
Source: Airport Charges Unit, Department of Air Transport, Cranfield University.
Note
Assumes 85 per cent passenger load factor, 398 tonnes MTOW and 3 hour parking.
Adjusted for seasonal charging peaks.
Exclude government and other taxes which are passed on directly to passengers.

normally passed on directly to passengers such taxes are not included in Figure 5.1. In the United Kingdom the airport passenger duty levied on a flight is in total much higher than the airports' own landing and passenger fees. Strictly speaking such government taxes should not be considered as an airline cost, but rather a transfer of funds collected by the airlines on behalf of governments. They are increasingly shown as a separate item on the tickets over and above the fare.

En-route charges are imposed by civil aviation authorities on aircraft flying through their air-space to cover the cost of air traffic control and navigational and other aids provided. The charges are generally levied on the basis of the weight of the aircraft and the distance flown within each country's airspace. But there are variations. Some countries, Egypt, India and Thailand among them, base the charge on distance alone and aircraft weight is ignored. A few, such as Japan and Kenya, have a fixed charge irrespective of aircraft size or distance travelled. As a result, while there is some uniformity in the method of charging the level of charges varies enormously, as can be seen in Table 5.4. By far the highest charges tend to be those in Japan, China and Europe.

For airlines, en-route charges are a set cost. They are not negotiable. A few state-owned airlines have been able to persuade their governments or airport authorities to give them preferential treatment on airport or en-route navigation charges. Such cases are relatively few, however, because such preferential treatment runs counter to Article 15 of the Chicago Convention and to the principle of equal treatment of each other's airlines which is enshrined in bilateral air services agreements.

Table 5.4 Comparative en-route charges in selected countries, 2007, for Boeing 737–400

	Charge for 700 km overflight with no landing	
	US $	Distance related
UK	910	
Spain	857	
Japan	768	NO
Italy	756	
China	700	
France	681	
Austria	649	
Russia	523	
India	332	
South Africa	318	
Kenya	190	NO
Chile	160	
Egypt	127	
Malaysia	22	

Source: Airport Charges Unit, Air Transport Department, Cranfield University.

5.3.3   *Commission payments for sales and distribution*

For most network or legacy airlines, distribution costs, namely the cost of sales, ticketing and promotional activities, represent around one tenth, generally between 8 and 10 per cent, of their total operating costs (see Tables 4.3 and 4.4). As pointed out earlier (Section 4.5), these costs have declined in significance over the last 10–15 years as airlines have increasingly switched to direct selling, to electronic tickets, and have also reduced or eliminated commissions paid to travel agents. Nevertheless, distribution costs remain an important cost element.

Historically, a major element of distribution costs is the payment of commission to third parties who assist the airlines in selling and reservations. The level of such payments or commissions is largely externally determined. Significant commissions are paid to three service providers – travel agents, the global distribution systems and credit card companies.

The highest commission payments have been those made to travel agents or other airlines. According to an IATA 1996 study, agents' commissions paid, net of commissions received, represented at that time almost 43 per cent of airlines' distribution costs. The rate of commission paid, expressed as a percentage of the ticket price, varies between markets and between countries. The rates for international ticket sales have tended to be between 5 and 6 per cent, but they are usually lower for domestic tickets. Where commissions are the norm, all airlines will pay agents identical or very similar rates in any particular market in order to remain competitive.

It is very difficult for an individual airline to negotiate a separate and lower commission rate than the prevailing rate in a market unless it is very dominant in that market. This may be possible in some smaller domestic markets where the one national carrier may be in a very powerful and possibly monopolistic situation. Elsewhere, if an airline tries to pay lower commissions than competing airlines it may well lose the loyalty or support of travel agents. Unilateral action on commission rates by one airline is generally avoided because it may prove counter-productive. Commission rates can only be cut effectively if there is concerted action by all airlines in a market.

Surprisingly, while airlines may have little discretion to pay lower commission rates, they are able to offer higher rates to generate or buy agents' loyalties. This is done by offering commission 'over-rides'. That is higher commission rates to larger agents when sales volumes in monetary terms surpass certain benchmark levels. However, in more competitive markets the over-ride rates offered by different carriers may end up being fairly similar.

While airlines operating in any particular market tend to end up paying agents the prevailing commission rates, pressures to cut costs have forced airlines in recent years to try to cut the overall level of agents' commissions. They have done this in two ways. First, in several key markets, airlines working in unison have cut agents' commissions to zero and now sell their tickets through agents as net of commission. They leave it to agents to add a service charge to customers for making the booking and providing the ticket. Second, airlines have tried to cut out agents wherever they can by selling direct to customers through their own sales offices, by phone or online through their websites. Both these trends accelerated after 2001 as a result of the strong pressures to cut costs and because of the example set by some low-cost carriers, such as easyJet, who only sold direct and ignored travel agents altogether.

In the 1980s and 1990s airlines became increasingly dependent on the global distribution systems (GDS), such as Amadeus, Sabre or Galileo, which provided agents and even the airlines themselves with a worldwide computer-based reservations facility. Airlines paid the GDS a fixed charge per sector booking made, even though most of the bookings were made by travel agents. The airlines even had to pay if they themselves booked passengers on their own flights using one of these global systems. Initially, all the GDS charged airlines the same booking fee. They matched each other on price and for obvious reasons they could not discriminate between airlines. While the sum paid appeared relatively small, in 2000 it was $3 per sector booked, and represented on average around 7 to 8 per cent of airline distribution costs in the mid-1990s. Once again the unit charge was not negotiable. It was determined by the GDS providers.

After 2000 the GDS commission fee per segment booked continued to rise in both absolute and relative terms, with no increase in value or quality of service to the airlines. This was at a time when many airlines were in crisis and desperate to cut costs. Northwest, for example, claimed in 2004 that its GDS fee per booking was averaging $12.50. To make matters worse, some of the fee paid by airlines was passed on by the GDS to travel agents as incentive payments to book through a particular GDS. But the agents were being paid commissions by the airlines as well. Especially disturbing for the airlines was the ability of the GDS to continue to generate high profit margins in the period 2001–3 when most airlines, especially those in North America, were suffering huge losses. Thus in 2002 the four US-based GDSs produced a net profit margin equivalent to 9.8 per cent of their revenues (*Airline Business*, March 2004). In 2003 the average net margin was lower at 6.1 per cent, but very few airlines were anywhere near this figure.

The GDSs faced increasing pressure to reduce segment fees and also found that they were largely by-passed by the low-cost carriers, by far the fastest growing sector of the airline industry. It was clear that the GDS needed to adapt to a changing market environment.

In 2002, in response to all these pressures and the impending deregulation of US and EU codes of practice for GDSs, they did begin to change their pricing structures. The first was Sabre, which introduced its 'Direct Connect Availability' in October 2002. This offered airlines discounts of between 12.5 and 15 per cent on the sector fees, if they were prepared to market all their available fares through Sabre for a three-year period, including their lowest online fares, which airlines previously offered only on their own websites as a way of luring customers to those sites. Galileo and Wordspan were forced to follow suit and offer similar deals. As a result, British Airways, for example, signed three-year deals with both Sabre and Galileo, which came into force in March 2004. It made all its fares, including its lowest fares, available to travel agents through these two GDSs. In Europe, Amadeus was more innovative on pricing. It did not offer lower fees in exchange for access to all fares. Instead, in January 2004 it launched its 'value pricing' scheme, whereby GDS booking fees were to be set according to the value of a particular booking to the airline. Amadeus was also planning to find ways of attracting the low-cost airlines on to its system.

All these GDS pricing changes were just the beginning. More innovation in pricing of GDS is inevitable. Most network airlines, despite developing their own reservation systems, are still dependent for the majority of their sales on the GDS. But as the GDSs have introduced more flexible pricing, fees paid have become a more controllable cost than they were in the past.

Finally, airlines need to pay commission to credit card companies and other handling intermediaries for any tickets bought directly from the airline sales offices, telephone sales or internet site and paid for by credit card. Again the commission rates have been largely non-negotiable. Commissions and associated fees on credit card sales take up to 2.0 to 2.5 per cent of the revenue earned on a ticket. As other distribution costs have declined, credit card fees have become a far larger percentage of the costs incurred in handling each booking. And, since direct online sales on airlines' own sites have increased dramatically the total cost of such fees has risen sharply. In June 2007, Chris Phillips, Director of Sales Development at Delta, claimed that credit card fees had become the airline's single highest distribution cost, surpassing agents' commissions and GDS fees (*Airlines International*, June 2007).

Taken together, these three types of commission payments, namely those paid to travel agents and other airlines, those exacted by computer reservations systems and payments to credit card companies may make up around 5–6 per cent of total operating costs. They tend to be highest among smaller international airlines who pay a lot of commission to agents and other airlines but have limited opportunities to earn commission themselves.

In conclusion, the three input costs which are largely externally determined, namely the costs of fuel, of airport and air navigation charges and of sales commissions paid to others, together represent between 35 and 40 per cent of most airlines' total expenditure – that is, when fuel prices are at 2007 levels. Because they are so significant, the prices or commission rates that any airline pays for these inputs have an important impact on its cost levels. Differences in these input prices may explain some of the variation in costs between airlines. Yet airlines can influence the level of these input prices only marginally.

5.4   The cost of labour

For most airlines wage costs and associated social security and pension payments for staff represent the largest single cost element, though, of course, it is split between different functional areas within the airline. In 2007, among major North American carriers, such costs, including social charges, on average accounted for around 20 to 25 per cent of total operating costs. Labour costs tend to be lower among those airlines, such as United, which, in the period 2004–7, went through Chapter 11 bankruptcy restructuring. This enabled them to renegotiate labour contracts and cut salaries. Among European airlines the average figure in 2006 was also around 25 per cent, though it was about half of that for low-cost carriers. In Asia, lower wage costs mean that airlines' labour costs are significantly lower than those of European or US network carriers they are competing against. For most Asian carriers, labour costs represent on average around 15 per cent of total costs. For example, for Singapore Airlines staff costs represented 16.6 per cent of total expenditure in the financial year 2007–8 (SIA, 2008). This compared to a figure of 27.5 per cent for British Airways in the same year. Among China's airlines, labour costs drop to 8–12 per cent. Since staff costs represent such a high proportion of overall costs, variations in the average level of wages paid has a direct effect on an airline's total costs and may also lead to appreciable cost differences between airlines.

In a country with free wage bargaining it is the interplay of supply and demand for the categories of labour required by the airline(s) together with the strength of particular unions which will broadly determine the level of wages that an airline has to pay for its various categories of staff. In other countries wage levels may be set by national agreements between governments or employers' associations and the trade unions. In some cases governments themselves virtually determine the levels to be paid and impose them on employers and employees alike. In all cases the prevailing wage levels are related to the standard and cost of living in the country concerned.

In addition to the basic cost of salaries and wages, airlines will normally also have to pay a variety of social charges such as social security or pension contributions or medical expenses. They are frequently enshrined in the social legislation of the country concerned and are mandatory and non-negotiable. Their impact on staff costs can be very substantial. For example in 2002, the average cost to Lufthansa for social charges was $20,800 for each of its employees. These social charges increased Lufthansa's wage bill by 39 per cent in that year. British Airways, on the other hand, paid much less, only $8,400 per employee, which increased its overall staff costs by 121 per cent (Doganis, 2006).

For most airlines, the three most expensive groups of employees tend to be the flight crews, the cabin attendants and the maintenance engineers. For British and many European airlines, the pilots and cabin attendants alone represent on average around 10–12 per cent of total operating costs (see Tables 4.4 and 4.5 in Chapter 4). The significant variations which exist in wage levels for similar categories of staff between regions and between airlines in the same region are illustrated in Table 5.5. This shows the average annual remuneration or wage for two of the three key groups of airline employees, pilots and cabin crew, for a selection of airlines including most of those airlines whose costs were given in Table 5.1. Some variation in pilot salaries maybe due to differences in flight equipment, since pilot salaries vary with type of aircraft flown, or with the age and seniority of the pilots. Nevertheless, allowing for this and other minor discrepancies, some interesting conclusions emerge.

Two trends have become apparent in recent years when comparing airline wage levels across the major aviation regions. First, European pilots and cabin crew, as well as those of the two major Japanese airlines, have become the highest paid in the world and are significantly better remunerated than their American colleagues. Two factors help explain this. The devaluation of the US dollar in the 2000s has made European and Japanese wages more expensive in dollar terms. At the same time, during and following the 2001–4 crisis, several US airlines were able to significantly reduce wage levels because of the

Table 5.5 Average annual remuneration for key staff of selected major airlines in 2006

	Average annual expenditure (US$000s) on:	
	Pilots/Co-pilots	Cabin attendants
North America		
American	138.3	47.2
Delta	127.3	37.0
Continental	123.6	41.9
Air Canada	119.1	38.4
Northwest	117.6	33.7
United	114.9	36.2
USAir	87.0	34.7
Europe		
Air France	316.7	83.3
SAS	233.8	97.2
Lufthansa	225.0	58.7
Iberia	213.1	78.1
British Airways	178.8	50.8
East Asia/Pacific		
JAL	189.2	71.6
All Nippon	184.1	44.0
Cathay	170.2	35.6
SIA	168.0	52.5
Thai Airways	105.4	25.1
Malaysia Airline	46.6	5.4

Source: Fleet and Personnel 2006, ICAO, Montreal.

depth of the crisis, especially those airlines which used Chapter 11 bankruptcy rules to force major concessions from employees. The second trend is that wage levels among US airlines which used to be fairly uniform now show much wider spread. This too is linked to Chapter 11 filings. When examining pilots' remuneration in 2006 among North American carriers (Table 5.5) it is noticeable that the lowest paid pilots were among airlines which had gone or were going through bankruptcy procedures such as Air Canada, US Air and United. The highest paid pilots and cabin crew were at American Airlines, which was among the few not to file for Chapter 11 bankruptcy protection.

Salary differentials were widest among East Asian airlines with airlines such as Malaysia or Thai having especially low wages. But other Asian carriers not listed here pay even lower salaries. Philippine Airlines and Garuda are among these. As seen earlier (in Table 5.1), the unit costs of Japan Airlines are very high compared to those of other Asian carriers. This is also true of All Nippon Airways. This is due in part to their high wage costs, made worse by the steady appreciation of the Yen over the last two decades. So, too, high salary levels among major European airlines is one explanation for their high unit costs seen earlier in Table 5.1.

Marked currency fluctuations can have a significant impact on salary levels when the latter are expressed in US dollars. For example, following marked currency devaluations in 1997, all Thai and Malaysia Airlines staff were paid less in US dollar terms, though their salaries did not change. They have remained low since then (Table 5.5).

The traditional view, long held within the airline industry, was that management could do little about the unit cost of labour because salaries and social charges were largely externally determined. As a consequence, airline executives focused their attention on improving labour productivity through the introduction of large aircraft, computerisation and so on, while holding back, as much as possible, any increases in staff numbers as output increased. But during the 1980s, management attitudes to labour began to change dramatically as a result of deregulation and the successive cyclical economic crises that affected the airline industry. Growing domestic and international competition, which was accompanied by falling fares and yields, made it increasingly clear that marginal improvements in labour productivity in themselves were not enough to contain labour costs. Airlines were forced to try to reduce both the unit cost of labour and the amount of labour used.

This trend was reinforced by the cyclical downturns and crisis years of the early 1990s and 2000s. These forced airline managers to rethink their approach to labour costs. They became much more aggressive in trying to control such costs. They focused on a four-pronged attack. First, they tried to freeze or reduce wages while also renegotiating terms and conditions of employment so as to increase labour productivity. Second, they made great efforts to reduce staff numbers, which also meant increased productivity from the remaining staff. Third, many airlines reduced labour costs by out-sourcing labour-intensive activities to low-wage countries. Finally, some went even further and used franchising of air services to smaller operators as a way of reducing all costs including labour.

The United States airlines had been the first to tackle the issue of labour costs head on in the early 1980s. But it was in the period after 2001, that US airline managers had the greatest impact on their labour costs. Using the threat of imminent collapse of their airlines and, in the case of four of the majors, Chapter 11 bankruptcy rules, many airlines were able to cut staff numbers by up to one third, while also reducing individual wage levels by 25 to 30 per cent (Doganis, 2006).

Achieving similar dramatic cutbacks in numbers and wages in Europe and elsewhere has proved more difficult because of legal, social or even political constraints. But, in Europe action came during the crisis years of the early to mid-1990s, when so many European airlines faced very large and mounting losses. Because of the constraints imposed by national labour regulations, the most common strategy adopted was to renegotiate terms and conditions of employment with the twin aims of cutting the unit cost of labour while also improving the productivity of labour. This meant attempting to freeze wages for one or two years or even to cut them, while at the same time reducing staff numbers or agreeing higher work loads with existing staff. This process was encouraged by major cash injections, the so-called 'state aid' granted by several governments to state-owned airlines to facilitate their restructuring (Doganis, 2006, Chapter 8). Part of the 'state aid' was normally used to offer attractive early retirement or redundancy packages to staff so as to cut staff numbers.

A different approach has been to transfer employment to countries where wage rates are much lower. This effectively means relocating certain activities away from an airline's home base. Swissair was the first to do this in the 1990s by moving some of its revenue accounting services to Mumbai in India and later its international call centres to Dublin and Cape Town. It was followed by others including Austrian Airlines. Meanwhile both British Airways and Singapore Airlines have transferred much of their software development for their management information systems to India. Another way of achieving lower wage costs is by employing flight or cabin crews who have as their base and point of employment countries with lower wage rates. Several European airlines have done this by employing Asian-based flight attendants. Conversely, Cathay Pacific has been trying to reduce its high pilot costs (Table 5.5 above) by taking on pilots based in London at UK pilot wage rates rather than having them based in Hong Kong, where salary levels are very high and the airline has to meet lodging and other costs for expatriate crews. In the mid-1990s Japan Airlines set up a subsidiary company Japan Air Charter which hired most of its pilots and cabin crew abroad, mainly in Thailand. The salaries of Thai pilots and stewardesses employed and based in Bangkok was about one fifth of those of Japanese pilots and stewardesses. JAL then leased in Japan Air Charter to operate scheduled services on holiday routes and JAL benefited from much lower unit labour costs. This trend to relocate airline jobs to lower-wage economies is bound to increase.

Some airlines have tried to overcome the adverse impact of their own high salary levels by setting up or acquiring low-wage airlines which are then used to operate services on their behalf, often with smaller aircraft. It may also be the case that the smaller carrier has lower costs in other areas as well as cheaper labour costs. Lufthansa, for instance, has for some years operated a separate subsidiary called Lufthansa CityLine which flies regional jet services on its behalf with staff employed on different terms from those of the parent company. Some airlines franchise smaller airlines to operate on their behalf again to take advantage of their lower wage rates. Early in 2007 British Airways had five franchisees flying services on its behalf while using British Airways aircraft livery and uniforms, though by 2009 these had been reduced to two. One was in Denmark and the other was Comair in South Africa. In the United States, regional airlines operate scheduled services on behalf of the majors. For instance, the Mesa Air Group in May 2005 clinched a 12-year deal to fly 30 aircraft for Delta Connection, yet it was already operating 70 aircraft for United Express. The effect of all of the above measures is not to reduce the major airlines' own unit labour costs but to mitigate their impact by utilising other airlines with lower wage rates to operate certain services.

The ultimate cost of labour depends not only on the average wage rates paid for different categories of staff but also on the productivity of that labour. This partly depends on institutional factors such as working days in the week, length of annual holidays, basic hours worked per week and so on, and partly on the ability of management to get more output per employee. This in turn is a function of the collective agreements between each airline and its staff which determine work practices, such as number of rest days for pilots or cabin crew after long-haul flights. It is also a function of the number of staff actually employed. Many airlines' response to the worsening crisis facing the industry after September 2001 included massive cuts in staff numbers, especially among US carriers. Where staff cuts were proportionally greater than the reduction in routes and frequencies then labour productivity would inevitably rise.

In summary, until the mid-1980s, wage costs seemed to be largely beyond management's control. However, the major economic crises faced by the airline industry in the early 1990s and after 2001 forced airline managers to take a more direct and active role in reducing staff costs. They were successful in showing that this could be done in many but not all cases. Thus, today one should consider labour as a factor input whose cost levels are largely determined by prevailing economic and social factors in an airline's home country but, where national labour laws and social pressures permit, wage levels can also be influenced by effective management action.

While airlines do have some flexibility in reducing the unit cost of labour, that is the average wage cost plus social charge per employee, they can also reduce the overall cost of labour by employing fewer employees to produce a given level of output. In other words they can strive to increase labour productivity. However, labour productivity is not only a function of the collective agreements and work practices or of the number of staff employed. It is also very much influenced by the type of aircraft being flown by the airline as well as the characteristics of the network which is being served.

5.5 Aircraft type and its characteristics

Many technological aspects of each aircraft type have a direct effect on that aircraft's operating costs. The most important from an economic viewpoint are likely to be the size of the aircraft, its cruising speed and the range or distance which that aircraft can fly with a full payload. The significance of size, speed and range is reinforced in that, taken together, they determine an aircraft's hourly productivity, which in turn also affects costs.

5.5.1 Aircraft size

As a general rule, though there are exceptions, the larger an aircraft the more it will cost to fly per block hour, but the lower will be cost per seat-km. This is because, other things being equal, the direct operating costs of aircraft increase less than in proportion to their size or their payload capacity.

One can illustrate this basic principle of airline economics by reference to the experience of US airlines. In 2007 Boeing 737–500 aircraft flown by US carriers with on average 114 seats incurred on average direct operating costs of about $3,034 per block hour (*Airline Monitor,* 2008). A larger Boeing 737–300 aircraft with 132 seats cost about $3,299 per block hour to fly. The larger aircraft's hourly costs were 9 per cent higher than those of the Boeing 737–500 but its capacity in terms of seats was about 16 per cent more. The greater capacity of the Boeing 737–300 more than compensated for its higher hourly cost. As a result its unit cost was 7.50 US cents per available seat-mile. This was less than the smaller and newer Boeing 737–500 whose seat-mile cost was on average US cents 8.25 or 10 per cent higher.

Aircraft size influences costs in two ways. In the first instance, there are certain aerodynamic benefits from increased size. Larger aircraft have proportionally lower drag and more payload per unit of weight. At the same time larger and more efficient engines can be used. Thus the 215–21-seater Boeing 767–300 has a maximum take-off weight which is nearly two-and-a-half times as great as that of the Boeing 737–800, yet its hourly fuel consumption is slightly less than twice as high (*Airline Monitor,* 2008). It is relatively easier and cheaper per unit of weight to push a large mass through the air than a smaller one. The same applies to mass in water. Hence the development of supertankers. Second, there are other economies of size related to the use of labour. Maintenance costs, a large part of which are the costs of labour, do not increase in proportion to increases in aircraft size. One can see this clearly when comparing two aircraft from the same manufacturer, the Airbus-321 and -320 aircraft. The hourly maintenance costs among United States airlines in 2007 of the larger Airbus A-321 and the smaller Airbus A-320 were very close, yet the A-321 aircraft were carrying 20 per cent more passengers. In addition large economies also arise in flight crew costs since larger aircraft do not require more flight crew, though the pilot and co-pilot may be paid slightly more for flying a larger aircraft.

The close relationship between aircraft size and unit costs for the major aircraft types operated by United States trunk airlines in 2007 can be seen in Figure 5.2. The right-hand axis shows how hourly direct operating costs increase in a linear progression as aircraft size, measured in seats, rises. However, since hourly costs increase less than

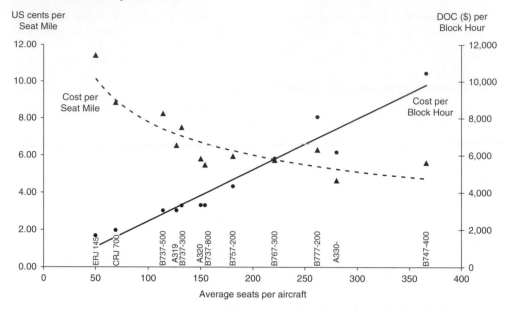

Figure 5.2 The impact of aircraft size on aircraft direct operating costs, US airlines in 2007.
Source: Compiled using data from *Airline Monitor* (2008).

proportionately to size when they are converted to costs per seat-mile, on the left-hand axis, there is a strongly downward sloping curve as aircraft size increases. In simple terms and as a general rule, larger aircraft cost more to fly per hour but should cost less per seat-mile or seat-km. In Figure 5.2 the relationship between increasing size or seating capacity and declining unit costs is clear, though there are deviations and outliers. Such deviations relate either to new and improved versions of existing aircraft types, or to the launch of a newer generation of twin-engine aircraft. Examples of the latter are the Boeing 737–800 and the Airbus A-320 that have unit costs significantly lower than the earlier generation but similar sized Boeing 737–400 they were designed to replace. Among larger aircraft it is the twin-engined Airbus A330–300 which shows the impact of new technology in reducing cost per seat-mile. It should always be borne in mind that the aircraft illustrated are in practice flown on different average sector lengths and this, as is discussed later, influences the unit costs shown in the diagram. The diagram also highlights the very high unit operating costs of the newer generation of small regional jets such as the Embraer 145 and, to a lesser extent, the Canadair CRJ-700. This cost disadvantage is largely a function of their small size. On the other hand their hourly costs are low so they may be suitable for thin routes provided fares are high enough to cover their higher seat-mile costs.

Finally, it is important to emphasise that while larger aircraft generally produce lower seat-km or tonne-km costs than smaller aircraft when flown on the same sectors, their total round-trip costs are in most cases higher. This creates the basic conundrum of airline economics and route planning. Does an airline choose the aircraft with the lower seat-km costs or the one with the lower trip costs? Clearly the choice will depend on the pattern and level of demand which it plans to satisfy.

5.5.2 *Aircraft speed*

Apart from size, aircraft speed also affects unit costs. It does this through its effect on an aircraft's hourly productivity. Since hourly productivity is the product of the payload and the speed, the greater an aircraft's cruising speed the greater will be its output per hour. If an aircraft flies at an average speed of 800 kmph and has a 20-tonne payload, its hourly output is 16,000 tonne-kms. An aircraft with a similar payload flying at 900 kmph would generate 18,000 tonne-kms per hour, or about 12.5 per cent more than the slower aircraft. Some elements of cost might be higher for a faster aircraft. Fuel consumption might be slightly higher unless the faster speed was due to improved aerodynamic design. But many costs, particularly those that are normally estimated on a per block hour basis, would be similar. Flight and cabin crew costs, maintenance costs, insurance, landing fees and depreciation would certainly be fairly similar. These similar hourly costs would be spread over 12.5 per cent more tonne-kms. Therefore, assuming other things are equal, the cost per tonne-km for the faster aircraft would be lower. Since in practice the faster aircraft are frequently larger as well, the cost advantages of size and speed may reinforce each other, producing the lowest seat-km or tonne-km costs.

5.5.3 *Take-off performance and range*

The lower unit costs of larger and faster aircraft does not mean that airlines should always choose to operate such aircraft in preference to smaller, slower aircraft. Airlines must resolve the conundrum previously mentioned. The larger aircraft with the lower unit costs per tonne-km will have higher trip costs than smaller aircraft. In making a choice between aircraft types other factors must also be considered, such as the level and pattern of demand on the routes for which aircraft are needed and the design characteristics of the aircraft in relation to those routes. Aircraft are designed to cater for particular traffic densities and stage lengths. As a result each aircraft type has different take-off and range characteristics and these in turn influence unit costs. An aircraft requiring particularly long runways or with engines adversely affected by high ambient temperatures at airports suffers cost penalties. In either case it can overcome its design handicap by reducing its payload so as to reduce its take-off weight. This would enable it to take off despite a runway or temperature limitation. But the reduced payload immediately results in higher costs per tonne-km since the same costs need to be spread over fewer units of output.

An aircraft's range performance is illustrated in payload-range diagrams such as the one in Figure 5.3. This shows the payload-range characteristics of two versions of the Airbus A-340. Aircraft are authorised to take off at a maximum take-off weight (MTOW). This weight cannot be exceeded for safety reasons. The MTOW is made up of the 'Operating Weight empty' of the aircraft, plus some combination of fuel and payload. With maximum payload the aircraft taking off at its MTOW will be able to fly up to a certain distance for which it has been designed. This is known as the 'range at maximum payload'. To fly beyond this distance the aircraft must lift more fuel and reduce payload, always ensuring that it does not exceed its MTOW. This is why for both versions of the A-340 payload is reduced if the aircraft flies beyond the 'range at maximum payload' and the payload curve declines. Initially the reduction in payload may be in terms of belly-hold freight rather than passengers. The aircraft's range can be progressively increased by further uplift of fuel and a continuing reduction in payload. This process continues until the fuel tanks are full and no extra fuel can be uplifted. The range at this point is known as

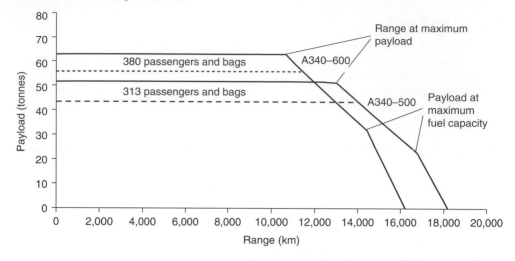

Figure 5.3 Payload–range diagrams for two versions of the Airbus A340.
Note: The 500 series has an extended-range version but achieves it by sacrificing payload. Both
       aircraft have a three-class layout. Passenger weight is 95 kg. Capacity above the dotted line
       is freight.

'range at maximum fuel capacity'. This is the effective maximum range of the aircraft. In
practice, an aircraft could fly further without more fuel by reducing its payload since a
lighter aircraft consumes less fuel per hour. This is why the payload line beyond maximum payload in Figure 5.2 is not exactly vertical but very steep sloping. The shape of
each aircraft's payload range line is different since aircraft have been designed to satisfy
particular market needs.

   Aircraft size, speed and range together determine an aircraft's productivity curve and
hence its unit costs. The relationships are illustrated in Figure 5.4. The top part shows a
hypothetical payload-range diagram for a certain aircraft. The middle diagram shows the
impact of increasing sector distance on that aircraft's hourly productivity, that is the available or capacity tonne-kms produced per block hour. Productivity rises with increasing
sector distance because average speeds rise.

   Hourly productivity is the product of aircraft size and speed. As sector length increases
average aircraft speed rises. This is because aircraft speed is calculated on the basis of the
block time for a journey. Block time is from engines on to engines off. It therefore
includes an amount of dead time on the ground. Ground time will vary with runway,
taxiway and apron layout at each airport and with the number of aircraft movements
during a given period. On departure at a very busy international airport such as London-
Heathrow or Frankfurt, aircraft may spend up to 20 minutes from engine start-up to
lift-off. This may be spent on being pulled out from the stand, disconnecting from the
ground tractor unit; waiting further clearance from ground traffic control; taxiing to the
end of the take-off runway, which may be some minutes from the stand; perhaps waiting
in a queue of aircraft for clearance to taxi onto the runway and take-off. On landing the
ground time is usually less, though at peak periods an aircraft may have to wait for a
taxiway to be clear or even for a departing aircraft to vacate a stand. The total ground
manoeuvre time at both ends of a flight may amount to 20 or 30 minutes at large and
busy airports and will rarely be less than 15 minutes on any international air services.

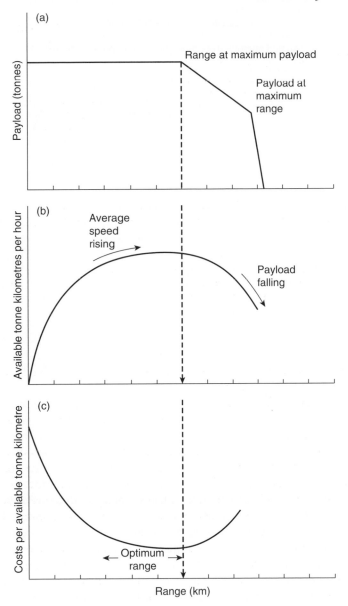

Figure 5.4 Payload–range, productivity and cost relationship: (a) payload–range, (b) hourly productivity, (c) unit cost.

When airborne, the aircraft may have to circle the airport of departure and it will then climb to its cruise altitude. The climb and descent speeds are relatively slow, especially if based on the horizontal distance travelled. On short sectors an aircraft may spend most of its airborne time either in climb or descent, that is at slow speeds, and may only fly at its higher cruising speed and altitude for a few minutes. As the stage distance increases more and more time is spent at the cruising speed and the ground manoeuvre, climb and

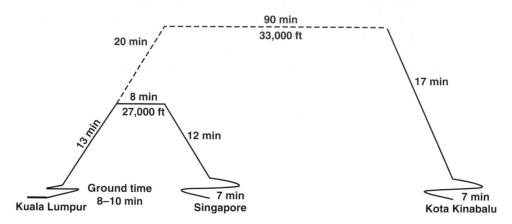

Figure 5.5 Impact of sector distance on block time and block fuel.

descent phases become a smaller proportion of block time. Average block speed therefore increases.

The flights as operated by Malaysia Airlines in 2007 from Kuala Lumpur to Singapore and Kota Kinabalu (on the island of Borneo) provide a vivid illustration of the impact of sector distance on average aircraft speed (Figure 5.5). On the very short sector Kuala Lumpur to Singapore the total block time with a Boeing 737–400 aircraft was on average 48 minutes. But of this 15–17 minutes was spent on the ground at either end of the route, with engines running. Around half the total block time, 25 minutes, was spent in the ascent (13 minutes) or descent (12 minutes) phases when speeds are relatively low. Only 8 minutes was spent at a cruise altitude and at close to a cruising speed. On the much longer sector from Kuala Lumpur to Kota Kinabalu the time on the ground was still the same, 15–17 minutes. Because the cruise altitude was higher it took a few minutes longer to climb and also to descend than it did on the Singapore flight. But once the cruise altitude was reached, the aircraft spent 90 minutes or 60 per cent of the block time flying at a relatively high cruising speed. The impact on average block speed was dramatic. The average block speed on Kuala Lumpur–Singapore is 400 km/hr while on the longer Kota Kinabalu sector it is 680 km/hr.

One could have used a different example, say Southwest Airlines flying from Dallas to Oklahoma City (302 kms) compared to its flight from Dallas to Miami (1,773 kms), but the block time analysis would have produced similar results.

The impact of increasing sector distance on average speed and in turn on hourly productivity is shown diagrammatically in the middle chart of Figure 5.4 above. Initially increasing sector distance has no impact on an aircraft's payload capacity. It remains at its maximum and constant. But as sector distance increases, the rising average speed ensures that hourly productivity rises, even though payload capacity remains constant. It continues to rise until the range at maximum payload is reached (shown by the dotted line in Figure 5.4). For distances beyond this, payload falls and though average speed may still be rising marginally the net effect is that hourly output (capacity multiplied by average speed) falls.

Hourly productivity directly affects unit costs because all the costs which are constant in hourly terms, such as flight crew costs, insurance, or depreciation, are spread over more units of output. Thus a unit cost curve can be derived from the productivity-range curve showing how unit costs decline as range and hourly productivity increase (bottom graph in Figure 5.4). Unit costs continue to decline until payload has to be sacrificed to fly further and hourly productivity begins to drop. The unit cost curve will vary for each aircraft type depending on its size, speed and range characteristics. For each aircraft type it is possible to identify a range of distance over which its unit costs are uniformly low. This might be considered the optimum cost range for that aircraft. The preceding discussion has assumed that total costs per hour are constant irrespective of sector length. The next section on the effect of stage length on costs will indicate that costs decrease relatively with distance. This reinforces the effect of increasing hourly productivity. More of this will be discussed later.

5.5.4   Engine performance

A key characteristic of any aircraft type is the engine it uses. Increasingly, the same engines or engines with similar thrust made by different manufacturers are being used by broadly similar types of aircraft. This is because there are only three major manufacturers of civil jet engines in the Western world and competition to get their engines into the same aircraft drives them to produce similar products. This should not obscure the fact that even similar engines may have different fuel consumption. In particular newer engines are likely to be more fuel efficient. Thus, early in 2000 BAE Systems launched the RJX, a new version of its successful Avro 100–120 seater regional jet powered by new Honeywell AS977 engines. It was claimed that these new engines would reduce fuel burn per sector by 10 to 15 per cent and cut maintenance costs by up to 20 per cent. It is clear that the type of engines in an airline's fleet and in particular whether they are new or old versions of the engine type may influence operating costs. In assessing the costs of different airlines one needs to consider the impact not only of the aircraft type being used but also the version of engine which powers it.

5.5.5   Impact of aircraft type on costs

In conclusion, there can be little doubt that the type and size of aircraft operated has a significant effect on cost levels. With this in mind the key questions are how far an airline has the freedom to choose any aircraft type it wishes or how far the choice is constrained by the sector lengths and the traffic densities on the routes concerned, or other factors. The choice of aircraft occurs in two planning stages and management influence is critical only in the second. The first stage is short-listing the possible aircraft types for a given operation. As previously emphasised, an international airline's route structure and demand pattern is dependent on its geographical location and on economic and political factors largely beyond its control. The route structure, the airports used, in particular the runway lengths available, and the traffic density on those routes will broadly delimit the type of aircraft that is needed or can be used. For particular parts of its network, the sector lengths and traffic densities taken together will reduce the options open to the airline to perhaps only two or three aircraft types.

In some cases only one type may fit the network characteristics and the anticipated demand levels. In the year 2009, airlines operating relatively long-haul routes of say over 5–6,000 kms but with traffic flows that were too thin to support a 400-seater Boeing 747 with a commercially acceptable frequency and planning to purchase new aircraft would have been looking for a 250–300-seater with a three-class cabin. Given these market constraints the choice would probably have been between an Airbus A-330, a Boeing 787 or, if the aircraft were not needed in the near future, an Airbus A-350. At another level, an airline planning to operate international charters from northern Europe into the larger Aegean islands of Greece, such as Mykonos or Santorini, may only be able to use Boeing 737–800 or Airbus A320 aircraft because of runway length limitations even if the traffic flows could support larger aircraft. In both the above examples it is a combination of external factors that produce the short-list of possible aircraft.

It is only when one moves to the second stage of fleet planning, that of choosing between the short-listed aircraft, that the role of management becomes critical. Management has to make several key and related decisions. It must not only choose the aircraft which best meets its airline's needs and objectives, but it must also choose the number of aircraft and optimise the mix of aircraft in the fleet. Fleet planning is pulled in opposite directions. On the one hand an airline needs to choose the optimum aircraft in terms of size and range characteristics for each route, but at the same time it must minimise the number of different types of aircraft in its fleet so as to reduce maintenance and crewing costs (Clark, 2007). Thus a compromise must be found between having a different aircraft type for each route and having only one aircraft type to serve all routes. Management must also decide on the engines which will power its aircraft, if more than one engine type is available. All these decisions will eventually affect the airline's cost levels.

Once an airline has made its choice and invested in particular aircraft types for various parts of its network then those aircraft types have to be considered as given. They cannot be changed from year to year. Because of investment in flight crew training, maintenance and ground facilities, aircraft types are unlikely to be changed except after several years. Once aircraft have been introduced into an airline's operation the most significant factor which will then affect their costs of operation, other than the level of input costs, is the route structure on which they will be operated.

5.6   Route structure and network characteristics

5.6.1   *Stage length*

Several aspects of an airline's operating pattern may influence its costs but the most critical are the stage or sector lengths over which it is operating its aircraft. The average stage lengths will vary within an airline by aircraft type since it is likely that different aircraft will have been chosen for different types of routes within the total network. For each aircraft type, nevertheless, the longer the stage length which can be flown the lower will be the direct operating costs per unit of output. This is so until sectors get so long that payload has to be sacrificed.

The rapid decline of unit costs as stage distance increases is a fundamental characteristic of airline economics. A number of factors help to explain this relationship. One of these, the effect of stage length on block speed and an aircraft's hourly productivity, has already been discussed in the previous section. It was pointed out that ground manoeuvre time and the relatively slow climb and descent phases of a flight become a decreasing proportion of the total block time as stage length increases. As a result, the average block speed increases. This, in turn, pushes up the hourly productivity in terms of tonne-kms or seat-kms also rises. Fixed costs, both direct and indirect, are spread over more units of output and therefore the total operating cost per available tonne-km or seat-km goes down.

The same considerations which affect block speed also influence block fuel. During ground manoeuvre time on departure or arrival aircraft are burning fuel. In 20 to 30 minutes on the ground they can burn a considerable amount of it (Figure 5.5 above). During climb and to a lesser extent during the descent phase, fuel consumption is relatively high in relation to the horizontal distance travelled. Conversely, fuel consumption is least in the cruise mode and is reduced at higher altitudes. The earlier example of the two flights out of Kuala Lumpur to Singapore and Kota Kinabalu highlight the impact of sector distance on fuel burn. On the longer sector to Kota Kinabalu, time on the ground and time spent in ascent and descent is a much smaller proportion of the total block time. More than half the block time is spent in cruise, when fuel consumption is lowest, but it is also spent at a much higher altitude than on the shorter sector, thereby further reducing fuel burn. In short, ground manoeuvre and climb and descent fuel becomes a decreasing proportion of total fuel burn as stage distance increases. The net result is that fuel consumption does not increase in proportion to distance. Thus if an Airbus A321 or a Boeing 737–800 doubles its stage distance from, say, 500km to 1,000km the fuel burnt will not double. Depending on the particular circumstances of the route the fuel consumed will only increase by about 60 per cent to 70 per cent.

Looking at an actual example, the Airbus A320–200 on London to Paris with a full passenger load and no cargo consumes about 1,700 kgs of fuel. Flying to Geneva, whose distance from London is 118 per cent greater, the Airbus burns about 2,800 kgs, an increase of only 65 per cent. As a result the fuel burnt per km and the fuel cost per km drops by up to 25 per cent. This is a major saving, given that fuel may be a significant proportion of total costs. On longer sectors beyond 2,500 kms the fuel savings from additional increases in sector distance become marginal. The fuel burn of the larger Airbus A321 on sectors out of London is shown in Figure 5.6.

Stage length not only affects fuel consumption but it also influences aircraft and crew utilisation and this too impacts on costs. An aircraft is a very expensive piece of capital equipment. It is only earning revenue and paying back its high initial cost when it is flying. The more flying it does the lower its hourly costs become. This is because the standing annual charges, notably depreciation and insurance, can be spread over a greater number of productive hours. It is much easier to keep aircraft in the air if stage lengths are longer. On short sectors such as New York–Boston, London–Paris or Singapore–Kuala Lumpur, where aircraft have to land after every 40–50 minutes of flight and then spend up to an hour on the ground, achieving more than 5 or 6 block hours per day with an aircraft becomes very difficult. Higher utilisation requires either a reduction in the aircraft turn-around time so as to carry out more flights within the operating day, or an extension of the operating day by scheduling very early morning or late evening departures. Charter airlines in Europe achieve very high utilisation on relatively short sectors by extending the operating day into the night hours. Low-cost no frills airlines achieve the same result by reducing turn-arounds to 30 minutes or less.

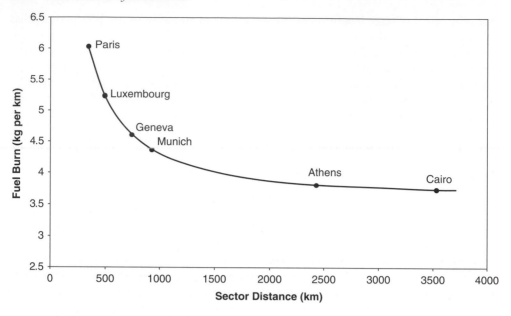

Figure 5.6 Impact of sector distance on fuel burn – Airbus A321–200 on routes from London.
Note: Fuel burn is average of outward and return trips based on 75 per cent passenger and
50 per cent cargo load factor.

When one looks at longer sectors involving, say, 5 block hours, an aircraft can fly out and back and with just two flight sectors achieve a daily utilisation of 10 block hours while spending only a couple of hours or so on the ground. The longer the sector distances, the easier it becomes to push up daily utilisation and thereby spread the aircraft's annual fixed costs over more block hours and more available tonne-kms. The close relationship between stage length and aircraft utilisation can be seen by examining British Airways' Airbus A-320 aircraft in 2007. BA's own A320s, flown on shorter sectors, averaging close to 1,000kms, achieved a daily utilisation of 8.6 hours. But BA's franchisee GB Airways flew the same aircraft as BA franchised flights but on longer sectors averaging about 2,000 kms. As a result it was able to achieve 12.5 hours each day on its A320s, that is, almost four hours longer each day than British Airways itself.

Flight and cabin crew, like aircraft, are a valuable and costly resource. A high proportion of crew costs are fixed and do not vary in the short term. The more flying that crews can actually do, the lower will be the crew costs per block hour. On short sectors crews spend relatively more of their time on the ground. On one to one-and-a-half-hour sectors, crews may actually only be flying for four to six hours during a 12–14 hour duty period. As stage lengths increase they should be able to spend more of their duty period actually flying.

A more obvious implication of short stages is that airport charges, station costs and any handling fees paid to others are incurred more frequently than on longer stages. Their impact on total costs is therefore greater. One can see this when examining the cost structure of short-haul airlines, whether international or domestic. In the financial year 2007–8 Bmi (British Midland), flying primarily UK domestic and European services, had an average stage length of only 760 kms. Its landing and other airport en-route charges, plus its station costs, including handling fees, came to a staggering 30.9 per cent

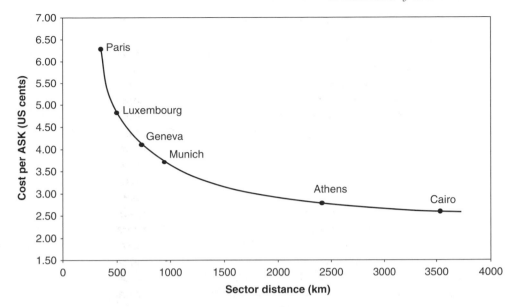

Figure 5.7 Impact of sector distance on unit costs for Airbus A321 on routes from London.

of its total costs. Yet in the same financial year British Airways, operating both a short and long-haul network with a much longer average sector distance of 2,380 kms, found that en-route and airport charges, station costs and handling fees accounted for 17.4 per cent of its total operating costs (CAA 2009a). For Virgin Atlantic, an exclusively long-haul airline, with an average sector distance of over 7,270 kms, these costs drop to only 12.5 per cent of their total costs (Table 4.4, Chapter 4).

Some elements of maintenance expenditure are also related to stage length. This is because certain maintenance checks and spare parts replacement schedules are related to the number of flight cycles, that is, take-offs and landings. These occur less frequently as stage length increases. The most obvious part of the aircraft whose maintenance is related to the number of flight cycles is the undercarriage, though there are others too.

All the above factors reinforce the more theoretical cost-range relationship, based on aircraft productivity, discussed in the preceding section. Together, they result in a typically U-shaped cost curve for every aircraft type. Unit costs fall rapidly at first as stage length increases, then gradually flatten out until they rise sharply as payload restrictions begin to push up costs. A cost curve based on a route costing study of the Airbus A321 is shown in Figure 5.7. The A321 study and other similar analyses indicate that the most significant economies with respect to distance occur by increasing stage lengths at the short to medium range. The implication for airlines is clear. They must avoid short sectors, because they impose much higher costs, and should try and operate each aircraft at or near the stage distances where costs are at their lowest. This means the distances for which each aircraft has been designed.

The relationship between sector distance and unit costs is one of the fundamental rules of airline economics. Short sectors are inherently more costly to operate, in terms of cost per seat-km or available tonne km, than longer sectors. Other things being equal, short-haul airlines will tend to have higher unit costs than airlines with longer average sector distances. This should be borne in mind when comparing airline costs. Several airlines'

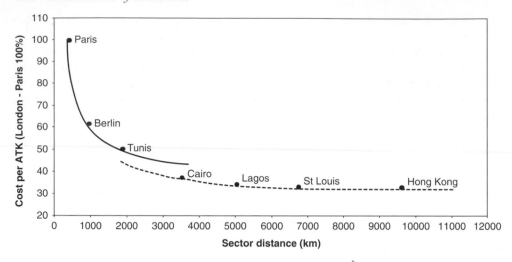

Figure 5.8 Impact of sector distance and aircraft size on unit costs: Airbus A320–200 and Airbus A340–600 on routes from London.

Note: The A320 is a 150-seater twin jet, the A340 is four-engined and here operated with around 300 seats.

unit costs were compared earlier in Table 5.1 above. Of these airlines, two, Singapore Airlines and Cathay Pacific, have average sector lengths that are very much higher than those of any other carrier. In 2007 they were 4,560 kms and 4,095 kms respectively. The average sector lengths of all the other carriers in Table 5.1 were close to or below 2,000 kms. This was due in part to the fact that they all operated a significant domestic network. Given that Singapore Airlines and Cathay Pacific are way ahead in terms of sector distance, it is hardly surprising to find that their unit costs are so low when compared to other airlines in Table 5.1. Though, of course, other factors also impact on costs.

In so far as larger aircraft tend to be used on longer stages the twin effects of aircraft size and stage length frequently reinforce each other. The result is that operating costs per tonne-km on long sectors flown by large wide-body aircraft may be as low as 20–25 per cent of the costs on short-haul sectors flown by smaller aircraft. This is vividly illustrated by comparing two Airbus aircraft on routes out of London, the 150-seat short-medium range A320 and the much larger 300-seater long-haul A340 (Figure 5.8). The larger aircraft's direct operating costs on long sectors are less than 40 per cent of those of the smaller aircraft on London–Paris. The unit cost discrepancy would be even greater if an older generation aircraft was being used on the shorter sectors.

Airlines operating primarily large aircraft over long sectors will always appear to have lower unit operating costs than airlines flying smaller aircraft on domestic and short-haul international services. But their lower costs will be primarily a function of aircraft size and sector distance rather than better managerial efficiency! It is no coincidence that two of the three airlines with the lowest unit costs in Table 5.1 above, namely Singapore Airlines and Cathay Pacific, operate, on average, very large aircraft over average sector distances which are well above the average.

If sector distances flown have such a critical impact on unit costs, to what extent can they be influenced by management decisions? As previously pointed out, an airline's route structure and therefore its sector distances are a function of the location of its home base(s), the geographical location of the markets it is serving and the degree to which the regulatory regimes within which it operates allow free access to those markets. But there is some scope for action. Management must constantly assess and re-assess the viability of short sectors to establish whether revenues generated exceed the high costs or at least make a sufficient contribution to fixed costs. Short sectors which have little prospect of achieving long-term profitability and do not generate significant transfer traffic onto other services at an airline's hub may be discontinued. Multi-sector services, especially those on domestic routes, can be re-examined to see if certain en-route stops can be cut out or replaced by non-stop services. Short hops at the end of long-haul routes are especially costly because the distances are usually very short and the aircraft used are large wide-bodies. For example, in May 2009 Malaysian Airlines was operating a twice-weekly service from Kuala Lumpur to Johannesburg, which continued on to Cape Town – a one-hour hop. Very costly!

5.6.2   Frequency of services

High frequencies provide airlines with greater flexibility in schedules planning, thereby enabling them to increase aircraft and crew utilisation. The availability of further schedules to be operated whenever an aircraft and crew return to base makes it much easier to keep them flying throughout the operating day. Airlines operating low frequencies on short to medium sectors face the problem of what to do with their aircraft when they have completed their first round trip of the day. This problem is especially acute if for commercial reasons most departures even for low frequency destinations need to be early in the morning. It follows that by early afternoon most aircraft will be back at their home base with insufficient further flights to absorb all of them. To avoid under-utilisation of aircraft and crews certain flights will be rescheduled to later in the day to utilise aircraft that have returned from early morning departures. But later departures may be at commercially less attractive times. On long-haul routes high frequencies also enable airlines to reduce the length and cost of crew stop-overs. Conversely, low frequencies prove costly.

Olympic Airways' route from Athens to Melbourne and Sydney in Australia in 1999 amply illustrates the cost problems created by low frequencies on long-haul services. Olympic operated the service with a Boeing 747 but only twice a week and with a stop in Bangkok. On the way out, after a nine-hour sector to Bangkok, a complete set of crew, 20 in all (a three-man cockpit crew and 16–17 cabin crew), would disembark. They would wait three or four days to take over the next outward flight on to Melbourne and Sydney. At Sydney they would spend a further three or four days before flying the return sector to Bangkok. Yet another three- or four-day stop-over in Bangkok waiting to take over the next returning flight back to Athens. Each set of crew were away for 13–14 days. The pilots were originally entitled to 11 rest days on their return! Thus during a 25-day period each pilot on this route would have undertaken only four duty periods. Not only was crew utilisation and productivity inevitably very low but crew expenses were extremely high. At all times there were two complete sets of crew, 40 or so people, staying in Bangkok, and another set in a Sydney hotel. This meant very substantial hotel costs plus associated daily out-of-base allowances and expenses for all 60 crew members. To make matters worse the Boeing 747 operated a very short and expensive one-and-a-quarter sector between Melbourne and Sydney in Australia. With very low yields and high costs this route inevitably lost money and should have been discontinued.

In 2000, Olympic switched from the Boeing 747 to a smaller A340. This enabled frequencies to be increased to three per week and rest days at the end of the rotation to be reduced. So crew utilisation improved marginally. But this was not enough to ensure profitability and the route was abandoned in 2002.

As mentioned earlier, in 2009, Malaysia Airlines was operating a similar twice-weekly service from Kuala Lumpur to Buenos Aires in Argentina with two stops in South Africa at Johannesburg and Cape Town, where crews were changed. Year-round there were two complete crew sets in South Africa and one in Buenos Aires, staying three or four days. This was a highcost operation due to the low frequency.

The aircraft which an airline has available, the demand patterns in the markets concerned, together with constraints imposed by bilateral air services agreements or inter-airline agreements influence or even determine the frequencies to be operated. But an airline has some scope to try to increase its frequencies by changes in the type of aircraft used or in the operating pattern or route structure. Higher frequencies also have marketing benefits.

5.6.3   *Length of passenger haul*

Many costs associated with sales, ticketing and the handling of passengers are related to the number of passengers rather than to the distance that each passenger travels with the airline on a particular journey. This is true with costs of reservation, of ticketing and of the handling of both passengers and their baggage. It is also frequently true of airport passenger charges when paid by airlines. In other words, a passenger who buys a single ticket and travels 3,000 kms on an airline network will cost less to the airline than three separate passengers each travelling 1,000 kms. In the latter case each of the three will impose his own ticketing and handling costs and the airline may have to pay a separate airport charge for each. From the cost point of view an airline is better off carrying fewer passengers travelling long distances rather than many more passengers on short journeys. However, the shorter-haul passengers may produce higher yields and generate more income because of the way fares are structured (see Chapter 11). Long-haul passengers pay much less per kilometre travelled because unit fares decline as distance increases, to mirror the drop in unit costs. But purely in cost terms the long-haul passenger is to be preferred. The average length of passenger haul, that is, distance travelled, on each airline's services depends primarily on two factors: first, the airline's average sector or stage distance, which is a function of its geographical location and network; second, on the airline's success in attracting passengers who travel on two or more sectors usually by transferring flights at the airline's hub.

Most of the major international airlines whose costs were compared earlier (Table 5.1) have an average passenger haul of between 2,000 and 4,500 kms, with European carriers generally having shorter hauls than Asian or US airlines. Among Europeans, British Airways (3,900 kms in 2007) has one of the longest passenger hauls. This is due to its success in generating online transfer passengers. In fact, in the early 2000s, British Airways' then chief executive claimed that the airline had been very successful in attracting transfer passengers but that this undermined the airline's profitability because average yields for much of this business were so low! The cost advantages of selling to passengers travelling long distances on the BA network were apparently not sufficient to offset the lower yields. As a result the airline then changed its strategy. It reduced capacity on many long-haul routes by switching from large Boeing 747 to smaller Boeing 777 aircraft and refocused its marketing on attracting Business Class passengers and away from Economy Class passengers transferring from short– to long–haul flights. These were the passengers who had been paying very low fares to travel thousands of kilometres but who had been needed to fill up the large Boeing 747s.

5.7   Airline marketing and product policy

Product and service quality is both an integral part of an airline's marketing strategy and a significant cost determinant. It is also an area of cost over which an airline has much greater control. But it does not have complete control except in those few cases where an airline operates on its own, as a monopolist, on all or most of its network. This is most likely to occur in domestic operations. On their international operations, where they face direct or indirect competition and in competitive domestic markets, airlines do not have an entirely free hand. The nature and strength of the competition which an airline faces in its main markets, together with its own positioning in those markets, will have a major influence on its product strategy and therefore on its costs. For example, network airlines facing direct competition from low-cost carriers and wishing to be more price-competitive will be forced to reduce their costs. This may well mean simplifying and cutting back on their product and service offering. It may also force them to adopt different pricing strategies. In long-haul markets the nature of the competition will be different and more diverse, especially since some of the competitors may be offering indirect services through their own hubs. But again, airlines will need to adapt their own marketing and product strategies in response to the competition they face.

Product and service standards are also dependent on the sector distances, or rather the trip travel times. Service standards must be different on a six-hour sector compared to a one-hour sector. They may also differ according to the time of day or night that a flight is operated. Above all, service quality must be responsive to competitive pressures from other carriers operating in the same or in parallel markets. Such pressures will even impact on routes where an airline may be the only operator, since it must offer the same consistent product throughout its network. It cannot afford to alienate customers by providing a poorer service on routes where it operates a monopoly.

Within the constraints imposed by sector times and by competitive pressures, an airline has considerable freedom to decide its marketing strategy. This means not only deciding which markets to service, it also includes pricing policy as well as decisions on the type of products and the quality of services that the airline wishes to offer in those markets. The whole issue of marketing is discussed in a later chapter (Chapter 8). But it is important to appreciate that several aspects of marketing policy impact directly on cost levels. They can be grouped under two headings: costs associated with product and service features and those costs more directly related to sales, distribution and related promotional activities.

5.7.1   *Product and service features*

Airlines have to decide on the nature and quality of the product they are going to offer in the various freight and passenger markets that they serve. This must be done within certain constraints. For commercial and competitive reasons airlines may have to conform to certain minimum standards of product quality. They must also conform to a variety of international or national safety and technical regulations. These affect many aspects of the cabin layout such as the seat pitch next to emergency exits, or the minimum number of cabin staff, and so on. Within these constraints airlines enjoy considerable freedom to decide on the quality of the product they are going to offer, both in the air and on the ground, and on the costs they are prepared to incur.

In the air, three aspects of cabin service standards are particularly important for passenger services. *Cabin layout and seating density* is frequently the most significant in terms of its impact on unit costs. Each aircraft type has a maximum design seating capacity based on an all-economy layout at a given minimum seat pitch. The actual number of seats that an airline has in its own aircraft of a particular type depends on a number of key decisions which the airline itself takes. It must decide whether it is going to offer a one, two or three class product in each part of its network. A large number of airlines such as Continental, Delta, SAS and KLM abandoned First Class on their long-haul routes some years ago and now only offer Business and Economy cabins. In so doing they have increased the seating density of their aircraft. Others offer fully reclining seats in First Class that turn into flat beds but take up a great deal of space. In 2000 British Airways was the first to launch fully reclining seats in their long-haul Business cabins and other airlines have gradually followed suit. By 2008 many of the larger US, European and some of the Asian airlines were also offering long-haul Business passengers seats that converted into flat or almost flat beds. A few airlines, again led by BA and Virgin Atlantic, have also introduced a small Premium Economy cabin on long-haul flights with 3–5 inches longer seat pitch than in the normal Economy cabin. In the mid-1990s many European airlines began to upgrade their short-haul business product – First Class had long been abandoned in Europe – by installing convertible seating in the front section of their narrow-bodied aircraft. This convertible seating is more expensive but it enables them to convert 6 abreast Economy seats (3 + 3) into five abreast (2 + 3) more spacious Business seating or even into two abreast (2 + 2). Moreover, by having a movable partition they can expand or contract the Business section in the aircraft by converting the seats in response to daily demand.

The distribution of space between fare classes, if there is more than one, the type of seating and the seat pitch adopted for each class and the numbers of seats abreast are the more crucial determinants of seating capacity. The distribution of cabin space between seating areas, galleys, toilets and storage is another factor. In certain wide-body aircraft extra space for seating can be provided by positioning one or more of the galleys in the freight hold, though this is at the expense of freight capacity. The fewer the number of seats on offer, the higher will be the cost per seat-km since the aircraft's trip costs need to be divided among the fewer seat-kms generated.

The range of seating densities used by international airlines in two aircraft types is illustrated in Table 5.6. Some scheduled airlines, as part of a superior product strategy, choose cabin and seating configurations which may result in a reduction in the number of seats by 20 per cent or more when compared to the seating capacity offered by other scheduled carriers in the same aircraft. The airline's product may be improved but the cost implications are serious. For example, in 2009 Lufthansa flew one version of its Airbus A340s in a three-class configuration with only 221 seats. This meant that costs were 31 per cent higher than if it had adopted Air France's two-class cabin with a much higher seating density. The impact of different scheduled seating densities on costs is normally not so marked and involves unit cost variations of up to 20 per cent. The charter airlines shown in Table 5.6 push their seating densities way above those found acceptable

Table 5.6 Impact of different airline seating density on costs per seat, 2009

Airline	AIRBUS A321		Airline	AIRBUS A340–300	
	No. of seats	Cost per seat*		No. of seats**	Cost per seat*
Scheduled airlines					
Lufthansa	186	100	Air France	289	100
British Airways	184	101	Cathay	286	101
USAir	183	102	SAA	269	107
Air France	175	106	Emirates (3)	267	108
Air Canada	174	107	SAS	245	118
Aeroflot	170	109	Cathay (3)	244	118
			Swiss (3)	228	127
			Lufthansa (3)	221	131
Charter or low-cost airlines					
Air Berlin	209	90			
Monarch	220	85			
Thomas Cook	220	85			

Notes

 * Assuming operating costs are the same, 'cost per seat' reflects each airline's seating density, a scheduled
   airline having most seats indexed at 100.
** Two class cabins except where indicated as three (3).

for scheduled services with a concomitant reduction of seat-km costs. Thomas Cook, a charter airline, offered 50 more seats in its Airbus A321 than Aeroflot. Very high seating densities are a key feature of the economics of both non-scheduled charter operations and of low-cost airlines.

A second aspect of cabin service standards which has important cost implications is the *number of cabin crew* used. Safety regulations impose a minimum number for each aircraft type. It is up to each airline to decide how many more than the minimum it wishes to use. This is partly a function of the number of cabin classes it decides to offer and partly a function of the sector distance. On short- to medium-haul sectors where there is less time for meals and other in-flight services, cabin crew numbers may be close to the minimum. On long-haul sectors airlines have more scope to try and differentiate their product through their in-flight services and one aspect of this may be more cabin staff. In 2007 Singapore Airlines were flying their Boeing 747–400 aircraft with 19 cabin crew when the minimum required was 11. Other South East Asian airlines had fewer cabin crew on their own 747s. Cathay Pacific had 18 while Thai International and Malaysian had 17. When an airline's cabin crew wages are comparatively low then the cost of improving the in-flight product by having more cabin staff is not high. This is the case with these Asian carriers. Conversely it is more costly for high-wage airlines to compete in terms of cabin staff numbers.

The third key element of cabin service standards is that of *in-flight catering and related cabin product features*. As a result of international liberalisation the need and the scope for management initiative in this area increased, particularly on long-haul services. Many airlines place great emphasis on trying to persuade potential customers that they offer the best meals, cooked by well-known master chefs, together with the most expensive and sought-after wines, the best spirits and the finest coffees. This is done despite the fact that passenger surveys repeatedly show that in–flight catering is way down in the list of factors that influence choice of airline. Moreover competitive pressures push most carriers to more or less match what their competitors are doing. For this reason, while in–flight catering costs may vary between airlines, they are unlikely to be important in explaining difference in total unit costs between those airlines. The same is also true of the minor elements of cabin service such as the range of newspapers and journals on offer, free give-aways, toiletry bags on long-haul flights and so on. There may be greater cost differentiation in the provision of in–flight entertainment because the options available to airlines are much greater. For instance, some long-haul carriers, such as Emirates in Dubai, have for some years offered seat-back screens for all Economy class passengers with a multiple choice of channels. This is clearly an expensive marketing decision since it means refurbishing all aircraft with complex and more expensive seats, as well as installing more expensive equipment. Moreover, the video and audio programmes are also expensive to buy and must be changed frequently.

There is also scope for product differentiation on the ground. Airlines can rent and operate more check-in desks to reduce passenger waiting times and they may also decide to provide more ground staff for passenger handling and assistance in general. Many international airlines go further and provide sometimes quite luxurious and costly First- or even Business-class lounges at airports, while their competitors may provide neither. An example is Singapore Airlines which has decided, as a matter of product policy, to provide its own exclusive First/Business-class lounges at virtually all the airports it serves irrespective of the frequency of its services or the number of First- or Business-class passengers handled. In this way it imprints its own brand and product style on the lounges. On the other hand, some other carriers share executive lounges with one or more different airlines in order to save costs.

It is difficult to assess the impact of the product quality decisions of different airlines on their comparative costs because of the paucity of reliable data. One way of doing this, however, is to establish the expenditure on passenger services per 1,000 passenger-kms of traffic carried. Passenger services expenditure essentially covers the costs of cabin crews and passenger service personnel as well as passenger-related costs such as in-flight catering and hotel accommodation. By expressing such expenditure per 1,000 passenger-kms rather than per passenger, one can partially adjust for the fact that there will be quite different average passenger hauls on the airlines selected.

The relative passenger services expenditure levels in 2005 on their intra-European services for a group of selected European carriers are shown in Table 5.7. The carriers selected all had broadly similar sector lengths on their intra-European routes, namely between 650 kms and 870 kms. The range of expenditure on passenger services is high, as illustrated by a comparison of Swiss and Czech Airlines from either end of the table. SAS, Swiss and British Airways spent almost twice as much per 1,000 passenger-kms as Czech Airlines or Olympic. This was reflected in part in higher wage costs for their cabin crews but also the fact that these three airlines branded themselves as high service quality airlines targeting the business passenger.

5.7.2   *Sales, distribution and promotion policies*

Scheduled airlines enjoy considerable discretion in the way they organise and run their sales and distribution activities. They decide on the extent to which they should sell their services through their own sales offices, telephone call centres and websites rather than

Table 5.7 Passenger services expenditure by European airlines in 2005 on intra-European services

Annual expenditure on passenger services	US $ per 1000 Pax-Kms
SAS	19.75
British Airways	19.71
Swiss Airlines	19.55
Air France	18.73
Lufthansa	16.61
Austrian	15.72
Alitalia	15.28
SN Brussels Airlines	15.23
Iberia	15.17
Finnair	14.15
LOT Polish Airlines	11.90
Olympic Airlines	10.93
Czech Airlines	9.91

Note
Expenditure includes cabin crews and passenger-related service costs.

through other airlines or travel agents. Such decisions have cost implications. While setting up and operating its own sales outlets costs money, the airline saves the commissions it would otherwise have to pay to travel agents. (The impact of commission payments on costs was discussed earlier in Section 5.3.)

A key issue in recent years has been the switch to online selling through an airline's own website. The low-cost no-frills airlines, such as easyJet in Europe, followed by Southwest in the USA, were the first to grasp fully the value of the internet in reducing distribution costs, by cutting out commissions to agents which in the past had represented between 6 and 10 per cent of total costs. As early as 2001 easyJet was selling close to 90 per cent of its tickets through its website. By 2009 the figure was over 95 per cent, with the balance being direct telephone sales. Conventional network carriers had been slow to follow. Few were achieving even 5 per cent of sales through their websites by 2001. But they grasped the message and, in recent years, most airlines have switched more and more of their sales to their own websites and call centres or to online travel agencies and away from retail travel agents. This is particularly true of European and US airlines. Airlines have also reduced the number and size of their own high street sales offices, especially in their home country.

Several other important decisions have to be made in relation to sales and distribution. An important issue is whether an international airline should set up off-line sales outlets, that is, outlets in cities or countries to which it does not fly. Equally crucial may be the decision on whether it should itself staff and operate sales offices at some of its less important overseas destinations or whether to appoint a general sales agent, who may or may not be another airline. When airlines enter cross-border alliances they may cut the costs of distribution by merging their sales offices and sales staff in each other's country or in third countries to which two or more of the alliance partners operate. This has been done by SAS and Lufthansa. Following their alliance in 1996, Lufthansa pulled out all its sales staff and closed its sales offices in Scandinavia. SAS did likewise in Germany. Each then sold and distributed for the other in its own home market. But this arrangement is now being re-assessed.

Table 5.8 Advertising spend in UK by selected Middle East and Asian airlines in 2006

	Annual spend 2006 £000	Flights per week to UK	Annual advertising spend per flight £000
Singapore Airlines	1,937	28	69
Cathay Pacific	1,266	21	60
ETIHAD	779	18	43
Emirates	2,717	70	39
Qantas	756	28	27
Sri Lankan	297	12	25
Thai Airways	306	14	22
Qatar Airways	40	28	14
All Nippon	90	7	13
Malaysia Airlines	96	18	5

Note
Includes advertising spend on television, radio and the press.

Having taken these decisions on whether to provide its own sales outlets, an airline has to decide on their location and size within each city. If opening a sales outlet in London, does it insist on its being with many of the other airlines in a small area bordered by Bond Street, Piccadilly or Regent Street, one of the most expensive shop locations in the world, or does it, like Philippine Airlines, choose a less expensive location in central London but somewhat away from the other airlines? Or could it follow Cyprus Airways' example and set up its sales outlet in much cheaper facilities well away from central London on the grounds that most sales are done through agents or its call centre?

Decisions on advertising and promotional activity are very much at management's discretion. It is open to airlines to decide themselves how much to spend on advertising and promoting their services and how to spend it. Numerous promotion channels are open to them from television, radio or national press advertising aimed at large numbers of potential customers at one end to promotional activities or trade press advertising involving relatively small numbers of freight and travel agents or travel journalists at the other. Many airlines target an advertising and promotional budget equivalent to about 2 per cent of their revenue. They may spend much more than this in particular markets, especially when they are launching a new service, or in foreign countries where they are less well known than the home-based carriers. Advertising spend is also likely to be higher in markets where competition is more intense.

Different management attitudes towards advertising can be seen in Table 5.8 which shows advertising expenditure in the UK press, radio and television of all the East Asian airlines in 2006. Some interesting differences emerge in airline policies. Some airlines, such as Emirates, are big spenders in absolute terms. But the key issue is not the total annual spend, since this should vary with the number of services or capacity operated in the market, but the annual expenditure per weekly frequency (column 3 in Table 5.8). Of the established carriers SIA and Cathay spent much more, in that year, per weekly flight than any of the other carriers. Because of their high advertising spend and excellent in-flight service Cathay and SIA were getting particularly good loads in First and Business class. They may also have been advertising more to reduce diversion of their own home market traffic via Middle East carriers such as Emirates or Qatar Airways. These airlines were flooding the UK market with capacity to their Middle East hubs in order to attract transfer traffic to/from East Asia. Some airlines were spending remarkably little on advertising, notably Malaysian, Japan Airlines and All Nippon Airways. The latter two did this partly because they clearly focus their marketing at the Japanese end of the route and partly because the bilateral agreement restricted capacity between Japan and the UK so the need to advertise was limited. Malaysia Airlines claimed it did not need to spend more as its load factors were already very high on the London–Kuala Lumpur route and it was the only operator with direct flights. These examples show that advertising spend, while it is influenced by competition, is very much at the discretion of management.

As a result of greater use of direct and online selling, of ticketless travel and of reduced commissions to agents and GDSs, ticketing, sales and promotion costs have gone down over the last 15 years (Table 4.3, Chapter 4). But they still represent around 8–10 per cent of total operating costs of most scheduled airlines and they become more significant on short-haul markets. They are clearly still a major item of expenditure, yet one that is very much influenced by the policies adopted by individual airlines.

5.8   Financial policies

5.8.1   Financial strategies

Aircraft ownership costs, that is, depreciation and/or lease payments and rentals, may represent up to 10 per cent or more of total costs. Management can influence such costs in three ways: first through the price it negotiates when buying or leasing aircraft; second through choosing the type of financing it uses to obtain the aircraft; and third by the depreciation policy it chooses to adopt.

5.8.2   Timing and size of aircraft orders

A number of variables determine the price of new or second-hand aircraft and of lease rates too. When the industry is booming financially, the demand for aircraft is high and this pushes up both prices and lease rates. The converse is true when the airline industry is in crisis, as in 2001–3 and again in 2008–9. Lease rates drop as airlines terminate or fail to renew leases. Aircraft are grounded, aircraft deliveries are delayed and options cancelled. By buying or leasing when demand for new capacity is low, airlines can significantly reduce their costs of purchase or lease. Timing is all. The size of orders is also critical. An airline ordering 30 or more aircraft at a time is bound to get a better price than if ordering just a handful. This may encourage management to delay orders until they need to replace a larger part of their fleet, perhaps even two different aircraft types.

A good example of perfect timing was easyJet's order in 2002 for 120 Airbus A319s with an option for a further 120 which could be swapped for A320s or A321s. The order was placed at a time when the airline industry was in deep crisis and orders for new aircraft had slumped. It was a very large order by an airline previously operating a small Boeing 737 fleet as all low-cost carriers were at the time. Airbus was desperate to establish its aircraft in the low-cost sector. This factor, plus the timing and the size of the order, meant that easyJet was able to negotiate a substantial reduction on the then list price. The reduction was reputed to be between a third and a half. Years later, in September 2007, British Airways placed an order for 19 Airbus A380s, of which seven were options. This, at a time when new orders for this new aircraft had slumped, because of two-year production delays. The need to revitalise its A380 order book and also to generate business from British Airways, an airline which had never ordered Airbus aircraft previously, is thought to have induced the manufacturer to sell this aircraft at as much as 50 per cent off the list price (*The Times*, 28 September 2007).

5.8.3   Methods of finance

Having decided on fleet expansion or renewal, management then has to get the finance in place. This is so even for cash–rich airlines such as Singapore Airlines or easyJet, since they are unlikely to be able or willing to finance all their purchases from cash.

Financing aircraft purchases or leases is too complex and dynamic a process to discuss in detail in the present book. Yet management has a crucial role to play in deciding between leasing and purchasing the aircraft it wishes to order and between the alternative financial models that are available for each (see Morrell, 2007).

Interest charges on loans are often considered within the airline industry as a non-operating item. As such they do not affect operating costs or the operating results. However, they do affect each airline's overall profit or loss after inclusion of interest and other non–operating items. The bulk of interest charges relate to loans raised to finance aircraft acquisitions though some airlines may also be paying interest on bank overdrafts arising from cash flow problems or from the need to finance losses incurred in previous years.

An airline can reduce or avoid interest charges by financing part or all of its aircraft purchases internally from self-generated funds. Self-financing is clearly cheaper than borrowing, especially at a time when interest charges are high. To do this, airlines must first build up their cash reserves from accumulated profits and possibly depreciation charges. But even highly profitable airlines may only be able to self-finance part of their capital expenditure. Singapore Airlines (SIA), through a policy of rapid depreciation previously referred to, and as a result of its high profits, has been able to build up substantial reserves during the last 15 years or so. Yet even SIA has been no more than 70 per cent self-financing in most years. There are few airlines in as favourable a position as SIA. Most are dependent on external sources of finance.

Airlines would prefer to be self-financing but may be unable to generate sufficient reserves from their depreciation charges and retained profits to do so except to a limited extent. Their remaining capital requirements can be met in one of two ways. First, there may be an injection of equity capital into the airline. The advantage of equity finance is that airlines only pay interest on it in the form of dividends if they make a profit. Many of the international airlines outside the United States are partly or totally government-owned, but governments have been loath to put in more capital to finance aircraft purchases, especially as the sums involved are very large. This is one of the reasons which has been pushing governments to partially or fully privatise their airlines. By injecting some of the funds raised through the privatisation back into the airlines concerned, the latter's debts and finance charges could be reduced.

If equity finance is unavailable, airlines must borrow in one form or another from commercial or government banks. Several different forms of loan finance are available, but either directly or indirectly they all involve interest charges. This is true even of finance or operating leases. In the past, the traditional reliance of state-owned airlines on external loan finance rather than self-financing or equity capital pushed them into having very high debt to equity ratios. In other words, too many of their investment requirements were financed by loan capital and too few by equity. Many airlines have been under-capitalised and have needed an injection of capital if the interest burden was to be kept within manageable proportions, and if they were to be in a position to order new aircraft without bankrupting themselves. It is generally believed that a debt to equity ratio of 25:75 is desirable and that a ratio of up to 50:50 is acceptable. Given the very high cost of new aircraft, airlines can only stay within acceptable limits by injections of new capital. Most governments have been loath to put more equity capital into their airlines. Their airlines' debt to equity ratios have consequently deteriorated, especially during each of the cyclical downturns.

As previously mentioned, an alternative solution for airlines with inadequate financial resources is to lease aircraft from specialist aircraft leasing companies, such as GECAS Capital, ILFC or smaller companies, such as Oryx, or from finance houses that provide the same facility. During the last 20 years there has been a marked trend towards greater use of leasing amongst all airlines including the largest. This solution is particularly attractive for airlines that are too small to obtain the best prices from the manufacturers or airlines that are not themselves in a position to get any tax advantages from direct purchase. The leasing companies, by doing both, can provide aircraft which in theory may be cheaper in real terms. But timing is critical here too. Lease rates inevitably rise when the demand for additional aircraft capacity outstrips the supply of available aircraft.

5.8.4   *Depreciation policy*

The hourly depreciation cost of an aircraft (as discussed in Section 4.3) depends on the length of the depreciation period, the residual value of the aircraft at the end of that period and the annual utilisation of the aircraft. The annual utilisation, that is, the block hours flown during the year, is dependent on the pattern of operations, on the stage lengths flown and on the scheduling efficiency of an airline's management. The depreciation period adopted and the residual value assumed are determined by an airline's financial policy. In many countries legislation or accounting convention may require the adoption of a particular depreciation policy or may impose certain minimum requirements. Most international airlines, however, have some flexibility in deciding on the effective commercial life of their aircraft and their residual value at the end of that life. This flexibility is important. If an airline adopts the practice of depreciating its aircraft over 20 years to a 10 per cent residual value, its hourly depreciation costs (assuming the same annual utilisation) will be 32 per cent less than they would have been had it used a 12-year life for the aircraft with a 20 per cent residual value.

Both these depreciation policies are currently in use by different airlines and they show the significant variations in depreciation costs that can result from the adoption of different policies. Since, for some airlines, depreciation charges may represent around 8 to 10 per cent of their total operating costs, then the depreciation policy adopted can influence total costs by as much as 3 per cent.

Many airlines change their depreciation policy in order to increase or reduce their costs. Depreciation periods are frequently lengthened or residual values increased in periods of falling profitability in order to reduce costs and improve financial results. It is less usual for depreciation periods to be shortened when times are good. In the 1970s Singapore Airlines had adopted a policy of using depreciation periods which were exceptionally short by international airline standards. They estimated the life of their aircraft to be between five and six years with zero residual value. The purpose appears to have been to build up reserves from the depreciation charges to finance the rapid renewal of the fleet and also to mask the large operating profits that were being made. When in 1979 the fortunes of the airline industry were hit by the rise in the price of fuel, Singapore Airlines promptly lengthened the life of its aircraft to eight years to reduce its costs. It thereby still managed to show a profit. During the 1980s Singapore Airlines (SIA) continued to use an eight-year life for its aircraft with appropriate residual values. This was still very short compared to most international airlines. It explains why Singapore Airlines' depreciation costs per tonne-km available were amongst the highest when compared to international airlines with roughly similar average stage lengths. Then in April 1989 SIA again lengthened its depreciation period to 10 years with 20 per cent residual value so as to be more in line with industry practice. SIA's rapid depreciation is also linked to its policy of rapid fleet renewal and the investment allowances available in Singapore which can be used to offset taxation. As the crisis of 2001 began to bite into airline profits, SIA announced that it would once again change its depreciation to bring it in line with industry practice. For the financial year 2001–2 it stretched its depreciation period from 10 to 15 years and halved the residual value from 20 to 10 per cent. These changes reduced its depreciation cost for the year by \$151 million! By 2006–7, SIA was still using the same depreciation policy for its aircraft; namely, straight-line depreciation over 15 years to 10 per cent residual value. But for its freighters the residual value used was 20 per cent. This was a shorter depreciation period than many other airlines were using in 2007 and meant that SIA's annual depreciation charge per aircraft would be higher.

An additional problem when considering depreciation costs is how to treat aircraft which have been leased rather than purchased since legally the airline is not the owner. One approach is to differentiate between *finance lease agreements* that give the airline rights approximating to ownership, often involving the transfer of ownership at the end of the lease period, and so-called *operating leases* which do not give such rights and are usually of shorter duration. In the case of finance leases the aircraft can be depreciated in the normal way so that its depreciation cost appears under the airline's direct operating costs in the profit and loss account. However, while the interest element which is included in the lease payment is added to the other finance charges in the airline's accounts, the capital repayment element is not charged to the profit and loss account but is shown only as a liability. This is to avoid double counting since the capital cost of the asset is already covered by a depreciation charge. Conversely, annual lease payments on operating leases would appear as a flight operating cost and there would be no separate depreciation charge. This is the approach adopted by Singapore Airlines. It follows that the type of aircraft leases that an airline negotiates will affect the absolute and relative level of its depreciation costs.

5.9   Corporate strategy

An airline's corporate strategy and objectives are likely to have a major impact on its cost structure and cost levels. It is self-evident that an international airline that sees its mission as being to operate primarily charter or non-scheduled services will have lower costs than a conventional scheduled network carrier. The same is also true of an airline that sees its prime mission to be a scheduled low-cost no-frills operator.

A key strategic decision is the degree to which an airline focuses on the carriage of freight as well as on the passenger business. On average, IATA's scheduled airlines generate around 39 per cent of their total international traffic from the carriage of freight (Table 1.6, Chapter 1). Yet several airlines as part of their corporate strategy are much more heavily involved in freight. In 2007, 66 per cent of Korean Airlines' revenue tonne-kms was generated from freight. For Lan Airlines in Chile it was 54 per cent, for Cathay 53 per cent and for Singapore Airlines 48 per cent. On the other hand, US carriers have more or less given up the carriage of freight as anything other than fill-up on their passenger services, especially on domestic flights, and even here they have been outsold by the integrators, such as Fedex and UPS. As a result freight is of little importance. For United and American in 2007 it represented 23 per cent of international traffic carried, and for Delta only 17 per cent. Since the costs of carrying freight are significantly lower than those of carrying an equivalent amount of passengers, then those airlines which focus on freight will have lower overall unit costs than those that focus primarily on carrying passengers. This is one further reason why Cathay Pacific and SIA have among the lowest unit operating costs of all the airlines shown earlier in Table 5.1.

Another strategic issue is whether an airline sets out to be a major network operator or whether it sees its role as being that of a more restricted 'niche' carrier. The 'niche' may be geographical in scope or it may be a particular type of operation such as providing feeder services into a network carrier's hub. The niche carrier may be able to reduce its costs through greater specialisation. For instance, it may operate only one type of aircraft and it may also be able to increase flight crew and staff productivity through the simple pattern of its operations. Airlines that try to be all things to all men and serve every possible market end up with very mixed fleets of aircraft and pilots, large transfer hubs, complex maintenance arrangements and large over-staffed head and regional offices. Inevitably their costs are pushed up.

Airlines with domestic networks in countries where there is only one major national carrier often find that their corporate mission is heavily influenced by government policies. This is particularly so if they are government owned. Such airlines may be required to provide domestic air links whose primary objective may be the social and economic cohesion of the country or the stimulation of domestic tourism rather than the provision of commercially justified and financially self-supporting air services. Services provided with social objectives in mind are usually on thin routes, with small aircraft and often at frequencies that are too high in relation to the demand. Olympic Airways, Malaysia Airlines and Air Algérie are among the many airlines whose corporative objectives have traditionally included the provision of services to isolated and small domestic communities. By their very nature such services are inherently high cost. Since in many cases the governments that expected this of their airlines also held back increases in domestic air fares, such social services became a constant financial haemorrhage on the airlines concerned.

Airlines, like most business enterprises, will normally have several, sometimes mutually conflicting corporate objectives. Invariably operating profitably is one of the objectives. But the key question is the degree to which profitability is pursued as the prime and key corporate objective. If it is, then airline managers will be under pressure to do all they can to reduce costs. This is the case with most privatised airlines or airlines which, though not fully privatised, such as Singapore Airlines, are nevertheless operated as fully commercial enterprises. Many government-owned airlines are expected to operate profitably. But this objective is often lost and blunted among a whole series of other corporate objectives which are often imposed by the government as the major or only shareholder. When profit is not clearly the prime corporate objective, then costs are likely to creep up as other objectives are pursued.

5.10   Does airline or fleet size matter?

Early studies of airline economics, particularly in relation to US airlines, had suggested that there might be significant economies of scale, particularly at the lower end of the size scale.

Such economies were expected to arise through the ability of larger carriers to gain the benefits of bulk buying and of spreading contingency provisions over more units of output. Large carriers would also benefit from their ability to themselves undertake discrete activities such as major maintenance checks or computerised reservations systems, for which a minimum scale of operations was necessary. Increasingly during the 1970s and 1980s the view that there are cost economies of scale in airline operations began to be questioned. Studies both in the United States (Reid and Mohrfeld, 1973) and elsewhere failed to establish any significant economies of scale in airline operations.

These findings were confirmed in practice following United States domestic deregulation in 1978 and liberalisation elsewhere. During the last 30 years many small new-entrant carriers have emerged in the USA, in Europe and in other deregulated markets. Many did not survive, but those that did have been able to be price competitive against very much larger and well-established airlines. Their unit costs, in many cases, have been actually lower because of leaner management and fewer administrative and other overheads.

The airline industry appears to be characterised by constant returns to scale. In other words, there are no marked cost economies of scale. Such a conclusion has important implications on regulatory policy and on merger and alliance strategies. It means that in the absence of entry or capacity controls new small carriers should be in a position to enter existing markets and be cost competitive with established carriers. On the cost side, the economics of the airline industry indicate a natural tendency towards competition rather than monopoly. In practice in international air transport, that tendency is distorted by bilateral agreements, by the lack of airport capacity at major airports and by other constraints discussed in earlier chapters on regulation.

If there are no significant economies of scale on the cost side, what has been driving the marked tendency in recent years for airlines to increase their size through acquisitions, mergers and alliances, such as the three global alliances? While cost advantages of larger size appear limited, larger airlines with a wide network spread enjoy distinct scale benefits in terms of marketing. It is primarily sales and marketing benefits which are driving consolidation, rather than cost synergies. The Air France take-over of KLM in 2004 is a good example of this. While cost benefits were being claimed, the size of each of the partners was such that most of the cost reductions could have been achieved by each independently of the other and without a merger! On the other hand, the marketing benefits of joining and co-ordinating their two networks were substantial. While new smaller entrants into an established market may be competitive in terms of costs, they may be less competitive in their marketing because of the small scale of their operations and because of brand loyalty towards larger and well-established carriers. As a result many new-entrant airlines have not survived long. This reinforces a tendency towards oligopolistic rather than perfect competition.

An IATA study in 2006 analysed the fiscal performance of 85 of the world's major airlines (IATA, 2006a). It found no evidence that scale creates higher profit margins. While some of the larger airlines had the largest absolute profits in financial year 2005, four of the five largest airlines, all in the USA, were unprofitable. But when one looked at profit margins, that is operating profit as a percentage of total revenue, only two of the largest carriers, Emirates and Southwest, achieved margins of 10 per cent or more. A 10 per cent margin would be considered necessary to cover the cost of capital. The 14 airlines which posted profit margins above 10 per cent were either low-cost carriers (Gol, Ryanair and Air Asia had the highest margins of 19 per cent of more), regional carriers such as

Mesa Airlines, SkyWest or American Eagle, or were smaller niche flag carriers such as Kenya Airlines or Philippine Airlines. It was clear that airlines in niche markets generated the highest profit margins. Airline size is not important in generating profitability. But clearly successful profitable airlines tend to grow faster as both Emirates and Singapore Airlines (profit margin of 9.1 per cent in 2005) have done. So, in summary, it appears that good profit margins generate larger scale, because they accelerate growth, whereas large size and scale do not necessarily bring financial success.

If there are no significant cost economies of scale related to airline size, what about the related question of fleet size? Varied stage lengths and differing traffic densities impose the need on many airlines to have quite mixed fleets. This in turn means that some airlines, especially smaller Third World airlines, may only operate two or three aircraft of each type. When the number of aircraft in a fleet of one type is so small there are likely to be higher costs. The cost of spares holding, expressed as a proportion of the purchase price of the aircraft, goes up as the number of aircraft of a particular type drops below a certain level. For instance, one spare engine may be enough whether an airline has three or fifteen aircraft of the same type. Flight crew training and engineering training costs have to be spread over fewer aircraft and are therefore higher. Maintenance costs would be particularly high for small fleets if engines or aircraft have to be sent elsewhere for major or even minor overhauls. The small numbers may preclude the installation of more advanced or very specific maintenance facilities. Conversely, if maintenance or ground handling equipment which is very specific for one aircraft type is installed to service only 2–3 aircraft it will push up the costs of maintenance or handling. Sets of flight crews per aircraft may be higher for very small mixed fleets because of the inability in emergencies to switch crews between aircraft if they are of different types. Pilots are certificated for only one aircraft type at a time. All the above considerations mean that it is relatively expensive to operate small fleets of aircraft.

Hourly direct operating costs go down by 5 to 10 per cent as the fleet size of aircraft of a particular type increases from 2 or 3 to 15 aircraft. Fleets larger than this do not appear to achieve further significant cost economies. This means that airlines with small and mixed fleets have a cost disadvantage. In 2009, Air Madagascar operated 12 aircraft of five different types, made by three different manufacturers. No fleet had more than four aircraft of the same type. They must have been costly to maintain and costly to crew. The low-cost airlines have learnt this lesson. Despite having large fleets they tend to fly only one or, at most, two aircraft types.

5.11   The quality of management

The analysis so far indicates that the most important variables affecting airline costs are the level of input prices, including the cost of labour, the type and size of aircraft used and the stage lengths over which these aircraft are operated. In so far as the last two of these variables are themselves influenced by the pattern and levels of demand that an airline is trying to satisfy, then demand may also be considered an important variable. Other, though less important, variables have also been discussed. Many of the latter are particularly prone to management decision and choice. But there is a further dimension of management whose importance may be absolutely crucial in establishing an airline's unit cost levels, but may be difficult to define or measure. One might broadly define it as the quality of management and it permeates through to most areas of an airline's activities.

The quality of management affects the efficiency with which the management of an airline brings together the various factors of production at its disposal in order to meet different levels and types of demand in different markets. In theory it is management ability or the lack of it which should explain cost differences between airlines which cannot be attributed to variations in input costs, aircraft types operated, stage lengths or any of the other cost variables.

In practice no airline management is likely to be equally efficient or inefficient in all areas of management. It may well be efficient in one area, such as flight crew scheduling, but relatively inefficient in the organisation of maintenance procedures. Thus the total unit cost of an airline may mask wide variations of performance in discrete areas of activity such as flight operations or maintenance management. Ideally, inter-airline comparisons should be on a disaggregate basis, looking at such discrete areas separately.

6 The low-cost model

The low-cost carriers are a far better place for investors to consider at this stage of the cycle than network carriers.

(Andrew Lobbenberg, Airline Analyst, RBS, April 2008)

6.1 Emergence of low-cost airlines

In the three or four years following 2000 traffic growth in many markets slowed down or collapsed while yields continued to fall. Numerous airlines around the world plunged into losses, some of them for several years. It was a turbulent time for the airline industry. In the USA in particular most airlines were in dire financial straits. It was not till 2006 that the industry as a whole began to look healthy again. Yet throughout the period Southwest, the largest so-called low-cost carrier in the United States, together with Ryanair and easyJet, Europe's largest low-cost airlines, continued to grow rapidly and profitably. While many smaller low-cost new entrants have collapsed in recent years, the largest operators, Southwest, Ryanair, easyJet and Gol in Brazil, have continued year in year out to generate profits and profit margins that are the envy of most traditional airlines. How have they achieved this?

The low-cost no frills airline business model is a relatively recent phenomenon whose emergence is linked directly to the spread of deregulation at first domestically in the United States and later in particular international markets.

The international airlines that grew in the decades up to the 1980s were essentially 'network' carriers. They operated radial networks centred on their main base or hub. Generally, they operated from one and occasionally two hubs if they were a national flag carrier. The major US carriers had secondary hubs as well. The international networks of the national flag carriers were relatively simple, with out and back routes radiating from their hubs. They were simple because of the constraints imposed by the bilateral regulatory regime (Chapter 2 above). The US majors operated hubs at their US international gateway airports but also had much more complex interconnected domestic route networks. A key aim of all these network carriers was to attract traffic by providing a wide range of possible destinations and linkages. They did this by offering transfer connections at their hubs for passengers wishing to fly between points that were not served by direct flights or could not be served because of the restricted air services agreements. In order to maximise the opportunities for such connections, airlines were forced to adopt complex and costly schedules and operating practices. (There is more on hubbing in Section 10.6 below.) These network carriers, in response to the domestic and international regulations they faced, such as those imposed by IATA, conformed to common service standards and pricing and fare strategies. They all operated their services very much in the same way. The traditional network airline model was characterised by considerable uniformity. It still is though to a lesser degree.

The characteristics of the traditional network model made it inherently costly and ensured that passenger fares were relatively high. In response, two other airline business models have emerged whose prime focus has been to offer lower fares by operating at lower cost. The older of the two models is that of the charter or non-scheduled airline. Such airlines expanded rapidly in the 1960s and 1970s, especially on European holiday routes and on the North Atlantic, and spread later to a few other markets such as that between North America and the Caribbean. Their impact elsewhere in the world was very limited. Their early success arose from the fact in certain markets they were less strictly regulated than scheduled services (Chapter 7 below).

The second and more recent airline model is that of low-cost no-frills airlines also referred to as budget airlines. These have a different product and market strategy from the charter carriers. But their focus is the same, namely to offer low-priced services. Their emergence is closely linked to the gradual liberalisation of domestic and later international regulations affecting the airline industry.

Deregulation offered carriers and entrepreneurs the opportunity to try out more innovative business models. One of the first to do this was Southwest Airlines. Launching services in 1971, it had operated purely within the state of Texas on short sectors offering low unrestricted fares, high point-to-point frequencies and excellent on-time performance. The essence of the model was simplicity. A simple product and simple operations. It worked. Southwest diverted passengers from other carriers and also generated new traffic by attracting travellers off the roads. It was the simplicity of the product and operating model which enabled Southwest to operate at much lower unit costs which, in turn, meant it could offer much lower fares and use these to stimulate demand. When US deregulation came in 1978 Southwest was well placed to export its low-cost model beyond Texas. It did this slowly, focusing initially on its traditional south-western and West Coast markets. It was only in the 1990s that it expanded beyond the sun belt. By the mid-2000s Southwest was the largest carrier in virtually all of its largest markets. Other US airlines adopted a low-cost no-frills strategy but few survived. The peak of low-cost new entry was between 1993 and 1995 when ten new low-cost carriers were launched. Only one or two of that group have survived to 2008, most notably AirTran (previously Valujet). More recent new entrants include JetBlue and Virgin America.

In Europe, the emergence of the low-cost model was dependent on the liberalisation of intra-European air services. This came with the 'Third Package' of aviation measures which came into force in January 1993. Though Ryanair had launched low-cost services between the UK and Ireland in 1992 it was not till after 1995 that Ryanair and new start-ups easyJet, Debonair, Go and Buzz launched intra-European low-cost services, which grew rapidly. Most of these early European low-cost carriers did not survive. The two that have, Ryanair and easyJet, continued to grow very rapidly and very profitably throughout the decade up to 2008. Being first in the field they have benefited from what economists call first mover advantage and have become well-known brands throughout Europe.

The successes of Ryanair and easyJet encouraged others to launch low-cost airlines in Europe. The major expansion came between 2001 and 2004 and by 2009 there were around 30 such carriers in Europe, though several had collapsed in the meantime. Their success in diverting passengers away from Europe's network and charter airlines

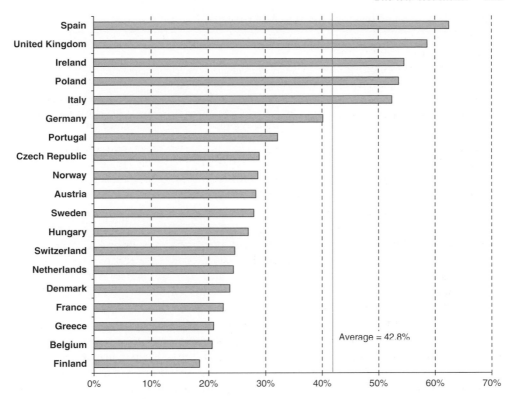

Figure 6.1 Low-cost airline seats as a percentage of total scheduled seats on domestic and intra-European routes to/from each country, September 2008.
Source: Compiled using the Official Airline Guide (OAG).
Note: Low-cost share in 2003 was 17 per cent.

and in developing new markets can be gauged from their market share in each country. The percentage of total seats on scheduled domestic or intra-European flights being offered in each country in September 2008 by low-cost carriers is shown in Figure 6.1. In five countries, Spain, United Kingdom, Ireland, Poland and Italy, more than 50 per cent of scheduled seats were available on low-cost airlines. In Europe as a whole, the latter provided 42.8 per cent of scheduled seat capacity. The speed of growth and penetration by the low-cost sector can be seen in the fact that five years earlier in 2003 its capacity share was only 17 per cent.

In other parts of the world, as in the USA and in Europe, the emergence of low-cost airlines was directly linked to the progressive liberalisation of the domestic and international regulations, which had hitherto constrained airline management. Thus, in the Asia-Pacific region five low-cost airlines were operating by 2001 but with purely domestic services. As governments slowly relaxed their bilateral air services agreements many new low-cost airlines were launched in that part of the world, especially in the period 2005 to 2007. By 2008 there were around 30 low-cost airlines operating in Asia and several were operating on international as well as domestic routes (Table 6.1). (For the early development of LCCs see Doganis, 2006.)

Table 6.1 The spread of low-cost carriers in Asia/Pacific

2001	*By 2008*	
Operating in liberalised domestic markets	*Many new entrants – more international routes*	
Air Asia	Air Arabia	Nok Air
Cebu Pacific	Air Do	One-Two-Go
Freedom Air	Air India Express	Spice Jet
Lion Air	Fly Pacificblue	Star Flyer
Virgin Blue	Go Air	Thai Air Asia
	Indigo	Tiger Air
	Indonesia Air Asia	Valuair
	Jeju Air	Virgin Blue Macau
	JetLite	
	Jetstar	and in China . . .
	Jetstar Asia	China United
	Kingfisher Red	Spring
	Lion Airlines	Okay
		East Star etc.

6.2   The essence of the low-cost model

The essence of the low-cost business model is twofold. First, 'Keep it simple' by providing a simple no-frills product or service based on simple operations and thereby minimise costs and maximise efficiency. Second, 'Create demand', which means 'Do not try merely to satisfy an existing passenger demand, but set out to generate and stimulate new demand both by offering very low fares and flying to destinations not previously served'.

The aim of the Southwest Airlines business model was to offer a simple, uncluttered, low-fare, point-to-point product using a single-type aircraft fleet, while achieving very high aircraft and crew utilisation by operating from secondary and uncongested airports. Ryanair, easyJet and the other low-cost airlines adopted the Southwest model. But each modified it to a lesser or greater extent to suit their own marketing needs. For example, unlike Southwest or Ryanair, easyJet from its very inception in 1995 ignored sales through travel agents and focused on 100 per cent direct sales, initially through its own telephone call centre and then increasingly online through its own website.

The essential features of the low-cost model are summarised in Table 6.2. Despite individual variations, low-cost airlines have generally adopted most of these features into their own operations. It is by adopting these features that low-cost carriers can achieve unit operating costs that are 30 to 60 per cent lower than those of network carriers flying on the same or similar routes with the same aircraft. The wide cost differential between the two airline business models in 2005 is amply illustrated in Figure 6.2. This compares the unit cost per seat-km on domestic and intra-European routes of Ryanair and easyJet with the costs, again on their domestic and European network, of a selection of European network carriers. The figure shows clearly how unit costs tend to decline as average sector distance increases. As a result, in 2005 some network carriers operating relatively long European sectors, such as Cyprus Airways, achieve low unit costs. But those flying on short sectors averaging 600–1,000 kms find that their unit costs are several times higher than those of Ryanair or easyJet. Or, expressed in another way, Ryanair's unit costs in 2005 were equivalent to as little as 40 per cent of the unit costs of large network airlines such as British Airways or Lufthansa or even less in some cases (Figure 6.1).

Table 6.2 Low-cost and network models compared – early/mid-2000s

	Low-cost carriers	Traditional network airlines – early 2000s*
	Simple product	*Complex product*
Fares	Low, simple – one-way Minimum restrictions Fares rise nearer departure	Round trip – complex Multiple restrictions Lower fares last minute
Distribution	Avoid travel agents Aim 100% direct: either online or call centre Ticketless	Dependent on travel agents Own ticket offices/call centre Paper tickets
In-flight	Single class High-density seating No seat assignment No meals or free drinks	2 or 3 classes Low seat density Assigned seats In-flight catering
	Simple operations	*Complex operations*
Aircraft	Single type – maximum two High utilisation (11 hours/day)	Multiple types – aircraft tailored to routes Low utilisation on short sectors
Sectors	Short – 500 to 1,000 kms Point-to-point No hubbing or connecting flights	From ultra-short to long Hub-based network Pax/flights connect at hub
Schedules	Used to shift demand	Response to current demand
Airports	Secondary or uncongested (where possible) 20–30 minute turn-arounds	Focus on larger airports 1 hour turn-around on short sectors
Staff	Competitive wages Profit-sharing High productivity	Higher wages Minimal profit-sharing Over-staffed

Note

* In the mid-2000s some legacy carriers, in response to low-cost competition, began to adopt several low-cost features, e.g. no paper tickets, one-way fares, online selling.

EasyJet's costs, though higher than Ryanair's, were only around 50 per cent of those of some of its major network competitors.

The average cost of European network carriers on their domestic and European services in 2005 was 10.46 US cents per available seat-km. Ryanair's unit cost was 3.60 US cents, that is, 34 per cent of the European average, while easyJet's 5.82 cents was 56 per cent of the average. By 2009 the cost gap between the two models had not closed appreciably.

In the United States the unit cost gap between legacy network carriers and their low-cost competitors is not as wide as in Europe but is still substantial. A 2006 study by IATA, using Bureau of Transportation Statistics for domestic operations, calculated the unit cost differences between the largest US network airlines (American, United and Delta) with those of three low-cost carriers, namely Southwest, JetBlue and AirTran. The analysis included all major operating costs but the comparison was undertaken after adjusting the reported cost data to an average sector length of 1,400 kms. Two adjustments were made to the unit costs to allow for operational differences between the two models. First, both JetBlue and the large network airlines had average domestic sectors well above 1,400 kms, whereas those of Southwest and AirTran were close to 1,000 kms. So the network airline's unit costs were adjusted upwards. Then the network carriers' costs were adjusted downwards, to allow for the fact that they fly fewer seats in comparable aircraft than

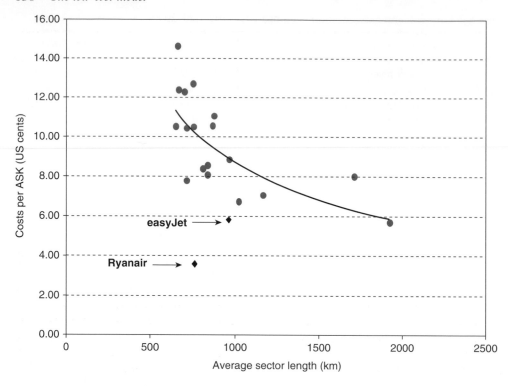

Figure 6.2 Unit costs of European network airlines compared to easyJet and Ryanair on intra-
European services, 2005.
Source: Compiled by author using various sources.

Note: Costs refer only to intra-European operations and exclude longer-haul.

low-cost airlines. Having made these two adjustments, the IATA report found that
JetBlue's unit costs were 75 per cent of those of the three network airlines, Air Tran's were
71 per cent and Southwest's were as low as 64 per cent (IATA, 2006b). A similar comparison a year later found that the cost gap between the two sectors had not closed despite
the fact that four of the network airlines had been able to undertake cost-cutting measures while under Chapter 11 bankruptcy protection.

6.3   More seats and higher aircraft utilisation

The lower unit operating costs of the low-cost model stem both from the simplicity of
the product offered to passengers and from the simplicity of the operations required to
generate that product. Central to the economics of this model are the *higher seat densities*
in the aircraft and the *higher daily utilisation* (that is block-hours per day) achieved with
these aircraft when compared to network airlines. These two features are important
because they increase both the hourly and the annual productivity of each aircraft measured in available seat-kms (ASK).

Hourly aircraft productivity in ASKs is the average distance flown in an hour multiplied by the number of seats on offer. Thus even if the hourly costs of the same aircraft
flown on the same sector were identical, the unit cost per seat-km of the low–cost operator
would be lower than those of the network operator because the former was generating

Table 6.3 Average daily utilisation of Airbus A-319 aircraft in 2008

European airlines	Block hours per day
Low-cost:	
EasyJet	11.1
Network:	
Lufthansa	10.3
Iberia	9.5
Swiss	8.6
British Airways	8.3
Air France	8.2
Alitalia	7.6
SAS (2007)	6.3

Source: Compiled from CAA (UK) and IATA data and airline annual reports.

Note
Four easyJet aircraft do the work of five Air France or BA aircraft.

more seat-kms by putting in more seats on the aircraft. Stated simply, if you offer more seats in the same aircraft the cost per seat will be less. By doing away with a two-class cabin, by reducing or removing galleys, especially hot galleys, and by reducing the seat pitch, that is the distance between seats, low-cost airlines can significantly increase the number of seats available in their aircraft. They may reduce the seat pitch to 28 or 29 inches compared to the 30–33 inches more common among conventional network carriers.

Thus in the United States in 2008 United operated its Airbus A-319 aircraft with 120 seats while Spirit Airlines, an LCC, offered 144 seats in the same aircraft. But in the same year in Europe, easyJet was flying its 319s with 156 seats, obviously with a shorter seat pitch than the US carriers. On several routes easyJet was competing against British Airways also flying Airbus 319s but with around 121 seats on average. Merely by putting in 29 per cent more seats easyJet would have reduced the cost per seat by 23 per cent, even if total trip costs were the same for both airlines. An IATA study has suggested that on average low-cost no frills airlines place 14 per cent more seats on the same aircraft than when flown by network carriers (IATA, 2007). This cost advantage, arising from higher seating density, is similar to that enjoyed by the other low-cost model, that of the charter airlines.

Equally, if LCCs fly their aircraft more hours each year, all those costs which are fixed annual costs are spread over more hours and therefore the cost per hour will be less. This is what happens. The use, where possible, of secondary airports, the rapid cleaning of aircraft by cabin crew rather than ground staff, more rapid embarkation as a result of free seating and the absence of catering or freight to load or off-load enables low-cost carriers to schedule for and achieve faster turn-around of their aircraft. Because they spend less time on the ground, aircraft can spend more time flying and so push up the daily utilisation achieved. Thus in 2008, while easyJet flew its Airbus 319 aircraft on average for 11.1 block hours per day, British Airways and Air France both managed under 9 hours for the same aircraft while Alitalia achieved even less, only 7.6 hours (Table 6.3). In brief, easyJet was getting much more flying out of its aircraft than its key competitors.

Or, in other words, easyJet aircraft flew each day at least one, and in some cases two, one-hour sectors more than its conventional airline counterparts. In essence, four easyJet aircraft were doing the same work as five BA or Air France aircraft. All those costs which

Table 6.4 Comparative operating costs, Boeing 737–300, United States airlines, 2007

	Cost per seat mile* (US cents)	Cost index**	Average sector (miles)	Daily utilisation (hours)	Seats per aircraft
	1	2	3	4	5
US Airways	9.55	100	498	7.96	128
United	8.88	93	657	9.07	122
Continental	7.66	80	934	9.55	124
Southwest	6.82	71	516	10.27	137

Source: Compiled by author from *Airline Monitor* (2008).

Note
 * Direct operating costs only (i.e. fuel, labour cost of flying, maintenance, aircraft depreciation and rentals).
** US Airways costs indexed at 100.

are fixed annual costs and are largely unaffected by the amount of flying done are spread over more flights and, therefore, the cost per seat-km is reduced. Depreciation, insurance, maintenance overheads and general administration costs clearly fall into this category. But some other costs too may be reduced. For instance, cabin and flight crew costs may be lower per seat-km since staff achieve higher productivity because shorter turnrounds mean they do more flying per duty period.

The higher seating density and higher aircraft utilisation achieved by low-cost carriers in the United States can be gauged from Table 6.4. This compares 2007 data for the Boeing 737–300 for low-cost carrier Southwest with three network carriers US Airways, United and Continental. By having a single-class cabin, doing away with hot galleys and perhaps reducing the seat pitch, Southwest can seat 10 to 15 more seats in the same aircraft than the network carriers (Table 6.4, Column 5). It also gets more block hours per day out of its aircraft. In 2007 Southwest flew its Boeing 737–300s two hours more each day than US Airways and an hour or so more than United or Continental (Table 6.4, Column 4).

The unit costs per seat-mile of the US Boeing 737–300 operators are shown in Table 6.4 (Column 1). This shows that Southwest's unit costs in 2007 for this aircraft were around 25 to 30 per cent lower than those of US Airways and United (Column 2). The gap with Continental was not so wide but this was due, in part, to the fact that Continental operated this aircraft on significantly longer sectors, 934 miles as opposed to Southwest's 516 miles, and obtained cost advantages from its longer sectors (Column 3).

Clearly, higher seating density and higher aircraft utilisation achieved by LCCs impact on their unit costs. But as will be discussed below, there are several additional factors which enable LCCs to produce lower costs though some of these factors are themselves affected by seat density and aircraft utilisation.

6.4   Cost advantages of LCCs – easyJet versus Bmi

The best way to appreciate where and how LCCs achieve their cost advantages is to compare the cost structure of a low-cost airline with that of a broadly similar network carrier. In Europe, the paucity of statistical data makes it quite difficult to make meaningful inter-company comparisons. While detailed aggregated cost data is available for Europe's conventional scheduled airlines, such data covers all their services including those on long-haul routes. It is virtually impossible to isolate the true costs of their purely

Table 6.5 Two UK network and low-cost airlines compared, 2007*

	British Midland (Bmi) network	EasyJet low cost
Total seat-kms available (million)	14,041	36,413
Average sector length (kms)	760	1,020
Average aircraft size (seats)	138	150
Passenger load factor	68.7%	81.6%
Fleet composition	2 Airbus 321	
	10 Airbus 320	31 Boeing 737–700
	11 Airbus 319	94 Airbus 319
	3 Airbus 330	
	15 Boeing 737–300	
	5 Boeing 737–500	
	3 Embraer RJ 135	
	13 Embraer RJ 145	
Cost per seat-km (US cents)	13.1	9.01
Cost difference		−31%
Cost per pax-km (US cents)	19.1	11.1
Cost difference		−42%

Source: Compiled by author using CAA airline data (CAA, 2008).

Note
* Data is for financial year ending 30 December 2007 for Bmi (British Midland) and 30 September 2007 for easyJet.

short-haul intra-European operations, similar to those of the low-cost carriers. One can overcome this difficulty by focusing any comparison on conventional scheduled airlines that only operate short-haul services or have very limited longer-haul operations.

In the UK in 2007 one such airline, British Midland (Bmi), was found to be comparable in many ways to easyJet in the nature of its operations (Table 6.5). While BMi operated three Airbus A330 long-haul aircraft in 2007, they were only a small part of a total fleet of 61 aircraft. Bmi was still primarily a domestic and short-haul intra-European operator, as was easyJet. In fact, despite the A330s, its average sector distance (760 kms) was shorter than easyJet's (1,020) but not too far off. While Bmi had a much more mixed fleet than easyJet, its average aircraft size in terms of seats at 138 was close to easyJet's 150 seats per aircraft (Table 6.5). In terms of size, easyJet was a little over twice as large as Bmi in terms of available seat-kms. However, in one sense, Bmi was not truly representative of a traditional network carrier. In 2002 it had launched a low-cost subsidiary 'Bmibaby'. By 2005 this was accounting for 25–30 per cent of Bmi's total traffic. It would undoubtedly have reduced Bmi's average unit cost but only to a limited extent. Bmibaby was not a newly-created, stand-alone, low-cost airline but one created by using the aircraft, crews and infrastructure of an established network carrier. As a result Bmibaby would not have obtained the full cost economies achievable by a low-cost operator.

Bmi and easyJet are sufficiently similar to provide a valid comparison. But in 2007 they did differ significantly in two key performance areas, which reflect their different business models (Table 6.5). First, easyJet's passenger load factor at 81.6 per cent was 12.9 percentage points higher than Bmi's, only 68.7 per cent. Second, easyJet's cost per seat-km was 31 per cent lower than Bmi's. Because of its much higher load factor when the cost per seat-km is converted to a cost per passenger-km, then easyJet's

Table 6.6 Cost comparison of easyJet and Bmi, financial year 2007

	Bmi	EasyJet	EasyJet saving	
	US cents/ ASK	US cents/ ASK	US cents/ ASK	as % of Bmi
Direct operating costs	1	2	3	4
1. Flight operations				
1.1 Flight and cabin crew expenses	1.50	1.07	−0.48	
1.2 Fuel	2.70	2.34	−0.36	
1.3 Airport landing/pax fees	2.04	1.61	−0.43	
1.4 En-route charges	0.67	0.78	+0.11	
2. Maintenance	1.47	0.54	−0.93	
3. Depreciation, leases, insurance	1.45	0.74	−0.71	
Total DOC	9.83	7.08	−2.75	−28%
Indirect operating costs				
4. Station and ground handling	1.34	0.93	−0.41	
5. Passenger services	0.27	0.05	−0.22	
6. Ticketing, sales, promotion	1.11	0.32	−0.79	
7. Admin and other	0.57	0.63	+0.06	
Total IOC	3.29	1.93	−1.36	−41%
Total costs per ASK	13.11	9.01	−4.10	−31%

Source: Compiled using data from CAA (2009a).

Note
ASK – available seat-km.

cost is 42 per cent below Bmi's. Without Bmibaby this cost difference would have been greater.

At a disaggregate level, the lower unit costs of easyJet compared to those of Bmi, or any other network carrier, are due in part to easyJet's higher seating density on similar aircraft and to its higher aircraft utilisation as discussed in the previous section. This should be borne in mind in the analysis of the detailed cost data which follows comparing Bmi (British Midland) and easyJet costs in 2007. This cost comparison relates to two European airlines. A similar comparison of LCCs and network carriers in the United States, Brazil or South East Asia would inevitably produce different figures, but the areas where the LCCs could make cost economies would be broadly the same.

Direct operating costs are all those costs which are dependent on the type of aircraft being flown. A comparison of these costs in the top half of Table 6.6 suggests that the low-cost airlines enjoy marked cost advantages in four areas.

First, easyJet's unit costs of *flight and cabin crew* are about one third lower, which represents a substantial saving. As in other cost areas this is partly because of the higher seating density and the higher aircraft utilisation achieved. But in addition low-cost carriers may use a smaller cabin crew because there are no meals or snacks to serve, or a Business class cabin. Whereas easyJet would have a cabin crew of three on one of its Boeing 737–300 aircraft, Bmi or other network carriers operating this aircraft would fly with a cabin crew of four, especially if they had a Business class cabin. Surprisingly, though flight crew salaries are similar in both easyJet and Bmi, cabin crew at easyJet get paid substantially more than their Bmi counterparts. On the other hand, easyJet pilots are not as well paid as pilots in most of the European network airlines, such as BA, against which easyJet competes.

Table 6.7 Short-haul pilot productivity – Europe all LCCs and network carriers, 2002

Average for pilots/ *1st officers*	*Network carriers*** €	*Low-cost carriers**** €	*LCC versus network* €
Variable pay	6,400	18,800	+195
Fixed pay	102,200	60,100	−41
Total gross	108,600	78,900	−27
Annual block hours	562	760	+35
Salary cost/hour	193	104	−46

Source: compiled using data from European Cockpit Association.

Notes
 * Network average, short-haul pilots of AF, BA, IB, LH and SK.
 ** Low-cost average for Buzz, DBA, easyJet, Germania and Ryanair.

Despite having similar pilot salaries and more expensive cabin crew than Bmi, easyJet's flight and cabin crew costs per ASK are still a third lower than Bmi's (Table 6.6, column 4). This is due primarily to the higher productivity achieved by both flight and cabin crew because crew are rostered to fly as close as possible to the maximum permitted annual hours. This is made easier by the faster turn-arounds at airports and the higher aircraft utilisation, by the point-to-point services and by the avoidance of night stops. On the other hand, network airlines, such as Bmi, BA or Air France invariably might stop their last evening flights out of their base at their destination since they need for competitive reasons an early morning return flight.

The impact of higher labour productivity on costs was well illustrated by a 2002 study of European pilot wages and work hours carried out by the European Cockpit Association (Table 6.7). This showed that pilots in the larger European LCCs were paid on average 27 per cent less than short-haul pilots flying for the major European network carriers. They were paid less but flew about 200 hours more in a year. More flying was encouraged in part by a wage structure in which variable pay provided a much more important share of the final salary than was the case with network pilots. Lower pay combined with more block hours meant that the salary cost per hour for LCC pilots in 2002 was 46 per cent lower than for network pilots on similar short-haul aircraft. Unfortunately, this study has not been repeated by the European Cockpit Association.

The relative figures will have changed since 2002 but the productivity advantage of LCC pilots in Europe remains, though it may not be as high as it was. The same picture of higher productivity emerges with cabin crew.

As one might expect, the second area where there is a significant LCC saving is in airport charges, that is, *aircraft landing fees and passenger-related charges*. EasyJet's airport charges per seat-km were a quarter less than those of British Midland. This is because it had negotiated relatively low rates as a new start-up carrier at its Luton base and other UK bases, as well as at several of its foreign destinations. Ryanair, by focusing all its network on small secondary and little-used airports, many of which were desperate to attract a new airline, makes even greater savings in this area. Ryanair's airport charges per passenger are substantially below those of easyJet. Because, on short-haul sectors in Europe, airport charges can represent 15 to 20 per cent of total costs, for Bmi they were 16 per cent in 2007, then reducing such charges by one quarter, as easyJet did in 2007 when compared to Bmi, can cut total unit costs by 4–5 per cent! In the early days of the low-cost revolution it was easier for LCCs to negotiate good 5–10 year deals with airports eager to attract them. This will become increasingly difficult, especially when flying into larger established airports, except where the LCCs can use cheaper and/or more Spartan terminals.

The third direct operating cost where LCCs can achieve some cost saving is *maintenance cost*, where again the saving seems to be up to two thirds (Table 6.6, Column 3). This is likely to be due to three factors: first, through operating newer, younger aircraft which are cheaper to maintain. High profits make it easier to invest in a young fleet. In 2008 the average age of the easyJet or Ryanair aircraft was 3–4 years, while for most network airlines short-haul fleets it was over 10 years. With many very new aircraft in their fleet, both easyJet and Ryanair in 2007 or 2008 would have relatively fewer of the expensive D-checks to undertake. These are needed only every 3, 4 or more years. Second, as a result of the decision by many low-cost carriers to get the lowest possible costs by outsourcing most of their maintenance requirements, in some cases even their line maintenance. They have no top-heavy maintenance administration or costly hangars and maintenance facilities of their own. Finally, low-cost carriers can keep their facilities and spare parts costs to a minimum by operating a single aircraft type or if they operate a second type ensuring that they have sufficiently large numbers of each type to obtain scale economies.

In 2007 easyJet had Airbus 319s and Boeing 737–700 series. This is in marked contrast to the very mixed fleet of Bmi (Table 6.5) with small numbers of eight different types from three manufacturers, though some of the types offered some commonality of engines or spare parts. In the USA, Southwest achieves lower maintenance costs than the legacy airlines by operating only three aircraft types and in large number, namely the Boeing 737–300 (of which it had 194 in 2007), the Boeing 737–700 (280 in fleet) and the 737–500, of which there are only 25, but which has much commonality with the 300 series. Its US competitors had much more mixed fleets with smaller numbers of aircraft of each type. For example, in 2007 Northwest operated six different single-aisle aircraft on its domestic routes with an average of 52 aircraft of each type.

Surprisingly, the fourth area of direct cost saving for LCCs appears to be that of *depreciation and rentals or lease costs*. Here easyJet achieved a cost saving of about half (Table 6.6, Column 3). Three factors may explain this. Higher daily aircraft utilisation is the key here since depreciation and certain types of leases are fixed annual costs. Some of the saving may also be due to the fact that easyJet may have negotiated much cheaper leasing contracts because market conditions were easier for those leases entered into in the period shortly after 2001. But a more important factor is likely to be the very large single order that easyJet was able to place by concentrating on one aircraft type and rapid expansion. In October 2002 after playing off Boeing against Airbus, easyJet ordered 120 Airbus 319 aircraft with price-protected options for another 120. This was Airbus's first major breakthrough into the LCC market. It was desperate to do this and dropped the price. It is thought that easyJet bought these aircraft at around 50 per cent below the notional sticker price (Jones, 2005), a huge saving. In November 2006 easyJet signed options for an additional 75 aircraft at substantially the same terms as the original 2002 contract. Many were acquired through leasing arrangements and enabled easyJet to post low lease costs. Bmi's more mixed fleet with small numbers of each type would have required higher leasing costs.

Ryanair, which has an all-Boeing fleet, has also achieved significant saving through placing very large orders for Boeing 737–800 aircraft. In January 2002, when the market was depressed, it ordered 100 of these aircraft with a further 50 on option. In the following four years firm orders or options were placed for about 200 additional aircraft of this type.

Southwest too was benefiting from huge orders. Early in 2005 it had outstanding firm orders for 91 Boeing 737–700 aircraft for delivery before the end of 2008 and options for another 259 for possible delivery before the end of 2012. With such large orders and options all these LCCs would have been able to negotiate low purchase prices which could not be matched by network airlines generally ordering much smaller numbers of narrow-body aircraft. However, it seems that a large differential in ownership costs can only be sustained by those LCCs buying large numbers of aircraft at one time. Smaller LCCs may be unable to benefit from lower ownership costs to the same extent, but their costs should be lower if they can ensure much higher daily aircraft utilisation than network carriers.

From an examination of Table 6.6 it is clear that there are two distinct categories of direct costs in which LCCs are unlikely to enjoy any marked cost advantages, namely fuel and en-route navigation charges. *Fuel* is a major cost item and for most short-haul airlines it is the single largest input cost after labour. But airlines pay very similar prices for aviation fuel. Though larger airlines may be able to negotiate marginally lower rates because of the larger volumes uplifted the price differences are small. There are marked variations in fuel prices between airports, so where airlines flew from or to will influence their cost of fuel but within Europe differences will be limited. Nevertheless, some LCCs have been able to obtain a marginally lower fuel cost per seat-km by operating newer aircraft with more fuel-efficient engines. This was the case with easyJet in 2007, when the average age of its fleet was around four years. But all LCCs can reduce their fuel cost per seat-km by putting more seats into their aircraft than do network airlines. EasyJet has a younger fleet and higher seat density but in relative terms the fuel cost saving compared to Bmi is only about 13 per cent (Table 6.6, Column 3).

The other cost area which offers no scope for savings is *en-route navigation charges*. This is because en-route charges for using air navigation facilities are non-negotiable. All airlines on a route flying the same aircraft will pay similar charges. So costs depend on which routes airlines are serving since in Europe each country's air navigation services have different charge rates. In fact, easyJet route charges are higher than BMI's and this must reflect the geographical spread of their flights. As with fuel, the only cost advantage arises from low-cost carriers' higher seating density.

Insurance costs, though not shown separately in Table 6.6 but included with depreciation, are another item which cannot be reduced significantly by LCCs. All they can achieve is marginal reductions through higher aircraft utilisation.

Overall, in 2007, easyJet *direct operating costs* were about one quarter (28 per cent) lower than Bmi's (Table 6.6). In proportional but not absolute terms, LCCs achieve their most dramatic savings vis-à-vis traditional network carriers in most categories of *indirect operating costs*.

Low-cost operators' reductions in indirect operating costs arise primarily in handling and marketing-related costs. A significant saving can be achieved in so-called *station and ground handling costs*, that is the costs associated with providing ground staff, check-in staff, equipment, business lounges, office space and related facilities at each of the airports served by an airline. While conventional airlines maintain significant numbers of staff and equipment and may rent considerable space for business lounges and offices, especially at their base airport(s), low-cost carriers do away with much of this expenditure by outsourcing much of their passenger and aircraft handling and maintaining only very minimal numbers of their own staff. Since they do not have online or interline connecting passengers or baggage, they do not need staff or facilities for such handling. Nor do they have to handle freight since most LCCs do not carry freight. And, of course, they do not require business lounges at all.

In Europe, LCCs outsource the ground handling wherever they can and this enables them further to reduce costs through competitive bidding. Another area of cost saving is in aircraft cleaning. Legacy network carriers normally have their own or sub-contracted ground staff who clean the interior of the aircraft during each turn-around. This in itself lengthens the turn-around time. LCCs in most cases ask the cabin crew to clean up the interior towards the end of each flight, by collecting all rubbish from passengers, and then just tidying the cabin as passengers disembark. All this is made easier because there is no free in-flight catering. Where they need to rent space for check-in desks, offices, etc., LCCs negotiate very low rentals or at small secondary airports they may pay no rent at all. Wherever they can, they minimise the space they require in the knowledge that their passengers will accept some degree of discomfort, for instance longer check-in queues, in exchange for the low fares. As Southwest does in the United States, they argue that their entry on to a route generates so much new traffic that smaller airports have much to gain by offering them free or very cheap space. Given all this it is hardly surprising that easyJet's station and ground handling costs in 2007 were about a third below Bmi's.

Another area of major indirect cost savings for low-cost carriers is that of *passenger services* which include the cost of meals, drinks and other services furnished to passengers as part of the trip experience as well as meals or accommodation for transit or delayed passengers. Since airlines such as easyJet or Ryanair do not offer any free meals or drinks on board, but only a trolley from which passengers can buy drinks or light snacks, their passenger service costs are negligible. In fact they aim to generate additional revenue and profit from on-board food sales. Also, since they offer only point-to-point services they do not have to cater for transfer or transit passengers or their baggage, or for connecting passengers who have missed their flight. In the event of delays, LCCs are unlikely to offer meal vouchers or hotel accommodation, while, if flights are cancelled, they may not be prepared to meet the high cost of putting passengers on other airlines' flights but will rebook them on their own flights on subsequent days. Passenger service costs are not a major item, but they are a cost which LCCs can reduce very significantly (Table 6.6, item 5).

Ticketing, sales and promotion, which basically represent the costs of distribution, is the cost area where historically LCCs have made the most significant savings both in absolute and relative terms. They have done this by introducing innovative distribution processes based on disintermediation and ticketless travel. Disintermediation meant cutting out all intermediaries in the sales process between the low-cost airline and its customers, thereby saving all commissions and fees which legacy carriers were having to pay. EasyJet was the pioneer. From its launch in 1995, it was the first airline both to cut out travel agents altogether and to sell 100 per cent direct, by-passing the global distribution systems (GDSs). In this way it saved all commissions to travel agents which by the early 2000s averaged around 8 per cent of costs for network airlines as well as the GDS fees, which were $3.00 or more per booking made. They also saved money by not setting up their own retail sales offices in expensive high street locations in the towns they flew to or even off-line offices in towns they did not serve! EasyJet introduced internet selling in the autumn of 1998 and they had hit 30 per cent of sales within a year. By 2007 internet sales were around 95 per cent of total sales with the balance of tickets being sold through the easyJet call centre. Other LCCs such as Ryanair or Southwest did not initially focus on 100 per cent direct selling. They did use travel agents, but they quickly began to follow easyJet and focused increasingly on direct sales through the internet. Southwest was the first US airline to introduce direct online booking.

However, at the end of 2007, easyJet allowed its seat inventory to be accessed for the first time through two of the GDSs. In this it was following the example of Jetblue in the USA which claimed that its average fare sold on the GDS was $35 higher than fares sold direct by the airline. EasyJet also wanted to target corporate business passengers who are very dependent on business travel agents. But the deal made with Galileo and Amadeus did not involve any costs to easyJet. The GDS fees would be borne by the agent or the passenger. This was a breakthrough on GDS service fees and other LCCs were likely to follow.

EasyJet, Go and other LCCs in Europe were the first to introduce ticketless travel; passengers just needed their reservation number and some form of identity to check in. This saves money on printing tickets, on collecting them and on checking them. Since low-cost carriers only sell point-to-point on their own services and do not issue for or receive tickets from other airlines for interline transfers, passenger revenue accounting is greatly simplified and can be almost totally computerised. On a normal scheduled airline, each paper ticket may be manually handled up to 13–15 times as it goes from issuing office to check-in and on to various stages of revenue accounting. A low-cost carrier such as easyJet from its very beginning was completely ticketless with all revenue accounting done on computers. It has been estimated that the cost of a printed ticket and the extra work it creates in collecting and feeding it into an airline's accounting system is around $9. Like easyJet, Southwest was the first airline in the USA to introduce ticketless travel system-wide, further reducing its operating costs. It was not till the mid-2000s that network airlines woke up to the advantages of paper-less electronic tickets (e-ticketing). They began to introduce it rapidly after IATA in November 2004 set a target for its members of 100 per cent e-ticketing by the end of 2007. In the event this was largely but not fully achieved by the target date partly because of the difficulty of implementation for multi-sector flights involving different airlines. Nevertheless, e-ticketing has now become the norm, at least for international air travel.

Advertising is another cost falling within the ticketing, sales and promotion area. To offset the absence of travel agents as a selling tool, low-cost carriers tend to be more dependent on advertising. In Europe, easyJet, Ryanair and Air Berlin tend to advertise heavily, especially in the press. However, when easyJet's advertising expenditure in 2007 is converted into a cost per seat-km it is substantially lower than that of British Midland. This may well be because as an airline with a more restricted geographical spread, easyJet can more easily focus and target its advertising spend. It also enjoys some economies of scale in advertising when compared to Bmi, a smaller airline. EasyJet has also been very successful in generating a great deal of free advertising including an annual prime-time UK television series made about the airline each year from 1998 till 2006. With growing competition among low-cost carriers themselves, high advertising spend is likely to continue, though they will increasingly enjoy economies of scale if they continue to grow as rapidly as in recent years.

Low-cost airlines have simplified the whole process of reservation and ticketing and as a result enjoy substantial savings in their costs of distribution. In 2007, easyJet's cost of ticketing, sales and promotion per seat-km was over 70 per cent lower than Bmi's and in absolute terms it represented the second largest category of saved cost (Table 6.6, item 6). Nevertheless, this wide cost differential is not sustainable. The gap between the low-cost and network airlines in this area will be reduced as the latter increasingly adopt some of the former's practices such as direct online selling and 100 per cent e-ticketing.

Finally, low-cost airlines' *administrative costs* per seat-km should be lower. By their very nature low-cost carriers are likely to have a smaller, tighter central administration partly because they outsource many activities and partly because, as new start-ups, they do not carry any of the administrative accretions that old established conventional airlines are burdened with. For instance, they do not have large numbers of planning and other staff dealing with IATA issues or bilateral air services negotiations. Their small size and flexible staff also mean that in many areas one person will be undertaking two or three functions which in a conventional airline may require two or three separate people or even departments. Low-cost carriers would expect to achieve administrative costs per seat-km which are half or less than those of their conventional competitors. In the search for lower costs, low-cost airlines can operate more or less as virtual airlines outsourcing many of the non-core functions to the cheapest suppliers. However, in 2007 easyJet's administration costs were marginally higher than Bmi's. This was probably caused by the mis-allocation of certain minor costs into this category. Certainly similar analyses for earlier years did show easyJet's costs to be lower.

In summary, in the financial year 2007 easyJet's total operating costs per seat-km were about a third (31 per cent) lower than Bmi's. While in absolute terms the low-cost airlines' savings were greater in the area of direct operating costs, proportionally, the savings were substantially greater in the area of indirect costs. EasyJet was able to reduce its indirect costs by close to half (41 per cent) compared to those of Bmi, whereas its direct operating costs were only a quarter (28 per cent) lower than Bmi's.

Since the cost structures of different low-cost and network airlines vary, then inevitably the cost savings may differ from those suggested in Table 6.6, which compares easyJet and Bmi. This is especially true if comparing United States airlines or others outside Europe. Nevertheless the above comparison highlights where low-cost airlines are most likely to achieve significant cost savings. In fact, because Bmi accounts include a low-cost subsidiary, Bmibaby, easyJet's cost saving is less than it would be compared to other pure network carriers. This is evident from Figure 6.1 above, which shows that easyJet's costs per seat-km were 50 to 60 per cent lower than those of several European network carriers' short-haul operations in 2005. Moreover Ryanair's unit cost was substantially lower than easyJet's.

6.5   The impact of high seat factors

In Europe, the major low-cost carriers, easyJet and Ryanair, enjoy one final cost advantage, namely much higher passenger load factors, that is seat factors. On average, they achieve passenger load factors, which, year-round, are about 80–85 per cent, whereas most European network carriers manage only around 65 to 75 per cent loads on their short-haul domestic and intra-European services. This means that when the LCC's lower costs per available seat-km are converted to a cost per passenger-km or passenger carried, the cost difference with network carriers is magnified. This was evident earlier when comparing easyJet and Bmi (Table 6.5). Because in 2007 easyJet achieved an average passenger load factor of 81.6 per cent, compared to Bmi's 68.7 per cent, its 31 per cent saving in cost per seat-km became a 42 per cent reduction in cost per passenger-km. In fact Bmi had one of the highest passenger load factors among network carriers in Europe (Table 6.8). In 2007 several operated at domestic/intra-European seat factors that were about 10–15 percentage points below those of Ryanair and easyJet. Such a large gap significantly reinforced the latter's cost advantage. Since 2007, the better network carriers

Table 6.8 Load factors – European low-cost and network airlines on domestic/intra-European services, 2007

	Passenger seat factor %
Low cost	
Ryanair	82.5
EasyJet	81.6
Network airlines	
KLM	75.7
Iberia	73.8
Swiss	71.8
Turkish Airlines	71.4
Lufthansa	70.2
SAS	70.0
European average	68.9
Air France	68.7
British Midland (Bmi)	68.0
British Airways	67.9
Alitalia	67.9
Finnair	67.0
Austrian Airlines	66.9
Olympic	66.1
Air Portugal	64.6
Czech Airlines	62.3

Source: Airline Annual reports and AEA (2008).

have focused on pushing up their seat factors on their intra-European services but they are still 10 per cent or so below those of the LCCs.

The LCCs' very high load factors are achieved through every effective and, at times, aggressive pricing and inventory management. In Asia, the larger more successful LCCs such as Air Asia also operate at very high seat factors. But not all low-cost airlines are as successful in doing this, especially some of the smaller ones. In the United States, achieving such very high seat factors is not part of the LCCs' business model. In fact in 2007 neither Southwest's nor Air Tran's passenger load factors were higher than those of network carriers operating similar aircraft. In some cases they were a little lower. In Brazil, too, Gol, the low-cost airline, does not achieve particularly high seat factors. It seems that while very high seat factors are an integral feature of the European and perhaps Asian low-cost model, it is not crucial in other parts of the world.

6.6 Is the LCC's cost advantage sustainable?

The preceding analysis suggests that well-managed European low-cost operators, and these also tend to be the largest, have seat-km costs which may be 40 to 50 per cent lower than those of the European network carriers against whom they are competing. In the case of Ryanair the cost gap may well be even greater. Where the LCCs can achieve year-round passenger load factors which are 5 to 20 percentage points higher than their competitors, then the cost differential is magnified. In the United States, however, the unit cost differential is lower, around 20 to 30 per cent. Surprisingly, since US low-cost carriers do not operate at higher seat-factors, this cost advantage is not reinforced.

In South East Asia and South America, the unit cost gaps between the two models are high, 40–60 per cent, that is similar to those in Europe.

A key question in a period of market instability for the airline industry, and which began in 2008, is whether and the degree to which such cost differentials can be sustained in the longer term. This appears to depend on two counter-veiling trends: on the one hand, on the ability of network airlines to cut their own costs sufficiently to appreciably reduce the cost gap; and on the other, on the degree to which LCCs can prevent their lower unit costs drifting up as they become larger and more established.

As far as the larger European LCCs are concerned, their unit costs, excluding fuel, have not drifted up in recent years, despite their continuous and very rapid growth. In fact in the case of easyJet and, more especially, Ryanair, non-fuel unit costs declined in the period 2002 to 2007. During this period, easyJet cut its non-fuel unit costs each year on average by about 3.8 per cent while for Ryanair the annual decline averaged slightly higher at 4.3 per cent (UBS, 2007).

In the USA, Southwest has managed to keep its non-fuel unit costs more or less constant, even though labour costs rose as a result of new union agreements which have made its pilots some of the best paid in the country. Southwest's ability to maintain its unit cost advantage can be gauged from Table 6.4 (above). Despite the fact that both US Airways and United had filed for Chapter 11 and had been able to renegotiate many of their supplier contracts, including labour agreements, their costs per seat-km on their Boeing 737–300 in 2007 were still 20–30 per cent above those of Southwest. Even Continental's unit cost was 10 per cent higher, despite operating its aircraft on much longer sectors.

LCCs appear to be able to control or even reduce their non-fuel costs. The one risk is that increasing competition between such carriers may force them to adopt product and service improvements, in an effort to differentiate themselves. This may mean introducing some in-flight catering, as Air Berlin has done in Europe, seat assignment, longer seat pitch, which reduces seat capacity, or even in-flight entertainment as JetBlue has done in the USA. In Australia Virgin Blue introduced a premium cabin in 2008 with four-abreast seating instead of six-abreast and with in-flight catering. Attempts by LCCs to differentiate their products in such ways do run the risk of pushing up their unit costs.

Nevertheless, whether the gap in unit costs between the two sectors can be reduced depends very much on the network carriers' ability to cut their own costs. They have been under great pressure not only because of the worldwide downturn in the airline industry in the early 2000s but also because the low-cost revolution impacted network carriers in two ways. In many short-haul markets they have lost passengers and market share to the rapidly growing low-cost carriers. At the same time in most of these markets low LCC fares have forced the network airlines to change their pricing policies and to cut their own fares in order to remain competitive. This has reinforced the previously existing downward pressure on fares and undermined the economics of short-haul operations since costs were not falling as rapidly as fares. In fact, when after 2005 and again in late 2007, fuel prices began to rise sharply, network airlines' non-fuel unit costs were also rising. Network airlines in Europe and the USA were forced to act to cut costs, especially those airlines most affected by low-cost competition. They tried, where possible, to learn from the low-cost model. This strong pressure to reduce costs was reinforced at the end of 2008 and in 2009 as a result of falling demand and further downward pressure on average yields.

For network airlines, cost reduction has focused on four areas. First, on *labour costs*. By cutting staff numbers, by increasing productivity, for instance by reducing cabin crew numbers on-board aircraft, and by outsourcing more of their maintenance or their ground handling at non-base airports, network airlines have been able to save on labour costs. In the United States, four airlines, United, US Airways, Delta and Northwest, filed for bankruptcy protection and operated under Chapter 11 rules for various periods between 2004 and 2007. This enabled them not only to cut staff numbers by close to a third but also to reduce wage levels significantly, especially for flight and cabin crew. Other US airlines were also able to negotiate lower wages through threatening bankruptcy and filing for Chapter 11. Air Canada, using Canadian bankruptcy rules, did the same thing. Lower flight and cabin crew costs at US network airlines combined with rising flight crew salaries at Southwest to largely eliminate Southwest's previous advantage in flight crew labour costs. This may be a short-term phenomenon. Previous experience suggests that as the US majors return to profit, labour unions will agitate to recoup past wage reductions. This began to happen in 2007 as profits started being posted. But labour expectations were dampened as high fuel prices in early 2008 and then falling demand in late 2008 and 2009 undermined airlines' profitability. In Europe airlines were unable to cut wages or reduce staff numbers as dramatically as in the USA so they focused much more on improving labour productivity.

Second, *aircraft ownership costs* have been reduced by delaying the purchase of new aircraft, especially single-aisle aircraft for short-haul sectors; also by major efforts to push up aircraft utilisation on short-haul routes. Third, *maintenance costs* have been cut through fleet rationalisation, which removed older and smaller aircraft and reduced the number of aircraft types in the fleet and through reducing maintenance staff numbers and/or out-sourcing more maintenance functions.

Finally, the most significant cost savings achieved in recent years by network airlines have been in *passenger-related costs*, where they have adopted practices and procedures largely pioneered by the LCCs. These are in ground handling, in passenger services and, above all, in sales and distribution. They have increasingly focused on more direct sales, especially online, and have moved over to fully electronic ticketing. At the same time they have cut or removed travel agents' commissions and renegotiated their fees with the global distribution systems. Electronic tickets have removed the high cost of dealing with paper tickets and have also reduced airport handling costs by allowing self-service check-in. This reduces the space and ground staff needed at airports. In the air, many airlines on their short-haul sectors have reduced or largely eliminated in-flight catering or, like the LCCs, they now charge for it. Some have moved from a double- to a single-class cabin on parts of their network. Less catering and single-class cabins both allow for a reduction in cabin crew numbers.

Leaving aside the cost of fuel, there is little doubt that traditional European and US airlines have been able to significantly reduce their non-fuel unit costs since 2003 on short-haul operations. But have they done enough to eliminate or substantially reduce the cost gap with low-cost no frills airlines in the markets where they compete? The answer appears to be no, at least not by 2006. A March 2007 report by IATA compared the unit costs of US network carriers with those of Southwest, JetBlue and Air Tran (IATA, 2007). The costs per seat-km were adjusted to the average class length of US domestic markets of 1,400 kms and also to take account of the fact that the no-frills air-line pack 14 per cent more seats into the same aircraft. The report then finds that from a peak cost gap in 2001 when Southwest's unit costs were 41 per cent lower than compet-ing network airlines, the gap had been narrowed to 37 per cent by 2005 – marginal progress! An updating of this analysis suggests there was no significant subsequent reduction

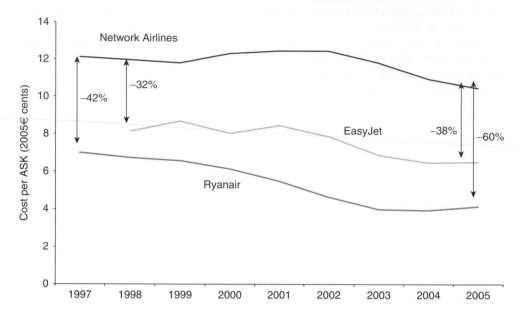

Figure 6.3 Comparing unit costs of European network and low-cost airlines, 1997–2005.
Source: IATA (2007).

in the unit cost gap. In fact, a 2008 comparative study of US airline unit costs (normalised for 1,000 mile sectors) showed that in the third quarter of 2008 Southwest's costs per available seat-mile were 33 per cent below Delta's, the best of the legacy carriers. So it was even lower when compared with that of the other legacy carriers. (Data from Oliver Wyman and Raymond James & Associates, Air Transport World, April 2009.) The cost gap has not been closing.

In Europe, too, the network carriers closed the cost gap in the three years up to 2005 but only marginally. Compared to the late 1990s the gap had actually widened. In 2005, Ryanair's unit costs per seat-km were 60 per cent below those of the network airlines while easyJet's were 38 per cent lower (Figure 6.3). The cost gap has closed only marginally since then.

Despite their efforts and partial success in reducing their own non-fuel costs, in the period since 2005 or 2006, network airlines have not significantly reduced the gap in unit costs between themselves and their low-cost competitors on short-haul operations for two reasons. First, because the LCCs have also been cutting their own non-fuel costs. Second, because, in essence, airlines operating a network business model are inevitably faced with higher costs because that model imposes certain costs. The model aims to provide connectivity allowing passengers to fly from anywhere to anywhere through a system of connected airport hubs. Since it requires high fare Business or First class passengers on its long-haul operations to ensure profitability, such passengers expect high service quality on short-haul connecting flights. This means that two-class cabins, some in-flight catering, lower seat densities and other costly product features have to be provided on short-haul sectors. The model also aims to ensure a high level of convenience and comfort for passengers. This means effective but costly processes for transferring passengers and baggage at the hubs. If incoming aircraft are delayed, departing aircraft have to be held back to pick up connecting passengers. In turn this requires good airport facilities and superior on-board and ground service. It also requires stand-by aircraft to deal with schedule disruption. Airports must be close to the markets they serve and easily accessible. They will tend to be larger airports and therefore prone to delay and congestion. In short, it is the complexity inherent in network operations that creates higher costs.

The network carriers can continue to do much to close the cost gap. They can increase seat density on some short-haul routes by going for a single-class cabin. They can further reduce in-flight catering standards. By switching all their sales to electronic tickets and by switching to automated machine check-in they can cut station and handling costs. They can negotiate to further reduce travel agents' commissions and fees paid to the GDS. Administrative and managerial staff numbers can be dramatically pruned as British Airways did in 2007 when it cut out 500 or so of its middle managers. Such actions will reduce the cost differential with low-cost airlines, but will not eliminate it. This is because the cost differential is linked to differences in the two models.

In the longer term, when competing on the same routes, well-run low-cost operators will continue to have seat-km costs 15 to 25 per cent lower than those of the most efficient network carriers, even after the latter have significantly reduced their own costs. If in particular markets, the LCCs are able to operate at higher seat factors then any cost differential will be further widened.

6.7   Revenue advantages

While low-cost no frills airlines enjoy substantial cost advantages which arise from the characteristics of the low-cost model, they also benefit from more limited advantages on the revenue side.

The first of these relates to revenue management. To break even at their very low average fares, low-cost carriers need to achieve very high load factors year round. This is difficult when offering relatively high daily frequencies on a scheduled basis. Daily and seasonal variations in demand mean that passenger load factors can fluctuate. Therefore low-cost carriers, like other scheduled carriers, need to practise yield management to try to maximise the revenue generated per flight. This is easier for them than for network carriers because low-cost airlines, with rare exceptions, only sell point-to-point single sector tickets. As a result they do not face yield assessment problems arising from multi-sector tickets, from having two or more cabin classes and from tickets sold in a wide range of different currencies and at different values. Revenue management with multi-sector fares paid in different and at times fluctuating currencies pose difficult problems for network carriers. Because of their more limited geographical spread, most low-cost carriers in Europe or North America tend to sell the bulk of their tickets in only one or two currencies. Southwest sells virtually all its inventory in US dollars. In easyJet's case in 2007, 92 per cent of its sales were in sterling or euros. Simpler fare structures make for simpler and more effective revenue management.

Because of the complexities of their fare structures, network carriers need to use up to 24 or more different booking classes in their revenue management systems. These are used to control the number of seats sold at different fares so as to maximise the revenue earned on each flight. Low-cost carriers can generally manage with 12 or less to reflect the separate fares they may offer on any individual flight as the departure date approaches. This makes effective yield management easier and cheaper to implement. Whereas network carriers have traditionally offered the same seat on a particular flight, at various different fares with different conditions attached and often as parts of various multi-sector trips, on most LCC flights there is in general only one ticket price available at any one time for each flight. Less frequently there may be two or three fares on offer, as is the case with Southwest or Air Berlin. Nevertheless, the low-cost airlines' fare structure remains simpler, making revenue management easier and more effective to implement.

The pricing strategy of both Ryanair and easyJet is simple. They start selling the cheapest advertised lead-in fares when bookings for flights open and then their booking system automatically moves to higher fares which are triggered as seats sold at each fare level for any particular flight pass certain pre-planned numbers or as the departure date approaches. At any one time there is only one fare available for purchase on each flight, though it will often vary between flights on the same route to reflect differences in demand levels between times of the day or week. During known or anticipated periods of high demand the early lead-in fares may start at a high level or may be offered only for a few seats. Conversely if sales are slow, an existing low fare may be offered for longer than previously planned or occasionally fares may even be reduced as the departure date approaches. The overall aim is to maximise the revenue per flight. In this process, effective yield management ensures that average yield per passenger on most flights is well above the level of the lowest fare. (See Section 11.8 for more details on LCC pricing.)

A further advantage of LCCs is that they do not suffer yield dilution from multi-sector tickets. For instance, on a sector such as London (Luton) to Amsterdam easyJet collects the full fare at which each ticket has been sold. But KLM on its flights from London (Heathrow) will be carrying a significant proportion of passengers transferring to a wide range of destinations on other KLM flights at Schiphol or even to another airline. Because of the way multi-sector tickets are pro-rated for each sector flown, KLM may receive much less per transfer passenger on the London–Amsterdam sector than it collects from a local point-to-point passenger. Moreover, these connecting passengers may have paid their fares in a variety of different currencies. Such revenue dilution can significantly reduce the average yield per passenger on many short-haul sectors, serving major hubs. Low-cost airlines do not face such revenue dilution. On the other hand, by offering Business Class the conventional airlines can generate some very high yields.

Another revenue advantage enjoyed by low-cost airlines is that where they sell direct to the public without using agents, passengers must pay by credit card when they make the booking. They cannot make a reservation without paying. This means that airlines such as easyJet, who sell only direct, generate all their cash revenue before flights are made. This contrasts with their conventional competitors who, selling through various agencies worldwide, may not receive all the payments for individual flights until some months after the departure date. This difference facilitates the low-cost airlines' cash flow and cash management and may enable them to generate substantial interest income from their cash deposits. This is an advantage also enjoyed by charter airlines.

A further advantage enjoyed by many LCCs is that bookings once made and paid for cannot be changed, except in some cases on payment of a surcharge, and tickets normally cannot be refunded. This means that there are very few 'no shows' on departure. When they do occur, the airline still collects the revenue from the ticket since an unused reservation cannot be changed or re-used subsequently. While some fares on network carriers have some refund or change conditions many do not.

Finally, low-cost airlines have always made major efforts to generate additional or so-called 'ancillary' revenues from non-ticket sources in order to supplement the low fares they were charging. With no free on-board catering, LCCs have been able to generate significant revenues from the on-board sale of food and beverages on which there is a high profit margin. Since most sales were direct through the LCCs website or call centre they had to be paid by credit cards and the LCCs charged fees for their use. Low-cost carriers also make a major effort to design their websites to facilitate the sale of additional products and services such as hotel and car hire bookings and travel insurance. They are then paid commission by the providers of these services. Some, like Ryanair, also sell advertising space on their websites or provide links to other websites for which they get a fee. Traditional airlines have also done much of this but hitherto have treated ancillary revenues as of marginal importance whereas for LCCs they have been central to their economic model.

As fuel prices rose sharply from 2004 onwards, network carriers responded by imposing fuel surcharges on the price of tickets. In Europe LCCs did not follow suit but tried to cover the cost increases by reducing their non-fuel costs and by using their yield management systems to try and maintain or even increase average fares. But in 2006 and 2007 further fuel price increases pushed the LCCs to introduce a variety of new sources of ancillary revenue. In Europe most began to charge for any checked-in baggage which had previously been carried free of charge up to a certain weight. For example, easyJet introduced a £2.00 ($4.00) per bag charge in October 2007 and within three months had doubled it. This airline also in 2007 introduced a speedy boarding charge for those passengers wishing to board their aircraft first and chose their preferred seat since there was no prior seat allocation.

In its financial year to end of September 2007, easyJet generated 9.5 per cent of its total income from ancillary revenue that is non-ticket sources. But the baggage charge introduced in October 2007 and increased revenues from other fees were expected to increase this figure to around 14 per cent in 2008. For Ryanair the share of non-ticket or ancillary revenues in its financial year 2006–7 was higher at around 16 per cent of total revenue. In profit terms the contribution of ancillary revenues was even greater, since these revenue sources have high profit margins.

US low-cost airlines have been slow to see the potential for generating ancillary revenues. The one exception was the small Las Vegas-based Allegiant Air, whose ancillary revenues per passenger have been close to those of Ryanair or easyJet (*Airline Business*, May 2007). The others, including Southwest, only began waking up to the potential in 2007. In November 2007, Southwest launched 'Business Select' which offers early boarding, a free cocktail and additional frequent flyer points at an additional cost of $10 to $30 each way depending on the route. Southwest claimed this would raise additional revenue of $100 million each year (Nuutinen, 2008). At about the same time, the airline also announced it was improving its website technology in order to be able to provide for hotel bookings, car hire and other sources of ancillary revenue.

While some low-cost carriers have been successful in generating revenue from ancillary sources, in general they do not carry freight so they forfeit this revenue source which some network carriers may enjoy. But they also escape any freight-related costs. In practice though, in Europe and the North America short-haul freight volumes are limited as they have to compete with road trucking and the integrators. Even if shipped by network carriers, much short-haul freight will often be trucked by the airline.

The revenue advantages enjoyed by LCCs hitherto can be eroded more easily by the network carriers than can their cost advantages. This has been happening since about 2005. Several network carriers, especially airlines facing the most competition from the low-cost sector, have begun to adopt many of the pricing and ancillary revenue practices of their competitors. For example, Aer Lingus while publishing very low up front fares on its website for intra-European markets, where it competes head on with Ryanair, then has a number of optional add-on charges. In 2008 on London–Dublin flights these included a high charge of £9 for checked-in baggage in each direction, £10 in each direction for a seat reservation in the two wider emergency exit rows, £5 each way for a seat in the first five rows or £2 for a pre-assigned seat anywhere else or no charge for getting a seat allocation on check in. There was also a ticket-handling charge of £4 even for those booking online. Air Canada is another airline that has adopted a similar strategy of complex charges and add-on fees, which generate substantial additional revenue (see Tables 11.4–11.5 below). Other network airlines, particularly in the United States and to a lesser extent in Europe, started introducing a variety of ancillary charges in 2008. So-called 'à la carte' pricing included charges for more than one item of baggage, for call centre as opposed to online bookings, for drinks in Economy class and so on. This practice will undoubtedly spread.

In conclusion, the cost advantages enjoyed by low-cost carriers are reinforced by more limited advantages on the revenue side. This is especially true for those airlines selling their entire inventory directly by telephone or the internet. These benefits are somewhat diluted for those low-cost airlines that continue to use travel agents as well.

6.8   Future trends

The unit cost gap between network and low-cost airlines may be reduced, but a marked gap will remain. This, combined with aggressive low-fare pricing, will ensure that LCCs around the world will grow rapidly and capture a growing share of short-haul domestic and international markets at the expense of network airlines. The less-well-managed network carriers may lose a large part of their short-haul domestic and international markets and be forced to pull out of many short-haul operations. Many short-haul routes will be increasingly dominated by low-cost carriers as already happens in the United States. Southwest is the largest carrier in over 90 of the top 100 routes it operates. Ryanair or easyJet are the dominant carriers on many of the routes they serve from London or other UK points. They have forced European network airlines out of many important markets. For example, Air France has long abandoned its flights from Bordeaux, Toulouse or Marseilles to London.

As a result of their lower costs and continued growth, the better LCCs are likely to achieve high profit margins. But there are too many smaller LCCs and many more new-entrant LCCs are likely to emerge as more markets are liberalised. Most of the smaller and newer LCCs are unlikely to be financially successful. The survivors will be the larger and older LCCs who enjoy what economists call 'first mover' advantage and have widespread brand recognition within the regions they operate. They also have the cash reserves and liquidity to see them through the economic downturn which started late in 2008, especially if this proves to be prolonged. In each region of the world there will be consolidation around the big players, such as Southwest, Ryanair, easyJet or Air Asia, as most of the smaller LCCs collapse or are taken over by the former.

But there are tough times ahead for all low-cost airlines, not only because of external factors, such as the financial crisis, which started in 2008, or any future spike in fuel prices, but also as a result of developments within the airline industry. First, the continued expansion of the existing large LCCs will inevitably mean that increasingly, on many short-haul routes, they will be competing not only against network carriers but also face-to-face against other large and powerful LCCs. Second, in several markets including Europe, South East Asia and India there are too many new LCCs flooding the market with capacity and adversely affecting yields. These will create market instability until they collapse or are merged with larger carriers. Third, as mentioned earlier, increasing competition between LCCs and more effective pricing strategies by network airlines may induce some LCCs to try to differentiate their products by offering one or more service improvements. These may prove costly and may erode some of the LCCs' unit cost advantage and in turn their price competitiveness. Finally, in the period 2007 to 2009 many LCCs, especially in Europe, have grown ancillary revenues from baggage and other charges very rapidly. The additional income generated has enabled them to maintain very low fares, even at times of high fuel prices. There must be some doubt as to whether the ancillary revenues per passenger can continue to increase or whether they will soon reach a level beyond which it becomes impossible to generate more additional revenue in this way from each passenger. If that happens, LCCs will become more dependent again on ticket revenue and on low fare pricing strategies.

7 The economics of passenger charters

Charter airlines are the original low-cost airlines . . . they must not be ignored.
(Robert Parker-Eaton, Deputy Managing Director,
Britannia Airways, November 2000)

7.1 Charters – the first low-cost model

Charter or non-scheduled airlines had been operating low-cost and low fare passenger services very successfully in some parts of the world long before the emergence of the so-called low-cost airlines. Like the latter they came into being in response to a particular regulatory environment prevailing in the 1960s and 1970s. During those two decades they expanded very rapidly especially on holiday routes between Northern and Mediterranean Europe, on trans-Atlantic routes and later on some other routes such as North America to the Caribbean. In other regions of the world such as Asia or South America passenger charters were less developed.

The global significance of passenger charters within the air transport industry can be gauged from the fact that in the mid-2000s around 11–12 per cent of the world's international passenger traffic, measured in passenger-kms, was being carried on charter flights. Interestingly, a marked proportion, about one third, of these charters was being operated by scheduled network airlines such as Austrian, Finnair or Tunis Air.

The early success and continued growth of passenger charters on European holiday routes and on the North Atlantic in the 1960s and 1970s was due primarily to two factors. First, on the ability of charter flights to circumvent both the tight bilateral regulations relating to scheduled flights and also the IATA controls on air fares. The second factor was the ability of charter airlines to offer significantly lower fares than the scheduled network carriers, because of their lower unit costs, and thereby attract a growing number of passengers. (For early regulations of passenger charters see Chapter 2, Section 2.8.) The economics of the charter model enabled charter operators to sell seats on particular holiday routes to tour operators or travel agents at 40 to 70 per cent lower than the cheapest scheduled fare. It was European charter airlines' ability to offer such low seat costs which enabled them by the mid-1990s and before the emergence of low-cost carriers to capture over 30 per cent of all international passenger traffic within the European Union. At that time, charters were dominant on most holiday routes between Northern Europe and the Mediterranean. On very many such routes, for instance those between the UK or Germany to the Greek Islands or to Turkish resorts such an Antalya or Dalaman, charter airlines were the only operators. The mid-1990s saw the peak penetration of charters in European short-haul international markets. Then the rapid growth of low-cost carriers, especially in the early 2000s, resulted in a relative decline of charters in Europe who were forced to adapt and change in order to meet the new competitive pressures. Yet still in 2008 in the United Kingdom, despite the marked inroads of low-cost carriers, charter airlines were generating 27.5 per cent of all passenger-kms produced by UK airlines, though it is true that this figure had been as high as 40 per cent or more 20 years earlier (CAA, 2009a). In several other countries in Northern Europe, such as Germany or Denmark, charters in 2007 or 2008 were still generating a quarter or more of the total intra-European passenger traffic when measured in passenger-kms.

On the North Atlantic the peak year for charter traffic penetration was 1977 when almost a third of trans-Atlantic passengers travelled on charters. Then after 1978 this market collapsed as several new entrants and lower fare scheduled airlines began operating following the liberalisation of entry regulations and fare controls on many routes. Charter flights declined in number but subsequently picked up again by focusing on many new holiday destinations such as Florida or the Caribbean islands. Today less than 5 per cent of passengers across the Atlantic are on charter flights, nevertheless this remains an important market for charters. Another important market is that from Canada or the North Eastern seaboard of the United States to Florida and the Caribbean.

A large niche charter market is that catering for the transfer of millions of pilgrims each year from countries with Muslim populations to Saudi Arabia during the Haj season. This is served both by charter airlines and by flights chartered from scheduled network carriers. In other parts of the world the charter market is less significant and is often linked to specific events such as festivals or sports fixtures. Also outside Europe and North America, a higher proportion of the charter flights in other markets are operated by the conventional scheduled airlines.

Another indicator of the continued importance of charter airlines is their relative size when compared to network or low-cost carriers. In Europe, where charters have been most developed, four of Europe's 15 largest airlines in 2006 in terms of passenger-kms were charter groups or carriers while only two were the newer low-cost airlines, Ryanair and easyJet. As a result of consolidation within the charter sector, in the early 2000s, the Tui and Thomas Cook groups, each owning several airlines, were significantly larger, in terms of passenger-kms, than many of the middle-ranking network carriers such as SAS, Swiss Airlines, Air Portugal or Bmi. Moreover, during 2007 both these charter groups moved to grow even larger through further acquisitions. Tui took over My Travel, the third largest charter airline, in September 2007 while in the same year Thomas Cook moved to acquire First Choice Airways, the fourth largest European charter carrier. In North America, charter airlines have faced strong competitive pressures from low-cost airlines for 15–20 years longer than in Europe. As a result, while there were several pure charter airlines in North America, of which the largest in 2007 were the Canadian airline Air Transat and the US-based World Airways and Omni Air Express, these are generally much smaller than their European counterparts. Though there are specialist passenger charter airlines in many parts of the world, large charter airlines today appear to be very much a European phenomenon, but one which, as discussed later, is having to respond to the challenge of the low-cost revolution. This has meant making many changes to the traditional charter business model.

7.2   The nature of the charter product

Two types of charter flights have emerged, namely *ad hoc* charters, that is, one-off flights where aircraft are chartered for a specific event such as a sports fixture, a religious festival or a sales promotion and 'series charters'. The latter are charters involving multiple flights which may be on behalf of tour operators, oil companies, the military or others requiring the regular systematic transfer of people. They normally have a set timetable and are operated as a regular series of flights though the series may be purely seasonal or of limited duration.

Traditionally, within the Europe–Mediterranean area, which is the world's largest charter market, the vast majority of series charter flights have been inclusive tour charters (ITCs). These are where the whole of an aircraft is chartered by one or more tour operators who combine the round-trip seats with hotel or other accommodation into 'package' holidays. The passenger buys a holiday package from a travel agent or tour operator at a single price and is unaware of the cost of travel within that total price. Some charter packages may involve minimal accommodation or may include car hire, boat hire, cruises, camping or other services in addition to or instead of hotel accommodation. A trend that emerged during the 1990s was the growth of self-catering inclusive tours, where the package does not include the hotel and meals but provides only for accommodation in houses or apartments. By 2006 one in five UK residents traveling on ITC packages were buying self-catering holidays. Since inclusive tour packages involved the provision by the tour operator of hotel, self-catering or other accommodation, which had to be tightly coordinated with aircraft seats, such holiday packages were mostly inflexible in terms of duration and departure days. People were mostly offered holidays of fixed duration, usually of just one or two weeks and they normally had to fly out and back on the same day of the week.

The majority of passengers on holiday charter flights have been on inclusive tours. In fact in 2006 about 13.5 million UK residents took inclusive tour holidays. Though about 15–20 per cent of these would have bought packages on traditional scheduled flights, around 11 million will have flown on charters. But in recent years inclusive tour package holidays have been declining in relative importance because travellers are increasingly demanding greater flexibility and choice when planning their holidays.

In order to fill up spare seats not booked by the tour operators who had chartered the flights, charter airlines introduced the innovation of selling such seats on a 'seat-only' basis without any holiday package or accommodation being attached. Tour operators also did this if they had unsold seats. This started in the 1980s but became more widespread after the 1993 Third Package of European Aviation liberalisation removed all restrictions on intra-EU charter flights. As a result seat-only sales, made either directly by the airline or through the tour-operator(s) who have chartered the flights, have become an important element of charter economics. They enable the charter airlines to push up their load factors and their revenues. The fares for seat-only tickets are generally very low but by generating additional traffic they have permitted charter airlines to fly larger and more economic aircraft on routes or at times when the demand for all-inclusive tour packages could not justify the larger aircraft. On some flights, especially out of Germany, seat-only sales may take up to 30 per cent or more of an aircraft's capacity. A good example of how the European charter market works can be seen in the way Condor, one of Europe's largest charter airlines and part of the Thomas Cook group, was selling its capacity in 2007. About 40 per cent of seats would be sold as holiday packages through the Thomas Cook group, another 36 per cent would be direct seat-only sale with no add-ons and the balance of around 24 per cent would be pre-sold to other smaller tour operators who were not part of the Thomas Cook group (Aviation Strategy, Issue No. 122, December 2007).

Such was the success of seat-only sales, that German charter airlines have re-designated their charter flights out of Germany as 'scheduled' flights, so they would appear in timetables and computer reservations systems. This facilitates seat-only sales but erodes the distinction between schedules and charters. Some charter airlines in the UK and elsewhere have followed suit more recently.

Another charter trend which emerged in Europe in the 1990s was a move away from dependence on short- or medium-haul markets between Northern Europe and the Mediterranean towards long-haul leisure markets previously the preserve of scheduled airlines. There has been above average growth in charter flights from Europe to Florida, the Caribbean, the Gulf and Indian Ocean destinations such as Sri Lanka and the Maldives. This change resulted in part from growing consumer demand for cheap access to new and more distant destinations and in part from the introduction of smaller long-haul twin jet aircraft with low operating costs. The use of Boeing 757–200 and Boeing 767–300 and more recently Airbus A330 aircraft has made the operation of long-haul charters more viable. Moreover, these aircraft could also be flown to denser Mediterranean resorts in summer months. For the airlines this change has resulted in a better balance of long- and short-haul markets. More importantly, the longer haul routes tend to peak in the European winter and can be used to generate cash flow in what, for charter carriers, is the low season. Long-haul charters have generally developed on routes where scheduled services cannot meet the highly seasonal demand for leisure travel.

Despite the spread of seat-only sales there are in essence two key features which distinguish most charter services from scheduled flights in Europe and in other parts of the world too. The first is that the majority of passengers do not buy a seat direct from the airline as scheduled passengers can do since most seats are sold as part of a holiday package. The whole package is bought through an intermediary such as a tour operator, travel agent, student union and so on. This distinction may be cosmetic rather than real, since in many cases the intermediary selling agent may be owned by the same parent company as the charter airline. Generally only a limited proportion of the seats will be available for direct sale to the public. On some flights there may be none at all. The second distinguishing feature is that flights are put on by the charter airlines not in the hope of generating demand from individual travellers but in response to specific advance contracts from tour operators. It is the latter and not the charter airlines themselves who determine the routes and frequencies to be served. This is true even when charter flights have been re-designated as scheduled.

7.3   Adapting to a changing market

Total charter traffic in Europe and North America reached a peak in the mid- to late 1990s and has not grown significantly since then, except in the new member states of the European Union that is in central and Eastern Europe. In some markets, such as out of the UK, charter traffic has actually declined in recent years. As a result, charters' relative market share of total passenger traffic has declined. At the same time there has been in recent years a gradual shift away from inclusive tour charters to the use of charters for more independent-type holidays. A number of factors have contributed to the relative decline in charters in both Europe and North America. First, increasing use of internet booking has enabled consumers to make simple price comparisons and also to make hotel, car hire or other reservations independently of their travel arrangements. Increasingly holidaymakers have rejected the inflexibility of the 7- or 14-day 'one-size-fits-all' holiday

Table 7.1 Impact of low-cost competition on charter traffic from London airports, 2000–5

Destination	Charter passengers (000s)		
	2000	*2005*	*Change %*
Served by no-frills and charter carriers			
Palma de Mallorca (Spain)	969	632	−35
Malaga (Spain)	802	288	−64
Mahon (Spain)	486	287	−41
Faro (Portugal)	618	274	−56
Ibiza (Spain)	437	222	−49
Alicante (Spain)	564	213	−62
Total	3,876	1,916	−51
Served only by charters			
Tenerife (Canaries)	916	682	−26
Arrecife (Canaries)	487	464	−5
Dalaman (Turkey)	227	441	+95
Paphos (Cyprus)	341	336	−1
Las Palmas (Canaries)	520	320	−38
Corfu (Greece)	372	293	−21
Fuerteventura (Canaries)	260	249	−4
Heraklion (Greece)	281	247	−12
Zakinthos (Greece)	216	206	−5
Total	3,619	3,239	−11

packages offered on charter inclusive tour packages. This demand for greater flexibility has been reinforced in Europe by the tendency for people to take more, shorter 3–5-day breaks instead of, or in addition to, the traditional two-week summer holiday and it was facilitated by the spread of internet selling. Second, the rapid growth of low-cost low fare airlines in Europe, more especially since about 2000, has undermined charter airlines' market base and reinforced the trend to more independent and self-organised holidays.

A 2006 study by the UK's Civil Aviation Authority showed the devastating impact of the low-cost challenge on charter routes from London (CAA, 2006). On those routes where charters competed head-on with low-cost carriers they lost around half of their traffic, 51 per cent or nearly 2 million passengers, in the five years between 2000 and 2005 (top half of Table 7.1). Surprisingly, even on routes, generally longer routes, where there was no low-cost competition, charters lost around 10 per cent of their passengers during this five-year period (bottom half of Table 7.1). The implication is clear. The low fares, the new destinations served and the flexibility offered by low-cost carriers has been diverting traditional charter passengers to the low-cost sector. This was so even in markets not served by low-cost carriers.

The impact of charging consumer tastes and increased consumer access to internet selling combined with an explosion of low-cost airlines created great instability for European charter airlines and their parent travel companies in the mid-2000s. Many posted losses for a year or more and any profits tended to be marginal. This was also a period of instability for North American charter carriers too. In response to their worsening market environment charter companies took a number of actions.

First, some set out to compete more directly with their low-cost competitors by offering more capacity for seat-only sales on those European sectors where low-cost competition was most severe. Some went further and launched their own low-cost airline. For example, in the UK Britannia Airways, part of the TUI Group, launched Thomsonfly, while in Germany charter carrier Hapag-Lloyd launched Hapag-Lloyd Express and Air Berlin switched many of its charter flights into low-cost scheduled operation and turned itself into a low-cost airline. In essence the charter carriers were accepting the fact that the European short-haul charter market based on the traditional inclusive tour holiday package could not survive except in some very dense markets such as those from Germany or the UK to Palma or to major Spanish destinations, on routes longer than three to three-and-a-half hours, or on very seasonal or thin markets which the low-cost carriers did not wish to attack. Monarch, the largest charter airline not linked to either of the two major groups, also switched away from charter flights so that by 2008 around 60 per cent of its capacity was being operated as scheduled low-cost flights. On the trans-Atlantic, Zoom Airlines, which had initially started as a charter airline serving tour operators, became a low-cost long-haul operator, but collapsed in summer 2008.

Second, charter airlines and more especially their parent holiday companies realised that they had to match the flexibility demanded by their customers and clearly offered by their low-cost competitors. So they 'unbundled' their airline product. Passengers were increasingly given many more options whether booking an inclusive holiday or just a seat-only. They were offered greater flexibility on the length of their holiday package, on their choice of hotels, and were also given the ability to split their stay between hotels. They could buy one-way seat-only tickets. They could choose seats with longer legroom, choose different types of in-flight meals in advance or get access to airport lounges, etc. – all at an additional cost. 'Dynamic packaging' is now the key to selling seats or holidays on charter flights. It allows consumers to bolt together a more or less complex and costly travel package based on their own choices.

Third, the earlier trend towards more distant longer-haul charter destinations has been strongly reinforced. More and more of the charter capacity both in Europe and North America is now offered to long-haul destinations, that is on sectors beyond 5 hours or so. For European charters these destinations include resorts in the Red Sea, East Africa, the Indian Ocean, South East Asia, Florida and the East coast of the United States, and to the Caribbean islands and Central America. Capacity is offered largely in conjunction with holiday packages but in many cases also on a seat-only basis. Charters are becoming the long-haul low-cost model.

The final response of the holiday travel companies and their associated charter airlines, when faced with so much uncertainty and market instability in the mid-2000s, was to undertake a new round of mergers and consolidation within their market sector.

7.4   Vertical integration – horizontal consolidation

Consolidation is not new in this sector of the travel industry. The European charter industry has long been characterised by a strong tendency towards *vertical integration* between travel companies or tour operators and charter airlines and in some cases with hotels or hotel groups as well. This is in marked contrast to the United States where antitrust regulations largely prevented this. Such vertical integration was inevitable since it was easier for a single company or organisation to order the charter seats required and tie them up with the hotel beds in each of many holiday destinations. If the same travel company owned or had long-term leases for large numbers of hotel beds or beds on cruise ships then the process of putting together holiday packages was facilitated. The travel companies also had a large number of retail travel agencies in key high street locations through which they could sell their holiday packages. Most of the larger tour operators in the major originating countries owned several travel agencies, often trading under different brand names as well as one or more charter airlines. Frequently, they also bought seats on airlines that were not their own. An example was the Thomson Travel Group. In the late 1990s it owned Britannia Airways, the UK's largest charter airline and several travel agencies or tour operating companies such as Lunn Poly, Pegasus, Sibbald Travel and others it had bought over time. In Germany and other major charter markets one found similar vertical integration within the leisure travel sector. It was generally the smaller charter airlines which were not vertically integrated through ownership. This was also true of those charter airlines based in the holiday destination countries. Though even these charter airlines were often dependent on and closely allied to one or more major tour operating companies.

An attempt in the summer of 1999 by Airtours to merge with First Choice, both tour companies operating their own aircraft, was turned down by the European Commission. The Commission felt that the combined group would be in a monopolistic position in the UK's short-haul leisure market, controlling 37 per cent of this market. If further integration and consolidation at the national level was likely to fall foul of the European Commission then the only way that the large leisure travel companies could expand was through cross-border acquisitions. There was a spate of these in Europe in 1999 and 2000. This was the first phase of *horizontal consolidation* in Europe. The major tour operating companies were hoping through mergers and acquisitions to achieve economies of scale in distribution, in the provision of charter flights and in the buying of hotel beds. Greater control of the various European markets would also enable them to squeeze out over-capacity and thereby push up the charter rates. Overcapacity seems to be endemic to the package holiday industry as the large operators fight for market share by offering more capacity.

While most of the larger charter airlines with linked tour operators were British, the drive for consolidation was driven by two large German companies, Preussag and C & N Touristic, which was then 50 per cent owned by Lufthansa. By early 2001 Preussag, a German conglomerate not previously heavily involved in tourism, had bought control of TUI, Germany's largest travel agent, and of the Thomson Travel Group in the UK. It also had a 34 per cent stake in the French travel company Nouvelles Frontières. Through these three travel companies, it also controlled three charter airlines, Hapag-Lloyd, Britannia and Corsair. Cross-border consolidation was also being undertaken by C & N Touristic. Towards the end of 2000, C & N acquired Thomas Cook, the UK's second largest tour operator. In the process it took over Thomas Cook's charter airline JMC, which was later renamed Thomas Cook Airlines. C & N also changed its own name to Thomas Cook. The European leisure travel industry was reflecting the trend towards consolidation and internationalisation in other sectors of industry.

Despite these changes the European charter industry did not grow very much in the years that followed. As pointed out earlier, the industry was adversely affected both by changing consumer tastes and more especially by the flexibility, low prices and new destinations offered by the low-cost sector. Stagnant or, in some markets, falling demand, together with mixed financial results for many tour operators and charter airlines, led to a second phase of horizontal consolidation in the period 2006 to 2008.

The economic drivers for this second phase of horizontal consolidation were similar to those of the earlier first phase. Large travel companies could see the need to rationalise their airline and hotel operations in order both to take capacity out of the market and to reduce competition between the major players. The aim was to push up average revenues per seat. At the same time by bringing together two or more travel companies and airlines one could also achieve significant cost synergies, especially as some of the larger travel companies had become bloated with too many retail outlets, and were over-staffed. Cost economies would also come from bulk buying of services, hotel beds, fuel and so on. Once again it was the large German companies that led the consolidation process.

The first to move was Thomas Cook, then Europe's second largest leisure group, which in February 2007 announced a merger with UK-based My Travel, the third largest leisure company. My Travel had almost collapsed in 2003 and was keen to join up with another party. The new Thomas Cook Group (TCG), which was listed on the London Stock Exchange in mid–2007, would operate a fleet of around 90 aircraft. The merger brought together Thomas Cook Airlines, My Travel Airways and Condor Flugdienst. In February 2009 Lufthansa sold its remaining minority stake in Condor to the Thomas Cook Group. TCG's UK airlines would continue to focus on providing most of the charter capacity for inclusive tour packages for the parent company. On the cost side, TCG claimed that cost savings arising from the merger with My Travel could be as much as $200 million a year. This would arise from closing some offices, substantial staff cuts and buying synergies and reduced distribution costs.

In September 2007, the European Commission approved the merger of TUI, by far the largest leisure group in Europe in terms of revenue, with First Choice, the fourth largest. This brought together seven airlines, with a combined fleet of around 140 aircraft, including Thomsonfly, TUIfly and First Choice Airways. Interestingly the TUI group in 2008 had 23 of the new Boeing 787 Dreamliner aircraft on order, emphasising the continued trend to longer-haul charter destinations.

The third force driving horizontal consolidation was Air Berlin. But here consolidation took a different form. Both TUI and Thomas Cook brought together travel companies and their associated charter airlines to create even larger leisure groups. Air Berlin's aggressive acquisition strategy aimed at creating a large hybrid airline group spanning traditional scheduled, low-cost and charter operations and focusing on both the leisure and business markets. Air Berlin had started life as a charter airline in 1978. In 1998 it introduced daily scheduled flights from 12 German airports to Palma in Mallorca and four years later launched what were in effect low-cost, scheduled services to major cities in Europe. But it continued operating charters for tour operators as well. In August 2006, using funds generated from its flotation on the German stock exchange earlier that year, Air Berlin bought dba, a Munich-based airline operating traditional and largely domestic scheduled services, which were later converted into a low-cost operation. Six months later, in March 2007, it bought LTU, then Germany's third largest charter airline. Though many of LTU's services were designated as scheduled flights, they were essentially catering for the leisure market with a high proportion of the seat capacity being packaged into inclusive tour holidays. In between Air Berlin had also acquired Belair, a small Swiss charter airline.

All this has made Air Berlin a true hybrid apparently operating all airline models – network, low-cost and charter – with a somewhat confused brand image or images. In the first half of 2007, 37 per cent of Air Berlin's flight revenues came from tour operator sales, mainly on charter flights, while 63 per cent were generated by scheduled services, which were a mix of low-cost and network airline operations (Johnson, 2007). Integrating and ration-alising the LTU and Air Berlin networks and operations during 2008 proved challenging. But there was more to come. In September 2007, Air Berlin announced it would be buying Condor, Germany's largest charter airline, from the Thomas Cook Group. The German competition authority signalled some concern and the deal collapsed. By 2008 Air Berlin with LTU had become the fourth largest European airline group in terms of available seat-kilometres. Only Air France/KLM, Lufthansa and BA were larger. Then in March 2009, TUI bought 19.9 per cent of Air Berlin's shares, while the latter bought an equivalent share in TUIfly, which is TUI's low-cost operation, which would henceforth be operated as part of Air Berlin's scheduled low-cost network.

Air Berlin epitomises the gradual blurring of distinctions between the three airline business models since it seems to have operated elements of all three in some form at the same time.

7.5   Cost advantages of charter operations

To appreciate the competitive advantages of the charter model one must analyse the cost and/or revenue advantages it can offer when compared to the traditional scheduled net-work model. But such comparisons have become more difficult in recent years as both models have mutated and changed in response to the challenge of the low-cost carriers. In the charter sector the most significant changes have been the spread of seat-only sales onto flights and routes which were previously wholly dominated by inclusive holiday packages and also the launch by some charter airlines of low-cost subsidiaries following the low-cost model. True charter flights in Europe, on the North Atlantic and other markets, can be defined by certain key characteristics. The flights are highly seasonal with very marked peaks and troughs and the bulk of the seats, and in many cases all the seats, are being packaged into holidays or sold through tour operators and travel companies who charter the flights and determine the routes and frequencies to be flown. Some of the capacity on certain routes may be sold on a seat-only basis, but it will be generally a third or less of the seats available.

It is the costs of these 'true' charter flights that need to be analysed and compared with those of scheduled network carriers. To eliminate the effect of differing aircraft types and stage lengths, any cost comparison should assume the use of similar aircraft on the same route or serving the same markets. Routes from the London area to Mediterranean points such as Barcelona, a two-hour sector, would provide a suitable example since in 2008 Airbus A320 aircraft were being flown by both charter and scheduled network airlines on this route.

7.5.1   *Direct operating costs*

Flight operations, that is flight and cabin crew costs, fuel and airport and en-route charges, insurance and depreciation, are the largest single element of direct costs. Here charter operators may enjoy some limited advantages.

As far as *flight crew* costs are concerned, charter flight crews, in the past, did receive lower salaries than those in scheduled airlines. However, the shortage of pilots in recent years has pushed up the salaries of charter pilots in Europe. There is now little difference in most cases in the salary levels of pilots flying the same aircraft whether on charter or scheduled services. This is so unless the charter airline is based in a destination country such as Turkey or Cyprus, where pilot salaries may be appreciably lower in the charter sector.

On the other hand charter airlines may have lower *cabin crew costs*. They will try to have fewer cabin staff than a scheduled airline would have in the same aircraft type, while providing the statutory minimum required for safety. While a charter airline may offer a premium service in the front of the cabin, it is unlikely to carry the extra staff that a scheduled airline would have to cater for its Business class. Moreover, a higher proportion of the cabin staff will be seasonally employed and will not be a cost burden for the rest of the year. Some charter airlines employ up to half of their staff for a six-month peak season only. Salary differentials are more marked in the case of cabin attendants than pilots. For instance, in 2007 British Airways was spending on average Sterling £28,700 per annum respectively on each cabin attendant. Yet the average cost per attendant for charter airlines First Choice was £18,400, for Monarch it was £16,100 and for Thomas Cook £18,200 (CAA, 2009a). This is possible because there is no shortage in the supply of new cabin staff, and they are easy and cheap to train. On short-haul sectors charter airlines also save money by scheduling crew rotations to avoid night stops for crew outside of their home country, thus eliminating crew overnight expenses. For instance, British Airways night stops crews and aircraft in Barcelona or other European points to provide early morning departures back to London for their business and connecting traffic. Charter airlines, on the other hand, would fly the aircraft back with the same crew even if it means night-time departures. Fewer cabin staff at lower average wages and with lower expenses helps charter carriers reduce their overall cabin crew costs.

Fuel costs should be similar for both charter and scheduled carriers if flying the same aircraft on the same route since they are likely to be paying very similar prices for fuel. The larger charter airlines should be able to negotiate just as favourable fuel prices at their home base, because their uplift will be very high, as the scheduled carriers do in their own bases. If, however, charter carriers have only a limited number of charter flights to a particular destination, their fuel uplift at that destination may be rather limited and they may be unable to negotiate as good a price as the scheduled carriers. In this case the charters may have a cost disadvantage. Conversely, there will be destination airports where charter flights may be more numerous than scheduled flights and the former may get a better fuel deal.

En-route navigation charges will be identical when charter and scheduled airlines are operating the same aircraft. On the other hand, charter operators may pay lower *airport charges* by using cheaper airports, especially in their home country. Scheduled services between London and Barcelona fly mostly from Heathrow and one or two from Gatwick. But charter flights might use either Gatwick or Luton, which are also in the London area. In summer 2008 a charter flight with an Airbus A-320 from Gatwick would have been charged around £1,425 for landing and passenger fees and one hour's parking and at Luton the charge would have been £1,507. A similar scheduled flight from Heathrow would have had to pay £2,261, substantially more. This could mean £6 to £8 more per passenger depending on the load. Charters will also choose the cheaper airport at the destination when there is a choice. So charter flights to Barcelona might well choose to fly to Gerona or Reus nearby, which have marginally lower airport charges.

Maintenance costs for both charter and scheduled operations would be broadly similar if using the same aircraft on the same routes. There is less variation in the wages of maintenance staff between carriers than other airline employees.

Insurance costs are only a very small part of total costs but large well-established operators (whether scheduled or charter) would both tend to benefit from lower rates.

Depreciation per hour, or lease costs per hour for leased aircraft, would also be the same if both charter and scheduled airlines achieved the same annual utilisation on their aircraft. In practice this is unlikely. First, aircraft used by the scheduled airlines will be used on different routes, many of which are relatively short. The need, for instance, to use the London–Barcelona aircraft on other shorter scheduled sectors, such as London–Amsterdam, inevitably reduces the annual utilisation which that aircraft could have achieved flying only on longer sectors such as London–Barcelona, London–Canary Islands, or London to Turkey, which is what the charter aircraft will be doing.

Second, during the peak summer months the charter airlines will be flying their aircraft night and day. Aircraft on scheduled short- to medium-haul routes have a limited 14–16-hour operating day since scheduled passengers do not like departing much before 0700 hours or arriving after 2200 hours. Also network carriers are often flying to/from airports which have night bans or restrictions, as is the case at London's Heathrow or many German airports. As a result of these two factors, scheduled short-haul aircraft frequently spend the night hours on the ground. Not so charter aircraft. Some charter passengers seem prepared to put up with considerable inconvenience in order to fly more cheaply. The flight departure time is also only one element in the overall package they are selecting. Leisure packages with night-time departures or arrivals are cheaper than day flights. Night flights also enable passengers to spend more time at their destination. Since some leisure passengers are prepared to accept departures or arrivals during night hours, charter airlines programme their aircraft to fly through the night during the peak months, except where constrained by night bans or limits. By doing this, they can frequently get three rotations, that is round trips, of the aircraft on a 2–3-hour sector during a 24-hour day. A scheduled airline would plan for only two rotations. On a longer sector such as between Northern Europe and Greece or Turkey, the charter airline will achieve two rotations while the network airline will only manage one or one-and-a-half.

However, in some short-haul leisure markets the availability of higher frequency LCC flights is reducing the attractiveness or need for night charters. Increasingly, the latter are concentrated into the two or three peak months.

Charter services, however, have much more marked seasonal peaks and troughs, so that in the off-peak winter months daily utilisation of aircraft may drop below that of scheduled aircraft. This can be compensated for by the very high peak utilisation achieved by using the night hours. In addition, some charter airlines are able to lease out aircraft during their own off-peak periods to airlines in other parts of the world that face peak demand at that time. Thus Monarch, My Travel and other UK charter airlines have often leased some of their aircraft to Canadian carriers who used them for winter charters to the Caribbean. As an alternative, airlines such as Condor or Thomsonfly, operating medium-range, wide-bodied aircraft on charters to the Mediterranean in the summer, can switch them to Caribbean, East African or Indian Ocean routes in the winter months.

The average annual aircraft utilisation in 2008 for a selection of UK charter airlines operating the Airbus A320 is compared to that of British Airways and Bmi (Table 7.2). It is clear that the net result of the above factors is heavily in the charter carriers' favour. They achieve between one and three hours per day more flying than their major scheduled counterparts when using the same aircraft on intra-European operations. As a result, their depreciation costs or lease rentals per hour will be reduced by up to 30 per cent. Higher aircraft utilisation can also lead to better utilisation of flight and cabin crew and therefore higher labour productivity.

Table 7.2 Aircraft utilisation rates, UK scheduled and charter airlines, 2008

	Average daily utilisation (hours)
	Airbus A320
Scheduled airlines	
Bmi (British Midland)	9.5
British Airways	8.4
Charter airlines	
Monarch	10.3
My Travel	11.4
First Choice	11.5

Source: Compiled using CAA (2009a) data.

In summary, a charter airline flying on the London–Barcelona market or on other short-haul markets in the Europe-Mediterranean region can achieve some limited direct cost economies compared to a scheduled operator. Through higher daily aircraft utilisation it can reduce its hourly depreciation or lease costs. By using fewer cabin crew and paying them less it can save costs here too, though this is a small cost item. If it can use cheaper airports at one or both ends of the route it can reduce the level of airport charges by half or more. Since on short-haul routes airport charges may represent 8–15 per cent of total costs, this cost saving can be important. These are the same areas in which low-cost operators save costs. But overall, the charter airlines' savings on direct costs are limited.

7.5.2   *Indirect operating costs*

The differences in direct operating costs between European network carriers and charters have been highlighted above. Such differences are not large. It is in the area of *indirect operating costs* that the costs of charter and scheduled services begin to diverge most markedly. These are station and ground expenses, passenger service costs, ticketing, sales and promotion costs and costs of administration.

Charters' *station costs* should be lower. Charter airlines can save money by sub-contracting out most of the aircraft, passenger and baggage handling activities at their destination airports. The seasonal nature of their operations means that they have no need for permanent staff or offices or other facilities at most of the out-stations they serve. At their larger destinations they may base one or a small number of their own staff to supervise local ground handling agents. Even where they do need staff dedicated to their operations, they may be in a better position to use seasonal staff. In contrast, most major scheduled airlines with daily or more frequent flights to most of their major European destinations will employ a station manager, together with assorted other station and handling staff. Even if they outsource much of the handling they will keep a small team of their own staff to supervise. They will have offices at the airport and perhaps off the airport as well, with associated rents and other costs. They will have cars and possibly their own ground handling equipment. Year-round station costs for scheduled carriers will tend to be higher. In Europe, as in many parts of the world, scheduled airlines now provide special dedicated lounges at airports for their business or executive club members, or they may pay for access to other airlines' business lounges. This is an additional expense avoided by charter companies. As a result of all these differences, charter airlines are likely to have lower station and ground costs.

One aspect of *passenger service costs* is cabin crew costs. In this analysis it has been included earlier as a direct cost of flight operations. A marked saving in passenger service costs arises because it is not necessary for charter airlines to offer a business class cabin with the more expensive business class catering, newspapers, magazines, etc., that are a feature of the scheduled airline's services, though some charter airlines now do offer some seat rows with more leg-room and better catering. Though meals and bar service on charter flights are generally good, attempts are made to provide simpler in-flight meals to reduce the costs of in-flight catering. In recent years many charter airlines charge separately for meals. Charter airlines will not normally have connecting passengers for whom they have responsibility. As a result, charters can escape the costs of transferring and handling passengers and baggage, which network airlines have to meet.

The greatest savings obtained by charter airlines arise in the areas of *ticketing, sales and promotion*. This is inherent in the charter model because most, and in many cases all, of the seats that the charter airline offers in any market have been chartered and paid for by tour operators and travel companies. The reservation of seats, ticketing and revenue accounting is the latter's responsibility, not the task of the airline. Even if the charter airline sells some seats on a seat-only basis, this may well be done either through the tour operator who chartered the flight or through the airline's website.

A charter airline also has minimal sales costs. Since all or the vast bulk of its capacity is not sold direct to the public, it needs no retail sales offices or staff, nor does it pay commission to others for selling its tickets. Yet commissions to agents, to GDS and credit card companies are an important cost for scheduled airlines. In the financial year 2007–8, commission paid (net of commission received) represented 3.8 per cent of British Airways' operating costs and 2.2 per cent of British Midland's costs. A charter airline sells most of its capacity not to passengers but to travel agents, tour organisers, or other charterers. There is no commission to be paid. Commission payments only arise when charter airlines sell capacity to the public on a seat-only basis, if any such sales are sold through agents. Here, too, charter airlines make great efforts to avoid or minimise commission payments.

In the UK, as in Germany, Canada or the United States, there are a small number of very large tour operators and a somewhat larger but diminishing number of medium ones. Most of a European charter airline's capacity is sold to the tour operator(s) in the same travel group. The balance is sold to other large travel companies or to a small number of independent tour operators. Thus a charter airline's annual selling and promotion costs may be no more than the cost of a few meetings and lunches with the key buyers of charter capacity. The charter airline's managing director, with a handful of back-up sales staff to do the detailed costings and negotiations, is probably all that is required. There is little need to sell or promote its services to the travelling public, so a charter airline is unlikely to have a promotion or advertising budget.

Overall, enormous cost savings accrue to charter airlines from the virtual absence of ticketing, sales and promotion expenditures. This is evident when one compares the marketing costs per passenger, including commissions paid, of a sample of UK scheduled and charter airlines (Table 7.3). While the larger scheduled airlines spend £7 to £27 for each passenger they carry, the two charter airlines shown spend less than £1.50 per passenger. Other UK charter airlines spend so little that it does not even appear in the CAA data. Virgin's spend is the highest, in part because it operates only long-haul flights with high revenues per passenger. But both Monarch and Thomson also operate many long-haul services.

Table 7.3 Marketing costs: UK scheduled and charter airlines, financial year 2007–8

	Ticketing, sales (including commission) and promotion costs per passenger £
Scheduled airlines	
Virgin Atlantic	27.81
British Airways	13.06
Bmi (British Midland)	7.89
Charter airlines	
Monarch	1.46
Thomson Airways	0.71

Source: Compiled by author using CAA (2009a) data.

Charter airlines tend to have very much lower general and administrative costs because they require fewer administrative and accounting staff. Many functions which are crucial to scheduled airlines and absorb significant resources either do not exist within a charter airline at all or, because of the different nature of charter operations, require relatively few staff. A charter airline, for example, does not need a large planning department with forecasting and yield management staff or large numbers of accountants to sort out revenue and sales accounting and inter-airline ticketing debts.

A charter airline can make economies in virtually all areas of indirect costs. Its station and handling costs are lower, as are its passenger service costs. Sales, ticketing and promotion costs, which for shorter-haul international scheduled airlines average around 8 to 12 per cent of total cost, are minimal for charter carriers. Administrative costs too are much lower. As a result, charter airlines' indirect costs may be up to half or less than those of network airlines operating on the same routes with the same aircraft.

Major savings in indirect costs, which in short-haul operations may represent about one third of total costs, together with slightly lower direct costs, which are two-thirds of total costs, suggest that flying similar aircraft a non-scheduled operator may have total round-trip costs between 20 and 25 per cent lower than those of a scheduled operator on the same route. However, the initial 20–25 per cent operating cost advantage is magnified by two key elements in the economics of non-scheduled air services: high seating densities and very high load factors. These are two advantages also enjoyed by low-cost airlines.

7.5.3   *High seating density*

In summer 2008 British Airways was flying many scheduled services in Europe using an Airbus A320 for some flights. Typically this had 152 seats in a two-class configuration. Air France had similar seating in its A320 on European routes. This is a popular aircraft with charter airlines but they put up to 180 seats in it. If BA and charter airlines had similar round-trip costs to a Mediterranean destination, merely by putting around 18 per cent more seats in the aircraft than their scheduled competitors, the charter airlines can reduce their seat-kilometre costs by about 15 per cent. In practice, seating on British Airways would be less than 152 since several additional rows of six-abreast Economy seats may well be reduced to four abreast to provide for a larger Business class cabin. Eight rows of Business class would reduce the seating capacity to 143. The scope for higher seating densities and therefore for even lower seat-kilometre costs is sometimes greater on wide-bodied aircraft. Non-scheduled airlines such as Monarch or Thomas Cook operating Boeing 767–300 aircraft would normally expect to have around 310 seats in a charter configuration. Yet the same aircraft flown on scheduled services by British Airways, on scheduled flights to Mediterranean points such as Athens, only has 247 to 256 seats. In this case, the charter configuration increases the seating capacity by nearly 25 per cent and reduces the seat-kilometre costs by about 20 per cent.

Several factors explain the ability of charter operators to push up the seating capacities on their aircraft. With very few exceptions, charter aircraft are in a single-class layout and at a constant seat pitch (the distance between each row of seats), though some rows in the front may offer marginally more leg room, especially on longer-haul charters. No space is lost accommodating first- or business-class passengers in separate cabins with greater leg room and low seat densities. If scheduled airlines operate a three-class cabin on medium- and long-haul scheduled flights this further reduces the total seating capacity.

Whatever the cabin layout, the charter configuration will also have a lower seat pitch, that is, less distance between each row of seats, so that more seat rows can be installed within the length of the cabin. A 29 inch seat pitch would be acceptable in a short-haul charter layout, whereas 31–34 inches would be more normal for economy-class seating on a scheduled flight. On wide-body aircraft an extra seat per seat row across the cabin (e.g. 10 abreast instead of 9 abreast) would be used on the wide-body Boeing 767 for charters. Charter airlines tend to increase the floor area on the main deck of their aircraft available for seating by reducing the number of toilets and galley space and by eliminating other space uses such as coat cupboards and so on. Galley space can be reduced because in-flight catering tends to be less lavish than on scheduled flights. The absence of first- or business-class passengers helps in this. In wide-bodied aircraft, such as Boeing 767, the galleys might even be placed on the lower deck with an internal lift providing access. This is possible because aircraft on non-scheduled flights generally carry little if any cargo.

7.5.4   *High load factors*

Not only do non-scheduled airlines put more seats into their aircraft, but they also fill substantially more of them. Whereas European network airlines would be pleased to achieve year-round passenger load factors on short- or medium-haul services of 70–75 per cent, especially for short-haul operations within Europe, charter airlines would be aiming for around 85 per cent or more. The stark contrast in the seat factors of the two sectors of the industry is illustrated in Table 7.4. In 2007 none of the scheduled European airlines listed achieved seat factors above 75 per cent (considered high by scheduled standards) on their short- and medium-haul services. The majority had seat factors between 65 and 75 per cent. By contrast, most of the major European charter operators shown achieved very high year-round seat factors of over 85 per cent while smaller European charter airlines achieved seat factors a few percentage points lower. One can conclude that, in general, passenger seat factors are at least 10–20 percentage points higher on non-scheduled than on comparable scheduled services, even if the charter flights are operated by network airlines. Finnair is a good example, with a seat factor of only 68 per cent on its short- to medium-haul scheduled flights but achieving a high 86 per cent on its non-scheduled operations, most of which were within Europe. Austrian Airlines provides a further example. While not shown in the table, it is noticeable that US charter carriers, in contrast to their European or Canadian counterparts, have much

Table 7.4 Charter and scheduled passenger load factors compared, 2007

Scheduled services		Non-scheduled/charters	
International short and medium-haul*	Seat factor %	All routes	Seat factor %
KLM	75	First Choice (UK)	92
Iberia	73	My Travel (UK)	90
Swiss	73	Condor (Germany)	88
Lufthansa	72	Thomas Cook (UK)	86
SAS	71	Thomsonfly (UK)	86
Air France	71	Finnair**	86
Alitalia	70	Iberworld (Spain)	82
BA	69	Monarch (UK)	82
Austrian	68	LTE (Spain)	81
Finnair	68	Austrian Airlines**	79
Bmi	66		
Olympic	65		
Air Portugal	64		

Sources: AEA (2008), CAA (2009), IATA (2008).

Notes
 * Scheduled covers cross-border European flights and services to North Africa and Middle East.
** Charters of scheduled airlines.

lower seat factors. For example, in 2007 World Airways' seat factor was 53 per cent, Omni's was 57 and Ryan International was 54 per cent. This is a function of the very different nature of their business, with less reliance on inclusive tour holiday packages.

The achievement of the very high load factors, shown in Table 7.4, is due not to the non-scheduled operators themselves but to the efforts of the tour operators and leisure companies, for it is they who have the responsibility for retailing the seats they have bought wholesale. By careful programming and scheduling of flights and other components of the total package such as hotel beds, self-catering apartments, ground transport and so on, the tour operators can achieve very high seat factors on the aircraft and high occupancy factors for the beds and other facilities they have booked. Vertical integration between tour organisers, which may be hotel owners too, and charter airlines facilitates the process of closely matching and programming the supply of and demand for hotel beds and aircraft seats. Load factors must be kept high to ensure low and competitive prices. Charter airlines which are not vertically integrated with major tour operators tend to achieve lower seat factors.

Several features of the charter market help in achieving such high load factors. Charter passengers are given limited flexibility in terms of choice of departure days and almost none on the choice of the return days. Particularly with inclusive tours, passengers can stay for only a fixed period at their destination – usually 7 or 14 days on intra-European charters, or perhaps 12 nights on some long-haul charters. Most of the travellers on an outward flight will come back together on the same return flight and on the same day of the week that they flew out on. Aircraft loads are not subject, as in scheduled operations, to the whims of different individual travellers who want to be away for different periods of time and travel on different days of the week. Moreover, once made and paid for, charter bookings are difficult to change and expensive to cancel. Ticket brokers are also used by aircraft charterers to fill up spare capacity on inclusive tour or advanced booking charters. Spare capacity can also be marketed for seat-only sales. If things go really badly, a tour operator with a large number of unsold seats on a flight it has chartered may cancel the flight (though it will pay a large penalty to the airline if it does that late in the day) and 'consolidate' its passengers onto someone else's flight where seats may be available. However, this practice is becoming less frequent. Both tour operators and charter airlines benefit from such an arrangement. Loads on individual flights are carefully monitored to ensure high load factors. A finely tuned and highly differentiated price structure for charter-based inclusive tours is used to induce a potential customer to travel on less popular days or times or seasons of the year.

Higher load factors substantially reduce the passenger-kilometre costs of charter as against scheduled services. The twin impact of higher seating densities and very much higher seat factors on the unit costs of charters can be illustrated by reference to two British airlines. British Airways and Thomsonfly in the mid-2000s were flying Boeing 767 aircraft on European routes such as London to Larnaca in Cyprus. Thomsonfly operated this aircraft in a charter configuration with 325 seats. Its average load factor in 2007 on international charter operations was 86 per cent. This would have resulted in a load of 280 passengers. British Airways' scheduled Boeing 767 aircraft on European services had 247 to 256 seats and its average load factor on intra-European operations within Europe was around 69 per cent (Table 7.4). This gives an average load of 170 passengers for a capacity of 247 seats. Even if on a particular route the operating costs of the two airlines were the same, and we have seen that they are not, the costs per passenger round trip or per passenger-kilometre for Thomsonfly would be about 39 per cent lower than for British Airways, purely because it was carrying 280 passengers instead of 170. On a smaller narrow-body aircraft where the capacity difference is not so great, the cost reduction would be less. In essence, by spreading the total round-trip operating costs over many more passengers, the non-scheduled operator can significantly reduce the trip cost per passenger. The above example shows that the higher charter seating densities and load factors together may have a greater impact on reducing the charter costs per passenger than do the savings in operating costs.

The preceding analysis indicates that non-scheduled operators start with an initial round-trip cost advantage of 20–25 per cent. This arises largely because of their lower indirect operating costs. By putting more seats into their aircraft they magnify this into an even greater cost advantage per seat-kilometre. Then, by filling 85–90 per cent of a larger number of seats, the costs per passenger-kilometre become even less vis-à-vis those of scheduled operators. The net effect may be to convert the round-trip cost advantage of only 20–25 per cent into a cost advantage per passenger carried which may range from 55 to over 65 per cent.

Using a cascade analysis, an attempt has been made in Table 7.5 to itemise the various potential cost savings which a charter airline might expect when competing head to head with a conventional scheduled airline on the same route and using a similar aircraft. With each cost reduction, the charter airline's costs per passenger cascade down to only 46 per cent of the scheduled cost. In practice the differential between scheduled and charter costs will depend on several factors such as the sector distance, whether night flying is allowed, the seat factors actually achieved by the scheduled or charter carriers, and so on. For example, if the scheduled seat factor was closer to 65 per cent, the charter seat cost differential would widen. But Table 7.5 summarises where cost savings are most likely to be achieved by a charter carrier competing head-on with a conventional scheduled airline. The areas of cost reduction are similar to those achieved by low-cost carriers, which raises the question of whether charters can compete effectively against the latter in short-haul markets.

Table 7.5 Cascade analysis: charter versus scheduled cost on route London to Barcelona area

	Charter adjustment to scheduled cost	Cost index
Total scheduled cost per passenger Assuming 72% year-round seat factor		100
1. Charter cost savings		
Direct operating costs		
Fewer cheaper cabin attendants	−1	99
Cheaper airports	−3	96
Higher aircraft utilisation	−3	93
Indirect operating costs		
More outsourcing at airports	−2	91
Economies in passenger services	−2	89
Minimal ticketing, sales, promotion or commissions	−8	81
Lower admin/overhead costs	−3	78
2. Higher charter seating density e.g. 20% more seats on narrow body	−17	61
3. Higher seat occupancy Assumed 88% on charter	−15	46
Derived charter cost as % of scheduled		46
But no compensating revenue from cargo		

7.6 Planning and financial advantages

Apart from a straightforward operating cost advantage, charter airlines enjoy other planning and financial advantages which are inherent in the workings of the charter market, particularly for inclusive tour charters (ITC). In Europe the peak period for ITC holidays is during the European summer from mid-June to mid-September. The marketing and retailing of those holidays begins the previous summer, with peak sales generally during the following January to March; though a number of passengers are booking even earlier, on return from their previous summer holiday! Because of early sales, the major tour operators have to produce their summer brochures and website displays with full details of their various package holidays a year or so earlier. To do this they must plan and schedule their flights and 'buy' the hotel beds they need some months earlier. This planning phase is carried out 12 to 15 months in advance. Tour companies would aim to have their routes and much of their summer flying capacity agreed with the charter airlines by the previous October, but finalised by February. The same pattern of charter contracts finalised a year in advance exists for winter inclusive tour charters to ski resorts or to long-haul destinations such as those in the Caribbean or the Indian Ocean.

The commercial pressure on tour operators and travel agents to plan and sell their holiday packages so far in advance works to the benefit of the non-scheduled operators. By May or early June of one year a charter operator would expect to negotiate several contracts for a 24–25-week summer season starting around the following April or Easter. Each contract may require numerous return flights per week and may involve hundreds or thousands of hours of flying. The routes to be flown, aircraft types, frequencies, days of the week and departure times will all have been specified. From one year to the next a large part of the flying programme will be the same. If the charterer is not the airline's in-house tour operator or a major travel company, staggered but high cancellation fees may also be agreed. Usually up to about 10 per cent of flights may be cancelled if this is done well in advance and before January or February when the agreed flying programme is finally firmed up. After that, cancellation fees may have to be paid. So there is a strong incentive not to cancel flights.

Charter operators are in an enviable position. Having negotiated contracts with their various customers they are in a position to know six to 12 months in advance the routes and frequencies they will be operating and the aircraft and crews they will need. They can plan their productive resources so as to ensure that supply precisely matches demand and that it does so as efficiently as possible. Knowing their total revenue in advance, charter airlines can adjust and re-organise their costs to ensure that costs do not exceed revenues. In contrast to this, network airlines normally do not know their revenues until the costs have been incurred and it is then too late to make any significant adjustments.

The charter airline has further safeguards. The negotiated price for the series of charter flights is normally a fixed fee per round trip or per block hour for a minimum number of trips or block hours per season. But the price is based on the airline's input costs at a datum point and will include actual or forecast fuel prices, airport fees and navigation charges and assumed exchange rates for relevant currencies. In the case of UK airlines this would be the sterling to dollar rate. The airline is obliged to advise the charterer, that is usually a tour operator, of any net change of costs in relation to the datum costs a certain number of days before a flight. If costs have gone up there will be a surcharge to pay. If they have gone down the charterer may be entitled to a rebate. This system of surcharges on the negotiated charter price in theory insulates charter airlines against any sudden and adverse variations in their input costs. In practice, since most charter passengers buy and pay for their flights several months in advance, imposing surcharges on package holiday prices is virtually impossible. So charterers generally prefer to hedge against fuel price escalation and adverse exchange rate fluctuations so as to reduce the need to pass on any increased costs to their customers. This is especially so if their major or only customer is their own in-house tour operator (for fuel hedging see Chapter 5, Section 5.3).

Another key feature of charter operations is that charter fees are paid rapidly. In a few cases involving small tour operators or one-off charters, flights are paid for before they take off. In most cases flights are paid for very soon after they take place. This contrasts with scheduled carriers who may wait for months after a particular flight to collect all the revenues due from ticket agents, credit-card companies and other airlines. Moreover, all payment accrues to the charter airline. There are no commissions or credit-card fees, no chasing of delinquent accounts. While charter flights are paid for quickly by the charterer, many charter airline inputs such as fuel may be paid in arrears. This creates large positive cash balances during peak periods which can earn substantial interest payments while on deposit with banks or financial institutions.

The charter operator's cash flow is also helped by the high volume of on-board sales of spirits, cigarettes, perfumes, watches, and so on. On-board sales per passenger in Europe are much higher for charter than for scheduled passengers. This may be due partly to the fact that many charter flights are to or from secondary airports, particularly in destination countries, with poor retail facilities of their own and partly to the high proportion of frequent travellers on scheduled flights, who may be less inclined to spend money on board. On-board sales also receive a lower priority on scheduled flights with more competing demands on the cabin crew's time. On charter flights, commission earned on in-flight sales may be a vital addition to the salaries of cabin crews, since their salaries in any case tend to be lower. After July 1999, when duty-free sales on flights within the European Union were abolished, charters tried to respond by focusing sales on high-value goods such as watches, jewellery, cosmetics. This has been a success but profit margins are lower. Nevertheless, there are many charter markets outside the European Union where on-board duty-free sales continue. These include Turkey, Egypt and other North and East African destinations, the Americas, the Indian Ocean and South East Asia. For flights to these destinations, many charter airlines have embarked on aggressive selling of their in-flight goods in advance of passengers' departures through mail order and other direct sales techniques. This enhances sales revenues. While duty-free sales on intra-European flights have declined, they may still contribute up to about 20 per cent of profits.

While in-flight sales are a positive element for non-scheduled operations, the absence of freight revenue clearly reduces the potential revenue from any one flight. Generally, charter operators cannot top up their passenger revenue with freight revenue as their scheduled competitors can. For the latter freight can add up to 10 to 15 per cent of the revenue on a passenger flight. The price at which the charter airlines sell their passenger capacity must therefore reflect this difference.

The charter airlines' planning and financial advantages described above are also the cause of their major headache, which is the constant fear of over-capacity in the market and intense price competition. Signed contracts to provide many hours of flying a year or so later can be used to facilitate the raising of loans to purchase aircraft to meet the charter contract. The ease with which finance can be raised once a contract has been signed may well induce new entrants into the market or existing airlines to expand their capacity too quickly. If there is over-capacity charter rates tend to drop and margins are squeezed. The fear that more new charter airlines will be set up reinforces the pressure towards vertical integration between airlines and the leisure companies. As more tour operators become financially linked with particular charter airlines, the scope for independent airlines and new entrants diminishes. Yet new and ever-hopeful charter airlines are regularly being set up, especially in newer destination markets, such as Turkey and North Africa.

The early negotiation of charter contracts and the ability to adjust charter rates in response to changes in input costs provide non-scheduled operators with a level of certainty and financial security that is unique in air transport. They can sell their product in advance, at a price which can be adjusted if their costs go up. They can then go out and procure the resources necessary to provide the capacity they have sold. Scheduled airlines, both network and low-cost carriers, are handicapped because they have to do the exact opposite. They first decide to provide a level of scheduled capacity which they judge necessary to meet the anticipated or targeted demand level; they then allocate resources to it and subsequently try to sell it. Scheduled operators must plan their output in advance, without knowing for certain how much of it they will sell. As a result, they face much greater problems in trying to match supply and demand than do the charter airlines.

7.7   Do series charters have a future?

Clearly one-off and short-series passenger charters, to meet short-term specific demand, will continue, for instance, for the transfer of pilgrims on the Haj flights to Saudi Arabia or for sports fixtures. The more critical question is whether leisure-based series charters in and from Europe or North America have a long-term future.

The charter business model appears to offer some competitive advantages. Charter airlines operating series charters on two to five hour sectors have costs per seat-km which may be as much as 50–60 per cent lower than those of traditional scheduled airlines operating on the same or parallel routes (Table 7.5). This cost advantage is similar to that enjoyed by low-cost airlines. On longer-haul sectors, the cost differential between charter and scheduled operators is likely to be less. The charter operators also enjoy the benefit of two unique features of the charter model. First, the bulk of their capacity is sold well in advance to tour operators or travel agents. This facilitates the close matching of supply and demand to ensure high load factors. Second, except for a limited proportion of the capacity on any flight which may be sold on a seat-only basis, the airline itself has no selling or marketing costs since it does not sell direct to passengers. Its sales effort is focused on the tour operators, who in any country are limited in number.

Despite these apparent advantages, both European and North American charter airlines have had a bumpy ride in the years up to 2008. They have faced strong competitive pressures and attacks from both their main competitors. Network carriers using the online travel agencies and their own websites have offered short-haul passengers much greater flexibility in terms of both pricing, with much lower and one-way fares, and the offer of do-it-yourself hotel and car-hire bookings. They have also become more price-competitive on long-haul leisure routes. As we have seen earlier, low-cost carriers have hit short-haul charters hard by also offering passengers greater flexibility and variety in fares, in destinations and in hotels. Above all their very cheap one-way fares and high frequencies have diverted large numbers of passengers previously flying on charters. It is low-cost airlines which have profited most from changing consumer tastes and desire for greater flexibility. LCCs undoubtedly pose the greatest threat to short-haul charter airlines.

Some charter airlines have responded to these competitive challenges and changing market conditions by launching their own low-cost services or subsidiaries, such as Thomsonfly, or by selling more of their seats on their charter flights on a seat-only basis or doing both, which is what Monarch has done. Air Berlin has done all this but also bought another charter airline, LTU, so as to offer both the charter and low-cost models. In the process of adapting to the new market conditions, the differences between the low-cost and charter models have become increasingly blurred.

The question which then arises is whether the traditional series charter model, where most of the capacity is sold by an airline to a leisure company or tour operator who then combines these seats with hotel beds, cruise-ship cabins or self-catering apartments into holiday packages which they themselves sell, will continue to have a future.

Traditional series leisure charters, in Europe at least, are likely to survive in two types of short-haul markets where they can offer some sustainable competitive advantage. First, on very dense holiday routes where the ability to package large numbers of hotel beds with seats on larger aircraft will enable tour operators to offer very low-priced and competitive all-inclusive holiday packages. By flying larger aircraft than low-cost airlines and possibly at higher seat factors charters may have a competitive edge over the LCCs. There appears to be a continuing but more limited demand for packaged inclusive holidays in markets where tourist flows are very dense even though LCCs may have captured a significant share. Routes from northern Europe to Palma and a dozen or so major resorts in Spain and the Mediterranean could fall into this category. Second, there will be many less dense leisure routes, where the traffic is too thin, for instance to small islands or isolated resorts, or so highly peaked into a relatively short holiday season that they are unattractive to low-cost carriers. Series charters may be able to meet the demand for holiday travel in such very thin or highly seasonal markets. These may include charter flights to the Greek islands, to smaller resorts in Tunisia or in the Red Sea and to some winter ski resorts.

In long-haul markets, charters will continue to be competitive against network airlines where there is relatively little higher yield Business or First class traffic. This is because network carriers' costs are too high to enable them to offer charter competitive fares or seat sales in the Economy cabin without a significant mix of high-yield traffic. Long-haul routes from Europe or Canada to several Caribbean or Central American destinations will continue to be served successfully by charters, offering both inclusive holiday packages and seat-only sales. So too will routes from Europe to East African and Indian Ocean holiday destinations, to Florida, to West African resorts and to a few destinations in South East Asia. Many of these leisure markets tend to be highly seasonal with very marked and often short peak periods and thin off-peak traffic. This also makes them more difficult and less attractive for network carriers. The stronger competitive position of charters in long-haul markets compared to short-haul sectors inevitably means that the trend for traditional style charters to increasingly focus on long-haul destinations will be reinforced. As a result, their short-haul operations will decline relatively.

In summary, there is a future for series charters, but a more limited future. Also, whether operating in those short- or long-haul markets suggested above, series charters will only survive if they continue to offer their passengers greater flexibility and choice. This means unbundling all aspects of the flight product and the holiday package, if any, so as to allow the passenger to choose what aspects of the product and service he wishes to pay for. Such 'dynamic packaging' is the key to the survival of series charters.

8 Airline marketing – the role of passenger demand

> Marketing is not just a bolt-on specialism which can be added to existing management structures, but an integrated approach to the whole conduct of profitable business. . . .
>
> (Sir Colin Marshall, Chief Executive, British Airways, 1988)

8.1 The interaction of supply and demand

As emphasised in the opening chapter, airline management is about matching the supply of air services, which management can largely control, with the demand for such services, which management can influence but cannot control. To be successful in this an airline can be a low-cost operator or a high-cost operator. What determines profitability is the airline's ability to produce unit revenues which are higher than its unit costs. Low unit costs are no guarantee of profit if an airline is unable to generate even the low unit revenues necessary to cover such costs.

In fact, profitability depends on the interplay of three key performance variables: unit cost, unit revenue and load factor. Unit cost is usually measured *per available tonne-km* (ATK), that is per unit of capacity or as *cost per available seat-km* (CASK); unit revenues or yields are measured *per revenue tonne-km* (RTK), *per available seat-km* (RASK), or *per passenger-km* (RPK), that is, per unit of output sold[1]. Load factor indicates how much of the capacity produced has actually been sold (it is the revenue tonne-kms expressed as a percentage of available tonne-kms) while the seat factor is the passenger-kms as a percentage of the seat-kms. Clearly, if yields are low they can be compensated for by higher seat or load factors. But high or very high load factors, in themselves, do not ensure profitability if yields are too low in relation to costs. Conversely, low load factors may not be critical if yields per unit sold are high (see Section 11.1 in Chapter 11).

To achieve a profitable matching of supply and demand airlines need to get the balance between unit costs, unit revenues and load factor right. For this, it is crucial for airline managers to have a thorough understanding of the demand they are trying to satisfy. Such an understanding is fundamental to every aspect of airline planning. Aircraft selection, route development, scheduling, product planning, pricing and advertising are just some of the many decision areas which ultimately are dependent on an analysis of demand for the transport of both passengers and freight. As in all industries, supply and demand for air

---

[1] Yield or revenue per seat-km (RASK) is a measure of revenue per unit of capacity rather than per passenger or seat sold. As such it is a revenue measure which is independent of the seat or load factor. But by measuring revenue per unit of capacity (RASK) one can compare it directly with the cost per seat-km (i.e. the CASK) on any route, while leaving aside the passenger load factor achieved.

services are not independent of each other. On the contrary, each affects the other. Aircraft types and speeds, departure and arrival times, frequency of service, the level of air fares, in-flight service, the quality of ground handling and other features of supply will influence demand for an airline's services. Conversely, the demand will itself affect those supply features. The density of passenger demand, its seasonality, the purpose of travel, the distance to be travelled, the nature of the freight demand and other demand aspects should influence the way in which air services are supplied and will impact on costs. (The impact of demand patterns on costs has been discussed briefly in Section 5.2 above.) Thus airline planning and management is a dynamic and iterative process.

An understanding and evaluation of the demand for air transport leads to the provision of services which themselves then affect the demand. New adjustments to the supply then take place to meet changes in the demand and this interactive process continues. The more competitive and unregulated the market, the more dynamic the interaction becomes and the greater are the headaches for airline managers. Marketing is concerned with this dynamic and interactive process of matching supply and demand in a manner which generates an adequate profit.

8.2   Key stages of airline marketing

There is a widely held misconception that marketing is about selling what is being produced. It is much more than that. Marketing is involved in deciding what should be produced as well as how it should be sold. As such it is the lynchpin of any industry. It is all-pervasive. It is important to recognise that virtually everyone within the airline can contribute to the marketing process.

The essence of marketing is to identify and satisfy customer needs; to be consumer or market oriented rather than production or supply oriented. If an airline concentrates on merely selling what is produced before identifying what customers want and are prepared to pay for, it is doomed to failure. A good example is supersonic air services. The supersonic Concorde aircraft was produced largely because it was technically feasible, with little reference to whether passengers would ultimately be prepared to pay the excessively high cost of travelling in the aircraft or whether people were prepared to pay the full cost of supersonic air travel to save two or three hours. A few were, but not enough to make the aircraft a commercial success. Launched in the mid–1970s, British Airways' and Air France's Concorde services survived only because they were not expected to cover their full costs since the capital costs were written off by their respective governments. No more Concorde aircraft were built after the initial batch of 16. After 27 years the last scheduled Concorde flight landed at London's Heathrow on 23 October 2003.

The first step in marketing is to identify markets and market segments that can be served profitably. To do this one uses the whole range of market research methods, from desk-based statistical analyses to surveys of current and prospective users of air services. The aim is to gain an understanding of the needs of different market segments and also the degree to which such needs are not currently being satisfied. This leads on naturally to the production of traffic forecasts, which should be as detailed and segmented as possible.

The second stage of marketing is to decide, in the light of the preceding market analyses, the air services that should be offered in the market and their product features both in the air and on the ground. This is product planning. Price is the most critical of the product features but, as discussed later in Chapter 10, there are many other aspects of the airline's product and service provision that must also be decided on. Product planning is related to three key factors: the market needs which have been identified, the current and expected product features of competing airlines and the costs of different product or service features. In assessing the costs of proposed products, the supply and demand sides of the industry are brought together, for there is a trade-off between the two. The product planners must balance the costs of alternative product and service features against what customers are prepared to pay for.

The third stage is to plan and organise the distribution and selling of the products on the basis of a marketing plan. This involves setting up and operating sales and distribution outlets both airline owned, such as sales offices, telephone call centres and online sites, and indirect outlets involving a range of agents, sub-agents and online travel agencies. In order to attract potential customers, the marketing plan will also include a detailed programme of advertising and promotion activities.

Lastly, marketing is concerned with reviewing and monitoring both the degree to which the airline has been able consistently to meet the service standards and product features planned and customers' responses to them. Such monitoring through weekly sales figures, customer surveys, analyses of computer data from online sales, reviews of complaints and other market research techniques should enable airlines to take short-term corrective action, where possible, and also to make longer-term changes in their service and product features.

The aim of this book is to assess the role of marketing in the process of matching supply of air services with the demand. Marketing starts with an understanding of demand. This chapter considers certain characteristics of the demand for air travel and examines the various factors which affect the level and growth of demand in any given market. This understanding of demand leads on naturally to an examination of the forecasting techniques most widely used by airlines (Chapter 9).This is followed by an assessment of product planning and distribution (Chapter 10), of which a key element is pricing (Chapter 11). The cost implications of marketing strategies have been considered earlier (Section 5.2).

8.3   The motivation for air travel

The bulk of air travel is either for business or for leisure. Business travel involves a journey necessitated by one's employment and paid for by the employer. The business traveller and the employer may in some cases be the same person, but even then the traveller will not be paying directly out of his own pocket but out of the firm's. The leisure market contains two broad categories, holiday travel and travel whose primary purpose is visiting friends or relatives (often referred to as VFR). Each of these can be further sub-divided. For instance, holiday travel can be for short- or long-stay holidays and can be further split between those flying on inclusive holiday packages and those who pay for travel and accommodation separately. Another distinct and growing category is travel to/from second homes, which is often for weekend trips. Some categorise this as VFR travel. But, whatever the nature of their holiday, leisure travellers, unlike those travelling on business, invariably pay their own fares out of their own pockets. A number of important differences between the business and leisure markets stem from the fact that in the former case the passengers are not paying for their own travel whereas in the latter they are. These are discussed later.

There is, finally, a small proportion of air passengers who do not fit into the business, holiday or VFR categories. These include students travelling to or from their place of

Table 8.1 Passengers (arrivals plus departures) by journey purpose at London's Heathrow and Gatwick airports in 2006

	London Heathrow %	*London Gatwick %*
Business		
Business	4.5	1.6
Attend internal company business	12.6	6.2
Meeting customers	10.8	5.4
Conferences	3.6	1.3
Other business	4.3	2.4
Total business	36.1	17.0
Holiday		
Holiday	18.1	25.8
Holiday inclusive tour/package	10.1	29.2
Total holiday	28.2	55.0
Visiting friends/relatives	31.9	26.0
Other (sports, studies, migration, etc.)	3.8	2.0
Total	100.00	100.0
Total pax (domestic and international)	67.1 million	33.7 million

Source: Compiled using CAA, 2007.

study, those travelling for medical reasons, and migrants moving to another country. They may be grouped together as a miscellaneous or 'other' category.

A 2006 survey of passengers at a selection of UK airports, which generated three quarters of UK passenger traffic, domestic and international, found that 26 per cent were travelling on business, 30 per cent to visit friends and relatives and 41 per cent were flying for holidays (CAA, 2007). The remaining 3 per cent were travelling for a variety of other reasons. These are very global figures. In any market or on any route the mix of passengers by purpose of travel will vary by country and also on whether it is a domestic or international route. Generally the proportion of business passengers is higher on domestic routes than on international ones because domestic distances are shorter and leisure passengers may find it cheaper to go by car, bus or train, especially if there are several people in the party.

Several other factors affect the passenger mix. These include whether the airline service is a network scheduled, a charter or a low-cost flight, the country of residence of the passengers, the nature of economic activities at each end of the route, the airports concerned, and so on. The two London airports provide contrasting examples (Table 8.1). In 2006 Heathrow handled 67 million domestic and international passengers, of whom 36.1 per cent, almost two out of five, were on business trips. Only 28.2 per cent were on holiday and slightly more, 31.9 per cent, were visiting friends and relatives. At London's second airport, Gatwick, handling almost 34 million passengers, the proportion of business passengers dropped to 17.0 per cent or just under half that of Heathrow. On the other hand, since charter and low-cost flights are significant at Gatwick but non-existent at Heathrow, one finds that 55.0 per cent of Gatwick flyers are on holiday and a further 26.0 are visiting friends and relatives. The total leisure segment is 81 per cent. At both these airports the proportion of business travellers on their domestic routes was significantly higher than on their international services.

It is noticeable also that at Gatwick nearly a third of passengers (29.2 per cent) were travelling on inclusive tour packages. The vast majority of these would have been flying on charters, for which Gatwick is an important base. At Heathrow, only 10.1 per cent were going on inclusive tours and all of these would have been on scheduled flights, since charters do not operate from this airport. The table also highlights different categories of business passenger.

While only about a quarter or so of UK residents flying abroad do so to visit friends or relatives, in some markets such VFR traffic can be more important. On routes to Canada, to the Caribbean or to South East Asia and Australia, the proportion of the UK originating traffic visiting friends or relatives rises significantly.

In other regions of the world the split between business, holiday, VFR and other trips will vary. As a general rule, the higher the personal disposable income of the population in a country, the greater is the proportion of holiday trips in the total international air travel generated by that country (unless, of course, travel or foreign exchange restrictions are imposed on its citizens). Low incomes in most countries of Africa mean that business trips dominate on international air routes within the continent. Conversely, rapidly rising personal incomes in Japan and the newly industrialised countries of East Asia during the last 35 years generated a rapid growth of leisure travel, which partly explains the unusually high growth rates enjoyed by airlines in the region during the last two decades (Table 1.4 in Chapter 1). VFR traffic tends to be significant on air routes joining countries between which there have been earlier population movements. Apart from the UK examples previously cited, there are many other air routes with an important VFR component. These include France to Algeria or Morocco, United States to the Philippines and Singapore to Southern India.

The variation in passenger motivation and mix which airline marketing managers have to deal with is illustrated by examining air travellers flying between the United Kingdom and the original 15 member states of the European Union in 2006 (Table 8.2). These 15 states are most of the countries in Western Europe before the enlargement of the Union. A close examination of Table 8.2 leads to the following broad conclusions:

- There are three times as many UK air visitors to Western European countries as visitors from these countries flying to the UK. A stark imbalance.
- Purpose of travel for air passengers varies significantly between UK residents going abroad and visitors to the UK.
- While almost 70 per cent of UK residents who fly to Europe do so on holiday, only 27.9 per cent of European air visitors to the UK come for a holiday.
- On the other hand, a higher proportion of European visitors (30.7 per cent) fly to the UK to visit friends and relatives compared to UK residents travelling for the same purpose (14.4 per cent).
- Whereas only one in eight or 12.8 per cent of UK residents fly to Western Europe on business, nearly a third of visitors, or one in three, to the UK come for business reasons.
- Finally one notes the high proportion of UK air passengers, 27.6 per cent or one in four, who flew to Europe in 2006 on inclusive tour packages. These are the ones who generate the substantial volumes of UK charter traffic (Chapter 7 above). But very few Europeans visiting the UK decide to travel on inclusive packages.

Directional imbalances in traffic volumes and marked variations in journey purpose from each end of the route are a common feature of most markets or individual routes. This is

Table 8.2 Purpose of travel for air passengers between UK and European Union (15 states) in 2006

Purpose of visit	Visits to Europe by UK residents %	Visits to UK from Europe %
Business	12.8	31.0
Holiday	69.8	27.9
(of which inclusive tour)	(27.6)	(2.8)
Visiting friends/relatives	14.4	30.7
Miscellaneous	3.0	10.4
All visits	100.0	100.0
Visitors	34.2 million	12.6 million

Source: Compiled using ONS, 2007.

Note
Visits to/from 15 European Union member states prior to 2006 enlargement.

Table 8.3 Traffic distribution and purpose of travel on selected London Heathrow air routes, 2006

London Heathrow to/from Total pax (million)	UK Residents		Foreign Residents		Total
	Business % 1	Leisure* % 2	Business % 3	Leisure* % 4	% 5
Short-haul					
Ireland (2.7)	22	18	22	38	100
Germany (3.9)	24	16	30	30	100
France (2.4)	21	21	24	34	100
Long-haul					
United States (11.2)	10	26	21	44	100
Australia (2.4)	3	40	9	48	100
Canada (2.5)	5	20	19	56	100

Source: Compiled by author using CAA, 2007.

Note
* Leisure here includes VFR and other non-business travel.

evident when examining five individual markets, two short- and three long-haul, from London-Heathrow in 2006 (Table 8.3). Unlike the earlier comparison of total UK to EU Europe visitors in Table 8.2, in these particular markets there is a marked imbalance with more foreign residents flying into London than UK residents flying out. The imbalance is particularly marked on services to/from the United States, by far the largest single market. It is also noticeable that business travellers generate a higher proportion of the total traffic on short-haul than long-haul markets. Business travel is particularly low on the routes to Australia, where only 12 per cent of all passengers were flying on business.

The preceding examples have illustrated the wide diversity in traffic mix between different markets and routes and also between different directions on the same route. In any market or route, the mix of passengers between business and leisure or VFR has important implications on marketing and pricing strategies and also on the average yield per passenger.

Thus a detailed knowledge and understanding of the passenger mix, in terms of purpose of travel from each end of each route, is crucially important.

The air travel market is smaller than the number of passenger trips recorded since each individual traveller will normally make more than one flight. The relationship between the number of travellers and the passenger trips recorded varies on a route-by-route basis. It is greatly influenced by the proportion of business travellers on the route, since they are the most likely to be frequent users of air services. On many inclusive tour charter routes, the number of travellers is probably close to half the number of passengers recorded on the route since each traveller will make both an outward and a return trip, while it is unlikely that they will make that round trip more than once a year. In scheduled markets, the position is more complex, with a small proportion of frequent travellers generating a high proportion of the total passenger trips recorded. Such frequent travellers will usually be flying on business, but some may also be on leisure trips.

Travel motivation has an impact on frequency of travel but also on the duration of the trip. While business travellers fly more frequently, they also take trips of shorter duration. Among leisure passengers, those on inclusive tour holidays have the longest trips since such holidays are normally of fixed duration, often in multiples of a week. As the journey distance increases so does the duration of the trip, whatever its purpose. A 2006 survey of Heathrow passengers (CAA, 2007) showed that, while 60 per cent of UK leisure passengers on international flights out of Heathrow stayed away for over one week, only 16 per cent of business travellers stayed away that long. In fact 14 per cent of business travellers on international routes flew back the same day or the next. On domestic flights nearly half of UK business travellers were away for less than a day. In other words, purpose of travel directly impacts on length of trip. This too has important implications for marketing of air services. Such figures also emphasise why high frequencies are important for business passengers.

8.4   Socio-economic characteristics of air travellers

Travel motivation and aspects of travel behaviour, such as frequency of travel, the number of people travelling together or the time when bookings are made, are linked to the socio-economic characteristics of the individual traveller. Sex, age, income level, stage in the life cycle, size of family and occupation are some of the many socio-economic variables that impact on travel patterns. The key variables affecting behaviour will clearly be different if one is travelling for business, or leisure, or visiting friends and relatives. They will also differ for the separate market segments within each of these categories. For an airline, the more it knows about its current or potential customers the easier it is to plan and target its services and products to meet the specific needs of each market segment. Surveys both of air passengers and those not currently using its services as well as more general surveys and market research are used to build up this understanding of what each market place needs. Airlines that fail to use and take account of surveys and market research are frequently the ones who lose their way. While an in-depth analysis of the socio-economic characteristics of different types of air travellers would need to be lengthy and is not appropriate here, it is nevertheless interesting to highlight some of these.

One would expect male passengers to make up the bulk of the business market, but the extent to which males still dominate is perhaps surprising. In the UK in 1999 only about 22 per cent of business air travellers were women (CAA, 2000b), but seven years later still only 26 per cent, one in four, of business travellers at Heathrow were women

(CAA, 2007). This pattern is indicative of the situation at other UK airports such as Manchester or Gatwick, with a significant share of business passengers. It is also indicative of the pattern elsewhere in Europe too. In the United States, the proportion of women among business air travellers is nearly twice as high at around 40–45 per cent.

As one would expect, the leisure market manifests a more even split of passengers between the two sexes, but there are variations and in some European and North American leisure markets women if anything predominate. The 2006 air passenger survey in the UK showed that at London's two major airports, Heathrow and Gatwick, leisure passengers were evenly divided between male and female, but at the other two London airports, Luton and Stansted, women represented 54–55 per cent of all leisure passengers (CAA, 2007). The proportion of women is even higher among international VFR passengers. In the United States, women are dominant in the leisure market, generating well over half the total air trips.

Traditionally, business travellers have been thought to be primarily middle and senior managers and executives and established lawyers, architects, consultants or other professionals. Their seniority inevitably meant that they would be in the middle to upper age groups. However, the business market has been undergoing a fundamental change. The internationalisation of the world's trade and industry and the fall in the real cost of air travel, together with the speed advantage offered, have resulted in recent years in a growth of business travel by more junior staff and skilled workers. Surveys of air passengers at London's airports have found that over one-third of business passengers were supervisory clerical and junior managerial or professional staff or skilled manual workers. Such passengers would tend to be younger and on lower incomes than the more traditional business passenger.

The most significant socio-economic variable affecting the demand for leisure travel is personal or household income, since leisure trips are paid for by the passenger, who may also be paying for a spouse and one or more children. As a result, those with higher incomes generate a disproportionately large share of the leisure market. A survey of UK passengers flying out of London's Heathrow airport on international flights in 2006 indicated that the 66 per cent of business trips and 43 per cent of leisure trips were generated by the 25 per cent of the population in the top A/B socio-economic groups.

The UK experience is mirrored in other European countries and in the United States. A small proportion of the population, the high earners, account for a disproportionately large share of international passenger travel and in most cases of domestic travel too. In many Third World countries with low average disposable incomes, international air travel may be limited entirely to the 5–10 per cent of the population with the highest incomes. Elsewhere, international leisure travel may be more widespread but still with a predominance of higher-income earners.

In the UK air travel market a key social variable is house ownership abroad. Those who own homes abroad undertake one and a half to two times as many international air trips for leisure as those without. This is true of people in all income bands (CAA, 2008).

The trend towards buying second homes abroad, which has been very marked in Europe during the last 20 years, has had an impact on travel frequencies. For example, in 2007 UK residents with an annual household income of over £115,000 and owning a home abroad each took 5.8 leisure air trips in the last 12 months, whereas those without a home abroad but with the same income only took 3.2 leisure trips (CAA, 2008). Owners of homes abroad who travel frequently are an important market segment for Europe's low-cost carriers.

An appreciation of the socio-economic characteristics of passenger demand in each market is helpful to airlines in planning their advertising, promotion and sales activity. It can help them in deciding which papers, magazines or television channels to advertise in and what features of their services to emphasise in their advertising campaigns. Such knowledge of the market may assist to a certain extent in product planning and in determining tariff policies and possibly even in forecasting.

8.5   Market segmentation

Traditionally airlines have segmented their markets on each route by trip purpose or motivation. Some airlines do this simply by dividing their passengers into business and non-business or leisure passengers. Others, as suggested earlier, make a three- or fourfold division into business, holiday, VFR and other. Market segmentation in this way is invaluable since the separate market segments have varied growth rates and respond differently to internal supply variables such as frequencies of flights, departure times, and fare changes or to external factors such as exchange rate fluctuations or economic recession. Understanding the size and the characteristics of each market segment on each route is essential for forecasting demand, for many aspects of product planning such as scheduling or in-flight service, and especially for pricing. Airlines without such detailed knowledge of their markets are likely to get into difficulties when trying to match supply and demand.

In recent years there has been a growing awareness among airline managers that this traditional and simple approach to market segmentation based on trip purpose has some shortcomings. First, it tends to place too much emphasis on the demographic and socio-economic features of the passengers. Age, sex or social class are perhaps less important than appreciating passenger needs and requirements when travelling by air. Surely it is more important for an airline to know whether a passenger will cancel their reservation at the last moment or whether they are prepared to pay a lower fare for an inconvenient departure than it is to know their sex or age? Except, of course, if age or sex does affect booking behaviour or attitudes to price. Second, air trips may increasingly be multipurpose. A business trip is combined with a holiday, or a wife accompanies a husband on a business trip, while many visits to friends and relatives are considered as holidays. Third, traditional market segmentation oversimplifies the motivational factors involved in travel decisions. All business air travellers cannot be grouped together and assumed to have similar demand characteristics and needs, any more than can all leisure passengers. A senior manager or engineer requiring to go to another country immediately because of an unexpected crisis has different transport needs from a salesman who plans his regular overseas sales trips months in advance. A businessman travelling to meet customers or a government official going to a conference are both considered business passengers, yet may have quite different travel requirements. Equally, the family holidaymaker buying an annual two-week inclusive tour package holiday at a sunshine resort places different demands on the air services from the holidaymaker going independently and making his or her own accommodation arrangements or the couple going for a weekend break from Montreal to New York or from Singapore to Hong Kong.

Most airline planners now believe that market segmentation should not be based on a straightforward fourfold division categorised by journey purpose but on a more complex division related partly to journey purpose but partly also to passenger needs and behaviour patterns. Thus the business segment may be further subdivided into routine business, emergency business, conference or trade fair travel, overseas employment, home leave, and so on. The holiday segment of the leisure market could be split initially into an inclusive tour segment, a multi-destination touring segment and a weekender segment. But each of these segments can be subdivided further. For instance, holiday packages may be to hotels, self-catering or on cruise ships. Other ways of segmenting the market can also be used depending on each airline's appreciation of what are the key segments of its own market. The point about more complex market segmentation is that each segment is likely to have distinctive needs and expectations, such as the freedom to change reservations or routings, the need to make stop-overs, or the ability to pay particular fare levels, or varying expectations in terms of in-flight service and comfort, and so on. Behaviour patterns are also important. Some passengers book very early, but others leave it to the last minute or may tend to change the day of travel.

Variations in needs for four of the many possible market segments on a medium-haul route such as London–Athens or Singapore–Hong Kong are shown in Figure 8.1. The contrasting needs of the emergency business traveller with those of the two-week holiday-maker stand out starkly. For the latter a low fare is critical. For the former, high service quality – seat availability, frequent flights and so on – is crucial and price is relatively unimportant. It can also be seen by comparing weekend and two-week holiday-makers that even in the leisure market there may be quite distinct segments with their own needs and expectations. It may well be that each of these groups also has different socio-economic characteristics which may help in targeting specific marketing efforts at them. But the key is their needs and expectations. What service and product features do they want or need?

The significance of this more sophisticated approach to market segmentation is that it can help airlines in their forecasting, but it can be especially helpful in product planning and pricing. It can help them in planning specific price and product combinations to attract each segment or at least those segments they wish to cater for. It can also be useful in relating fares more closely to the costs imposed by the different segments and also in working out the various conditions attached to different fares to prevent slippage of passengers from high- to low-fare categories.

Another approach is to segment markets both in terms of motivation and requirements but also in terms of psychological make-up of passengers. One British airline has categorised its business passengers into 'attention seekers', 'comfort cravers' or 'schedule seekers', each with different demands and flying behaviour. Leisure travellers were either 'schedule seekers', 'service seekers' or 'nervous nellies', though the latter were unlikely to be told this! Some other airlines have also tried to categorise their passengers in a similar fashion. The aim of such market segmentation is to gain a better insight and understanding of passenger needs so as to make the correct marketing decisions. There is a problem, however. The more complex and sophisticated the market segmentation, the more complex and costly is the market research which is necessary to establish and monitor the market segments and their needs. Smaller airlines will tend to stick to a simpler and more traditional approach.

Initially, low-cost airlines also tended to adopt a simple approach focusing on very low fares as their prime product feature and relying on such fares to stimulate demand from all market segments without worrying too much about identifying the specific needs of individual segments except in choosing the points to serve. But increasingly they too have focused on developing product features to target specific market segments. For instance, Southwest and easyJet have used high flight frequencies to attract business travellers.

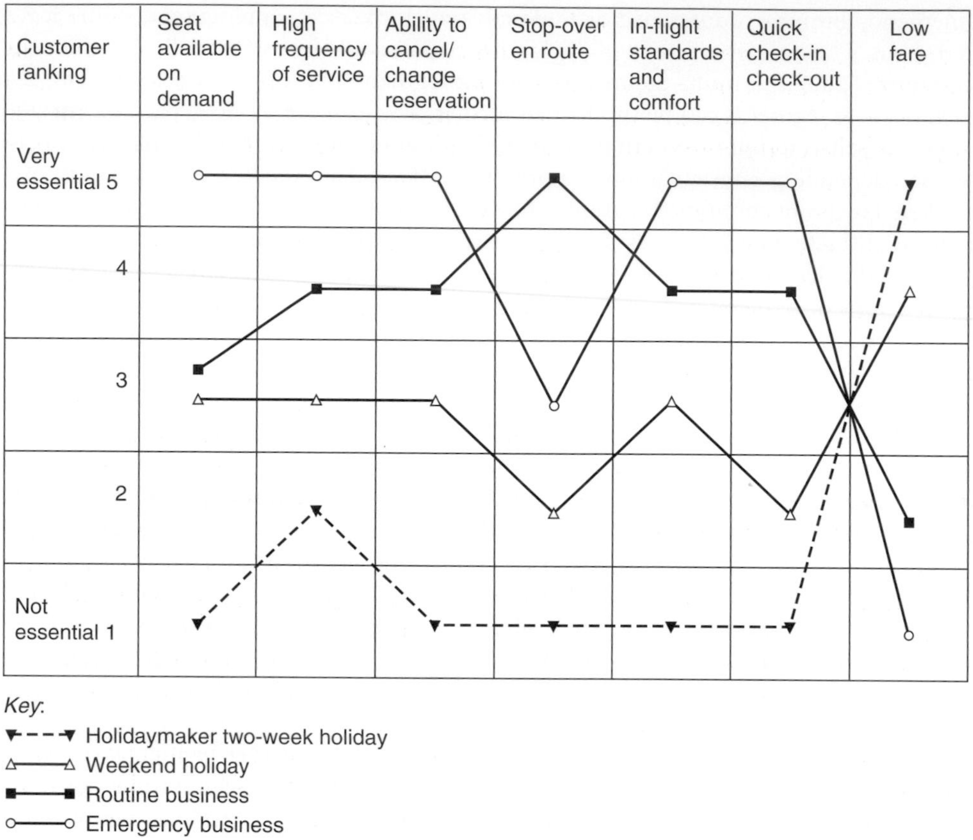

Customer ranking	Seat available on demand	High frequency of service	Ability to cancel/ change reservation	Stop-over en route	In-flight standards and comfort	Quick check-in check-out	Low fare
Very essential 5							
4							
3							
2							
Not essential 1							

Key:
▼--- ▼ Holidaymaker two-week holiday
△——△ Weekend holiday
■——■ Routine business
○——○ Emergency business

Figure 8.1 Market segmentation by trip purpose and passenger needs. Only a sample of possible market segments is shown.

8.6   The seasonality problem

Like many transport industries, particularly those dealing with passengers, the airline industry is characterised by marked daily, weekly and seasonal peaks and troughs of demand. The pattern and intensity of the peaks and troughs vary by route and geographical area. Peak flows become a serious problem when they begin to impose cost penalties on the airlines involved. In meeting demand at peak periods an airline may have to provide extra capacity not only in terms of aircraft and flight crews or cabin staff but also in terms of staff, equipment and facilities in areas such as ground handling or sales. Such extra capacity will be under-utilised during the off-peak periods. The greater the ratio of peak to trough traffic, the more difficult it becomes to ensure utilisation of peak capacity in off-peak periods. Such peak capacity then becomes very costly to operate since it must cover all its fixed and overhead costs during the short period that it is actually in use. Expressed another way, one finds costly equipment and staff required for the peak sitting around virtually unutilised or, at best, under-utilised in periods of low demand.

Where the peak traffic season corresponds with the school holiday period in an airline's home country even more extra staff are needed in the peak since many staff with children want to take their own holidays during the same period and are away from work. It may be possible in some areas to overcome the peak problem by using seasonal staff employed for three to six months. For instance, Olympic Airways in the year 2000 had 7,200 permanent staff based in Greece, but employed an additional 3,190 staff for several months during the summer peak, mainly in ground handling and a much smaller number as cabin crew. While the number appears very high in proportion to the permanent staff, the increase in total labour costs was only around 10 per cent since seasonals were paid at much lower rates.

Seasonal peaks in demand for air services to and from each country or on particular routes arise as a result of either institutional or climatic factors. The distribution and length of school holidays, the patterns of annual holidays for factories and offices, religious festivals such as Christmas, the Chinese New Year or the Haj pilgrimage, and the distribution of major cultural and sporting events are the main institutional factors creating seasonal traffic peaks. Climatic factors are important through their effect on holiday patterns or by disrupting surface modes of travel. Where institutional and climatic factors coalesce then seasonal peaks become very marked. In the European area, traditional summer holidays for schoolchildren and employees coincide with climatic conditions in the Mediterranean basin which are ideal for seaside holidays and which are markedly better than those in Northern Europe. As a result, during the summer months there is an outpouring of people moving southwards from Northern Europe. The effect on airline peaks is dramatic, particularly for the non-scheduled or charter operators who focus on catering for this demand. In North America, the Christmas holiday season coincides with very cold winter weather in Canada and parts of the United States while Florida and the Caribbean bask in warm sunshine. These conditions create a peak of demand for air services to the Caribbean area in late December and early January.

Daily or weekly peaks are related to the pattern of working times and days during the week. Business travel creates daily demand peaks usually in the early morning and early evening and weekly peaks on Mondays or possibly Tuesdays and on Fridays. In those Muslim countries which have Thursdays and/or Fridays as days of rest, the business peaks will be different. On the other hand, leisure traffic is responsible for a peaking of demand at weekends, particularly during the holiday seasons. Inevitably, the split of traffic on any route between business and leisure influences the nature of the daily, weekly and seasonal variations in demand.

The daily and weekly peaks in demand generally pose a less severe handicap than the seasonal peaks, since there is enough flexibility in most airlines' operations to enable them to make sensible use of spare capacity during particular periods of the day or the week. Maintenance and training flights can be programmed for such slack periods, or aircraft can be leased out for charter work. Many international airlines find that, on scheduled routes with a high business component, demand falls off at the weekend and they can reduce their frequencies on Saturdays and Sundays. A few, such as Tunis Air or Finnair, use this spare weekend capacity on charter flights to meet the needs of the leisure market, which prefers weekend travel.

It is the seasonal peaks of demand which create more problems and impose the greatest costs. The monthly variations in demand levels vary considerably between different types of international routes. As a consequence they pose varying problems for the airlines operating each type of route and may require somewhat different responses. The passenger traffic in the peak and trough months in the year 2008 for a selection of routes radiating from London are shown in Table 8.4. Two are long-haul routes to Singapore and New York and the other three are European short- to medium-haul routes.

Table 8.4 Seasonality problem – monthly peak–trough passenger flows, selected London
routes, 2008

London to/from:	Lowest month Pax (000)		Highest month Pax (000)		Increase high to low
Short-haul/scheduled					
Athens	Feb	54.9	July	121.9	+ 122%
Munich	Jan	95.5	July	127.2	+ 33%
Palma (charters only)	Feb	0.2	Aug	111.1	n.a.
Long-haul/scheduled					
Singapore	Feb	76.3	Aug	93.6	+ 23%
New York	Feb	281.9	July	422.9	+ 50%

Source: Compiled by author from CAA, 2009(b) data.

As expected, a really problematic traffic flow manifesting the most acute seasonal
peaking problem is that of charter passengers to Palma in Mallorca, a major holiday
destination well served by non-scheduled charter flights but also by low-cost operators.
While monthly charter passenger flows were over 100,000 for the three summer months,
with a peak of 111,100 in August 2008, they collapsed to a few hundred in the winter
months January and February. This is symptomatic of demand pattern on holiday routes
with a clearly defined peak season related to climate. Many routes from Northern Europe
to the Mediterranean and also from Canada to the Caribbean fall into this pattern though
in the latter case the peak is during the northern winter months. As previously pointed
out (Chapter 7, Section 7.5), charter airlines partly overcome their seasonality problem
by flying their aircraft and crews intensively day and night during the peak period, thereby
achieving very high annual utilisation for both aircraft and crew. Some may also try to
lease their aircraft during their low season to carriers (scheduled or non-scheduled) in
other parts of the world who may have a different seasonal pattern of demand.

Charter markets face the greatest seasonality problems. But scheduled traffic flows
to or from holiday destinations, which are again dependent on seasonal variations in
climate, also tend to exhibit very marked seasonal peaks. London–Athens is an example
(Table 8.4). In 2008 traffic was uniformly high during the Mediterranean summer months
from May to October but these levels were more than twice as high as in the weakest
winter month, February. This contrasts with London–Munich, which also peaks in the
summer holiday season but the peak to trough variation is much lower. On London–
Munich the peak month was only 33 per cent higher than the lowest month. This is
because of the higher business component on the latter route and because leisure traffic
on this route is less dependent on the search for good seaside weather!

The two long-haul routes examined also exhibit contrasting patterns. London–
Singapore manifests only limited seasonal variation. Monthly traffic appears to be steady
year-round and the peak month in 2008 was only 23 per cent higher than the lowest
month. On the other hand, London–New York appears to have a much more marked
summer peak. The absolute traffic levels to and from New York are so high that having
extra capacity to cater for 120,000 to 145,000 passengers for the peak months means that
such capacity is heavily under-utilised during January and February. This places an economic strain on airlines operating this or other similar routes.

Airlines operating in markets with very marked seasonal variations in traffic face a
major strategic dilemma. If they try to offer the capacity needed during the peak months,

they may find much of their productive capacity (aircraft and crews) is underutilised in off-peak months and therefore costly. If on the other hand they limit the extra capacity they need to offer in the busiest months when demand is greatest they may lose some high-yield passengers and also market share. Different sectors of the airline industry deal with this dilemma differently.

Low-cost airlines try to offer a fairly similar level of capacity year-round even on highly seasonal routes, so as not to carry too much under-used capacity in the off-peak seasons. This inevitably means that off-peak capacity may be too high, in relation to per-ceived demand, but the response of low-cost carriers is to fill these extra low season seats by marketing very low fares and through successive low-fare promotions. In the process they can maintain high year-round utilisation of both aircraft and flight/cabin crews and thereby reduce their costs. European charter airlines' strategy, as mentioned in Chapter 7, is to use their aircraft very intensively during the summer peak season, achieving, where possible, high daily utilisation by flying during night hours. Then they switch many air-craft to longer-haul charters during the European winter or lease them to North American airlines to operate winter charters to the Caribbean.

The legacy or traditional scheduled carriers have been less successful at dealing with marked season traffic peaks. A scheduled legacy airline operating on routes with different peak periods can try and shift aircraft and other resources between routes according to the season so as to ensure high utilisation. However, Table 8.4 shows that an airline such as British Airways operating a range of services out of London, its home base, would have only limited scope to do this since on so many London routes peaks and troughs of demand fall at the same time of the year. Many other airlines face the same problem. But competitive pressures and the need to target the higher yields that can be generated at peak periods, generally push such airlines to increase their flight frequencies during the peak seasons. As a result, the capacity provided by most scheduled airlines on international services in the peak season is substantially higher than in the low season. US airlines seem to face a particularly acute capacity peak, with airlines such as Northwest offering almost twice as many international seat-kilometres in their peak month as in their lowest month. Conversely, Asian carriers are the least governed by peaks and troughs and this may be an added cost advantage for them.

Peak problems also exist in the movement of freight by air, but they are frequently less of a problem than peaks on passenger services. The use on longer sectors of the wide-bodied passenger jets which have very considerable freight capacity in their holds means that peaks in the flow of air cargo can be met on many routes without the provision of extra peak capacity. A more serious problem in air freighting is the directional imbalance of flows which arises because freight travels only one way, unlike passengers, who gener-ally make a round trip (see Chapter 12).

Coping with the seasonal variations in demand is a major headache for some airline managements since they affect so many aspects of airline operations. Pricing policies, operating schedules, maintenance and overhaul checks and advertising campaigns all need to be carefully manipulated in order to minimise the adverse effect of traffic peaks and slumps on aircraft and crew utilisation and on load factors, and through these on unit costs. (Peak pricing is discussed in Chapter 11.) To mitigate the adverse impact of highly peaked demand, airlines may also lease in aircraft or try to use seasonally employed labour during peak periods. Whatever techniques are used to diminish its impact, the seasonality of demand remains a problem to a greater or lesser extent for all airlines and is an under-lying constraint in many aspects of airline planning and marketing.

Table 8.5 Factors affecting levels and growth of passenger demand

Factors affecting all markets	*Factors affecting particular routes*

Level of personal disposable income
Supply conditions:
   Fare levels
   Speed of air travel
   Convenience of air travel
	Level of tourist attraction:
	   Scenic/climatic/historical/religious
	     attributes
	   Adequacy of tourist infrastructure
	   Comparative prices
	Exchange rate fluctuations

Level of economic activity/trade
Population size and growth rate
Social environment
   Length of paid holidays
   Attitudes to travel
	Travel restrictions
	Historical/cultural links
	Earlier population movements
	
	Current labour flows
	
	Nature of economic activity

8.7   Factors affecting passenger demand

The demand for passenger services arises from the complex interaction of a large number of factors which affect the different market segments differentially. Those factors fall broadly into two groups, which are summarised in Table 8.5: the general economic and supply-related factors that influence demand in all markets and the more particular factors that may influence demand on some routes but may be totally absent on others.

Of the general factors affecting demand, the price of air transport and the level and distribution of personal income in the markets served are perhaps the most important. Much of the growth of air travel during the last 40 years can be explained by the falling real price of air transport (as discussed in Chapter 1) and more especially by growth in the world's economies and rising personal incomes. A more detailed discussion of the impact of price changes follows in the next section.

As far as the impact of economic growth is concerned, Figure 8.2 shows that there appears to be a very strong correlation between the annual rates of growth in the world's Gross Domestic Product (right-hand scale) and the growth rates in air travel, measured in revenue passenger-kms (left-hand scale). Bearing in mind that the left-hand scale measuring annual changes in revenue passenger-kms is double the right-hand scale of GDP growth, Figure 8.2 suggests that, broadly speaking, there is a two to one relationship between demand for air travel and world GDP. In other words, demand grows or declines around twice as fast as any change in GDP. This is why, when in early 2009 economic forecasters were predicting that world GDP would decline in that year by 2.5 to 3.0 per cent, airlines were predicting a 5 to 6 per cent drop in air travel in that year.

Accelerated rates of traffic growth in particular markets at particular times have usually been due either to rapid growth in personal incomes or to falling air fares. The more general economic conditions also impact on traffic growth. The world economic climate and the rate of economic growth in particular countries or regions of the world influence demand in a variety of complex ways. They determine the level of industrial and economic activity in each country and more generally the level and nature of international trade. The level of economic activity and trade directly influences the growth of demand for business travel. Indirectly, it also influences leisure demand since it affects the level and growth of personal incomes.

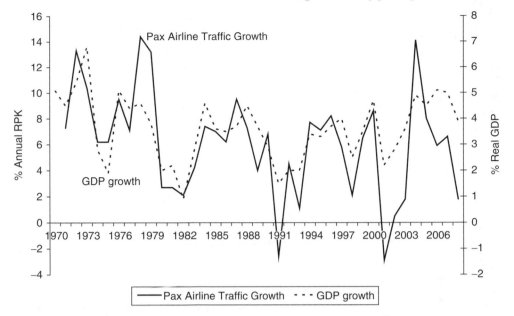

Figure 8.2 Annual changes in world gross domestic product compared to changes in revenue passenger-kms, 1970 to 2006.

Economic factors such as personal incomes or industrial activity have to be understood within a demographic context. The size and the distribution of the populations served by a route impose a major constraint on the level of potential demand. Thus, despite rapidly rising personal incomes in Singapore, the potential demand for Singapore originating air travel is strictly limited by the small size of the island's population of only 4.6 million. This explains Singapore Airlines' critical need to develop fifth and sixth freedom traffic, if it is to remain a big player in international air transport. Conversely, Japan originating leisure traffic has barely scratched the surface of the potential demand, given Japan's population of about 125 million and its rapid economic growth up to the mid-1990s. While rapid population growth may in theory increase the size of the air market, in practice it may have an adverse effect if it results in lower per capita incomes or in a larger population but one with a disproportionate share of young children who are unlikely to be air travellers. Both these phenomena have been evident in Morocco and Algeria, countries with birth rates well above average.

The social environment is also important in all markets since it determines the number of days of holiday available for travel or leisure and social attitudes towards travel. Thus one finds in Japan that workers do not take all the holidays they are entitled to but stay at work. In the same country, though there are many working women with relatively high disposable incomes, it is only in the last 20 years or so that social attitudes have begun to accept the idea of women holidaymaking on their own, though this is acceptable for men. For both these reasons, and given its high wage levels, Japan represents a huge potential market for air travel which will boom as social attitudes change and people start taking more of their holiday entitlement and as the notion that women can travel on their own becomes more widely accepted. At the other extreme, in much of Western Europe two long holidays away from home, one in the summer and a shorter one in winter, have traditionally been the social expectation of the middle- and upper-income groups. However, in recent years this too is changing with a trend to take more shorter leisure breaks. This has been stimulated by the very low and simple fares offered by low-cost carriers.

Demand and supply do not interact only through the price mechanism. As previously mentioned, various supply conditions other than price affect demand. In the short term, frequency, seat availability, departure and arrival times, number of en-route stops and other supply features influence the level of demand and the distribution of that demand between competing carriers.

In addition to the above general considerations affecting all markets, several other factors, which may be particular to individual routes, also influence demand levels. These are factors which may explain growth on some routes but not on others (Table 8.5 above). Demand for holiday trips is related to the tourist attractiveness of particular destinations. In order to be attractive and have tourist potential, resort areas or towns need two things: they must enjoy certain attractive and preferably unique scenic, climatic, historical or cultural advantages; they must also have the right infrastructure to cater for tourist needs such as sufficient hotel beds of the required standard, adequate ground transport, restaurants, entertainments, shopping facilities and so on. An attractive tourist location without the necessary infrastructure is not enough to generate a significant volume of demand for holiday travel, as many Third World countries have found. The two must go hand in hand.

Tourist facilities in themselves may not be enough. They must be priced correctly for the market they hope to attract and in relation to competing destinations. Changes in the relative price levels of hotels and other facilities in a tourist resort area may accelerate or retard traffic growth on particular air routes. Changes in the relative costs of holidays in a country may come about as a result of internal economic conditions or even government decisions. But they may also be generated by fluctuations in the exchange rates. Often, switching of tourist demand from one destination to another or the acceleration of outward-bound tourists from a particular country can be related to changes in the relevant exchange rates. Early in 2008, as the value of sterling fell sharply in relation to the Euro, many European destinations became less attractive to British tourists. Conversely, travel to Britain appeared much cheaper for many in Europe. The falling value of the US dollar in the mid-2000s attracted many Europeans to the United States.

Exchange rate fluctuations or even political factors may induce governments to impose travel restrictions on their own citizens. These may take the form of bans on external travel, the imposition of travel taxes for outgoing travellers or restrictions on the amount of foreign exchange which can be taken out for travel purposes. Following the economic crisis which hit several East Asian countries in late 1997, South Korea, the Philippines, Indonesia and Thailand all restricted travel for some time by one or more of these measures. Conversely, when in 1989 Taiwan allowed its citizens to travel to mainland China (via Hong Kong) for the first time there was a sudden boom in air traffic between Taipei and Hong Kong.

Ultimately, of course, leisure travel is also related to taste. Tourist destinations can inexplicably fall into or out of favour. In 2006, when air travel from the UK to most Mediterranean destinations held steady, the number of passengers flying to Turkey dropped by 4 per cent. Yet in the following year, 2007, Turkey was the fastest growing air travel market out of the UK, rising by 14 per cent, much of it on inclusive tour charter flights. Very competitive inclusive holiday prices, new hotels and a falling currency may have favoured Turkey, but it was also a question of changing tastes.

The visiting friends and relatives (VFR) demand is clearly affected by earlier population movements and migrations, which are very specific to particular routes. The heavy volume of demand on routes between France and Morocco, Algeria or Tunisia is related to the large number of immigrants from these countries living and working in France. There is little VFR traffic on routes between North Africa and the UK. On the other hand traffic demand between the UK and Canada, the West Indies, Pakistan or Australia and from Singapore to southern India or Sri Lanka can be explained only by earlier population movements. The same is true of the demand between the United States and Israel or the United States and Ireland. Many earlier migrations of population were related to the colonial period of history. Colonial ties have also resulted in linguistic and cultural links between particular pairs of countries which generate certain types of leisure travel but also considerable student travel. Large numbers of Singaporean, Malaysian or Hong Kong students go to English-speaking countries such as Australia, the UK or the United States to study. Students are an important component of demand on the air routes between their home countries and their place of study.

Cultural and linguistic ties also generate travel for cultural events, for conferences, and so on. Such ties affect trading patterns and thereby they may also influence business travel. Population migrations for work or settlement are still going on. The United States, Canada and Australia are still attracting and allowing immigrants from certain other countries and these swell the number of air passengers on the respective routes and subsequently generate VFR traffic. In other parts of the world since the 1980s relatively dense traffic flows have been generated by movements of migrant labour, such as those from the Philippines, India or Pakistan to Saudi Arabia and other Middle East states. More recently the migration of large numbers of Polish workers to the UK and Ireland has stimulated dense air passenger flows often catered for by low-cost carriers.

The demand for business travel is related to several factors, not just the level of trade and commercial interaction between two city pairs. It would seem that the nature of industrial, commercial and other activities in an airport's hinterland is an important determinant of the level of business travel demand. Certain activities appear to generate more business trips than others. At the London airports, banking and finance generate a disproportionately high level, around 25 per cent or more, of UK-originating business travel but account for well below 10 per cent of employment. This reflects London's role as a global financial centre. Administrative capitals obviously generate a great deal of government-related travel. Equally there is some evidence that major international ports generate a disproportionate amount of business air travel. Then there are very specific industrial situations which may stimulate, often for a short term, a rapid growth in demand for air services. The exploration and development of a new oilfield or the construction and commissioning of a new industrial complex would be two such examples.

The pattern and growth of demand on any route can be understood only by reference to the economic and demographic characteristics of the markets at either end of the route and to the supply features of the air services provided, of which price is the most important. However, when examining traffic growth on an individual route one must also consider any particular or localised factors such as those mentioned earlier which may affect demand on that route. These may include the tourist attractiveness of one or both ends of the route, the historical and cultural ties between the two markets served, the impact of exchange rate fluctuations, earlier or current population movements, and so on. These various factors provide an explanation of the growth and current level of demand on a route. Changes in any of them will affect the growth of traffic in the future. None the less, the overall demand for air travel, like that for most goods or services, seems ultimately to be most closely related to its price and to the income levels of its potential consumers. The impact of price and income on demand are therefore worthy of more detailed consideration.

8.8   Income and price elasticities of demand

Historically, leisure travel has shown a marked responsiveness to personal income levels. Early surveys of air passengers, such as those done at the University of Michigan more than 45 years ago, established that two things happen as people's personal incomes rise (Lansing and Blood, 1964). First, they spend more on all non-essentials. This includes greater expenditure on travel by all modes. Second, air transport, which is the high-cost but more comfortable and convenient mode for longer journeys, becomes more competitive with surface travel and there is a shift of demand from surface modes to air. In other words, higher incomes result in greater expenditure on longer-distance holiday and VFR travel, and at the same time a higher proportion of that expenditure goes on travel by air rather than surface. That trend still holds true today.

The relationship between income changes and demand for air travel can be measured by what economists call the income elasticity. This is arrived at quite simply by dividing the percentage change in demand generated by an income change by the percentage change in personal income which brought about that shift in demand:

$$\text{income elasticity} = \frac{\%\ \text{change in demand}}{\%\ \text{change in income}}$$

Thus, if a 3 per cent increase in personal income results in a 6 per cent growth in demand for air travel, then the income elasticity is 6 per cent divided by 3 per cent, which is +2.0. This means that every 1 per cent variation in income will induce a 2 per cent change in demand. Our earlier comparison of annual changes in world GDP and air travel over the period 1980 to 2008 does indeed suggest a GDP elasticity of around +2.0 (Figure 8.2).

In examining traffic development on a route or group of routes over time in order to establish what the impact of income changes has been, a number of problems arise. The first is how to isolate or exclude the impact of other variables, such as fare changes, on demand. This is done by using multiple regression techniques, which in turn pose certain methodological problems discussed in the next chapter. Second, there is the question of how to measure personal income. Ideally one would like to use a measure of the personal disposable income (after adjustment for inflation) of the population in a market or of the populations served at either end of a route. But disposable income data are not always available and countries tend to calculate it differently. Proxy measures have to be used for disposable income. Gross national product (GNP) or gross domestic product (GDP) are frequently used but they may be converted into per capita GDP. The latter is itself problematical in that it assumes a fairly even distribution of income among a country's population, which frequently is not the case. Both the British Airports Authority (BAA PLC) and the UK's Civil Aviation Authority (CAA) in their forecasts use an index of consumer expenditure as a readily accessible measure of the income available to consumers in different countries. Third, since air travel for leisure is a relatively new form of expenditure, one can assume a higher rate of growth in the early stages of increasing incomes and then a gradual saturation as people on high incomes get to the stage where they cannot easily consume more leisure travel.

A UK study of international leisure trips by air from the UK found that whereas income elasticities ranging from 2.2 to 2.5 were obtained for the period 1970 to 1998, they were considerably lower for the more recent period 1984 to 1998 (Graham, 2000). For the short-haul holiday market they had fallen from 2.2 to 1.5, indicating increasing saturation. If income elasticities are changing over time, it may be misleading to base forecasts on elasticities derived from past data. Lastly, there may be difficulties in establishing different income elasticities for the different segments of the leisure market, such as inclusive tours or independent holidays, or for VFR travel.

One would not expect the demand for business travel to be closely related to per capita income since business travellers' expenditure patterns are related not to their own personal incomes but to the needs of their employers. On the other hand, several studies have found that gross domestic product or some other measure of a country's national income or wealth does correlate with the volume of business traffic generated. It is not difficult to accept that business activity and travel will increase as a nation's total wealth grows. Thus it has proved possible to establish income elasticities for business travel but based on changes in national rather than in per capita income.

In the United Kingdom, most demand studies in the 1980s and 1990s produced results indicating income elasticities for various categories of passengers which were usually between +1.5 and +2.5. As one would expect, these studies indicated lower income elasticities for business as opposed to leisure travel. These were a feature of most studies (e.g. DoT, 1978, 1981; CAA, 1989 and Maiden, 1995). They also highlighted that short-haul travel is more income-elastic than long-haul travel.

A later 2005 study of outbound leisure passengers from the UK found that long-run income elasticities for the period 1993 to 2003 were in the range of +1.5 to +1.8 depending on the geographical markets concerned (CAA, 2005). Income elasticity was highest, +1.8, on routes to North America and lowest at +1.5 on routes to Western Europe. Long-haul income elasticities on travel to North America and the rest of the world appeared to have declined after 2000. This was possibly due to the various shocks in those markets in the period 2000 to 2003 such as the September 2001 attack on the twin towers in New York, the Iraq war and the SARS epidemic in 2003. Interestingly, an earlier UK Department of Transport forecast had in fact assumed that income elasticities of leisure travel were likely to decline over time as leisure markets reach maturity (DoT, 2000).

A number of forecasters have found that other economic variables such as volumes of trade or exchange rates could help explain changes in demand on particular markets in addition to or in place of income, usually measured in terms of gross domestic product (GDP) or per capita GDP. After the mid-1990s, the British airports company BAA PLC no longer calculated income elasticities for business demand since it found that other independent variables were more significant for business travel than income. Domestic business travel seemed to be more affected by the UK's gross domestic product, while international business travel seemed to be linked to changes in the volume of trade between the UK and major overseas markets. Yet, even when using trade as an income-related variable, one finds that business travel is relatively trade inelastic. Amsterdam airport has found that the trade elasticity of business travel is between 0.8 and 1.0 (Veldhuis, 1988).

Apart from income, price is the other variable which has, historically, had a major impact on the growth of air travel. The responsiveness of demand to price or fare changes can also be measured in terms of an elasticity coefficient:

$$\text{price elasticity} = \frac{\text{\% change in demand}}{\text{\% change in price/fare}}$$

Unlike income elasticity, price elasticity is always negative since price and demand must move in opposite directions. If the fare goes up, demand is expected to fall and vice versa. So there is invariably a negative sign in the equation. If fares go up 3 per cent and demand drops 6 per cent, then the price elasticity is $(-6\%) \div (+3\%) = -2.0$.

Most of the problems previously mentioned which have to be faced when estimating income elasticities also arise in price elasticity studies, but there are some additional ones too. In examining traffic and fare data, for a route or several routes over a period of time, which fare should one choose to indicate price changes? Not only will there be several fares on each route, but the number of fares and their relative levels may have changed over time. Problems multiply when fares vary by season of the year. Some analysts might use the basic economy fare or the most widely used fare or, if it is available, the average yield obtained by the airline. Alternatively, some have overcome this problem by establishing different price elasticities for different fare groups. It is the real level of the fare, in constant value terms, that is significant, not the current level. Therefore fares have to be adjusted for price inflation so as to establish the real cost of air travel in relation to the cost of other goods and services. On international routes this means making different adjustments at each end of the route. An additional problem in establishing fare elasticities in leisure markets is posed by the inclusive tour (IT) passengers, who have no knowledge of the cost of the fare within their total holiday package price. Moreover, fare changes within an IT package will have a disproportionately small impact on the total holiday price paid by the prospective IT consumer.

In so far as business travellers do not pay for their own travel, one would expect them to be relatively insensitive to fare changes. This should be reflected in lower price elasticities for business travellers or for high-fare traffic categories which are composed primarily of business travellers. An examination of price elasticities in some studies shows this to be true. Whereas non-business travel tends to have price elasticities greater than -1.0, the price elasticity of business travel is often less than -1.0. Conversely, the most price-sensitive market segments are those at the lower end of the market, that is, the high-discount fare groups and, in Europe, the inclusive tour segment of the market.

It is the high elasticity of demand to price changes at the bottom end of the leisure market that appears to explain the very rapid growth of demand for low-cost airlines such as Southwest in the United States and Ryanair and easyJet in Europe. But another factor has also played a part. This is the so-called price cross-elasticity of demand. This measures the responsiveness of demand for product A (say a low-cost airline) to the price of product B (say the fares of a legacy network carrier). In other words, if LCC fares are much lower they will divert passengers from higher fare airlines.

Economics textbooks deal at length with the concept and the mathematics of elasticity. It is not opportune to discuss the complexities of the concept here. Suffice it to say that, in order to make pricing and other marketing decisions, airline managers need to have a feel for the price elasticity of the various market segments on the route or routes they are dealing with. Without such a feel, they may make major planning and pricing errors. They basically need to know whether their markets, or rather different segments of each

Table 8.6 Short-haul international return flight – 200 seats and $100 single fare

Total seats offered per day (200 each way)	= 400
Business passengers (approx. 50 each way)	− 100
Leisure passengers (approx. 50 each way)	= 100
Daily seat factor (200 pax in 400 seats)	50%
Revenue from business market (100 × $100)	= $10,000
Revenue from leisure market (100 × $100)	= $10,000
Total revenue per day	= $20,000

market, are price elastic or inelastic. They also need to have an awareness of the fare cross-elasticities affecting these markets.

If the price elasticity of demand in a particular market is greater than − 1.0, that is, if it is − 1.1, − 1.2 or more, the market is considered to be elastic. This means that a change in the price or fare has a more than proportional impact on demand. If the fare is reduced, demand will grow more than in proportion. Though each passenger will be paying less than before, many more passengers will be travelling, with the result that the total revenue generated will go up. Conversely, a fare increase in an elastic market has such an adverse effect on demand that total revenue will decline despite the fare increase. When the price elasticity is less than − 1.0, as in the case of many business markets, demand is inelastic. Fare changes have a proportionally smaller impact on demand levels. In such market conditions, fare increases will generate greater total revenue because demand will not fall off very much. On the other hand, fare reductions will stimulate some traffic growth, but it will be proportionally less than the drop in fare, so total revenue will decline.

The easiest way of appreciating the pricing and revenue implications of different price elasticities is to consider a simple example. Let us assume that on a short-haul international route an airline is flying a daily return service with a 200-seater aircraft. It is the only operator and there is a single fare of $100 one way. The daily traffic and revenue on the route can be summarised as in Table 8.6.

Because of an unexpected increase in jet fuel prices, the airline needs to increase revenue on the route by about 4 per cent. In the short term, costs cannot be reduced in other areas, so the marketing manager is required to generate the additional revenue through tariff changes. The instinctive reaction would be to increase fares to cover the increase in costs. However, earlier market research had established that, while business demand is relatively inelastic to fare changes, with an elasticity of − 0.8, the leisure market is price elastic with an elasticity of − 2.0. Using these price elasticities the marketing manager estimates the traffic and revenue impact of a 10 per cent increase in the fare from $100 to $110.

The business price elasticity of − 0.8 tells him that, for every 1 per cent increase in the fare, the airline will lose 0.8 per cent of its market. Thus a 10 per cent fare rise results in an 8 per cent loss of business travellers (i.e. change in demand = + 10% × − 0.8 = − 8%). So their daily number will decline by 8 per cent, from 100 to 92. Leisure traffic, being more elastic to price changes, will drop more, by 20 per cent (or − 2.0 per cent for each 1 per cent increase in fare), to 80 passengers on average each day. Surprisingly, even a 10 per cent fare increase results in a drop in revenues, not an increase (Table 8.7).

Revenue from business travellers would go up because, though fewer would travel, the drop in traffic is more than compensated for by the higher fare they are all paying. But leisure passengers react in larger numbers to the higher fare and total revenue from

Table 8.7 Impact of $110 single fare

---

92 business passengers at $110 = $10,120
80 leisure passengers at $110 = $ 8,800

172 passengers: total revenue $18,920

Seat factor: 172 as percentage of 400 seats = 43%

Table 8.8 Impact of $90 single fare

---

108 business passengers at $90 = $ 9,720
120 leisure passengers at $90 = $10,800

228 passengers: total revenue = $20,520

Seat factor: 228 as percentage of 400 seats = 57%

---

this segment of the market would go down markedly. The net result is that, if the airline followed an instinctive reaction and increased the fare by, say, 10 per cent, it would end up with a significant fall in traffic, and a collapse of the seat factor from 50 per cent to 43 per cent. This in turn would lead to a drop in total revenue. Too often airlines fail to appreciate that increasing fares may reduce rather than increase their total revenues.

What would be the effect of reducing the fare by 10 per cent to $90? Both business and leisure demand would increase – the former by 8 per cent (i.e.– 10% ×–0.8 = +8%) and the latter by 20 per cent. Using the price elasticities as before, the traffic and revenue implications can be calculated (Table 8.8).

The lower fare would generate 28 more passengers each day and the seat factor would jump to 57 per cent, a creditable improvement from the current 50 per cent. Most of the additional passengers would be leisure passengers, who are more price elastic, and revenue from this sector of the market would increase. While there would also be more business travellers, business revenue would decline because the 8 per cent increase in passenger numbers would not be sufficient to compensate for the 10 per cent drop in the fare paid. However, total revenue would increase by only $520. This might do little more than cover any additional costs such as in-flight catering imposed by the extra 28 passengers. Cutting fares would produce a better revenue result than increasing the fares. It would increase total revenue by 2.6 per cent. But this is still less than the 4 per cent required.

Examination of the above figures suggests that revenue could be maximised by a two-fare price structure (Table 8.9). The airline should charge the business travellers more because their demand is relatively inelastic to price. But it should charge less to the price-elastic leisure market, knowing that lower fares will generate proportionally more demand and thereby increase total revenue from this market segment.

By introducing separate fares for each market segment, the airline can increase its total revenue by $920 or 4.6 per cent and its seat factor by three points to 53 per cent. The net revenue gain might be less because there may be some extra costs involved in carrying 12 more passengers. This solution also presupposes that the airline can create effective tariff 'fences' to prevent slippage of business passengers into the low-fare market. Simply put, the above example illustrates the principle that, in price-elastic markets, low fares may

Table 8.9 Impact of two-fare price structure

92 business passengers at $110 = $10,120
120 leisure passengers at $ 90 = $10,800

212 passengers: total revenue = $20,920

Seat factor: 212 as percentage of 400 seats = 53%

increase total revenue and that conversely, where demand is price inelastic, higher fares will generate higher total revenue.

It must be emphasised that even on a simple route the best pricing solution is dependent on two variables, the price elasticities of the different market segments and the market mix, that is the proportion of the total market represented by each segment. In the above example, the pricing policy adopted might be different if business travellers represented 90 per cent of the market or if the price elasticity of leisure demand was −2.4 instead of −2.0.

The study of outgoing UK leisure air travellers mentioned earlier (CAA, 2005) estimated their long-term price elasticity on routes to North America, Western Europe and the rest of the world. It found that the demand for leisure air travel was relatively inelastic to changes in air fares. The price or fare elasticity of demand to North America was − 0.8 and to Europe and the rest of the world it was −0.7. Most studies have found, as one might expect, that businessmen are even less responsive to fare changes than leisure travellers, while both groups are less elastic to fare changes on long-haul international routes than on shorter routes.

A comparative analysis of 21 studies of price elasticities for air travel in different countries found significant variations in elasticities between markets and, as one would expect, between business and leisure. This analysis estimated the median values from the range of elasticities shown in the various studies. For long-haul business travel the median price elasticity was − 0.48, indicating very inelastic demand. Short-haul business travel demand was also relatively inelastic with a median value of − 0.7, whereas short-haul leisure demand appeared to be very price elastic with a median elasticity of − 1.52 (Gillen *et al.*, 2003).

A more recent comprehensive analysis of price and income elasticities in different markets, and using US, IATA and UK data bases, found much higher price elasticities of − 1.5 to − 2.0 in many markets than previous studies. But it did not differentiate between business and leisure passengers. Long-haul price elasticities were only marginally lower than short-haul. The income elasticities produced, ranging between +1.5 to +2.7 in different markets and countries, were more consistent with findings by others (IATA, 2008b).

Low price or fare elasticities suggest that demand is unresponsive to fare changes. But this assumes relatively small or marginal changes in fares. Southwest and later the European low-cost carriers realised that dramatic deep fare cuts of the order of 50–70 per cent or more could generate an explosion of demand even if the fare elasticity was −0.8 or even less. In Europe in the 1990s and early 2000s Ryanair and easyJet were increasing their traffic by 20 to 30 per cent each year by entering new markets and slashing the prevailing fare levels. Not only would much lower fares generate new demand, but the price cross-elasticity, which was strongly in their favour, would divert passengers away from network carriers who continued to offer higher, complex and inflexible fares. Ryanair and easyJet, like Southwest before them, clearly understood the concept of price elasticity.

The concept of demand elasticity can be taken further to establish the reaction of passenger demand to changes in other variables. For instance, it is possible to calculate the demand elasticities of service elements such as frequency or journey time. Journey-time elasticities would show that business travel is the most responsive to reductions in journey time and VFR demand probably least responsive. There is also the concept of price cross-elasticity mentioned earlier. This measures the impact on the demand for air travel of changes in the price of competing goods or services. Changes in fare structure and levels on the North Atlantic and other markets have resulted not only in changes in the total demand but also in significant shifts of demand between fare types, between cabin classes and also to some extent between seasons, since fares vary by season.

Different studies even of the same markets seem to produce different income and price elasticities. Airlines may have difficulties in choosing between them. Larger ones may carry out their own studies to establish elasticities on the routes they are most interested in. If they can overcome the data and methodological problems, they must still face up to the fact that the elasticities are based on historical traffic data, which may be influenced by particular variables other than fare or income which have not been included in their analysis. There is the additional problem that price, income or other elasticities are changing over time. This is inherent and inevitable. Since elasticities are based on proportional changes in demand, such proportions change as the total demand changes. In the simple example used above, once the fares have changed from the $100 starting level to a new fare generating a different level of demand, then the price elasticities at that new demand level will have changed too. Though the change may be a relatively small one.

The pragmatic and methodological problems involved in establishing elasticities should not induce airlines to abandon the concept. Some understanding of elasticities is so crucial for pricing, marketing and forecasting that they cannot be ignored. Even an approximate appreciation of price and income elasticities for the major market segments will help airlines make more soundly-based decisions.

9 Forecasting demand

9.1 The need for forecasts

Forecasting is the most critical area of airline management. An airline forecasts demand in order to plan the supply of services required to meet that demand. Broadly speaking, tactical or operational decisions stem from short-term traffic forecasts covering the next 6–18 months or so, and are included in the airline's operating plan and budget for the current and the coming financial year. Aircraft scheduling decisions, maintenance planning, advertising and sales campaigns, the opening of new sales offices are among the many decisions which ultimately are dependent on these shorter-term forecasts. There are in addition a range of strategic decisions, many related to an airline's corporate plan and objectives, which stem from long-term forecasts. Decisions on aircraft procurement and the airline's fleet plan, the opening-up of new routes or markets, the training of additional flight crews, investment in new maintenance facilities and similar strategic decisions all stem from longer-term forecasts of up to five years or longer. Almost every tactical or strategic decision taken within an airline stems ultimately from a forecast. At the same time, forecasting is the area in which mistakes are most frequently made and the one about which there is least certainty. There is no absolute truth in forecasting, no optimum method that can guarantee accuracy. Instead, airline forecasters use any one of a range of forecasting techniques, of varying mathematical complexity, each of which has advantages and disadvantages, none of which can ensure consistent accuracy. Yet forecasts have to be made since so many decisions flow from them.

The annual budgets and the longer-term plans on which so many supply decisions hinge start with forecasts of passenger and freight traffic. Forecasting involves different types of forecasts, each of which pose different methodological problems. In the first instance, airlines need to forecast traffic growth assuming a continuation of current operating conditions with no dramatic changes in fares or in other supply factors. They will forecast the global growth of passenger and/or freight traffic on a route, group of routes or geographical region. Such forecasts represent the total demand, from which the airline then has to predict its own share and its own traffic. Essentially they involve an assumption that, all other things being equal, traffic growth will continue in the future very much as it has done in the past.

But frequently 'all other things' are not equal. They do not remain unchanged. The economic climate, exchange rates, tourism trends are among the many external factors which impact on demand and which may change over time or very quickly, as in the case of terrorist attacks. Many external factors which impact directly on the demand for air travel or air freight are unforeseeable. Their impact may be local or much wider.

Because external factors are unpredictable, they create much of the uncertainty in airline forecasting.

Demand is also dependent on numerous internal factors and changes. Airlines need to be able to forecast the response of demand to a change in the conditions of supply. Such changes may include an increase or reduction in the real level of fares, a change from narrow- to wide-bodied aircraft, a market increase in frequencies or a change in departure times. A significant change in supply conditions may be under consideration by the airline itself or change may be imposed by one or more of its competitors. In either case, an airline must be in a position to forecast traffic reaction to such change.

A somewhat different forecasting problem exists when an airline is trying to forecast demand on a new route which is under evaluation. This may frequently be a route on which there have been no direct air services at all previously, or it may be a route on which the airline concerned is a new entrant. In either case the airline has no experience and little or no historical traffic data on which to base its forecasts. This is particularly so if the route has had no previous air services at all. Forecasting in such circumstances is clearly very difficult, with a high risk of error, and may require different forecasting techniques from those normally used.

Lastly, there is the question of segmental forecasting. Passenger traffic on a route is composed of identifiable market segments related partly to purpose of travel and partly to service requirements. Such segments may be further categorised by point of origin. The earlier analysis of demand factors indicated that each market segment is likely to have differing demand elasticities and to be growing at different rates. It should therefore be possible to produce more accurate forecasts by forecasting the growth in each market segment separately and then aggregating them, rather than by forecasting the total traffic from the start. Many traditional network airlines already produce forecasts using two market segments, business and leisure, or possibly three based on fare type. Only a small number of airlines have the resources to carry out more extensive segmental forecasting. In the future, however, planning requirements and the need to improve the accuracy of forecasts may push more airlines to consider this disaggregate forecasting. In many airlines there is a dichotomy in forecasting methods. If an airline has a yield management system, its revenue planners may be using very detailed forecasts disaggregated by fare type but with a very short time horizon of a year or so. Yet in the same airline route and fleet planners will be basing their own three-to-five-year forecasts on less detailed models with fewer market segments.

The aim of this chapter is not to suggest the best way of forecasting but to review and assess some of the problems of forecasting and the alternative techniques which are most commonly used in the international airline industry, without going too deeply into their mathematics. As a result, this is not an exhaustive review, since some forecasting tools, little used by airlines, are not examined. The forecasting methods more widely used by airlines, often in combination, fall broadly into three groups of growing complexity: qualitative methods, time-series projections and causal or econometric methods.

9.2 Qualitative methods

9.2.1 *Executive judgement*

Of the numerous forecasting techniques available to airlines, executive judgement is one of the most widely used, usually to modify and adapt other more mathematical forecasts.

Such judgement is based on the insight and assessment of a person, who often may not be a forecaster, but who has special knowledge of the route or market in question. For instance, the country or area managers of an airline are frequently asked to predict traffic growth on their routes. Their knowledge will include an understanding of recent and current traffic growth and of economic and other developments likely to affect future demand. They also have first-hand knowledge of their own market and its peculiarities. They weigh up the factors involved and therefore their judgement and their predictions may be quite soundly based, but the approach is basically crude and unscientific. The more detailed and the more long-term the forecast, the more likely it is that executive judgement will prove inadequate. On the other hand, executive judgement as a forecasting tool has two distinct advantages. It is quick. Forecasts can be made almost instantaneously and do not require any detailed assessment or working out of data. In addition, the person making the forecast may be aware of extraneous and particular factors which may affect future demand on a route, which the more data-based techniques would not pick up. It is for this reason that many airlines subject their data-based forecasts to assessment and possible modification by certain key managers and executives.

9.2.2 *Market research*

A wide range of market research techniques can be used by airlines in order to analyse the characteristics of demand for both passengers and freight. These techniques will include attitudinal and behavioural surveys of passengers and, it is hoped, those not travelling by air. They will also involve studies of hotel and tourism facilities, surveys of travel agents and business houses, analyses of trade flows and other business interaction, and so on. Such studies might be commissioned from specialist market research companies or they might be carried out by the airlines themselves. Many larger airlines in any case carry out regular and systematic surveys of their own passengers so as to build up a profile of their needs and characteristics. Others carry out such surveys on an *ad hoc* basis when a specific question needs to be resolved. Airlines also build up market knowledge through data collected from their reservation systems, especially from direct online bookings, and from them frequent flyer programmes. The aim of all this is to derive empirically an understanding of how demand for air transport varies between different sectors of the population or, in the case of air freight, between different industrial sectors. This knowledge can then be used in combination with forecasts, by others, of sociological, demographic or economic change to predict future levels of demand.

In many circumstances such an empirical approach to forecasting may be more appropriate than the more econometric methods. On an air route where the demand for air travel is suppressed by the inadequate number of hotel beds at the destination, a study of hotel and tourism infrastructure projects at that destination may produce a better indication of future travel flows than would an analysis of past traffic trends. Equally the forecasting of air freight demand often lends itself to the use of market research studies, especially on routes where freight flows are relatively thin. On many routes the erratic and irregular growth of air freight makes time-series analyses or other econometric techniques difficult to use. Air freight forecasting models have generally been less successful than models for forecasting passenger demand. On most air routes, the goods freighted by air fall into a limited number of clearly-defined commodities. Exports by air from many developing countries are usually confined to one or two commodities, while imports are quite different and cover a wider, though still limited, range of goods. As a result, air freight forecasts may often fruitfully be based on market research analysis of trade developments in a few key commodities.

Market studies are particularly useful as a forecasting tool when past traffic data are inadequate or non-existent, thereby prohibiting the use of time-series and possibly of econometric forecasts too. This happens on many routes from developing countries and is obviously the case on entirely new routes. In these circumstances market research may be the only way of evaluating future demand. Market research also helps airlines to forecast demand reaction to changes in supply conditions, such as a change of timing, and to gain an appreciation of their different market segments if they wish to get involved in segmental forecasting.

9.2.3   Delphi techniques

The Delphi approach requires the building up of a consensus forecast based on the views of individuals who are considered to have sufficient expertise to be able to anticipate future trends. The process is an iterative one, possibly involving several rounds of consultation. In simple terms, a group of experts may be asked to give their forecasts of growth in a region or market. These forecasts are used to build up a composite forecast. This is then communicated to each expert who may wish to revise his own original forecast in the light of what other experts are predicting. The individual forecast from this second round of consultations can be used to arrive at an agreed or consensus forecast. This is the principle of the Delphi method. In practice, the consultative process can be more or less complex depending on the amount of information exchanged between the experts.

The Delphi technique is more suitable for aggregate forecasts of growth in major markets or regions than for individual route forecasts. As a result it is little used internally by airlines, but it has been the basis for the industry-wide forecasts produced annually by the International Air Transport Association (IATA). These are regional forecasts for nearly 20 route areas such as Europe–Middle East or Middle East–Far East. Forecasts by direction are produced for freight traffic too. The forecasts cover the current year and a five-year period ahead and are revised each June, sometimes with interim revisions during the winter. Up to 1986 these IATA forecasts were Delphi forecasts based on a consensus of expert opinion and were arrived at in a series of steps.

The first step involved the development of explicit forecasting assumptions at a meeting of airline forecasters and key experts from outside the airline industry. The airlines were requested to submit their own forecasts for the industry as a whole and for each route area or market in which they operated. Airlines were free to use whatever forecasting method they preferred in arriving at their own forecasts and could even make alternative key assumptions if they wished to. The results of this first round were distributed to all participating airlines for review before the finalisation meeting. This took place in early June. The experts reviewed the consolidated regional forecasts and made adjustments in the light of more recent developments. The IATA forecasts were then finalised and represented a consensus of expertise within the airline industry.

However, this Delphi approach was very time-consuming and since 1986 IATA has reverted to a simpler approach. Preliminary meetings to agree basic assumptions are no longer held. Instead, individual airlines submit their own forecasts for individual routes or markets. A consensus forecast based on a compilation of individual airline forecasts is then prepared by IATA. It is still in essence a Delphi forecast based on a consensus of expert opinion. The IATA annual forecasts are used by smaller airlines as inputs into their own forecasting processes and by larger airlines as a counter-check to their own internal forecasts. Airport authorities, aircraft manufacturers and governments also refer to the IATA forecasts.

9.3   Time-series projections

Time-series or trend projections represent the forecasting technique most widely used by airlines. Many smaller airlines do little else. Essentially the technique involves a projection into the future of what has happened in the past. It assumes that whatever factors affected air traffic in the past will continue to operate in the same manner in the future. The only independent variable affecting traffic is time, and as time progresses so will traffic.

To establish the relationship between traffic (the dependent variable) and time (the independent variable), it is essential to have accurate and detailed traffic statistics for the route in question. Without such data, trend projections cannot be used. The first step in the forecasting process is to plot the time-series data on a graph so as to show monthly or annual traffic totals against the appropriate month or year. Drawing a freehand curve through the points should indicate whether the traffic trend on the route is exponential or linear (Figure 9.1). An exponential trend is one where traffic seems to grow by a constant percentage with each unit of time. This means that the absolute increase in each time period in passenger numbers or freight tonnes is greater than in the previous period. This is because each successive growth is a constant percentage but of a larger preceding total. The equation of the exponential curve is given by

$$\text{traffic } (y) = a(1 + b)^t$$

where a is constant and b is the rate of growth and t is time. A linear or straight-line trend is one where the traffic increases by a constant absolute amount with each unit of time. It is expressed in the form

$$\text{traffic } (y) = a + bt$$

where a and b are constants and t is again time. Because changes for each unit of time are by a constant amount and the total traffic is growing, the percentage growth is gradually declining. There is therefore a fundamental difference between the impact of exponential as opposed to a linear growth trend on forecasts of traffic growth. Exponential growth means ever greater annual or monthly traffic increments, though the percentage change may be more or less constant. Linear growth would indicate constant increments in terms of numbers but declining percentage changes. Deciding which trend best represents developments of a route will therefore have a major impact on forecasts, especially longer-term ones. There is also the possibility that growth on a route may be linear in its early stages and then become exponential or vice versa. An added problem is that at times it might be difficult to decide whether an exponential or linear trend fits the data best, yet choosing between them will produce quite different forecasts.

It has been observed that some air routes or markets, after achieving very rapid growth for a number of years, reach a plateau where traffic growth flattens off. It is frequently assumed that this plateau level is reached when the market has matured and is in some

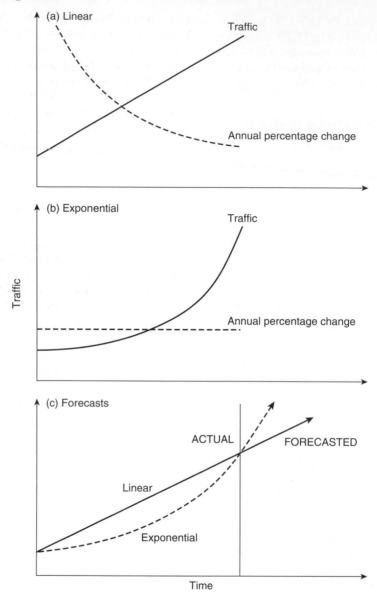

Figure 9.1 Types of traffic growth: (a) Linear: $y = a+bt$, (b) Exponential: $y = a (1+b)^t$, (c) Forecasts: linear and exponential.

sense saturated. If this has happened or is happening on a route, the trend of past traffic data may best be described by growth curves which asymptotically approach an upper limit such as a logistic curve or a Gompertz curve. Both of these are S-shaped and indicate declining absolute and relative growth as markets reach maturity. In practice, international airlines tend not to use logistic or Gompertz trend curves for forecasting. Most time-series forecasting is either exponential or linear. Of these, the former is probably

Table 9.1 Total passenger traffic, London–Nice (both ways), 1972–83

Year	Terminal passengers 000	Annual change %	Three-year moving average passengers 000	Annual change %
	1	2	3	4
1972	140.6			
1973	148.5	+ 5.6	143.8	
1974	142.4	− 4.1	151.6	+ 5.4
1975	163.8	+15.0	158.6	+ 4.6
1976	169.6	+ 3.5	166.9	+ 5.2
1977	167.4	− 1.3	174.0	+ 4.3
1978	185.0	+10.5	187.4	+ 7.7
1979	209.9	+13.5	206.7	+10.3
1980	225.1	+ 7.2	225.4	+ 9.0
1981	241.2	+ 7.2	245.0	+ 8.7
1982	268.8	+11.4	259.3	+ 5.8
1983	268.0	− 0.3		

Source: *UK Airports: Annual Statements of Movements, Passengers and Cargo*, UK Civil Aviation Authority, 2000a.

more widely used both because of its simplicity and also because past air traffic trends do often appear to be exponential.

The workings and implications of different time-series techniques can best be appreciated by using them to make forecasts for an actual route. The case study chosen is London to Nice on the French Mediterranean, a short-haul scheduled route with relatively little charter traffic and little indirect traffic transiting via Paris or elsewhere. The case study assumes that one is living in 1984 and wishing to forecast the traffic on the route for 1988, four years hence. For reasons of simplicity the forecasts for individual years from 1984 to 1988 are not discussed.

To make time-series forecasts, a minimum of 7–10 years of past traffic data is required and some forecasters suggest that one should not forecast for a longer period ahead than about half the number of past years for which statistics are available. For the London–Nice route, traffic data for 12 years to 1983 were examined (Table 9.1). This indicated that, though passenger movements almost doubled between 1972 and 1983, growth was at times erratic, with two years, 1974 and 1977, in which traffic actually declined. In practice, many larger airlines would hesitate to forecast so far ahead on the basis of time-series projections alone. Nevertheless, a five-year forecast does enable one to see clearly the impact of different techniques. While the analysis which follows relates to annual traffic volumes and forecasts annual traffic for 1988, the same forecasting methods could be used with monthly or weekly traffic data. Problems of seasonal traffic fluctuations would arise, but these can be adjusted for.

The London–Nice data underline some of the difficulties faced in forecasting. To start with, examination and plotting of the past traffic data do not make it easy to decide whether past growth is linear or exponential. As a result, both exponential and linear forecasts will be made in the analysis which follows. Another major problem facing forecasters using time-series analysis is how far back they should go in examining past traffic data. In the case of London–Nice, 10-year data to 1983 meant 1974 would be the first year.

This was known to be a year in which traffic slumped because of the first oil crisis. There was subsequently a very large jump in traffic in 1975. Using a maverick low year as the starting point might produce less accurate forecasts. So forecasters may decide, as has been done here, to go back and extend the time series by two years to 1972. This then raises a different question. Are data and traffic so far in the past a good reflection of what will happen five years in the future? Would it not be logical to take a shorter time series? Is the recent past a better indicator of the future than the more distant past? There is no absolute answer to this enigma. Forecasters must choose the time series which they feel in each case will best allow them to make a realistic forecast. To do this they must ensure that their stream of data embodies the underlying trends and encompasses complete cyclical variations if any exist.

9.3.1   *Exponential forecasts*

9.3.1.1   *Average rate of growth*

Many airlines, especially the smaller ones and those that have relatively new routes with only a short stream of data, base their forecasts on the average of the past rates of growth. This approach has the advantage of simplicity. In the London–Nice case, adding up the annual percentage change each year from 1972 to 1983 and dividing by 11, which is the number of observations, produced an average annual growth of +6.2 per cent. Using the formula

$$y = a(1 + b)^t$$

where a is the actual traffic in 1983, b is the growth rate and t is the number of years forecast, then

$$1988 \text{ traffic} = 268 \times (1.062)^5 = 362.0.$$

In this and subsequent equations, traffic volumes are in thousands.

In the London–Nice case, the number of observations is relatively small, and only 12; and this is so with many airline forecasts. But it does raise some doubt about whether +6.2 per cent is the true average growth rate. It is possible to estimate mathematically what the possible range of values for the true growth rate might be. The true growth rate at a 95 per cent level of confidence would be 6.2 ± 4.2. If one were to adjust the 1988 forecast accordingly, the range would be very wide. It is for this reason that most airline forecasters tend to ignore the implications of having a relatively small number of observations.

9.3.1.2   *Moving average growth*

The use of annual average growth rates should be based, in theory, on data series which are long enough to show what are the random variations and what are shifts in underlying trends. Where the time series is not very long and where there are very marked fluctuations in traffic growth from year to year, as in the case of the London–Nice data (Table 9.1), some forecasters will use moving averages as a way of flattening out wild traffic variations so as to understand the underlying trends. In order to do this, normally three (or more) observations are added together and the average calculated. This is then given as the actual observation for the middle of the three years (or months if one is using monthly data). For London–Nice the actual traffics for 1972, 1973 and 1974 were added together and divided by three. This produced a three-year moving average of 143,800, which was the traffic attributed to 1973, the middle year (column 3 of Table 9.1). Then 1972 was dropped and the average for 1973, 1974 and 1975 calculated and attributed to 1974 and so on, the final moving average being for 1982. The choice of the number of observations for the moving average is up to the forecaster, whose aim is to eliminate sudden short-term traffic variations without losing sight of longer-term changes. But moving averages cannot be used with small data sets since one effectively loses data at each end. Examination of the moving average data for London–Nice in Table 9.1 (columns 3 and 4) shows a flattening out effect. Traffic does not decline in any single year and the growth in the good years is not as high as the unadjusted annual figure would suggest. The highest growth was 10.3 per cent in 1979, following which there seems to have been a downward trend in the underlying growth rate.

The annual average rate of growth can be calculated from the annual changes in the moving average figures (column 4 in Table 9.1). In this case it was 6.8 per cent. Using this to forecast 1988 traffic, then,

$$1988 \text{ traffic} = 259.3 \times (1.068)^6 = 384.8.$$

The use of a moving average here seems to have identified a faster underlying growth than was evident previously.

9.3.1.3   *Exponential smoothing*

Some forecasters believe that the recent past is a better pointer to the future than the more distant past. It follows that, in projecting past traffic growth into the future, greater weight should be given to the more recent observations. Mathematically, the technique for doing this is similar to the moving average but adjusted to give a particular weighting to recent as opposed to more distant observations. In a simple form,

$$y + 1 = \alpha y + \alpha(1 - \alpha)y_{-1} + \alpha(1 - \alpha)^2 y_{-2} + \alpha(1 - \alpha)^3 y_{-3} \dots$$

where α is a smoothing factor ($10 < \alpha < 1$), y is the number of passengers in year y, and $y + 1$ is the first-year forecast.

The greater the value given to α, the greater will be the weight given to the more recent observations. The forecaster can decide the value of α. The above formulation is relatively simple but some smoothing techniques can be quite complex. The best known is the Box-Jenkins model. This is a sophisticated and complex model requiring a large number of observations. Though airline forecasters make reference to Box-Jenkins (Nguyen Dai, 1982), few actually use it. Simpler formulations are available. One of these is Brown's double exponential smoothing model and another the Holt-Winters model. Both use a smoothing technique to deal with time-series data containing a trend variation. Since the London–Nice traffic data showed a clear trend pattern, the Holt-Winters model was used. The 1988 forecast produced on this basis was 326,200 passengers. This is much lower than the other exponential forecasts because the effect of the smoothing technique is to give much greater weight to the fact that in 1983, the most recent year, traffic declined marginally. While exponential smoothing techniques have been widely used in some other industries, their use is still fairly limited within the airline industry. There is, however, a growing awareness that, by giving greater weight to the more recent observations, forecasters may be in a position to improve the accuracy of time-series projections.

9.3.2   Linear trend projections

9.3.2.1   Simple trend

The underlying assumption is that a straight line best represents the trend of the traffic over time and that traffic increases by a constant amount with each unit of time. The technique involves drawing a straight line through the time series so as to produce a best fit. This is normally done by the least squares method, though other mathematical techniques are also available. The least squares criterion requires that the line fitted to the data should be the one which minimises the sum of the squares of the vertical deviations of the individual data points from the line. Some of the points are likely to be above the line, and therefore positive, and some below the line, and so negative. These would cancel each other out if one were merely trying to minimise the sum of the deviations. By using the squares of the deviations this problem is avoided.

In fitting a line of the form $y = a + bt$ to the time-series data so as to satisfy the least squares criterion, there remains the problem of how closely the straight line corresponds to those data. The goodness of fit is measured by an index known as the coefficient of correlation (R), or the square of this quantity (R^2), which is strictly speaking the coefficient of determination. In practice the R^2 coefficient is used most frequently. If the fit of the straight line to the data is very poor, the value of R^2 approaches zero. If the fit is very good, the value of R^2 will be close to 1.0. Within the airline industry, experience suggests that accurate predictions using linear trend lines require very high coefficients of determination. They should be above 0.90 and preferably higher.

Fitting a trend line to the London–Nice data produced the following result:

$$y = 111.9 + 12.7t, \quad R^2 = 0.939.$$

This indicates that a trend line starting at 111,900 passengers and growing by 12,700 passengers per year (t) produces a good fit with the actual traffic in each year since the coefficient of determination at 0.939 is high. To forecast traffic in 1988 one needs to add 12,700 passengers for each year of the 17 years from 1972 to 1988 to the starting figure of 111,900:

$$1988 \text{ traffic} = 111.9 + (12.7 \times 17) = 327.8.$$

Trend projections are simple and easy to use. But they can be used only if the data exhibit some regularity without wide fluctuations. Many air routes, however, do exhibit very pronounced traffic variations, with large jumps in traffic followed inexplicably by sudden slumps. In such conditions, fitting trend lines with an adequately high coefficient of determination may prove difficult. One possible solution is to use moving averages.

9.3.2.2   Moving average trend

Unusually large variations in the past traffic volumes can be reduced by calculating moving averages and establishing a new time series. This should now contain only the trend

Table 9.2 Alternative time-series forecasts (made in 1984) of London–Nice traffic for 1988

Forecasting method	Number of passengers forecast
Exponential forecasts:	
Average annual rate of growth	362,000
Moving average	384,800
Exponential smoothing (Holt–Winters)	326,200
Linear trend projections:	
Simple trend	327,800
Moving average trend	329,500
Difference between highest and lowest forecast	58,600

component in the traffic and it should be easier to fit a trend line. Using the moving average data for London–Nice (as previously given in column 3 of Table 9.1), the following trend line and forecast were calculated:

$$y = 119.9 + 13.1t, \qquad R^2 = 0.961$$

$$1988 \text{ traffic} = 119.9 + (13.1 \times 16) = 329.5.$$

On London–Nice, the use of a moving average trend produces a forecast which is very close to the one based on the unadjusted trend. This is because the London–Nice traffic did not exhibit wide fluctuations and therefore using a moving average trend has relatively little impact. It has been done here only for illustrative purposes.

As a result of using alternative time-series techniques, five different forecasts of the London–Nice passenger traffic in 1988 could have been produced. They are summarised in Table 9.2. The difference between the highest and the lowest forecast is around 58,000 passengers a year, equivalent to five round-trip flights a week in an Airbus A320 at about a 65 per cent seat factor. The range is very wide and could play havoc with any airline's strategic fleet planning decisions. Which forecast should the forecasters and planners go for? As a group, the exponential techniques in this particular case produced higher forecasts than the linear trends. This seems to be frequently so in airline forecasts and may be an additional reason why airlines prefer working with exponential rather than linear projections. They prefer to be optimistic in their forecasts.

What did happen on the London–Nice market by 1988? The year-by-year growth after 1983 seems to have been relatively rapid (Table 9.3). Only in 1986, the year of the nuclear power station disaster in Chernobyl and a poor year in many markets, did traffic growth slow down. By 1988, 392,800 passengers were travelling on the route. Comparison with the summary of forecasts (Table 9.2) suggests that growth in this market was clearly exponential rather than linear. The linear forecasts were much too low, while two of the exponential forecasts, based on the annual or the three-year moving annual rates of growth, were relatively close to the 1988 outcome. Despite the very high values of R^2 obtained for the linear trends they proved poor predictors of future traffic. This suggests that one should not accept very high values of R^2 uncritically when forecasting.

The exponential smoothing forecast was not very accurate, but this was no doubt due to the fact that 1983 had been a year of slight decline. Had one used 1982 as the final year, when traffic grew 11.4 per cent, then an exponentially smoothed forecast, which places

Table 9.3 Actual London–Nice traffic, 1983–8

Year	Terminating passengers '000	Annual change %
1983	268.0	
1984	278.1	+ 3.8
1985	305.6	+ 9.9
1986	308.7	+ 1.0
1987	341.4	+10.6
1988	392.8	+15.0

Source: *UK Airports: Annual Statements of Movements, Passengers and Cargo*, UK Civil Aviation Authority, 2000a.

greater weight on the most recent years, would have produced a much higher forecast. This suggests that exponential smoothing may be too dependent on what has happened most recently and may distort the longer-term trend. Moreover, this technique, though called *exponential* smoothing, is mathematically more akin to linear forecasting. This may explain its low 1988 forecast.

A similar exercise for the London–Nice route carried out ten years later in 1995 to forecast passengers numbers for 1999 produced similar conclusions (Table 9.4). The forecasts were based on annual traffic volumes for the period 1983 to 1994. Once again the exponential forecasts proved to be much closer to the actual out-turn than the linear projections. The exponential forecast, using a moving average, predicted traffic of around 921,000 passengers in 1999 compared to the actual traffic of 980,300. This proved remarkably close given that in 1996 there was a dramatic change in the supply conditions. In that year, easyJet, a low-cost carrier, launched services from Luton, one of the London area airports, to Nice, offering very low fares. This had a dramatic impact on demand levels. In 1998, by which time easyJet was well established on the route, passenger numbers grew nearly 30 per cent. All carriers between London and Nice increased their traffic that year, though growth in the following year 1999 was down to 13 per cent. Exponential forecasts appear better able to allow for sudden surges in demand due to changes in market conditions.

As markets mature it is likely that annual growth will slow down and as a result exponential forecasts will over time need to reflect this maturity. The London–Nice market shows the onset of maturity very clearly. In the 11 years from 1988, when passengers on this route numbered 392,800, to 1999 traffic grew by 150 per cent to 980,300. As mentioned above this high growth was due in part to the impact of the entry of a low-cost carrier in this market. But in the following nine years to 2008 traffic grew by only 31 per cent to just under 1.3 million. The market had matured and low fares were no longer stimulating demand as previously. Executive judgement may be needed to assess when markets are maturing and to adjust exponential forecasts downward.

Nevertheless, the London–Nice case study supports the view of many airlines that traffic growth is more likely to be exponential than linear. But there will be routes where linear trend projections may produce more reliable forecasts. In practice, every airline's forecasting group has developed in the light of its own experience a preference for a particular approach to forecasting involving only one or two of the methods proposed above. Few airlines would bother to calculate more than a couple of time-series forecasts.

Throughout the world the majority of airlines use time-series projections as the starting point for their forecasting exercises. They are simple to use provided that adequate

Table 9.4 Alternative time-series forecasts (made in 1994) of the London–Nice scheduled traffic for 1999

Forecasting method	Number of passengers forecast
Exponential forecasts	
Average annual rate of growth	859,700
Moving average	920,700
Exponential smoothing (Holt–Winters)	743,400
Linear trend projections	
Simple trend	764,200
Moving average trend	745,800
Actual traffic in 1999	**980,300**

statistical information on past traffic flows is available. They require little else. They are also likely to be reasonably accurate for short-term forecasts. It is relatively easy to forecast tomorrow's traffic if you know today's, or to forecast next week's traffic if you know the average traffic handled in recent weeks. Beyond 18 months or so, the risk of error with time-series forecasts increases as various external factors begin to impact on demand. Time-series projections allow airlines to make individual forecasts for each route. Annual forecasts can be disaggregated into monthly forecasts reflecting seasonal variations without too much difficulty. Alternatively, time-series forecasts can be built up using monthly rather than annual data.

Although they are widely used, time-series forecasting methods do have a fundamental underlying weakness. They are based on the assumption that traffic growth and development are merely functions of time. As time changes, so does demand. Yet our earlier analysis of demand showed that many factors affect the level of demand, such as the level of trade or of personal income, and that these factors are themselves changing over time. Even if these did not do so, there are numerous supply factors, of which the most critical is the tariff level, which are invariably changing and affecting demand in the process. It is clearly an over-simplification to relate demand purely to changes in time. Time can be only a very poor proxy for a host of other critical variables. The longer ahead the time-series projection, the less likely it is to be accurate, as there is more time and scope for demand to have been influenced by changes in one or more of the many independent variables.

There are two ways in which airline forecasters can try to overcome this underlying weakness. Most airlines start by making time-series projections. They then modify these projections on the basis of market research findings and executive judgement and turn them into forecasts. In this way they can allow for the impact of the expected changes in demand factors and of planned changes in supply which they themselves control. As an alternative, a few airlines, usually larger ones, may try to use econometric or causal forecasting techniques, which relate traffic growth not to time but to a series of assumed causal factors.

9.4   Econometric or causal models

The underlying principle of all such models is that the demand for passenger transport or for air freight services is related to and affected by one or more economic, social or supply factors. Economic theory suggests that the demand for any product or service depends primarily on its price, on the prices of competing products or services, on the nature of the product and the degree to which it is essential for consumers, on levels of personal income and on consumers' taste. Changes in any one of these variables will affect demand. Econometric models attempt to measure that causal relationship so that by forecasting or even implementing change in any one of the variables one can predict the consequent impact on demand levels.

The starting point in causal modelling must be to identify and select the factors, known as the independent variables, which must be assessed in order to forecast the dependent variable, which is the level of passenger or possibly freight traffic. The second step is to determine the functional relationship between the dependent variables and the independent variables selected. This means specifying the form of the model to be used. Normally for airline forecasting it will be a regression model. Other model forms such as gravity-type models are used in other areas of transport but less frequently in air transport. The third step in the forecasting process involves the calibration of the model and the testing of the mathematical expression for the relationship between the dependent and the independent variables. Should the tests show that the relationship established through the model is significant and statistically robust then one can move on to the final step. This involves forecasting the independent variables or using other people's forecasts in order to derive from them the forecasts of air traffic.

9.4.1   Regression models

Most econometric forecasts of air traffic tend to be based on simple or multiple regression models, where traffic is a function of one or more independent variables. The two variables most frequently used are the air fare and some measure of per capita income. Thus, for a route such as London to Nice, one might consider a model of the form:

$$T = f(F, \ Y, \ t) \tag{9.1}$$

where T is the annual number of passengers travelling between London and Nice; F is the average fare in real terms; Y is an income measure such as gross domestic product or consumer expenditure per head; and t is some underlying time trend. Fare level, income levels or other economic variables have to be adjusted for inflation and expressed in constant value or real terms. The choice of fare is critical. Ideally only change in the lowest fare should be considered as only this should affect the total market; changes in other fares would affect only the market mix. On many routes it is not as clear-cut as that, since the number of seats for sale at the lowest fare may be strictly limited in number. Many analyses will choose the average yield rather than the lowest fare as the fare variable. Income levels pose the additional problem of identifying those whose income one considers is the variable affecting demand. In the above case, should one use a global figure of UK per capita income and another for French income or should one try to establish the income levels in London and those in Nice? If one adjusts the fare level for inflation, one would have to make adjustments to the fare in Euros for Nice-originating traffic and a different adjustment to express the sterling fare in constant terms. This kind of problem would induce many forecasters to develop two separate directional models for the route based on origin of travel. For London-originating passenger traffic going to Nice the formulation would be:

$$T_\mathrm{L} = f(F_\mathrm{L}, \ Y_\mathrm{UK}, t_\mathrm{L}) \tag{9.2}$$

where T_L is the London-originating passenger traffic on London–Nice; F_L is the real sterling air fare from London; Y_{UK} is the per capita income in the UK; and t_L is the time trend for London-originating traffic.

In order to convert fares, income or other independent variables into number of passengers, a constant (K) has to be incorporated into the equation

$$T_L = K f (F_L, Y_{UK}, t_L) \tag{9.3}$$

Most airline forecasting models assume that the relationship between the independent variables is multiplicative, that is to say, the effects of each of the variables on traffic tend to multiply rather than to add up. The independent variables must represent quite different influences on demand, otherwise the multiplicative relationship may not apply. Expressing the multiplicative relationship between the dependent and the independent variables in logarithmic form turns the relationship between the logarithms into a linear one:

$$\text{Log } T_L = K + a \log F_L + b \log Y_{UK} + c \log t_L + u \tag{9.4}$$

where u is an error term and a, b and c are model parameters, and the higher their value the more impact changes in the corresponding variables will have on the traffic level.

It is not essential for the model to be log-linear, but many empirical studies of demand have found this to be a useful and relevant form.

Many forecasters may decide to go further and relate the percentage change of traffic from one year to the next to the corresponding percentage change in the independent variables, in this case fare and income. The model is then expressed as follows:

$$\Delta \log T_L = K + a \Delta \log F_L + b \Delta \log Y_{UK} + c \log t_L + u \tag{9.5}$$

where Δ is the logarithm of the percentage change in the variable in question over the previous year. Effectively a and b are now the demand or traffic elasticities. The value of a is, in fact, the fare elasticity of UK-originating traffic on the London to Nice route, and b is the income elasticity of that traffic. It is through regression models of this kind that the price and income elasticities discussed in the preceding chapter are derived.

Having specified the regression model and the independent variables to be initially included, the model is calibrated to past traffic levels and changes in the independent variables. It is usual for time-series data to be used, that is, past data over a period of time. Less frequently a model may be calibrated using cross-sectional data, that is, data at one point in time but covering many routes. Using an iterative process based on the estimation of ordinary least squares, the regression model establishes the value of the constant term (K) and of the coefficients a, b and c.

It is normal for several model formulations to be tested before the independent variables to be used for forecasting are finally selected. While fare and income levels are the most frequently used, many others have also been found to give good results on particular routes or markets. Models for forecasting business travel may well use trade as an index of industrial production instead of income as a variable (CAA, 1989). Models on routes where holiday traffic is dominant may include hotel prices, currency exchange rates or some other variable that is especially relevant to tourism flows. Quality of service variables may also be introduced into the model. The simplest of these is a speed or journey time variable, though a few more complex models have included frequency, load factor or some other service variable.

Having fitted the data and established the value of the constant (K) and of the coefficients, forecasters need to find out how statistically sound their model is. They can use it as a forecasting tool only if they are convinced of the reliability of the relationships the model purports to have established. A number of statistical tests can be used for this purpose. The most straightforward is the coefficient of multiple determination (R^2), which measures the closeness of fit of the time-series data to the regression model. A very close fit will produce a coefficient approaching 1.0, whereas a low coefficient of, say, 0.5 or less would indicate a poor fit. Using time-series data one would ideally expect to obtain a coefficient of 0.9 or more if one wanted to use the model for forecasting with some degree of confidence. The R^2 coefficient may also be used to choose between models with different combinations of independent variables.

While the R^2 value tells forecasters how well traffic variations fit variations in the independent variable, it does not tell them how traffic is related statistically to each of the independent variables separately. This is done by partial correlation coefficients. These measure how closely traffic is related to any one of the independent variables when all other variables are held constant.

Other tests to establish the validity of the model and the significance of the relationships it purports to measure include Student's t test and the F statistic. The latter is an alternative to the coefficient of multiple determination and is found by comparing the explained variance of the data with the unexplained variance. It is not the aim of the present book to deal in detail with the conduct and significance of the various statistical tests which can be carried out. These are covered adequately in many statistics textbooks and in one or two specialist air transport texts (Vasigh *et al.*, 2008).

While academic economists have developed quite sophisticated and apparently robust econometric models for forecasting air traffic, airlines tend to use fairly simple models, which often may not be as statistically sound as, in theory, one might wish. An early example of one such model was developed in 1977 for forecasting Air Algérie's traffic between Algeria and France. The model took the form:

$$\text{Log } T = K + a \log GNP + b \log F + C \log S \qquad (9.6)$$

where T is the number of passengers carried by Air Algérie between Algiers and Paris; GNP is a measure of the combined real GNP of France and Algeria weighted in proportion to the share of Algerians in the total traffic; F is the average yield per passenger-kilometre on all Algeria–France routes; S is the average speed of all Algeria–France air services.

Effectively the independent variables were income, price and a quality of service variable which was speed. The time series on which the model was based was for the eight years 1968–75, which was rather short. Using the ordinary least squares method, the coefficient worked out as follows:

$$\log T = 1.0963 + 1.4476 \log GNP - 1.4135 \log F + 0.2471 \log S \qquad (9.7)$$
$$\quad (0.7890) \quad (8.3352) \quad\quad (-2.3490) \quad\quad (0.6656)$$

where the respective Student t-values are given in parentheses below the main equation, $R^2 = 0.9732$, the standard error is 0.0381, $F(3.5) = 60.60$ and the value of the Durbin-Watson statistic is 3.24.

The model established a price elasticity of -1.4 on the Algiers–Paris route and an income elasticity of $+1.4$. Since the high t-test values validated the significance of the coefficients, the model was used to carry out 10-year forecasts to be used for fleet planning purposes.

While models similar to the Air Algérie model may be useful for specific route forecasts, econometric models are used to forecast traffic development in wider markets. For example, the UK Department of Transport, in its 2000 forecast of air traffic for the whole of the UK, divided the traffic flows to, from and within the UK into 16 discrete international and three domestic market segments based on purpose of travel, place of residence of passengers, that is UK or foreign, and whether short- or long-haul. Each market segment had its own causal model and its traffic was forecast separately. This was done because the strength of the independent variables affecting air traffic differs between sectors. For all 19 sectors, elasticities were developed on the basis of past data for air fares, exchange rates, GDP and trade volumes. Using these elasticities and forecast changes in the level of the independent variables, forecasts of air traffic in each segment were produced up to the year 2020. The segmental forecasts were then aggregated to generate the total air traffic for the UK year by year (DoT, 2000).

Econometric models can become very detailed and complex, especially if the forecaster splits the market into numerous discrete segments. A good example is provided by BAA PLC, which runs seven airports in Britain, including the three largest London airports. For its investment planning it needs long-term forecasts for which it uses causal models. When forecasting traffic for the London area market the BAA breaks down its passenger forecasts into 14 separate route or market areas such as domestic, European Union, other European, North Atlantic, Asian and Pacific, and so on. For each of these route areas it produces forecasts for four separate passenger segments, that is UK residents on business, UK residents on leisure trips and foreign residents travelling on business and leisure. This results in a matrix of 56 separate forecasts or cells (four passenger segments for each of 14 route areas). The BAA's forecasting model has been developed and calibrated over time. For each of the 36 cells a distinct combination of independent economic variables has been formulated as the basic forecasting equation. Non-economic variables can also be included. For instance, UK leisure trips to other short-haul destinations are forecast as a function of UK consumer expenditure and the cost of air fares and package tour holiday prices. On the other hand, an important variable affecting UK domestic business and leisure air travel is domestic rail competition (Maiden, 1995).

But for shorter-term forecasts, BAA PLC finds econometric models less helpful. For planning facilities in the near future, that is for the next two or three years, the BAA bases its forecasts on a variety of inputs. These include the fleet plans and schedules of its airline customers, their planned load factors, assessment of recent traffic trends, and so on, together with BAA PLC's executives' own judgement of economic or other developments which may impact on traffic levels.

Forecasters must bear in mind that very high coefficients of multiple determination are not in themselves a guarantee of causality or even of a close relationship between the independent and the dependent variables. A high coefficient of determination may be produced if the error terms produced by the regression equation fall into a pattern. This is called autocorrelation, and may occur either when a significant independent variable has been left out or when there is a marked cyclical variation in the dependent variable. One can test for autocorrelation using the Durbin–Watson d statistic. The values of d which will enable one to assess whether autocorrelation is present are related to the number of observations and the number of independent variables. As a general rule, if the Durbin–Watson statistics are below 1.5 or above 2.5 the forecaster will be concerned with the possibility of autocorrelation. The high Durbin–Watson statistic of 3.24 on the Algiers–Paris model (equation 9.7 above) would suggest the existence of negative serial correlation.

Another problem which might exist despite high coefficients of determination is that of multicollinearity. This occurs if the independent variables are not statistically independent of each other. For example, air fares and fuel prices may move more or less in unison. Therefore including both as independent variables would result in multicollinearity and would pose difficulties in interpreting the regression coefficients. In particular, they could no longer be strictly considered as elasticities. One can test for multicollinearity by using a matrix showing the correlation between the independent variables. Independent variables showing a high correlation, say 0.86 or higher, should not really be included in the same model. The possibility of autocorrelation and multicollinearity are two key problems for the airline forecaster using econometric models. There are other more obscure ones, such as heteroscedasticity, which are dealt with in detail in the specialist texts (Taneja, 1978).

Having developed and tested models such as those described above, an airline needs to obtain forecasts of the independent variables used in order to be able to derive from them forecasts of future air traffic. In doing this, particularly for longer-term forecasts, one should not necessarily assume that the elasticities remain constant over time. It is inherent in the way that elasticity is measured that it must change over time as total traffic grows. Because of this, many forecasters build changing elasticities into their predictive processes. Changes in elasticity values can be derived mathematically or they can be assumed. The BAA, for example, in its own forecasts assumes a decline in the income elasticities of most market groups (Maiden, 1995).

It is while forecasting the independent variables that some form of sensitivity test may be introduced into the forecasting process. Airlines might consider what would happen to the economy of a particular country and its per capita income if industrial growth did not turn out to be as fast as predicted by the government concerned. Alternatively, they might evaluate the impact of a disruption of oil production in the Middle East on the price of fuel and ultimately on economic growth or on the future level of air fares. These sensitivity tests may produce band forecasts suggesting a range of possible traffic outcomes rather than point forecasts.

For decisions dependent on forecasts over a two-year time span or less, airline managers tend to prefer point rather than band forecasts. Decisions have to be taken and giving a range of forecasts is no help to the decision makers. They want precise traffic estimates. They expect the forecasters to have assessed the risks and the sensitivity of the forecasts to external variables and to have made the point forecasts in the light of such assessment. When it comes to strategic decisions stemming from the airline's corporate plan, band forecasts become useful. They should force the airline to maintain flexibility in its long-term planning decisions. An airline must avoid taking decisions which lock it into a size and level of production which it cannot easily vary. This is particularly true of aircraft purchase or other major investments. Band forecasts emphasise the uncertainty inherent in forecasting.

9.4.2   *Air freight models*

The factors affecting the growth of air freight are complex and often fickle. The tonnage of freight moving on any route is subject to sudden and unexplained variations. There is the added complication that, unlike passengers, who tend to return to their point origin, freight movements are unidirectional. There is a multitude of commodity freight rates on any route and such rates have also tended to be less stable than passenger fares. Much freight capacity is produced as a by-product of passenger capacity, and as a consequence there is frequently an overprovision of freight capacity with a strong downward pressure on freight rates. Tariffs charged often bear little relationship to the published tariff, so that even establishing tariff levels is difficult. As a result of all these complexities, it has often been found difficult to relate past freight growth to one or more independent variables, particularly in relation to individual routes, though one of the early studies did develop a model relating freight tonne-kilometres to freight rates, an index of US industrial production and a time trend (Sletmo, 1972).

The few causal freight models which have been developed have tended to be used for forecasting global air freight demand or demand in large markets rather than on individual routes. Both Boeing and Airbus use such models. In 2008 Airbus Industrie derived its long-term forecasts of global air-freight traffic, measured in freight tonne-kms, primarily from econometric analyses of 144 directional air freight flows. Independent variables driving air freight include economic growth, international trade, air freight yields and industrial production. However, traffic in each direction on every market is analysed separately because freight movements in opposite directions are often imbalanced and involve different types of goods. The Airbus forecast therefore includes an extensive analysis of the type of goods traded (Airbus, 2008).

The International Civil Aviation Organisation (ICAO) has used econometric models for its long-term forecasts of the world's scheduled air traffic (ICAO, 1997). For instance, using data for the period 1960–91, ICAO developed two separate models, one for passenger traffic and one for air freight. The freight model took the form:

$$\log FTK = -0.41 + 1.58 \log EXP - 0.37 \log FYIELD \tag{9.8}$$
$$(20.3) (5.1)$$

where *FTK* is freight tonne-kilometres, *EXP* is world exports in real terms, *FYIELD* is freight revenue per freight tonne-kilometre in real terms, and figures in brackets are the *t*-statistics and the $R^2 = 0.996$. This clearly suggested that air freight was much more responsive to growth in world trade than to changes in freight tariffs.

Most route-by-route forecasts for freight are based on a combination of executive judgement, market research and, where appropriate, time-series projections. Frequently such forecasts are on a commodity-by-commodity basis since the number of separate commodities being freighted by air on any route is usually fairly limited. The development of causal models of individual commodity flows may ultimately prove more rewarding than attempts to model total freight flows on particular routes.

9.4.3 Gravity models

Time-series analyses or regression models are of little use when trying to forecast traffic on new routes, where there are no historic traffic data, or on routes where traffic records are inadequate or non-existent. Traditionally, this problem has been overcome by using a combination of market research or executive judgement. Another possible approach is to use a gravity model. This was the earliest of the causal models developed for traffic forecasting. It has been relatively little used in aviation, even though gravity formulations have played a crucial part in many road traffic forecasting and assignment models.

The gravity model concept has a long history. It was in 1858 that Henry Carey first formulated what has become known as the 'gravity concept of human interaction'. He suggested that social phenomena are based on the same fundamental law as physical phenomena and that 'gravitation is here, as everywhere else in the material world, in the direct ratio of the mass and in the inverse one of the distance' (Carey, 1858). One of the first applications to transport was by Lill (1889), studying movements on the Austrian state railways in 1889. Subsequently the concept was taken over by highway engineers who developed gravity models for forecasting road traffic. The first recorded use for aviation was in 1951, when D'Arcy Harvey, working for the US Civil Aeronautics Administration, developed the gravity concept to evaluate the air traffic flow between two communities (D'Arcy Harvey, 1951).

Translating the concept into aviation terms, one starts with the simple formulation that the air traffic between two points is proportional to the product of their populations and inversely proportional to the distance between them; so that:

$$T_{ij} = K \frac{P_i P_j}{D_{ij}} \tag{9.9}$$

where T_{ij} is the traffic between two towns i and j, K is a constant, P_i and P_j are the populations of the two towns, and D_{ij} is the distance between them.

The top half of the equation, namely the populations, contains the generative variables while the bottom half contains the impedance variables, in this case distance. This is a simple causal model with population size and distance as the independent variables affecting traffic flow. As the concept has been developed, both generative and impedance factors have been modified and the model has become more complex. For instance, the level of air fares has often been considered a better measure of impedance than distance. It has also been thought necessary to modify crude population numbers to take account of purchasing power, nature of economic activity of that population, and so on.

An early study in 1966 involved replacing the population in the interactive formula by the product of the total air traffic of each of the cities concerned (Doganis, 1966). Total airport traffic was thought to provide a good measure of a region's income levels, of the type of economic activities within it and of the effective catchment area of its airport. Using airport traffic obviated the need to incorporate other economic variables into the model. It was also found that raising the distance term to a power other than unity improved the correlation of the model when tested against actual traffic levels. This model took the form:

$$T_{ij} = K \frac{A_i A_j}{D_{ij}^p} \tag{9.10}$$

where T_{ij}, K and D_{ij} are as before, but A_i and A_j are the total passenger traffics of the two airports at either end of the route and P is distance raised to a power of between 1 and 1½.

Subsequent studies using gravity models to predict traffic on new or potential routes include one in 1989 carried out for the European Commission, which involved forecasts of air traffic between airports in the southern regions of the European Community, some of which did not already have direct air links (Westminster, 1989). Various model formulations were calibrated on 47 existing air services for 1987. The one which produced the highest correlation of 0.97 took the following form:

$$T_{ij} = K \, \frac{(A_i \, A_j) \, Q^{3/4}}{F^{1/2}} \tag{9.11}$$

where K is a constant, A_i and A_j are the scheduled passenger traffics at each of the two airports, $Q^{3/4}$ is a service quality variable raised to the power of three-quarters, and $F^{1/2}$ is the normal economy fare raised to the power of half. The quality of service variable *(Q)* was a measure of equivalent weekly frequencies which makes allowance for intermediate stops and type of aircraft. Whereas a weekly non-stop jet service is given a *Q* value of 1.0, a one-stop service is valued at 0.5 and a turbo-prop service at 0.7. Services involving two or more en-route stops are ignored.

The value of a gravity model approach is its ability to forecast demand on new routes. Thus, using the model just described, it was possible to forecast the passenger demand between two cities such as Venice and Madrid which did not have air services in 1989 by feeding into the equation the projected forecasts of total air traffic for each of these airports in that year, the current economy air fare and the likely types of air services that could be viably provided. The latter is the quality of service variable and involved some iteration to arrive at the optimum combination of traffic and service level. While using airport traffics as one of the generative factors in a gravity model appears to improve the robustness of the model, it has a major disadvantage in that the model cannot be used where there is no existing airport traffic at one or both ends of the route. In such circumstances one has to revert to using population size perhaps weighted by income levels.

The great advantage of gravity models is their ability to forecast traffic between airports which have not been served by air links previously. Consultants frequently use such models. Lufthansa Consulting, for example, has developed a complex gravity model for forecasting passenger traffic for new air services in Europe. It's a complex model in which the generative variables are the populations, the gross domestic product and the tourist numbers of the two regions, and the total passenger traffic of the airports to be served (Solomko, 2009).

Over the last ten years in Europe it has been above all the low-cost airlines that have launched new air services between numerous airports, often very small ones, not previously served. In the case of Ryanair the strategy has been described as one of flying from 'nowhere to nowhere'. But the LCCs did not use gravity models to assess the potential demand on the new routes they were launching. Nor did they use other models. They used a combination of executive judgement and limited market research, for instance to establish the number of migrant workers from one end of the route who were working at the other, or patterns of holiday home ownership. But above all they relied on the impact of extremely low fares in generating demand and new travel patterns. When evaluating the launch of services on routes already served by others, low-cost carriers, while examining historical traffic data on the route, focused on the impact their very low fares would have on diverting traffic from existing carriers. With a strategy of very low fares, they had less need for sophisticated forecasting tools, but they were flexible. If they got it wrong they were quick to pull out of a new route if it did not meet their traffic targets.

9.4.4 *Assessment of econometric models*

The strength of causal forecasting models is that they are logical. They relate demand to changes in factors which one would expect to have an impact on demand. The models chosen must therefore be logical too, despite the findings of any statistical tests. A model with a high coefficient of determination should not be used if the independent variables are intuitively wrong. The forecaster's direct experience of market conditions and knowledge gained through market research can provide an insight into demand behaviour which may ultimately be more useful than that obtained through statistical analysis and mathematical correlation. The models used must be logically consistent. If they are, it follows that, if one can forecast the independent variables for three or more years, then one should be able to derive longer-term traffic forecasts with a lower risk of error than if one were using time-series projections where demand is related purely to changes in time. Herein lies the strength of causal forecasting but also its weakness. For, by using a causal model in the interests of logical consistency and greater accuracy, airline forecasters transpose their problem. Instead of having to forecast air traffic, they must now use someone else's forecasts of the independent variables and, if these are not available, they must make their own. Many governments, central banks and other institutions do make forecasts of gross domestic product, consumer expenditure, trade and other economic indicators which might be used as independent variables. Such economic forecasts are not always reliable, nor are they necessarily long term. No forecasters in 2006 or 2007 were predicting the melt-down of key economies in 2009. Where more than one institution is forecasting a particular variable, the forecasts do not always agree. If the air fare is one of the independent variables used, then this should in theory be easy for an airline to forecast since it is under airline control. In practice it is difficult for the airlines to predict fare levels more than two or three years hence, without getting embroiled in forecasting oil prices or changes in other factors that may affect future fare levels.

Causal techniques pose some further problems too. Like time-series analyses they also depend on the availability of historical data. Clearly, to calibrate regression models in particular one needs not only good air traffic data but also adequate and accurate statistics going back many years of independent variables being used in the model. In most developed countries these should be available. In many Third World countries, adequate data is either unavailable or possibly unreliable. Where data is available, the complexity of the modelling work is daunting and time-consuming, especially if an airline wishes to develop separate forecasts for key markets or major routes, each requiring separate models.

It should be borne in mind that econometric forecasting, despite its inherent logic and mathematical complexity, is not a mechanistic exercise. Judgement is involved at all stages, from the model specification to the choice of independent variables, and more especially in the choice between alternative forecasts of those independent variables.

9.5 Choice of forecasting technique

It is clear from the preceding analysis that there is no certainty in forecasting; no forecasting tool that can guarantee the accuracy of its predictions. Even very similar forecasting methods may produce widely diverging forecasts. Whatever the uncertainties, however, airlines cannot avoid making forecasts because so many other decisions stem from them. Their forecasters must make a choice between the numerous forecasting techniques open to them. Several factors will determine that choice.

Table 9.5 Attributes of airline passenger forecasting techniques

	Qualitative methods			Time-series projections				Causal models	
	Executive judgement	Market research	Delphi	Annual average growth	Exponential smoothing	Linear trend	Linear trend on moving average	Regression analysis	Gravity model
Accuracy:									
0–6 months	Good	Good	Fair/good	Fair/good	Good	Fair/good	Good	Good	Good
6–24 months	Fair	Good	Fair/good	Poor/fair	Fair/good	Poor/fair	Fair	Fair/good	Fair/good
5 years	Poor	Poor/fair	Fair	Poor	Poor/fair	Poor	Poor/fair	Poor/fair	Poor/fair
Suitability for forecasting:									
Traffic growth	Good	Good	Good	Good	Good	Good	Good	Good	Good
Traffic reaction	Fair	Good	Fair	n.a.	n.a.	n.a.	n.a.	Good	Poor
Traffic new routes	Poor	Fair	Poor	n.a.	n.a.	n.a.	n.a.	Fair	Good
Ability to identify turning points	Poor/fair	Fair/good	Fair/good	Poor	Fair	Poor	Poor/fair	Good	Poor
Ready availability of input data	Good	Poor/fair	Poor	Good	Good	Good	Good	Poor/fair	Fair
Days required to produce forecast	1–2	90+	30–180	1–2	1–2	1–2	1–2	30–90	20–60
Cost	Very low	Very high	Moderate	Low	Low	Low	Low	High	High

Note: n.a. = not applicable.

The starting point is to determine the prime objective of the forecast. Is it to forecast traffic growth; is it to predict the reaction of demand to some new development such as a fare increase or frequency change; or is it to forecast the traffic on a new route? While all techniques enable one to make a forecast of traffic growth under normal conditions, only a few are suitable for forecasting traffic reaction or demand on a new route (Table 9.5). If an airline is planning to open up an entirely new route, it has little choice but to use a qualitative technique or a gravity model.

Having determined the forecasting techniques suitable for the type of forecast being undertaken, then speed and data availability become important criteria. A quick forecast means either executive judgement or a straightforward time-series projection. Data availability is crucial for certain of the techniques. Time-series projections need accurate and detailed traffic data over a reasonable period of time. Regression models need all that but also adequate data on the independent variables included in the model. If either traffic data or data on the various socio-economic variables are unavailable and unobtainable, then the forecaster is obliged to turn to qualitative methods. Cost may be an important consideration too. Smaller international airlines may not be prepared to meet the high costs of market research, while sophisticated causal forecasting for them would mean using consultants, and consultants do not come cheaply. In fact, some smaller airlines are dependent on aircraft manufacturers for their long-term forecasts or use IATA forecasts combined with their own executive judgement for shorter-term planning.

If speed, data availability and cost are not a constraint, then airlines might choose between the forecasting techniques open to them on the basis of their predictive accuracy. This is a difficult judgement to make. The various techniques are listed in Table 9.5 and their accuracy for short-, medium- and long-term forecasts is indicated on a three-point grading of poor, fair and good. However, the gradings are to a certain extent subjective and influenced by one's personal experience and judgement. Different forecasters would use different gradings. Inevitably most techniques are fairly accurate for short-term forecasts and some are also reasonable for two-year forecasts. Beyond that time span there is some doubt, but it is likely that qualitative or causal techniques will produce the more accurate forecasts. These techniques are also the most likely to be able to identify and predict turning points in the underlying growth trends. In theory, causal models should produce the better results, but some aviation experts suggest that there is no compelling evidence that econometric techniques produce more accurate air traffic forecasts than do the simpler and more straightforward approaches.

Within most international airlines a range of forecasting techniques is used. Faced with differing planning requirements, airlines carry out both short- to medium- and longer-term forecasts. The former tend to be based on time-series projections, frequently modified by executive judgement and by market research findings. The precise time-series technique or techniques used by each airline will depend on its experience and the judgement of its forecasters. Where new routes are being evaluated, the airline's preference may well be to use market research methods to forecast potential demand. For longer-term forecasts beyond a year or two, many smaller airlines continue to use time-series projections, despite doubts about the accuracy of such methods for longer time spans, while some of the larger airlines switch to causal models. Ultimately, so many exogenous and unpredictable factors may affect air transport demand that forecasts beyond 3–5 years ahead must be thought of as being very tentative.

10 Product planning

Our product must be so excellent as to clearly differentiate us from our competitors
(Tony Tyler, CEO, Cathay Pacific, February 2009[1])

10.1 Key product features

Product planning is about deciding what product and service features an airline should offer in each of its markets. It is also about ensuring their delivery. For each airline, product planning is crucial in two respects. First, it is the key tool in the process of matching potential demand for air services with the actual supply of services which it offers in the markets it serves. Each airline controls its own supply of services but can influence the demand only through its product planning. Much, therefore, depends on product planning. Second, as previously mentioned, product planning has a direct impact on operating costs (see Sections 5.5 and 5.7 in Chapter 5). It is important as a cost factor because it is an area of costs where airlines have considerable discretion.

In deciding what products to offer in the different markets it has entered, an airline has to bear in mind a number of objectives. It must consider its overall marketing strategy, which will have emerged as a result of its demand analyses and forecasts (see Chapters 8 and 9). It must set out to attract and satisfy potential customers in the different market segments that it has identified. This means using its understanding of the needs and requirements of these different market segments. Such understanding will have been acquired through a range of market research activities, including passenger and other surveys, the monitoring of its own and its competitors' past performance in each market or route, and so on. Lastly, an airline will want to maximise its revenues and profits, not always in the short term but certainly in the long run. In brief, the ultimate aim of product planning is to attract and hold customers from the market segments that an airline is targeting and to do this profitably.

Experience suggests that an airline's potential customers will be influenced by five key product features in making travel decisions and, more important, in choosing between airlines. (These are summarised in Table 10.1.) An airline must therefore decide how to combine these various product features to meet customer needs in different markets. This is a complex process because customer requirements will vary not only between different market segments on the same route but also between neighbouring routes and geographical areas. For any particular airline product in a given market, different combinations of these five product features can be offered. To a certain extent there may even be a

---

[1] *Air Transport World*, February 2009.

Table 10.1 Key product features affecting travel decisions and choice of airline – but also operating costs

1	Price	Fare levels and conditions
2	Schedule based	Points served and routings
		Frequency
		Timings
		Connections
		Punctuality
3	Comfort based	Type of aircraft
		Interior configuration
		Individual space
		On-board service
		Ground/terminal service
		Airline lounges
		In-flight entertainment (IFE)
4	Convenience	Distribution/reservations system
		Capacity management policy
		Seat availability
		Ability to change reservations
5	Image	Reputation for safety
		Branding
		Frequent flyer loyalty schemes
		Promotion and advertising
		Market positioning

trade-off between them. Greater comfort can be offered, for instance, by reducing the number of seats in an aircraft, but this may necessitate selling at higher fares.

It would seem that the fare level is the most critical product feature for many market segments, especially in many price-sensitive leisure or VFR markets. It may be less important for business markets which are relatively price inelastic, though even here marked fare differentials between airlines or between different fares on the same airline may have an impact. Fares are also the most dynamic product feature in that they can be changed almost daily, at least in deregulated markets. Moreover, in those short-haul markets and routes where low-cost airlines have made a major impact, air travel has begun to resemble a commodity, in that price or fare has become the dominant product variable. Thus the whole question of pricing and revenue generation merits the more detailed examination provided in Chapter 11. If markets are price inelastic or where fares of different carriers are very similar, then product features other than price become relatively more important in determining the market penetration of different airlines. They also tend to become more important in medium and especially long-haul routes.

10.2   Schedule-based features

From a consumer viewpoint, the critical schedule-based features in any market are the number of frequencies operated, their departure and arrival times, the points served and in particular whether flights are direct or involve one or more stops or change of aircraft en route at a hub. Conversely, aircraft type is not seen as important, though on some short-haul routes a jet may be preferred to a turbo-prop. Different market segments will have differing schedule requirements. Short-haul business markets generally require at least a morning and an early evening flight in each direction on weekdays so as to allow business trips to be completed in a day. But the ideal is several flights each day. Weekend flights may be less important for business travellers but crucial for short-stay weekend holiday markets. Frequency requirements will also vary depending on the type of market, the length of haul and the level of competition. For instance, offering a once-daily service when a competitor has 10 flights a day is unlikely to make much impact on the market.

In the early 1980s, the Scandinavian airline SAS asked its passengers what were the most important factors for them in choosing a flight when making their reservations. More than two-thirds of those surveyed said that departure/arrival times were very important and two-thirds claimed that non-stop direct services were also very important. Other factors were relatively unimportant in travellers' choices. Interestingly, only 3 per cent claimed aircraft type as an important factor in their decision. It was in response to such surveys that SAS effectively grounded their four new large A300 Airbuses in 1982 and concentrated on using their smaller DC-9s and later MD 81s and MD 82s with less than half the seats of the Airbuses. The smaller aircraft enabled SAS to offer higher frequencies and to operate direct services on thinner routes for which the Airbuses would have been too large. SAS has continued this strategy to the present day. It is still flying relatively small aircraft on intra-European services. Since smaller aircraft have higher unit operating costs (Chapter 5, Section 5.5) such a marketing strategy has inevitably pushed SAS into operating with very high unit costs on its intra-European services. However, by concentrating on schedule-based product features, SAS was able to attract a significant share of business traffic which was prepared to pay the higher fares that such a strategy necessitated. But in the 2000s this strategy began to unravel. First the growth of low-cost airlines made SAS's high fares increasingly unattractive even to business passengers on which SAS had been very dependent. Second, SAS was especially badly affected by escalating fuel prices after 2004 since over a quarter of its short-haul fleet in 2007–8 was still gas-guzzling MD-87s and MD-81s.

Most surveys reinforce the importance of schedule-related features. Such features appear to be the core element of the scheduled airline product on short-haul routes and are probably the most important factor for business travellers. Comfort features, as one would expect, become more important on long-haul flights.

A survey, in 1999, of 3,000 business air travellers from around the world, including the USA, Europe, Singapore and Australia, emphasised the importance of convenient schedules when it comes to choosing an airline. It was the most frequently mentioned factor. Reputation for safety was the second most highly rated. Since most major international airlines have equally good safety records it is difficult to appreciate how this factor influences choice of airline. Presumably it is a negative reaction to one or two airlines which may have had a recent accident. Membership of a frequent flyer programme was the third most important factor. Among comfort-based features extra on-board comfort and legroom as well as efficiency of the check-in procedures were highly rated. On the other hand, features that airlines spent much money advertising such as the quality of food and drink, their executive lounges or the awards they have won did not feature highly when business passengers chose an airline. It was also evident that such travellers were not at that time concerned about obtaining the cheapest fare (OAG, 2000).

By the late 2000s, nearly ten years later, passenger preferences appear to have changed, according to an IATA survey of just over 10,000 business air travellers. This survey highlighted some interesting changes in the factors influencing travellers' choice of airline for business trips (Table 10.2). First, membership of a frequent flyer mileage programme has

Table 10.2 Most important factors in choice of airline for business trips, 2007

Percentage of travellers who mentioned each factor

For long-haul	%	For short-haul	%
FF/mileage programme	51	FF/mileage programme	44
Seat comfort C	32	Most convenient dept/arr. times S	31
Non-stop flights S	30	Non-stop flights S	30
Sleeping comfort C	25	Punctuality S	28
Most convenient dept/arrivals S	25	Value for money	25
Quality of service C	24	Seat comfort C	21
Previous good experience C	22	Offered lowest fare	19
Safety standards	20	Safety standards	18
Value for money	19	Quality of service C	17
Punctuality S	18	Connection time S	16
Route network S	16	Route network S	16
Best for connections S	15	Previous good experience C	15
Airport lounges C	15	E-ticketing available	15
Airline reputation	15	Convenient airport S	15
		Best for connections S	15

Several other factors all below 15% mention.

Source: IATA (2008c).

Notes
Respondents asked to name five most important factors so % added to more than 100.
Choice of 29 factors offered in questionnaire.
S = Schedule-based factor, C = Comfort-based factor.

now become by far the most frequently mentioned factor for both long- and short-haul trips. Second, safety considerations, while still important, appear less critical than they did in the late 1990s – perhaps because perceptions have changed and air transport is now seen as being much safer.

The 2008 IATA corporate travel survey also contrasts the different factors influencing choice of airline when travelling on short- as opposed to long-haul business trips. For the latter, *comfort-based* factors, such as seat or sleeping comfort, appear to be the most frequently mentioned and tend to be in the top half of Table 10.2. Fewer scheduled-based factors are in the top 12 for long-haul trips.

On the other hand, for short-haul trips, *schedule-based* factors predominate. Convenient departure and arrival times, non-stop flights, punctuality and other schedule-related service features are mentioned by a high proportion of travellers. There are few comfort-based features which are rated as important for short journeys. The fare level, measured in terms of value for money and 'being offered lowest fare', also appear more important for short- as opposed to long-haul trips. These findings are not unexpected. But the IATA survey provides a good measure of the significance of different factors in choice of airline and can help airline executives to focus on different priorities when product planning.

Interestingly, some factors vary between regions of residence of business travellers. North Americans are much more influenced by the frequent flyer programmes they belong to than travellers in other parts of the world, though it is the most frequently mentioned factor too. Safety is a relatively unimportant consideration in North America or Europe, but is one of the key factors in airline choice in Africa, the Middle East, Asia and the Pacific. Airline marketing directors must take such variations into account when marketing and advertising their services in different parts of the world.

The IATA survey also highlighted the importance of marketing to business travellers because they are such frequent travellers. The average number of short-haul trips by survey respondents in the last year was 10 for American passengers, 13 for Europeans, 9 for those in Africa-Middle East and 10 for Asian-Pacific business travellers. Annual long-haul trips were about half these levels (IATA, 2008c).

The South African Airways (SAA) services between London and Johannesburg provide an interesting case study of the power of frequent flyer programmes. In the early 2000s on this prime route SAA had a First class product as good as British Airways and a Business class which was only marginally poorer. Despite undercutting BA's fares in both classes, SAA's traffic was disproportionately small. Efforts to boost loads all failed. With lower load factors in these two classes and at lower fares it was losing money. Then it discovered FFPs were the problem. Well over half the Business/First class passengers in this market were UK originating. Flying BA, they could earn points which they and their families could redeem to fly to anywhere in the world BA flew to. If they flew SAA to Johannesburg, any points earned would only enable them to fly back to South Africa. The lack of attractiveness of its frequent flyer programme (FFP) for UK passengers was a major factor in inducing SAA to join the STAR alliance in 2005. By so doing it linked SAA's FFP to British Midlands's, to which many UK business travellers belong, as well as that of Lufthansa. Earning points on SAA flights to Johannesburg now became more attractive to UK passengers since they were able to redeem their awards by flying with British Midland, Lufthansa or other STAR airlines flying to and from the United Kingdom.

The survey results in Table 10.2 show the factors affecting the choice of airlines among business travellers. Surveys of leisure passengers indicate that price and value for money is the most important factor in decision-making. The relative importance of other factors varies, but the overall pattern is consistent with that of the business travel survey. Schedule-based factors are relatively more important for short leisure trips and comfort and convenience become more important for long trips.

Passenger surveys frequently highlight the importance of punctuality (Table 10.2). Numerous surveys, especially in the United States, have emphasised growing passenger concern with poor on-time performance. It was this which in 1987 induced the then US Transportation Secretary, Elizabeth Dole, to introduce a ruling requiring airlines to submit on-time performance records which would be publicly available so that they could be seen, if required, by passengers when booking flights. The second leading cause of consumer complaints in the United States was lost or delayed baggage. Here, too, airlines were required to provide comparative statistics on how often they lose, delay or damage baggage. The UK Civil Aviation Authority (CAA) followed the US lead on punctuality but not on baggage, which is less of a problem in European markets. Currently, UK airlines have to submit punctuality data to the CAA which is then published. The Association of European Airlines in Brussels also publishes quarterly data on delays and lost baggage rates for its member airlines, as well as on delays at each of the major European airports.

In the last two decades, a key product development which has affected many scheduled-based features has been the restructuring of many airlines' operations so as to enable passengers to travel between two points, without direct services, by transferring through a central hub airport. Schedules are planned to minimise the connecting time at the hub.

The concept of hubbing is now central to most network airlines' international operations and to US domestic air services. Moreover, one aim of the emerging global alliances is to link major hubs in different continents. On the other hand, low-cost airlines focus on point-to-point services and eschew hubbing. The importance and economic impact of hubbing is such that it is examined in greater detail in Section 10.6 below.

The main reason why schedule-based features together with the fare are generally the most important factors affecting airline choice for many market segments is that they can be seen and quantified objectively. They are explicit and precise: one can compare one scheduled departure time with another, or the total journey time of a direct as opposed to a one-stop service. By comparison, assessment of comfort, convenience or image-based product features, such as the quality of an airline's in-flight entertainment or of its distribution system, is more subjective. Customer perception of these product features will vary for each trip and between different customers on the same trip. They cannot easily be quantified or compared between different airlines.

10.3   Comfort-based product features

The schedule-related features of an air service are important in all markets, while in short-haul markets they appear to be more significant than comfort-based features. But schedule features cannot be adjusted rapidly. In many cases they cannot be changed at all, either because an airline already has a network and schedules which meet market needs or because of external constraints such as the bilateral air services agreements or possibly an absence of available runway slots. Yet, as markets become more competitive, the need for product innovation has intensified. Since schedules, in most cases, can be changed only in the medium term, if at all, airline product development has often concentrated on improving comfort-based features, which can be changed more readily and quickly. Three aspects of the airline product are important in determining passenger perceptions of comfort.

The first is the *interior layout and configuration* of the aircraft, which affects the width and pitch of each seat and thereby determines the space available for each passenger. Individual space seems to be the key comfort variable, but so too is the quality of the seating provided. Comfort is particularly important for long-haul passengers both for those flying on business, as evidenced from the IATA surveys (Table 10.2), and those on leisure trips. But, there is a trade-off between seating density and unit costs in that the more seats that can be put into the aircraft the lower are the operating costs per seat. Thus deciding on seating density has major cost implications (see Table 5.8 in Chapter 5).

A key aspect of comfort relates to the width and pitch of each seat. Pitch is the distance between the back of one seat and the same point on the seat in front, and is a measure of the leg-room available. Seat pitch and width and the type of seat provided has a major impact on perceived comfort, especially on long-haul services. But more spacious seats mean fewer seats per aircraft. Thus in 2000 when British Airways announced the introduction of fully flat sleeper seats for its Club World and a new World Traveller Plus cabin area, for full-fare long-haul economy passengers, with a 38-inch pitch instead of the normal economy 31-inch pitch, the number of seats in its Boeing 747s dropped sharply. The standard 747–400 aircraft previously had 376 seats – 14 First, 64 Club World and 298 in the World Traveller and economy cabin. The new configuration, part of a $860 million investment in the interiors of its whole fleet, would offer only 291 seats – 14 First, 70 Club World, 30 World Traveller Plus and only 177 in World Traveller or normal Economy. Effectively a quarter of the seats were lost in order to upgrade the product.

But as economic pressures and fuel costs mounted, British Airways had by 2009 reconfigured many of its 747–400s so as to reduce Club World seats to 52 while increasing the number of Economy and World Traveller Plus seats. As a result the total seats rose to 329. Because totally flat seats take up more space than angled lie-back seats, many airlines, such as Air France, KLM and Delta, delayed following British Airways in adopting totally flat and horizontal beds in their Business class. These airlines had still not done so by mid-2008.

Other aspects of the interior lay-out which an airline must decide on, since they affect the nature of the product it is offering, include the number of separate classes of cabin and service, the number of toilets, the types of seats installed, interior design and colour schemes, the size and suitability of overhead lockers, and so on.

The second important area where decisions have to be made is that of *in-flight service and catering standards*. This covers the nature and quality of food and beverages provided, the number of cabin staff for each class of cabin, the availability and range of newspapers and magazines, in-flight entertainment and communications, give-aways for first- and business-class passengers as well as for children, and so on. A great deal of effort goes into planning airline meals and meeting target catering standards. Again there are cost implications and as a result the composition of meals is planned down to the precise weight in milligrams of a pat of butter or the weight of the sauce going on a meat dish. While airlines place much emphasis in their advertising on the quality of their food and wines, there is little evidence that gastronomic preferences determine choice of airline for a journey. Nevertheless, catering standards together with the quality and attentiveness of the cabin staff may create a certain image for a particular airline which may be important in marketing or branding terms. However, during recent years in an effort to cut costs and in response to the challenge of low-cost no-frills airlines, many legacy network carriers reduced or cut altogether their free in-flight catering in the economy cabin on short-haul sectors. The US legacy carriers have done this on most of their domestic services as have many European airlines. Swiss Airlines did this in 2005 but passenger reaction was so adverse that Lufthansa quickly re-introduced light catering in 2006 after taking over Swiss. Lufthansa wanted Swiss to position itself as a premium service airline like Lufthansa itself.

In recent years much effort has gone into improving the quality and range of in-flight entertainment (IFE) facilities in all cabins, but especially for Business and First class on long-haul flights. Aircraft seats are now expected to provide interactive multi-channel music and films, as well as sockets for computers, in-flight telephone and facsimile access, and electronic games. Increasingly passengers will be looking to have live TV or radio. But all this costs money to install in the seat, and also creates substantial running costs to buy and prepare film and sound programmes which need to be changed monthly. Airline annual investments in IFE were less than $400 million in 1990. By 1999 this figure had risen to $2,300 million. Seats also become more costly in order to incorporate all the electronic gadgetry. In 1990 airlines were investing $1,800 per seat to install IFE. Ten years later in 2000 the cost was around $10,000 per seat, which means about $3–4 million per long-haul aircraft (*Airline Business*, January 1999). This figure has more than doubled since. IFE may add up to 2 per cent to the total purchase price of a new wide-body aircraft. Pro-active, innovative airlines, such as Emirates, which was one of the first to introduce seat-back screens and multi-channel films in Economy class, gain some initial marketing benefit. But it is a short-term benefit. IFE improvements can be introduced fairly quickly and any competitive advantage is soon lost, but the high costs remain.

Currently, most quality airlines have personal IFE systems in First and Business class. Therefore it is becoming an expected airline feature by passengers travelling in these cabins. This is why, despite the high spend on IFE, most surveys show that it is not an important factor in choosing between airlines. In the 2008 IATA business passenger survey, mentioned earlier, only 13 per cent of long-haul passengers mentioned 'on-board facilities and entertainment' as one of the five factors affecting their choice of airline. For short-haul flights this dropped to 3 per cent (IATA, 2008c).

The third key comfort component of an airline's product is the *services offered to passengers on the ground*. An airline has to consider whether to provide its own check-in and handling staff at out-stations or to use another airline or handling agent. It must decide what is an acceptable average waiting time for check-in for its passengers, since this will determine how many check-in desks and staff it needs for each flight. More desks cost more money. Then the airline must determine the nature of any special ground facilities for First- and Business-class passengers, such as special lounges, office services, car parking valets, or the provision of limousine service to collect and deliver passengers from their homes or offices. Surveys suggest that many business travellers are primarily concerned with speed through the terminal rather than comfort as such. This means separate, well-manned check-in desks for Business and First class passengers. To speed up the check-in process, particularly when baggage is involved, airlines have in recent years progressively introduced online check-in and self-service kiosks at the airport as well as off-airport check-in at hotels (SAS) or at railway stations (Lufthansa). IATA's success in implementing 100 per cent electronic tickets by its member airlines by mid-2008 has made all this much easier. Airlines have also started to introduce arrival lounges for First- or Business-class passengers on long-haul flights.

The ground environment and quality of service provided can have an important influence on a passenger's perception of an airline, but they are inevitably also affected by the actions and efficiency of the airport authority. This is why more and more airlines now wish to operate and possibly own the terminals they use. This is fairly common in the United States but rare elsewhere.

A non-measurable and intangible aspect of comfort which underpins all the areas mentioned above is the efficiency, helpfulness and friendliness of staff, both the cabin crew in the air and also the ground staff at check-in, in the airline lounges and at the boarding gates. This appears to be dependent on three factors. First, the quality of the training received by all staff in contact with the public, but also the degree to which they are constantly being retrained. In the late 1980s British Airways transformed itself from an airline with a poor reputation for quality of service to one being very highly thought of by ensuring all its staff from the Chief Executive down went through a programme entitled 'Putting People First'. This was a training programme originally introduced at SAS. Its success at BA was such that other airlines followed suit.

The second factor is the success of management in motivating and empowering staff at all levels. Staff need to feel that they 'own' any problems that arise and are empowered to deal with them, rather than pass them on to someone else higher up the management chain. British Airways were successful in this area too, helped, no doubt, by the fact that many staff became shareholders when the airline was privatised in 1987. Giving shares to staff can be an important motivator (Doganis, 2006). But then British Airways blew it. An acrimonious confrontation with cabin crew in 1997 undermined much of their previous success in improving service and motivating staff.

Finally, the number of staff employed in each functional area is important. In an aircraft such as a Boeing 747–400 does an airline carry the legal minimum of cabin crew, which is 11, or something close to it, or does it go for 18–19, so as to ensure higher service, though at a higher cost? Similarly, decisions have to be made for the ground staff. The motivation and quality of staff in contact with clients is crucial. Poor staff attitudes can destroy the best-planned product. On the other hand, friendly, warm, welcoming staff, who are obviously trying hard, can overcome shortcomings in the product and win over customer support. Singapore Airlines at one time had a small poster, which could not be seen by passengers, at check-in desks, which simply said: 'If you see someone without a smile, give them one.'

Product and service planning is a complex task. Product planners must work in two dimensions. They must ensure that their product and service standards match or are better than those of their key competitors. But they must also try to differentiate the products offered in their own aircraft in such a way that passengers in each class feel that they are getting value for money.

It is primarily in the comfort-based aspects of the airline product that distinctions between the products offered to different cabin classes by the same airline become most apparent to passengers. This means that airline product planners have a complex task. They must specify differing comfort-based features for the different market segments they are trying to attract. Not only may product features have to be varied by class of cabin and type of ticket but the same cabin class may require different product features on different routes, different sector lengths, or in various geographical areas. Thus Business class in Europe does not have the same product specification as Business class on Europe to Asia services.

Because they can be more easily changed and more readily advertised, comfort-based product features are continuously being monitored and revised. There is a constant requirement to respond to product changes introduced by competitors and an even greater need for an airline to be the first to introduce innovative changes. Airlines that are innovative can enjoy a competitive advantage until their new product is copied by others. In 1989 Virgin Atlantic made a major break-through by introducing its so-called Upper class on services from London to New York and later to Tokyo and its other long-haul routes. This was an upgraded product, but at Business class fares. Seat pitch was 55 inches, when all other long-haul carriers were offering only 38 to 42 inches. This, together with a cabin service which was equivalent to other airlines' First class, gave Virgin a major competitive advantage on the long-haul routes it served. It enabled Virgin to expand against head-on competition from British Airways in markets where others, notably British Caledonian, had failed. Virgin offered and still offers its Upper class at Business class fares, but has no First class. During the 1990s several airlines, such as Continental, Delta, SAS or Air New Zealand, followed suit and abandoned First class on long-haul routes in favour of an enhanced Business class. Over this period all airlines gradually improved their Business class product in various ways – more leg-room, better seating, interactive IFE, improved catering, and so on.

The next major innovation in long-haul Business class was the introduction of seats which converted into fully flat beds. British Airways began the trend by introducing seats with a 72-inch pitch converting into fully flat horizontal beds. Initially, as no other carrier had flat beds in Business class, BA was able to charge a premium above the prevailing Business class fare on routes where they were available. That is, until its direct competitors also provided beds. Virgin was the first to match BA when it began offering sleeper seats in its Upper class (i.e. Business class) in mid-2001. But initially these were angled beds, not fully flat, and less comfortable.

Some airlines, Air France, Japan Airlines and Cathay Pacific among them, were slower to adopt sleeper seats and when they did they used cradle or angled beds rather than the more comfortable fully flat beds introduced by British Airways. By 2007–8 they began converting from angled to fully flat beds.

Another relatively recent produce innovation has been the introduction of a Premium Economy class by some airlines on long-haul routes. Virgin Atlantic was the first to do this in the mid-1990s. The aim is to offer passengers paying the full Economy fare a dedicated and quieter cabin with several inches more leg-room than the normal Economy cabin and better in-flight catering. This development, combined with the spread of flat beds in Business class, has encouraged more airlines to abandon First class altogether, or to keep it only on a few dense business routes where there may be sufficient passengers prepared to pay the very high First class fares. By 2008 less than half the airlines operating long-haul services still offered a First class cabin. This trend reflected not only the improvements in the Business class product but also the fact that First class services were generally loss-making unless load factors were very high (see Chapter 11 on pricing).

Some airlines, among them Virgin Atlantic, Emirates, British Airways and Singapore Airlines, have a reputation as innovators. In Virgin Atlantic's case it arises from a corporate strategy of trying to satisfy passenger needs. Its Managing Director, Steven Ridgeway, explained the strategy as follows:

> *Our aim is to orient the airline so that it is totally driven by customer needs. As we all fly the same aircraft it is even more important to be different, and we are always trying to do things on the ground and in the air that have not been done before.*

> (Pilling, 2001)

In planning new product or service improvements airlines have to balance three factors – the cost of the innovation, its marketing benefits in terms of revenue generation and the speed with which it can be copied. It is not an easy balance to calculate. The costs involved may be substantial. For example, not only in initial capital outlay but also in terms of cost of operation, in October 2007 Singapore Airlines launched the first scheduled Airbus A380 services which included First class suites. These were 12 separate large cabins which included a stand-alone bed (28 by 78 inches) in addition to a separate seat. The space used and therefore not available for more seating was very significant. In Business class, SIA offered seats/beds which were around 50 per cent wider than most and therefore requiring considerably more space. These major product innovations were costly but would take time for competitors to match given the slow delivery rate for the new A380s.

10.4   Convenience features

Convenience, as a product feature, is concerned both with availability of seats when requested by customers as well as their ability to change or cancel bookings. It is also about the ease of customer access to airline reservation and ticketing services and the quality of such services. Frequent flyer programmes and airline clubs may also play a role both in enhancing convenience and accessibility as well as in improving an airline's image.

Each airline has considerable freedom of action in deciding its capacity management policy, though it will be influenced by what its competitors are doing. Capacity management is a key tool for airline executives. There are two broad challenges. The first is how to plan capacity, that is frequencies and seats offered on a year-round basis, so as to deal with seasonal variations in demand. The traditional approach of legacy network airlines has been to offer more capacity by increasing frequencies in the peak holiday periods, which usually are the summer and/or times of religious festivals. They hope that the higher fares and greater passenger volumes generated during periods of peak demand will more than compensate for the fact that some assets, such as aircraft and crews, may be underutilised and therefore more costly in the off-peak periods. The low-cost carriers have generally adopted a different approach. To ensure high utilisation of all assets on a year-round basis, they do not vary their capacity or frequencies so much between seasons. Instead they use the pricing mechanism to stimulate demand in the periods of low demand to fill up their capacity. In other words, very low fares and seat sale campaigns in off seasons are used to fill up what would otherwise be empty seats. For example, Ryanair at the start of each European winter suddenly advertises millions of seats available at £1 or €1 each plus airport taxes. In this way aircraft utilisation can be kept high on a year-round basis.

The second challenge is how to manage capacity on each route so as to ensure passenger convenience in terms of seat availability while maximising revenue per flight. Again the approach of legacy and low-cost carriers has differed. Traditionally, the former using more complex fare structures and yield management systems have aimed to push up load factors and revenues in advance. But if seats were empty as departure dates approached, legacy airlines tended to drop their fares or sell off seats cheaply through travel agents or seat brokers. In other words, the lowest fares were often the last minute fares or deals. The low-cost carriers have adopted a simpler fare structure but one in which the lowest fares are available for the earliest bookings. As the departure date for each flight approaches fares tend to rise. Compared to the fares of early bookers, the fares for late or last-minute bookings are very high. In essence, passengers are required to pay a high price for the convenience of booking late. In recent years some network carriers, such as British Airways, have also started to adopt the low-cost approach of pushing up fares as the departure date approaches.

Another aspect of capacity management is the degree to which over-booking is practised and, more especially, the airline's success in accurately predicting the pattern and number of 'no-show' passengers and cancellations so as to end up with a very high load factor without the need to deny boarding to any passenger. If its predictions are consistently wrong it may end up paying costly denied-boarding compensation to its over-booked passengers. Its image inevitably suffers too. From a passenger's point of view, especially if travelling for business or some kind of emergency, availability of a seat when required is an important convenience factor that may well differentiate one airline from another.

Another aspect of convenience is the ability of passengers to change or cancel their reservations once made. From the airline's point of view a cancelled or changed booking may mean that that particular seat on the flight concerned may not be sold later. This means lost revenue. This must be balanced against the need to attract bookings by not imposing too many onerous conditions. This requires a fine balance. On network carriers the cheapest fares offer the least flexibility and impose the highest penalties if changes are required. Many will be non-changeable and non-refundable in the event of cancellation.

Others will allow changes but at a cost to the passenger. Total flexibility requires paying the highest fares. This applies to all classes. Thus British Airways, Lufthansa and others in 2008 offered two fares in Business class on most routes, one offering total flexibility including a refund for cancellation and a cheaper Business fare with severe restrictions which might include paying a charge to change the booking or no refund in the event of cancellation. Initially in Europe fares on low-cost airlines allowed for little flexibility. But airlines, such as easyJet, soon realised that the convenience of having more flexible booking conditions was an important product feature. Though easyJet does not give refunds for cancelled tickets or a missed flight it allows passengers to change flights, by paying a small fee and any increase in the fare, and even allows them to change the name of the person booked, so someone else can use the booking. Passengers may also get on an earlier flight on the day of their booking at no extra cost if seats are available.

A key decision area in any airline's marketing is how to distribute and sell its products and, in particular, how far it should use its own sales outlets in addition to independent travel agents, including online agents such as Opodo, Orbitz, Travelocity, e-bookers or Expedia. Since traditionally airlines paid commission on sales through travel agents, they had a vested interest in trying to sell directly through their own sales offices, through their own telephone call centres or their own website. But airlines also relied heavily on travel agents and they still do in some markets. The major benefit of travel agents was that they were and still are very numerous and widely scattered, giving airlines a much wider distribution network at relatively lower cost than they could achieve themselves. But high commissions paid to agents, together with the development of online selling since the late 1990s, has undermined and changed the role of high street travel agents. Online distribution has also led to a reduction in airlines' own high street sales outlets. In the mid-2000s IATA mounted a major drive to get its members to switch from paper to electronic ticketing by the end of 2007 and had achieved this by mid-2008. The death of paper tickets not only reduced costs but further undermined the need for travel agents or airline sales offices.

Easy online access to schedules, routings and price information as well as reservations, combined with tickets that can be issued electronically, have significantly improved the accessibility and convenience of air travel to both business and leisure passengers. Airlines now compete through the speed, quality and user-friendliness of their websites. They also compete in terms of the speed and quality of ancillary services, such as hotel booking, car hire, car parking and so on, that can be accessed through their websites. It is the low-cost carriers who have led the field. EasyJet was the front runner because, from its launch in 1995, it insisted on selling 100 per cent of its seats direct to passengers and did not use travel agents or other intermediaries. Initially it focused on its telephone call centre and then switched rapidly to selling online through its own website. It was not till late 2007 that it also began to sell through the Apollo and Sabre global distribution systems (GDS) with the aim of attracting business and corporate passengers. By 2008 Ryanair, which in its early years had been using travel agents, and easyJet together with younger low-cost airlines such as Clickair, were selling around 95 or more per cent of their seats online. In the United States, the figures were lower, around 75 per cent for Southwest and closer to 80 per cent for JetBlue.

Network airlines were much slower in switching to direct online selling. It was the financial losses of the early 2000s and the competitive pressures from low-cost competitors that forced them to focus on online selling. In 2000, ticketing, sales and promotion together represented 16.3 per cent of the total operating costs of IATA member airlines.

Table 10.3 Share of direct sales in airlines' total sales

	Own airline website %	Other online %	All online channels %	Airline's call centre %
2003	9.7	6.1	15.8	n.a.
2004	11.0	3.5	14.5	17.1
2005	16.4	3.7	20.1	20.3
2006	24.4	8.0	32.4	18.6
2007	26.6	8.6	35.2	13.4

Source: SITA, 2008.

Only fuel was marginally higher at 16.8 per cent. But unlike fuel, distribution costs could be cut. The quickest way of doing this was to develop online selling, which provided an improved level of service, while at the same time cutting the high commission rates then being paid to travel agencies. The results of this policy can be seen in Table 10.3. Whereas in 2003 less than 10 per cent of airline ticket sales were direct online, this figure had risen to 26.6 per cent by 2007. The total online sales, including on-airline sites, had risen to 35.2 per cent by 2007. But at the same time as airlines switched to online selling, sales through airlines' call centres were gradually declining. This needed to be done because such centres were labour-intensive and costly.

There are significant regional variations in the use of online distribution by network carriers. In 2007, 63.6 per cent of sales in North America were through online outlets both airline-owned and independent. The figures for other regions were substantially lower, around 29 per cent for European and South American airlines, 14 per cent for airlines in Africa and the Middle East (*Airline Business*, March 2008). But wherever it has been implemented the switch to direct online sales has had a major impact on distribution costs. Speaking at the Airline Distribution Conference in Fort Lauderdale in April 2007, Oliver King, British Airways Senior VP Latin America, said, '*It used to cost $24–25 to distribute our product. Now it is less than $5*' (*Airline Business*, June 2007). While distribution costs have been cut substantially, there has been a downside. By giving consumers easier access and transparency to all airlines fares data, online selling has created strong downward pressure on yields.

The internet itself offers airlines several choices in distribution strategies. They can sell purely on their own website as easyJet does or they can combine this with selling through a variety of additional web-based service providers. One option is to sell through sites shared with other airlines or alliance partners. In the United States, Orbitz, in which American, Continental, Delta, Northwest and United invested $145 million, started selling tickets in mid-2001. Later in the same year a group of nine European airlines launched their own joint website, 'Opodo'. Orbitz was floated in December 2003 and eventually sold to Cendant in September 2004, who owned the Galileo GDS. So airlines are no longer involved. The European airlines owning Opodo have meanwhile brought in Amadeus, the large European-based GDS, as a shareholder.

There are numerous other non-airline-owned online sales outlets. Large traditional travel agencies such as Thomas Cook or American Express have their own websites which offer numerous services such as hotels or cruises in addition to travel. These websites complement their high street sales office and telephone call centres. In addition there are specialist online-only agencies, some of which are owned by or linked with the global distribution systems (GDS). For instance, Travelocity, the second largest of these agencies, in 2008 was owned by the Sabre GDS. There are, of course, many smaller online agencies scattered around the world.

A key issue for airlines has been whether to allow the GDS or other online or high street agents to access their cheapest fares. They have been concerned for two reasons. First, they felt that such indirect agents might oversell the cheapest fares despite any internal yield management controls. Second, they did not want to pay fixed commission on what would be very low fares. As a result, some airlines have restricted the seat inventory and fares available to indirect agents. Airlines such as Lufthansa, KLM or British Airways have created schemes that compel travel agents in their major markets to pay a surcharge to access each airline's lowest fares. Others have allowed the sale of their cheapest fares but on a non-commission basis. Managing relationships with online and other indirect sales agents is a key part of distribution planning.

The role of traditional travel agents is declining as airline-owned websites and online travel agencies get better known and more frequently used. But it is also declining because airlines, during the 1990s, realised that agents, and more especially commissions paid to agents, were a controllable cost rather than an externally determined cost. In 1993 the US airlines were paying out on average 10.9 per cent of their revenue as commission to agents. A similar level of commissions was being paid by European carriers. In some US markets by 1990, airlines were having to pay 20 per cent or more of the ticket price to agents. This was particularly the case for the smaller airlines and for foreign carriers with only a limited marketing base in the United States such as Thai International or Malaysia Airlines. After the mid-1990s airlines around the world made major efforts to cut commission rates on a country-by-country basis. As a result, by the early 2000s commission expenses had dropped to between 4 and 6 per cent of revenues for the major US carriers. Among European airlines they had also dropped, though they still ranged between 6 and 8 per cent. But during the crisis years of the early 2000s, many airlines moved to cancel commissions altogether, especially in their home markets. They sold net fares, that is, with no commission to pay, to agents who were then expected to charge their customers a handling fee. But in distant or foreign markets where they are less well known, airlines continue to pay commission to attract business through travel agents.

As a result of airline pressure to cut or reduce commission rates, especially in their home markets, airline distribution costs have also been reduced. In the financial year 1996–97, British Airways commission payments absorbed 14 per cent of sales revenue. Eleven years later in 2007–8, this figure was 4 per cent.

There can be no doubt that the role of the travel agent in airline distribution will continue to be crucially important. But it is changing in character. High street travel agents will tend to focus increasingly either on leisure travel, where they can more easily offer customers greater choice and various add-ons – hotels, car hire, cruises, specialist holidays – as well as more personalised service or on business travel for large corporate clients. In the latter case they will also provide specialist services such as travel planning, tracking business travellers' expenses, or ensuring company travel policies are adhered to. Increasingly, they will charge a management fee to the corporate client while buying seats from airlines net of commission. Despite the fact that they have no direct control over travel agents or their staff, airline marketing managers need to ensure two things: first, that agency staff provide an efficient, speedy and reliable service to any potential customer; second, that, where alternative airline products are available, agents' sales staff give preference to their own particular airline. Not easy!

10.5   Airline image and branding

The final group of product features are those associated with the image that an airline wishes to create, both among its own customers and among the public at large. This is done in a variety of ways: through the nature of its advertising and promotions, through the airline's logo, its colour schemes, and the design of its aircraft interiors, sales offices and airport lounges, and through the quality of service provided by its staff in the air and on the ground. Ensuring an excellent safety record is also an important consideration. The success of Singapore Airlines' (SIA) 'Singapore Girl' advertising campaigns during the 1980s created the image not only of helpful, smiling, attentive cabin staff but also of an airline that took care of its passengers. This image was an important factor in enabling SIA to maintain unusually high passenger load factors throughout the period and up to the present day. A key element in brand building is to ensure that what is promised before the flight actually materialises and meets passenger expectations when the flight takes place. SIA's ability to do this has been crucial for its success. In other words, an eye-catching logo and an attractive colour scheme in themselves are not enough to establish an attractive brand. The airline has to offer a good product and service standards which are delivered consistently in all aspects of its operation. This is why marketing and product planning must be all-embracing, covering what is produced and how it is produced as well as how it is sold.

In order to establish an image, an airline needs to first identify its market position and marketing strategy. Clearly Southwest Airlines in the USA or easyJet in Europe position themselves quite differently from, say, United Airlines or British Airways. The former are low-cost no-frills airlines who would need to project a different image from the latter. But even within the same sector airlines may adopt a different market position. Among low-cost budget carriers in Europe, easyJet positions itself at the top end in terms of service standards, whereas Ryanair has branded itself as the lowest fare airline. Its rather indifferent service standards are counterbalanced by very low fares. Passengers know this and many, many millions of them choose to fly with Ryanair. As a result, Ryanair is highly profitable and very successful. Charter airlines, in yet another market niche, need to develop a separate and different image from scheduled carriers.

Airline services have been commoditised. An airline seat from point A to point B on a scheduled airline is perceived as being very similar by the passenger irrespective of which airline actually flies the service. Fares may differ, but otherwise the essential product is very much a commodity. Product planning as discussed earlier tries to differentiate an airline's product from that of its competitors. But it can only be partially successful since so many service elements, such as the quality of in-flight catering or of ground handling, are subjective. This is where the concept of branding comes in. Through product and service improvements, combined with targeted and effective advertising and promotion, airlines attempt to change their product from being a common commodity to being a 'brand'. As a unique brand it becomes more attractive and may even, on certain routes, attract a higher fare than that prevailing in the market. A brand is exemplified not only by service and product standards but also by designs and colours used in the aircraft interior and exterior and on the ground, as well as in more mundane aspects such as crockery, cutlery, ticket covers and so on. A distinctive logo and colour scheme may differentiate an airline product, but to establish a successful brand one needs to deliver what is promised. Employees are crucial in this process and in conveying the brand image to customers.

A first step in this process of branding on international flights was seen in the mid-1980s when airlines began to give their Business class distinctive names, even though what the product offered in terms of space and comfort was broadly similar. As previously mentioned, Virgin Atlantic called its Business class 'Upper class', and was successful in creating a high-quality brand image, which it still maintains. Many passengers think of it as a First class product at Business class fares. Later in 1988 British Airways set up brand teams to develop and launch two distinct Business class products, Club Europe and Club World. The aim was to plan and produce two separate products, each of which would have the same distinctive British Airways product features and quality on whichever route or geographical area they were being offered. These product features would differentiate Club Europe and Club World from other airlines' Business class by creating a distinct image and product. British Airways claimed this policy was highly successful. Passenger numbers in Club World increased by 27 per cent in the first two years after its introduction. On a number of routes, notably on the North Atlantic, where Club World passenger load factors regularly exceeded 80 per cent, British Airways was forced to increase capacity in response to demand. In some markets the airline was able to charge a premium over the normal Business class fare for its own distinctive product. Subsequent product improvements, such as the lie-flat bed seats introduced in 2000, have tried to sustain the Club World brand. Its latest upgrading was in 2007–8. Other airlines followed in branding their Business class service by giving it a distinctive name. For instance, Singapore Airlines has 'Raffles class', Air France has 'L'Espace Affaires' and Etihad has 'Pearl class'.

Changing the brand or mixing brands within the same airline can be problematic. Aer Lingus in the period after 2006 managed to overcome the problems. It managed successfully to rebrand itself as a low-cost airline for its short-haul intra-European services while maintaining a traditional legacy airline brand for its long-haul services, though this was not enough to ensure its long-term profitability. On the other hand, Air Berlin, having bought a disparate group of scheduled and charter airlines in the mid-2000s, was having great difficulty by 2009 in sorting out its brand or brands.

The ever-growing global alliances pose a particular branding and image problem. That is, how to try and create an alliance brand, which can be an effective marketing tool, while not diluting the strength of any existing airline brands. The problem becomes especially acute when there are many airlines within an alliance since they are then less likely all to have the same high service standards and an equally good image. The STAR alliance faced exactly this problem by 2009 because it had 20 or so members with differing service quality. This is evident from Table 10.4, which shows how UK passengers travelling for personal not business purposes rated 9 of the largest STAR airlines for their most recent long-haul trip (*Which*, 2008). While the best two, SIA and Air New Zealand, achieved very high customer satisfaction scores and quite similar ratings, for cleanliness, comfort and value for money, others were rated as relatively poor in all these categories, especially South African, United and US Airways. They also earned low overall satisfaction scores. Surprising also was the poor showing of Lufthansa which had spent the previous five years developing a brand based on offering a premium product (Arnoult, 2008). The very different service standards of STAR alliance members clearly poses a problem.

During 2008 and 2009 British Airways was discussing a proposed merger with Iberia. Branding here would also be a real problem. Whereas the 2008 passenger survey mentioned above had ranked BA in the middle in terms of customer satisfaction for both

Table 10.4 UK leisure customers' rating of STAR Alliance long-haul services, 2008

	Cleanliness	Comfort	Value for Money	Customer Satisfaction Score %
Singapore Airlines	✳✳✳✳✳	✳✳✳✳✳	✳✳✳✳✳	85
Air New Zealand	✳✳✳✳✳	✳✳✳✳✳	✳✳✳✳✳	80
British Midland (Bmi)	✳✳✳✳✳	✳✳✳✳	✳✳✳✳	70
Thai Airways	✳✳✳✳✳	✳✳✳✳✳	✳✳✳✳	66
Air Canada	✳✳✳	✳✳✳	✳✳✳	57
Lufthansa	✳✳✳	✳✳✳	✳✳✳	57
South African	✳✳✳	✳✳	✳✳	49
United	✳✳✳	✳✳✳	✳✳✳	48
US Airways	✳✳	✳	✳✳	40

Source: *Which*, 2008.

Note
Survey of 9,300 passengers assessment of most recent personal (not business) long-haul trip.

long- and short-haul travel, Iberia was at or near the bottom for both. Its customer satisfaction score for short-haul trips was 38 per cent and for long-haul 27 per cent, the lowest of 42 airlines. On long-haul it was deemed to have the worst food and the poorest entertainment (*Which*, 2008). How would one brand the merged airline or business when the passenger perceptions of each partner were so different?

In the mid-1980s airlines began to develop Frequent Flyer Programmes (FFPs) both as a way of ensuring passenger loyalty and as a way of improving their image. Under such schemes, passengers are awarded points for each flight with the airline whose FFP they have joined. The number of points depends on the length of the flight and the class of travel and sometimes the type or price of the ticket. As the points build up, passengers can redeem them for free flights for themselves or family members, for upgrades to a higher class when they buy a paid ticket or for a variety of other travel or related benefits. However, there may be strict conditions as to when and on which flights such redemptions can be made. This minimises the costs of redemption in terms of lost revenues. The number of points awarded for specific flights or their value when redeemed varies from airline to airline. The FFPs are normally operated as clubs, giving higher grades of membership and more privileges as the number of points earned or journeys made with the parent airline within a year climbs above certain thresholds. In theory it is the combination of more points and greater potential awards, together with increased privileges associated with higher grades of club membership, such as access to an airline's airport lounges, that ensure passenger loyalty.

Certainly, as mentioned earlier (Section 10.2 and Table 10.2) FFP membership has become a dominant factor in airline choice at least for business travel despite the fact that most business travellers normally belong to three or four separate FFPs. FFPs are targeting the frequent flyers who are primarily those flying on business, though many leisure and VFR passengers also fly frequently and belong to FFPs. The main objective of all loyalty schemes has been to sell more seats. Airlines appreciate that it is much more expensive in marketing terms to attract a new customer than to obtain repeat business from an existing one. As a result, the efficiency, flexibility and user friendliness of FFPs are a key marketing tool. For example, how easy is it to redeem award miles or points for one's chosen destination, or to use miles to upgrade class of travel?

In recent years airlines have been focusing increasingly on a second objective of FFPs. Loyalty schemes can provide the data base on which airlines can build effective customer relationship management (CRM) while the internet provides the means for communicating with customers. Airlines with long-established FFPs have considerable data on their customers' travel patterns and preferences, family, residence, place of work and so on. This data can be leveraged either to prevent defections or to encourage repeat business. The latter can be done by developing an inter-active relationship with FFP members by offering them discounted fares to their favourite destinations, special fares for family members, and so on. By using the internet to question customers about needs and preferences, by setting up customer panels and through other survey techniques airlines can develop customer bonding and loyalty. Customer relationship management is playing an increasingly important part in airline marketing.

As competition has intensified, brand and customer loyalty have become key product features. With the strengthening of airline alliances and global networks they will become even more important. Lufthansa, among other airlines, appreciates this. According to Nicola Lange, the Director-marketing, Lufthansa North America, 'We have some values we defined five years ago, premium being one, along with innovation and customer focused service. Whatever we do with the customers we try to bring that brand' (Arnoult, 2008).

10.6   The 'hubbing' concept

In the 1980s, following deregulation in the United States, 'hubbing' was developed by all the major companies as a crucial schedule-based product feature. Hub and spoke networks in themselves were not new. After all, European and most airlines outside the United States had always operated radial networks because the international regulations prevented them from doing anything else. What was new was the way in which hubs came to be operated. Hubbing has major implications both for airline economics and for competition policy and thus merits more detailed examination.

The concept of hubbing was first developed in the 1970s by Federal Express for the carriage of overnight express parcels throughout the United States, using its hub at Memphis. Effective hubbing requires that flights from different airports, which are at the spokes of a network, arrive at the hub at approximately the same time. The aircraft then wait on the ground simultaneously. This facilitates the interchange of passengers and baggage or, in the case of Federal Express, of express parcels between aircraft in a short period of time before they depart in quick succession back out along the spokes. This process, which involves a wave or 'bank' of arrivals followed shortly after by a wave of departures, is described as a complex. The transfer time between flights in the same complex should be close to the best attainable. A US airline with a major hub will operate several complexes during the day. American Airlines schedules about eight complexes daily at Dallas-Fort Worth. Air France in 2008 had six at Paris Charles de Gaulle, while KLM and Lufthansa operated five complexes each at their respective hubs.

An airline able to develop and operate a hub-and-spoke system with a series of complexes enjoys numerous potential advantages. The increase in city-pair coverage that can be obtained as a result of hubbing is much more dramatic than is often realised. If three point-to-point direct links from cities A to B, C to D and E to F are replaced by six direct

Table 10.5 Impact of hubbing on the number of city pairs serviced

Number of spokes from the hub n	Number of points connected via the hub $n(n-1) \div 2$	Number of points linked to the hub by direct flights n	Total city pairs served $n(n+1) \div 2$
2	1	2	3
6	15	6	21
10	45	10	55
50	1,225	50	1,275
75	2,775	75	2,850
100	4,950	100	5,050

services from each of these six airports to a new hub at an intermediate point G, the number of city-pair markets that can be served jumps from three to 21. This advantage increases in proportion to the *square* of the number of routes or spokes operated from the hub. Thus, if a hub has n spokes, the number of direct links is n to which must be added $n(n-1) \div 2$ connecting links via the hub.

The progressively greater impact of adding more links through a hub can be seen in Table 10.5. The ability to reach a large number of destinations from any one origin gives the airline operating the hub system considerable market appeal. Effective hubbing generates substantial volumes of additional traffic, and revenue, but most of it is transferring through the hub airport.

A number of further marketing advantages flow from the increase in city pairs served. By channelling what may be a large number of separate but thin city-pair flows originating at an outlying airport but going to different destinations onto a service going into the hub airport, the density of traffic on that particular spoke may be built up. The additional traffic generated by the connecting passengers may allow an airline to use larger and more economical aircraft, but also to operate more frequent flights along the spokes. As this will happen on many spokes, the frequencies of possible connecting services via the hub linking two distant spokes, with low traffic between them, increases. Not only does this stimulate traffic but it also inhibits potential competitors from starting a direct service between the two spokes, since they may be unable to compete in terms of frequencies or departure times.

The hub operator may also drop its fares on connecting services if it needs to undermine any new competition from an airline offering direct point-to-point services bypassing a hub. It can do this easily by cross-subsidising this service from other routes where it faces no direct competition. Moreover, once traffic between two airports at the periphery of a hub-and-spoke system builds up, the hub airline may offer a direct service between them to pre-empt a new entrant.

The power of an effective hub to build up dense traffic flows on key routes by attracting passengers from a wide range of origins linked to the hub is well illustrated by the case study of a Lufthansa Boeing 747 flight from Frankfurt to Hong Kong in October 2006 (Table 10.6). Nearly two thirds of the capacity of the aircraft (364 seats) was filled by the 224 passengers who came in on feeder flights from 50 different European airports. Without such volumes of feed Lufthansa would have had difficulty supporting a once-daily Boeing 747 flight to Hong Kong. It would have been forced to reduce frequencies or cut them altogether or fly daily with a smaller aircraft, with higher unit costs.

Table 10.6 Power of hubbing – connecting passengers on Lufthansa LH-738 Frankfurt–Hong Kong on 4 October 2006

ORIGINS to Frankfurt	Flight LH-738	FINAL DESTINATION
No. of transfer pax from:	FRA. to Hong Kong Boeing 747	No. of pax going to
16 Hamburg		
15 Lisbon		
13 Milan		
11 Munich		
10 Dusseldorf		
9 Madrid		
9 Oslo		
8 Bremen	Seats	
8 Brussels		31 Taipei
8 Copenhagen	First 13	5 Manila
8 Manchester	Business 64	2 Brisbane
7 Bologna		
7 Berlin	Economy 287	2 Guangzhou
6 Paris CDG	Total 364	1 Sydney
6 Rome		1 Shanghai
6 Heathrow		
5 St Petersburg		
5 Nuremberg		
4 Amsterdam		
4 Athens		
4 Hanover		
4 Venice		
4 Zurich		
67 various other origins		
TOTAL FEED		TOTAL ONWARD FEED
244 pax from 50 origins		44 pax to 8 destinations

Source: Lufthansa.

One of the most important benefits to arise from effective hub-and-spoke operations is the extent to which individual airline networks can become self-sufficient in meeting demand, enabling operators to keep passengers on their own services rather than lose them to interline connections to another airline. This has been illustrated clearly since deregulation in the USA. The proportion of all passengers making an online transfer connection with the same carrier or regional affiliates has risen from 25 per cent in 1977 to over 90 per cent of all transfer passengers. At London's Heathrow airport 27 per cent of transfer passengers were British Airways to British Airways in 1984. By 2008 this had grown to over 65 per cent.

Complexing of flight schedules ensures that the probability of the first outgoing service to any particular destination being by the same airline as the delivering flight is disproportionately high. Interlineable fares, involving transfer from one airline to another, therefore no longer become necessary. Even if a parallel journey from a competitor exists on one leg of a connecting journey, there will now usually be a severe financial penalty for using it. In other words, the hub carrier will offer a lower through fare on its own services than can be obtained by transferring to or from another carrier at the hub. The passenger also gains in terms of convenience and reliability from single airline service. Frequent-flyer incentive programmes further encourage the use of online connections with the same airline rather than interlining onto a different carrier.

Certain pairs of links created by hubbing will generate substantially more traffic than others. Such demand can be stimulated by offering through services. Unlike traditional scheduling methods, whereby aircraft return on the same route from which they originated, they can now proceed on through the hub to the location with which there is most market potential. This is often done in the United States but rarely in Europe.

The result of all this is to ensure that a major airline at a particular hub in terms of routes and frequencies will become even more dominant in its share of transfer passengers, as its operations develop. In the early 1980s as 'hubbing' began to be implemented in the USA, there were only a couple of the 15 or so larger airports where a single operator had more than 50 per cent market share in terms of flights. By the late 2000s, about half of these airports had a dominant carrier who, together with an owned or contracted regional airline, generated 60 per cent or more of the flights and at most of the remaining airports the major hub operator had a 40 to 50 per cent share of departures. The dominance was least marked at major international gateways such as Los Angeles and New York-JFK. This is inevitable as many foreign carriers also operate into these airports.

The European airlines, despite operating radial networks, were much slower than their US counterparts in developing schedules to provide effective hubbing. However, the European experience in developing powerful hubs contrasts with that of US airlines in three respects. First, the dominance is not so marked. At only two of the major European airports did the base airline operate close to 60 per cent of the flights in 2007. This was the case at Frankfurt where Lufthansa and its subsidiaries had 60 per cent of the departures and at Amsterdam where KLM and various subsidiaries operated 59 per cent of all flights. At London-Heathrow British Airways' share of flights was only 41.3 per cent. This is partly due to the fact that all the European airports are also international gateways with many foreign airlines flying in. Second, European airlines have generally only operated one hub. Those with two such as the former Swissair (Zurich and Geneva) or Alitalia (Rome and Milan) have faced serious problems in the past. Lufthansa has been developing a second hub at Munich but this is in part because Frankfurt is full. The US majors tend to operate multi-hub networks with two or more hubs each. For instance, Northwest operates its major hubs at Minneapolis-St. Paul and Detroit with a smaller one at Memphis. Partly to overcome their focus on single hubs, European airlines have embarked on alliances and, more recently, acquisitions, with other European carriers in order to develop multi-hub systems. For instance, Air France-KLM have two major hubs, Paris and Amsterdam, while the STAR alliance partners have seven hubs in central Europe of varying size – Frankfurt, Munich, Zurich, Copenhagen, Vienna, Warsaw and Brussels. Perhaps too many! Finally, Europe has no shared hubs with two carriers each having a significant market share at the same airport. This is what American and United do at Chicago O'Hare and US Airways and Southwest at Phoenix. Asian carriers too tend to focus on one major hub which is also their country's international gateway.

Once airlines have established dominance at a hub through control of a disproportionate share of the flights offered and traffic uplifted, it is very difficult for another airline to set up a rival hub at the same airport, because it is unlikely to get enough runway slots to offer a similar range of destinations. In the United States the hub operator will also control most of the terminal gates. If the new entrant chooses to compete on just a few direct routes from the hub airport, it will face a competitive disadvantage vis-à-vis the hub airline in terms of ensuring adequate feed for its own services. Hence the notion of the 'fortress hub'. This raises competition issues. For instance, in 2006 US Airways controlled 72 of the 85 gates at its main hub at Charlotte. This made it very difficult, if not impossible, for any new entrant to mount any effective competition.

Consumers clearly benefit from hub-and-spoke systems in that they can fly to many more points with higher frequencies and, where necessary, shorter connecting times than was the case before hubbing became so finely developed. On the other hand, passengers who as a result of hubbing are deprived of direct services which might otherwise be operated are clearly worse off. Their journey times may be longer and their fares may be higher if there is no alternative routing. There may be other disadvantages too. Hubbing is very dependent on excellent punctuality, and delays anywhere can throw whole 'complexes' into disarray, with serious knock-on effects. This is because a delayed flight may be carrying passengers transferring to a dozen or more departing flights, all of which may have to be held back. The short transit time between arriving and departing flights can create havoc in trying to handle large volumes of connecting baggage. It is not surprising that passenger awareness of and concern with punctuality and misdirected baggage has increased significantly in the United States as hubbing has spread.

There is also considerable concern about the high fares on routes to fortress hubs as a result of market concentration. The US Department of Justice uses the Herfindahl-Hirschman Index (HHI) to assess levels of concentration for anti-trust reviews. The HHI is calculated by summing the square of individual market shares of all companies operating in a market. For example, if three airlines at an airport have 10, 30 and 60 per cent of the traffic the HHI is 4,600 ($10^2 + 30^2 + 60^2 = 100 + 900 + 3,600$). If there is only a single operator the HHI is 10,000 (100×100), suggesting total concentration, that is, a monopoly. The Justice Department considers markets with an HHI of 1,001–1,800 as moderately concentrated and those above 1,800 as highly concentrated. Of the 15 largest US airports in 2007, in terms of passengers, only two, Los Angeles and New York JFK, both major international gateways, had an HHI below 1,800. Six had HHIs above 4,000, indicating very high concentration. The others' HHIs were between 2,000 and 4,000, which is still very concentrated in Justice Department terms.

10.7   The economics of hubbing

Hubbing can be an effective schedule-based marketing tool providing wider market spread, generating increased revenues and resulting in market dominance on many routes. But the economics of hubbing are quite complex, since it imposes certain cost penalties on the operating airlines. These are largely of two kinds: those associated with the extra flying required and those arising from the extra passenger handling that is involved compared with direct flights.

An example of the extra flying involved can be seen in Swiss Airlines' efforts in 2008 to sell London to Rome services via Zurich in the London market. This involved carrying passengers on two sectors London–Zurich, with an aircraft block-time of 1 hr 40 min and Zurich–Rome with a block-time of 1 hr 35 min, making a total block-time of 3 hr 15 min. Yet a direct flight London–Rome requires a block-time of only 2 hr 30 min. In other words 40 minutes of extra block-time is required for the passenger hubbing through Zurich. Carrying online transfer passengers through a hub as opposed to a direct flight creates higher costs in a number of areas. Fuel costs will be higher both because of the longer flight time and the extra landing and take-off when fuel consumption is highest. In fact, all direct operating costs will be higher, including airport landing charges since landings will be more frequent. In a European context, where airport charges are especially high, this may be a severe cost penalty. En-route navigation charges will also be higher. In order to provide feeder traffic for the first bank of departures from the hub airlines must night-stop aircraft and crews at the end of the shorter spoke routes and schedule early morning departures to the hub. Such night stops are expensive.

Each passenger making a transfer connection at the hub is involved in two boardings and disembarkations, a transfer of baggage at the hub and the use of two or three departure or arrival lounges. The costs of handling must be high. The airline may also have to pay two airport charges for him. Moreover, the complexing of flights at the hub and the need to transfer passengers and baggage in the shortest possible time create tremendous peak pressure on staff and facilities compared with a normal operation where demand is spread through the day. To meet such peaks of demand, extra staff will be needed and not only additional but also more sophisticated baggage- and passenger-handling equipment and facilities.

The cost disadvantages of hubbing are particularly severe if one is trying to operate a short- to medium-haul hub such as one linking European points. On gateway hub services connecting short- to long-haul services the cost penalties are less marked because the total increase of in-flight distances as a result of hubbing are less pronounced.

The economics of hubbing hinges on whether the higher flying and passenger-related costs of indirect services via a hub are off-set by the ability to operate larger aircraft with lower unit costs, as in the case of the Lufthansa Frankfurt–Hong Kong services cited earlier. Larger aircraft should result from combining several thin flows into a single radial service from the spoke to the hub. It may also be possible to increase aircraft utilisation because of the higher frequencies resulting from the denser traffic flows. On the cost side it is a fine balance. The emergence of small but regional jets able to offer low-cost point-to-point services on thin routes joining the spokes of a radial network has made the cost economies of hubbing for shot-haul services more precarious. A 1999 study compared the costs of connecting two points via a hub using an Airbus A321 aircraft, offering around 200 seats, with the cost of down-sizing to Boeing 737–300 aircraft, with around 120 seats, on the flights through the hub, while also offering a direct service between the two outlying points with a Canadair 50-seater regional jet. The first spoke was assumed to be 300 kms in length. It was only when the length of the second spoke (sector) reached 900 kms or more that hubbing with larger A321s produced lower unit costs than a direct link with a regional jet combined with smaller aircraft on services through the hub. The implications are clear: if the spokes of a hubbing operation are relatively short the unit costs are likely to be higher than offering direct services with small regional aircraft (Eggert, 1999).

To what extent can increased revenues through improved passenger loads and/or higher yields per passenger counter-balance the higher costs? Certainly, airlines have tried to off-set the diseconomies of hubbing by trying to increase their fares on services through the hub. They can do this in two ways. First by charging a premium for purely local traffic travelling only between a spoke and the hub, and not connecting, especially if they are the only operator on the spoke. For instance, following its purchase of Swiss Airline in 2006, Lufthansa has an effective monopoly on the local feeder routes from Zurich and

a to its hubs at Frankfurt and Munich. It can, and does, charge high fares for local
on these routes. In the United States, a 1998 report by the Department of
sportation found that 'in the absence of competition, the major carrier is able to
charge direct fares that exceed its fares in non-hub markets of comparable distance and
density by upwards of 40 per cent' (DoT 1998).

Second, by trying to exact high fares when offering hub services between two points
that have no direct links. There may not be many of those. On the other hand, if there is
a direct link offered by another carrier or if it is possible to travel via another carrier's hub,
then competition for this point-to-point traffic will be intense. Fares are then likely to
drop, particularly if one of the sectors is long-haul. For example, in August 2008, British
Airways was selling its lowest Business class return for London-Singapore for the following October, for a flight out on Monday and return Friday, for Sterling £5,137, but
Lufthansa was offering the same route via their Frankfurt hub for only £2,552. This
£2,552 revenue had to be split between the two sectors London–Frankfurt and Frankfurt–
Singapore, diluting the average yield on both. In fact, Lufthansa separate Business fares on
the two sectors for the relevant sectors were £656 and £3,059 respectively, making a total
of £3,715. Selling these seats for £2,552 meant substantial yield dilution.

The economics of hubbing depend largely on having sufficient local traffic from each
spoke to the hub, paying a premium price to compensate for the lower yield on hub
transfer traffic. This means that a hub which is itself a major traffic generator or attractor
has a distinct advantage. It also means that the proportion of transfer traffic on each spoke
route should ideally not rise to more than 55–60 per cent.

US experience, and more recent experience in Europe and at long-haul hubs such as
Singapore or Dubai, suggests that for an airport to become an effective hub it must possess
five attributes: a central geographical position in relation to the markets it is to serve,
whether this is purely short-medium haul or intercontinental; ample runway capacity; a
single terminal building for the hub airline and, ideally, strong local demand to and from
the hub. Many airports satisfy these criteria. Where the latter does not exist one may try
to create it by building up local industry, business or tourist infrastructure as both Singapore
and Dubai have done. The fifth and most critical requirement is to have a strong hub-
based airline prepared to develop effective hubbing by operating banks of arriving flights
followed by banks of departures.

During the 1980s and 1990s more and more international airlines, following the US
example, restructured their networks and rescheduled their flights so as to operate their
base airports as effective hubs. But by the early 2000s there were some signs that hubbing
could be problematical. Increased competition, especially in long-haul markets as a result
of hubbing and the new alliances, was pushing down yields at a time when unit costs were
being affected by rising fuel prices. Another consequence of competition between hubs
was that capacity in many markets was rising too rapidly. Extra seats could only be filled
by lowering fares. In developing a turn-around strategy, following losses in 1999–2000, the
first for some time, BA came to the conclusion that its biggest losses were coming from
Economy class passengers transferring between short- and long-haul services in London
and, to a lesser extent, from short- to short-haul economy transfers. It would reduce
its exposure in these two areas. It would above all reduce capacity on long-haul routes
by cutting frequencies and, in some routes, reducing aircraft seating and/or size.
Henceforward BA would focus on selling fewer seats but at premium fares. The introduction of fully reclining sleeper seats in long-haul Business class in 2001 was part of
that strategy.

It is also clear that in Europe, attempts by some airlines to build both operationally and economically successful hubs have failed. A case in point is Sabena, the Belgian airline. As an ailing state-owned airline it received $1,800 million of government aid in 1991 to fund its restructuring and a further injection of capital in 1995. In the following year, 1996, Swissair bought a 49.6 per cent shareholding. Under Swissair guidance Sabena began to develop Brussels as a European hub. This meant opening routes to new and sometimes quite small European points, increased frequencies and a concomitant expansion of the fleet. Rescheduling produced three complexes of arrivals and departures each day. This strategy was mismanaged. It proved a disaster. After making a small profit in 1998, Sabena went into the red again in 1999 and slumped to a $170 million loss in 2000. It was then announced that the cost of saving the airline would be around $850 million. The hubbing concept had backfired. Sabena had opened too many new routes in Europe. Many had little local traffic and were too dependent on transfer traffic. For instance, on the flights from Dusseldorf or Luxembourg to Brussels, over 85 per cent of passengers were transferring to other flights in Brussels. The higher frequencies required to support three daily complexes meant a substantial increase in the seats available and which needed to be sold. New thin spoke routes, over-capacity, insufficient higher yield business traffic – within Europe only 1 in 10 Sabena passengers in 1999 were in Business class compared to 2 in 10 for its major competitors and 3 out of 10 at SAS – and competition from other European hubs meant that Sabena's average yields fell to levels that were quite unprofitable. By mid-2001 it was apparent that only by cutting out 15 to 20 of its European destinations plus most of its long-haul routes and reducing its hub, could Sabena achieve long-term profitability. But time ran out. The losses could not be stemmed fast enough. In November 2001 Sabena collapsed. Swissair did the same a few months later.

By pushing its hubbing strategy too far, Sabena ended up 'flying off course'. This example (and there are others, such as Alitalia) highlights the need to keep hubbing in perspective. The risks of failure are high because of the higher costs of operating a 'complexed' hub.

In the United States, during the early and mid-2000s some airlines reduced their secondary hubs, as Delta did with its Cincinnati hub, or de-complexed their hub schedules so as to get better utilisation of aircraft and ground facilities by having less marked peaks during the day. American Airlines followed the latter strategy. In Europe, Swiss downgraded its Geneva hub where it had offered 25 domestic and European services in early 2002 to just a handful by 2008, plus a few where it code-shared on foreign carriers. Alitalia in 2008 more or less abandoned its Milan-Malpensa hub. Of growing concern, in North America, Europe and elsewhere, is the impact of low-cost airlines on hub feeder routes. As network carriers lose traffic to low-cost competitors on routes feeding their major hubs some of these routes will become less viable once higher yielding local point-to-point traffic is lost. Some routes may have to be abandoned making their hubs even more dependent on locally-generated traffic.

11 Pricing for profit?

We have been doing à-la-carte pricing for six years and it is popular with our customers
. . . About 47 per cent of our customers choose a higher fare product for its attributes – even
with lower fares available . . . .

(Montie Brewer, CEO, Air Canada, April 2009)

11.1 Objectives of airline pricing policy

Pricing is a crucial element in airline management. It is only one of several product and
service features which are planned and combined together in order to generate demand.
But it is the key mechanism whereby the demand for air services is matched with the
supply. An airline's primary aim must be to sell the capacity it is prepared and able to offer
at prices which will generate sufficient demand to ensure an adequate level of profit.
A great deal hinges on what each airline considers an adequate profit. For some state-
owned airlines it may mean little more than breaking even. For others it may be measured
in terms of an adequate rate of return to shareholders or a target rate of return on the
value of the assets employed. Some airlines may go further and set out not only to produce
a target rate of return on their current assets but also to generate an adequate reserve fund
to self-finance, as far as possible, the acquisition of new assets such as aircraft. Singapore
Airlines appears in recent years to have followed this latter objective. Thus even the profit
objective in airline pricing may have different implications for different airlines.

There is also a temporal dimension to the profit objective. While some airlines may be
concerned more with current profits, others may place the emphasis on longer-term
profitability. They may be prepared to forgo profits in the short term to ensure their
longer-term objective. When launching new services or entering fresh markets airlines
will often accept losses in the short term, in the expectation of long-term profits. Short-
term losses may be exacerbated by the need to offer low fares in order to capture market
share and get established.

For many government-owned airlines, particularly in their early years, profit has been
less important than achieving other indirect benefits such as stimulating incoming tourism and related employment or ensuring adequate international air connections. Profit
may be seen as a desirable longer-term objective rather than a short-term priority. This
was certainly the case with the newer Gulf area airlines such as Qatar Airways, established
1993, and Etihad Airways launched by Abu Dhabi in 2003.

Most international airlines will normally have a clear profit objective but it will only
be one of a number of corporate objectives. These other objectives may also impinge on

pricing policy. Expansion into new routes and new markets figures large in many airlines' corporate objectives. Expansion may be an objective in its own right or the ultimate aim may be rapid growth or the attainment of a particular size of operation. Many airlines want to be big! There may be cost advantages from growth but ultimately the purpose of growth seems to be more akin to a revenue-maximising objective. But revenue-maximising may not be the same as profit-maximising, as Malaysian Airlines found out in the late 1990s. Under new private management it set out on a course of very rapid expansion only to see its profits evaporate to such an extent that in 2000 control was bought back by the Malaysian Government. If development of new markets or rapid growth are objectives of an airline's pricing policy then the pricing strategies it adopts must be coloured by this fact. In Europe during the 1990s Sabena, the small Belgian airline, tried to grow rapidly in long-haul international markets, competing with larger established carriers by offering lower tariffs, especially for transfer passengers through its Brussels hub. But it went too far with disastrous results. The airline collapsed at the end of 2001.

The adverse cost impact of large seasonal or even daily variations in demand may induce airlines to use the pricing mechanism as a way of reducing those fluctuations. This might be done by using high tariffs to restrain or dampen peak demand and lower tariffs to stimulate off-peak traffic. Such a policy may reduce the total revenue that could be generated by a policy of expanding the supply of services at the peak periods so as to carry all the potential demand. But revenue maximisation may be less important in the short term than restraining peak period demand in order to reduce unit costs by not providing too much capacity at the peak. Such capacity is costly because it remains under-utilised in the off-peak periods. In other words, a policy of revenue-maximisation may reduce profits.

Pricing has a further role. It should in theory be a guide to new investment. Where the number of consumers who are prepared to pay the full cost, including a reasonable profit, of the goods or services they consume exceeds the supply, then the producers have a clear indication that if they can supply more at the same or a lower price demand will be sufficient to generate further profits. Conversely, if consumers in total do not generate sufficient revenue to cover the full costs of particular services then it would be foolhardy to invest in the expansion of such services. If pricing is to be used as a guide to further investment then the prices of different services should broadly reflect their costs of production. If not, demand may be artificially high or it may be suppressed. On two or three occasions falling tariffs on the North Atlantic have generated a surge in demand which pushed up load factors to high levels. Some airlines misread the signs and increased the capacity on offer. Here, as on numerous other occasions, airlines have found that adding more seats, which can only be filled at very low fares, proved a recipe for financial distress! The low tariffs were only feasible if mixed with a certain proportion of high-fare business and First class traffic. Putting on extra services to cater exclusively for the low-yield traffic could prove ruinous since the revenue generated may be insufficient to cover the costs. The pricing mechanism, if used as a guide to further investment, must be used with care.

In short, few international airlines have a single overriding objective in their pricing policy, though the attainment of profitability looms large, especially for privately-owned airlines. Most want their pricing policy to achieve a number of internal objectives. But they may also have externally imposed objectives. Some national airlines are required by their governments to stimulate incoming tourism. This may well require a low-fare policy irrespective of its repercussions on the financial fortunes of the airline itself. The attempt to attain different pricing objectives simultaneously may produce conflicts and contradictions in pricing policy. Such conflicts and complexities in pricing are further increased because the same airline may be pursuing different objectives on different parts of its network. It may be trying to maximise profits on some routes, especially those on which there is little or no tariff competition, while on other routes its prime objective may be increasing its market share or its rate of growth. Inevitably within any airline different pricing objectives will prevail at different times and in different parts of their operations.

11.2   Three key variables

The theme of the present book is that airline management is about matching the supply of air services, which airline executives can largely control, with the demand for such services, which executives can influence but cannot control, in a way which generates adequate levels of profit. Profitability, which appears to be an important objective for most airlines, depends in turn on the interplay of three variables, the unit costs, which are a function of supply conditions, the unit revenues or yields and the load factors achieved, both of which are related to demand. The interplay of these three variables can be illustrated by reference to a specific example.

In summer 2004, before the huge escalation of oil prices, a West European airline flying a daily Boeing 747–400, with 400 seats, from its base airport to New York may have incurred a total one-way operating cost of, say, $80,000. On this basis it would be possible to draw a break-even load factor curve (Figure 11.1). This shows the load factor which the airline would have needed to achieve to break even at different average fare levels or yields (the average being the weighted average of all fares paid). At any point along the curve, the average fare shown (on the vertical scale) times the number of passengers carried or the load factor (horizontal scale) equals $80,000. By plotting on the graph the average fare and the average load achieved on each day's flight in each month or season it is possible to see whether the flight is profitable or not. The plots for just three days in the first month of the summer season are shown in the diagram. On both Mondays and Saturdays the combination of average fare and passenger load were clearly above the break-even curve. These flights are profitable. The Thursday flight was problematic! Average yields were low and so were loads, averaging close to 40 per cent.

What could be done? Two obvious strategies come to mind immediately – push up the loads or increase the fares. At the then existing one-way fares, which on Thursdays were averaging just over $200, the average load factor would need to be pushed up to more than 85 per cent to cross the break-even load factor curve. This seems unrealistic. On the other hand, to break even at the current 40 per cent load factor, the average fare would have to more than double to $500 to achieve a profitable operation. But if fares went up so much there would be a passenger reaction and it would be difficult to maintain the same volume of passenger traffic. Clearly the easiest task for Thursday flights would be to try to cross the break-even curve at the nearest point. In other words, try to increase both average yields and average loads. This could be done by targeting high-yield Business class passengers, thereby improving the traffic mix, by focused advertising and so on. There is a further solution: which is to try to move the break-even curve downward and to the right by reducing total operating costs, through tighter cost control or, if available, by operating the Thursday service with a smaller 260–300-seater aircraft, such as a Boeing 777–200, with lower trip costs. The airline's planners have three variables to play with in order to achieve profitability – unit costs, fares and load factors.

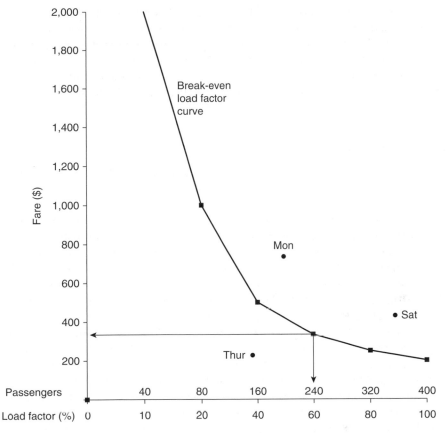

Figure 11.1 Unit cost, yield and load factor trade-off (total operating cost, Europe to New York. one-way=$80,000).

11.3 Inherent instability of airline fares

As in the simple case above, airline managers must juggle with costs, fares and load factors to produce a profitable combination. This is a very dynamic and interactive process, made more difficult by the pricing instability inherent in the airline industry. The industry is characterised by short-run marginal costs which are close to zero. In other words, the marginal cost of carrying an extra passenger on a flight which is due to leave with empty seats is no more than the cost of an additional meal, an airport passenger charge, the cost of ground handling and a few pounds of fuel burnt as a result of the extra weight. The problem is that even when operating with high load factors of 70 per cent or more there will be many empty seats. These cannot be stored or sold later. If they are not sold at the moment of production, the seats and the seat-kms generated are lost for ever. The same considerations apply to unsold freight capacity. An airline committed to operate a published schedule of services for a particular season or a tour operator committed to a series of charter flights find that their short-run total costs are fixed and cannot be varied. Therefore it makes business sense to try to maximise revenues. Having sold as much capacity as possible at normal tariffs, the airline or tour operator is tempted to sell any remaining empty seats at virtually any price above the very low marginal cost of carrying the additional passengers.

The problem is how to prevent slippage or diversion of passengers, prepared to book early and pay the normal tariffs, into paying the lower tariffs. If that happens then the total revenue generated may decline. In markets where tariff rules are regulated and enforced, diversion is prevented or minimised by the conditions, the so-called 'fences', which circumscribe the availability of the very low tariffs (see Section 11.5 below). In markets where tariffs are not regulated or, if regulated, regulations are not enforced, the low marginal cost of carrying an additional passenger (or freight consignment) has a strong downward pressure on all tariffs, including the normal Economy, Business or First class fares. The inherent instability in such markets is made much worse if they are largely liberalised and there are no controls on the seat capacity offered or if the entry of new carriers is easy. It is in conditions of over-capacity that airlines are most likely to resort to marginal cost pricing. Following the total deregulation of the United States domestic system the relationship between costs and tariffs in the early 1980s largely disappeared. Tariffs were determined by competitive factors and on many routes tariffs approached long-run marginal costs while on others only short-run marginal costs had any relevance to pricing.

In international markets the price instability is aggravated by a number of additional factors. One of these has already been mentioned and that is the tendency of new airlines entering established markets to try to capture market share by undercutting existing tariffs. The most significant factor and the most widespread, even affecting regulated markets, is the availability of sixth freedom capacity. While the point-to-point, third and fourth freedom carriers on a route may be trying to maintain an adequate mix and level of different tariffs, sixth freedom carriers operating via their own home base may be prepared to charge almost anything to fill empty seats with traffic that they would otherwise not have had. The sixth freedom operators' tariffs will be particularly low if they want to compensate passengers for having a lengthy stop-over en route to their destination. The development of hubbing (Section 10.6 in the previous chapter) has aggravated this problem as it has increased the number of convenient routings and timings available for many journeys. This, together with so much additional capacity being available, has intensified competition. In most long-haul international markets there is a great amount of spare sixth freedom and sometimes fifth freedom capacity slushing around and depressing tariffs. On some routes there may be the additional problem of the marginal carrier, that is the airline for whom the route is marginal to its total operation. It may therefore be unconcerned by low fares on the route, particularly if it sees them as a way of attracting traffic onto the rest of its network.

Examples of these and various pressures on price could be found early in 2009 on the London to Singapore route (Table 11.1). The table shows the lowest return Business class fares available direct from each airline late in 2008 for travel in February 2009. The two third and fourth freedom carriers, on the route, British Airways (£3,988) and Singapore Airlines (£3,709), had the higher fares. BA was actually higher than SIA because it had fewer seats on offer with two flights per day, compared to SIA's three daily, of which two were Airbus A380s. Most of BA's flights were going on to Australian points, so it had even fewer seats available for local London to Singapore traffic. Qantas has fifth freedom rights on this sector and, as a member of the oneworld alliance and BA's partner, its lowest business fare was the same as BA's.

The various sixth freedom operators, except Malaysia Airlines, all had low fares about half of those of BA or SIA. In the case of the European carriers this was despite the fact that they had to carry passengers on high-cost, short sectors from London to their European hubs. These very low sixth freedom fares were to encourage passengers despite

Table 11.1 Business class fares London to Singapore – February 2009

	Lowest return fare (£)
Malaysia Airlines	4,320
British Airways	3,988
Qantas	3,988
Singapore Airlines	3,709
Swiss	2,331
Lufthansa	2,065
Emirates	2,058
Qatar Airways	2,001
Air France	1,829
Turkish Airlines	1,669

Note
Fares offered by airlines in November 2008 for travel in early February 2009.

the inconvenience of changing aircraft at an intermediate hub on the way to Singapore. The exception among sixth freedom carriers was Malaysian Airlines, whose fares were surprisingly higher than those of BA and SIA (£4,320). It is difficult to understand why. While Table 11.1 shows the apparent price structure, the availability of so many low fares and so much capacity inevitably meant that all carriers, but especially the home carriers BA and SIA, were under tremendous pressure to cut fares, especially on flights when loads were poor. They did this by offering lower fares through internet travel agencies such as Expedia or Opodo. Economy class fares were even more varied and fluid with constant price changes in response to changing market conditions.

On other routes, price instability may be increased by the actions of financially weak or government-supported carriers. Surprisingly it is often the weak or loss-making airlines which drop their prices most in competitive markets in order to generate sufficient cash flow to meet their day-to-day payments. In 2000 and 2001, the Belgian airline Sabena, which was facing growing financial pressures, was offering by far the lowest fares across the Atlantic and to Africa for passengers from elsewhere in Europe prepared to transfer through its Brussels hub. It was desperate for cash. It nevertheless collapsed by the end of 2001. Some state-owned airlines may continue operating on certain routes at yields and load factors which are uneconomic because of government pressure or because they can rely on subsidies to cover their losses. In the process, however, they depress the market for other carriers. Finally, the willingness of some airlines to sell seats en bloc or on a part-charter basis to tour operators, consolidators or travel agents reduces the airlines' ability to control the tariffs at which those seats will ultimately be sold to the public.

The low marginal cost of carrying additional traffic, together with the other factors, which undermine price stability, means that international airlines often have a strong incentive to reduce tariffs often to very low levels. The characteristics of international airline operations are such that even published and agreed tariffs such as those negotiated through IATA are not enforceable unless the airlines themselves decide to enforce them. Even government controls, where they still exist, are ineffective without airline acquiescence since airlines can find countless ways in which to circumvent regulatory tariff restrictions. Without airline self-control and enforcement of tariffs and tariff conditions the inherent instability of air transport markets may well push tariffs to levels at which no operator can make a profit except for short periods. It is this fear above all else that pushes airlines to try to reach agreement between themselves on tariffs and on enforcement. One way of removing real price competition on routes where there are only two competitors, or where two airlines carry most of the traffic, is for these two airlines to enter into a code-share agreement or even a full alliance, as SAS and Lufthansa did in 1995. As a result, for many years afterwards there was little downward pressure on yields on the six major routes between Scandinavia and Germany, that is from Copenhagen, Oslo and Stockholm to Frankfurt and Dusseldorf. These were subsequently operated by these two airlines as a joint code-share with no other competing carriers, that is, as a monopoly (Doganis, 2006). It was not until 2002 that Ryanair launched the first competing service between Frankfurt and Stockholm, but from airports each of which was over 120 kms from the two cities served. By late 2008 there were still no competitors against SAS/ Lufthansa on either Frankfurt–Copenhagen or Dusseldorf–Stockholm.

11.4   Impact of the internet on airline pricing

The inherent instability in airline pricing has been made worse, particularly in short-haul domestic or international markets, by the advent of the internet and its rapidly spreading use over the last ten years or so. Its impact has been twofold. First, by giving potential travellers, who have online access, easy and immediate knowledge of all airlines' fares. In by-passing the traditional travel agents, the internet has shifted market power from the suppliers, the airlines, to the consumer. Using airline websites and online travel agencies the consumer can quickly obtain nearly perfect knowledge of what different airlines can offer in terms of fares, schedules, seat availability and service offers. There is full transparency. This gives the consumer considerable power. He can make his choice of airline with all the knowledge of the various options at his fingertips. Since on most routes service standards of different airlines are fairly similar or unimportant if on short sectors, consumer awareness of all the fare options has reinforced price as a differentiator between airlines. In fact, in many short-haul markets the internet has turned air travel into a commodity where price is the only variable on which many if not most consumers make their choice. All this has made it more critical for airlines to get their pricing levels and strategies right.

The second impact of the internet is that it has made airline pricing much more dynamic in real time. The development of computerised reservation systems and later automated revenue management programmes working in real time has given airline revenue controllers, at least those in the largest airlines, instant knowledge of fare changes introduced by their competitors. They can also monitor how well different fares are selling. The internet has given them the ability to respond immediately with new or matching fares which can be communicated worldwide in seconds through their website and those of the GDSs. The speed with which new fares can be introduced but also matched in many markets is a new and additional cause of instability in airline fares. The more truly competitive the market, the greater is the inherent instability.

In markets with several competitors and where product and service standards are not that different, attempts by any one or more carriers to gain competitive advantage by dropping fares will inevitably be matched by all the others. They all end up with similar fares but at a lower level and no one airline is better off in competitive terms. The internet facilitates this downward drift in fare levels.

11.5   Cost-related or market pricing?

In developing their pricing strategies international airlines must bear in mind both their pricing objectives and the inherent instability of airline tariffs. Broadly speaking, two alternative strategies have been open to them. The first is to relate each tariff to the costs incurred in providing the services used by those paying that tariff. This is 'cost of service' pricing, more frequently referred to as cost-related pricing. The alternative is to base tariffs for different categories of service not on costs but on what consumers are able and willing to pay. This is market pricing or demand-related pricing. Market pricing does not ignore costs but the aim is to ensure revenues in total cover costs rather than attempting to ensure that individual customers or groups cover their own particular costs.

In the four decades up to the mid-1980s most international and domestic fares around the world were regulated by IATA and/or governments to a greater or lesser extent (see Section 2.7 in Chapter 2). If fares were to be controlled the only logical and quantifiable basis on which this could be done appeared to be by linking approved fare levels to costs. Several regulatory authorities and European governments (CEC, 1983) or the Commission of the European Communities (CEC, 1984) argued most strongly in favour of cost-related pricing. The UK's Civil Aviation Authority had earlier outlined the fundamental principles to be pursued in developing airline pricing policies (CAA, 1977). It suggested that '*charges . . . should be at the lowest level which will cover the costs of efficient operators, including an adequate return on capital; each charge should be related to costs, and that tariff provisions should be rational, simple and enforceable . . .*'. Before 1978, the Civil Aeronautics Board in the United States had also based its tariff approvals on the concept of cost-related pricing.

The arguments in favour of cost-related pricing in utilities and transport services hinge on the twin issues of equity and economic efficiency. It was considered inequitable that some consumers of air services should be charged more than the cost of providing those services either to generate excess profits or in order to cross-subsidise consumers who are paying less than the full cost of the services they consume. If tariffs are not cost-related then they may well be discriminatory. That means that certain consumers will be discriminated against not on the basis of costs they impose but on the basis of their age, or their marital status or, for instance, because they want to spend less than six nights at their destination.

There are efficiency implications as well. If fares are above cost for some services, then demand for those services will be suppressed even though it might be profitable to supply that demand at prices that were cost-related. Conversely, fares below cost may generate excess demand for particular services and induce airlines to expand such services even though consumers are not meeting their full costs. This would clearly be a misallocation of resources. In truly competitive markets where there are several existing airlines or potential new entrants, tariffs for different services will tend to the level of the most efficient operator, as happened in the 1980s in the European charter market. In markets where real competition is restricted or where there are barriers to the entry of new carriers, there are no competitive forces to push tariffs to the level of the most efficient and lowest cost operator. There may also be a tendency to charge what are effectively monopoly prices for certain inelastic market segments. Market forces cannot ensure that tariffs reflect the costs of the most efficient suppliers. Regulatory authorities and other bodies, such as consumer associations, argued that it was primarily in regulated markets that cost-related pricing was needed to ensure that both equity and tariffs reflect the costs of efficient suppliers. Cost-related pricing was supported both on social grounds, in order to reduce discrimination between consumers, and on economic grounds, in the belief that it created pressures towards improved airline efficiency and a sounder allocation of productive resources.

On the other hand, several arguments can be used to question the principle of cost pricing. The first of these is that there is no satisfactory way for transport industries to allocate costs to particular users because of the incidence of joint costs. This means that a high proportion of fixed costs have to be allocated arbitrarily. Joint costs arise when in producing one service another is inadvertently provided. A daily scheduled flight aimed at a business market produces freight capacity whether or not there is a demand for freight services. Its operations will also inevitably result in vacant seats which might be sold off to meet tourism demand. How is one to allocate the costs of that flight between business passengers who were the prime objective in setting up the flight, and freight or holiday travellers? Any allocation of joint costs must have an element of arbitrariness in it. The same applies to certain fixed direct operating costs and to indirect costs. In practice, many but not all of the problems of airline cost allocation can be overcome, to some extent, as indicated later. But some arbitrariness remains and it is argued that airlines pursuing cost-based pricing would end up calculating what is more akin to an average cost for all users rather than a separate cost specific to different categories of users.

Another argument against cost-related pricing is that on some routes such a pricing strategy would not generate sufficient revenue to cover costs and would therefore fail to ensure the continued operation of services. On a simple route with one fare and one class of service a cost-related fare may not generate sufficient demand to ensure profitability. On the other hand, if two market segments with different price elasticities can be identified, then the airline concerned may generate higher revenue by charging two separate fares to the two market groups even though there may be no significant difference in the cost of transporting them. Without discriminatory but market-related tariffs the services might be abandoned and all consumers would be worse off. Such a hypothetical case was illustrated earlier (Chapter 8, Section 8.8) when discussing the concept of price elasticity.

Finally, attempting to improve efficiency by setting tariffs at the levels of the lowest cost operator may be meaningless in international air transport. Many international air routes, particularly on short- or medium-haul sectors, are dominated by the third and fourth freedom carriers of the two countries at either end of the route. These airlines may have quite different costs for reasons quite unconnected with questions of efficiency. The prevailing wage levels in each country may be different as may the price of fuel or other factor inputs. Exchange rate movements may also have an adverse impact on one airline's costs. Cost-related pricing would produce a different set of tariffs for each airline, yet the lower tariffs may not necessarily be those of the most efficient carrier in terms of the resources used.

It is important to bear in mind that demand or market pricing does not ignore costs, but its focus is to try to ensure that total costs of a route or a flight are covered, rather than to try to ensure that every user pay his own identifiable costs. From an airline viewpoint, demand-related pricing strategies make sense. A scheduled airline that is committed to a published timetable of flights and has brought together the productive resources to operate that timetable finds that its short-run total costs are more or less fixed. In those circumstances it needs the freedom to price its services in such a way as to be able to generate sufficient revenues to cover its costs. This may mean charging more than cost to price-inelastic segments of the market and less than cost to elastic market segments. In liberalised competitive markets, competition between carriers should ensure that market-related pricing is not abused to produce excessive profit for the airline. Where effective competition does not exist and market entry of new airlines is difficult, then there may well be a danger of excessive profits being made through discriminatory pricing. In such situations regulatory or government intervention to monitor costs, tariffs and airline profits may be necessary to prevent this happening, though there must be some doubt as to how effective such intervention can be. Deregulation of tariffs, of capacity controls and of market access would be the most effective way of minimising the likelihood of excessive profits.

As liberalisation of prices, traffic rights and market access has spread, first domestically in the United States after 1978 and subsequently in a growing number of international markets, the airline industry has moved increasingly from cost-based to market or demand-related pricing. In the United States and Europe this switch was accelerated by the rapid growth of low-cost airlines with their innovatory pricing policies. Today in most liberalised markets demand-related pricing prevails, though this does not mean that airlines do not constantly monitor the profitability of different market segments such as that of First or Business class passengers in long-haul aircraft. It is only in countries or markets where governments wish to control fares that attempts may be made to link fares with costs.

A simple, hypothetical example illustrates the basic differences in approach between cost-based and market-based pricing. The daily demand for air services between Athens and a small but important Greek island is shown in the first column of Table 11.2. This shows how much each potential passengers is prepared to pay to be able to fly to the island. It is a measure of the value or benefit to each passenger of this service. Some wealthy Athenians have holiday homes on the island and would be prepared to pay $300 or more to fly in 35 minutes and so avoid the four-hour boat services. Effectively column 1 is the downward sloping demand curve and shows how the demand increases as the cost or fare goes down.

The total one-way operating cost of this service with a small ten seater twin is $1,200 for a 35-minute sector. This means that the average cost per seat is $120. If a fare of $120 is charged, there would be seven passengers daily, that is, all those who, based on their willingness to pay (as shown in column 1), value the trip more than $120. The seat factor is good, 70 per cent, but the service would make a loss (column 2) of $360 per trip. Clearly the airlines' planners should not base the fare on the cost per seat but on the cost per passenger. If they target a 60 per cent seat factor, then the cost per passenger would be $200 (that is, $1,200 divided by six passengers). The airline could build in a profit margin of $10 per passenger and charge $210. It would then get six passengers and total revenue would rise to $1,260, producing a small profit. However, it is clear by comparing columns 3 and 1 that several passengers are paying a lot less than the value to them of the service. What economists call the 'consumers' surplus', which they enjoy, is substantial. Two who are prepared to pay $310 for the flight are getting it for only $210. Market-related pricing aims at ensuring that producers do not lose out in this way. If one introduced a three-tier fare structure, as indicated in the final column (4), where fares were more closely aligned to market demand rather than to costs, then seat factor and revenue can be pushed up markedly. In this case study a significant surplus of $330 per flight and a seat factor of 90 per cent would result from the proposed fare structure.

In practice, pricing is not as simple as the example would suggest. But the basic principle still applies. Market-related pricing may, in most but not all markets, enable airlines to generate higher revenues. The complexities of implementing such pricing are

Table 11.2 Pricing case study: Athens to Greek island
10-seater aircraft
Total operating cost = $1,200 (one way)

Passengers' willingness to pay, i.e. the demand curve	Average cost pricing		Market pricing
	Fare based on cost per seat = $120	Fare based on cost per pax at 60% seat factor = $210*	Three separate fares: $300, $150 and $90
(1)	(2)	(3)	(4)
	Fares paid by passengers willing to travel		
	$	$	$
1 310	120	210	300
2 310	120	210	300
3 280	120	210	150
4 260	120	210	150
5 230	120	210	150
6 210	120	210	150
7 160	120		150
8 110			90
9 90			90
10 55			
11 55			
12 50			
13 40			
etc			
Total revenue	$840	$1,260	$1,530
Surplus-deficit	−$360	+$60	+$330
Seat factor	70%	60%	90%

Note
* Cost per pax $200 plus $10 profit margin.

discussed later. For instance, in the case study above, barriers or fare fences would need to be devised to prevent high-fare passengers using the lower fares. Another complication may be government intervention to try and keep fares low. Up to the year 2001, on routes from Athens to smaller islands, the reality was that the Greek Government would not allow the airlines to charge even average cost fares. Government pressure over the years had resulted in single fares that were below average cost per passenger. As a result most such routes were loss-making.

While in the short term a strategy of market-oriented tariffs makes sense as a way of maximising revenues, it does not in itself guarantee profitability, especially in price-competitive markets. Because of the inherent instability in airline tariffs, discussed earlier, which is due to very low short-run marginal costs, market-related tariffs may reach such low levels that the total revenue generated is insufficient to cover total costs. This is particularly so if extra capacity is provided to cater for the demand generated by the low tariffs. While revenue maximising might be a short-term pricing objective in the longer term airlines are likely to adopt a profit-generating or loss-minimising objective. This means they should abandon routes where revenues do not cover costs or change their pricing policies to ensure that they do.

In order to achieve such objectives through their pricing strategies airlines must be in a position to do three things. First, they must have a fundamental understanding of the different market segments in each of their markets and of customer needs and requirements, both in terms of product features and price (as discussed earlier in Chapter 8, Section 8.5). Second, in markets where airlines decide or are forced to introduce fares which are market-related rather than cost-based, they must implement effective yield or revenue management. This is needed to ensure both that revenue dilution does not occur through slippage of high-fare passengers into lower-fare categories and that their revenues are maximised.

Finally, where market segments are fairly distinct, they should monitor the degree to which each major market category or traffic group covers the costs which it imposes on the airline. This, together with the need to evaluate the feasibility of aircraft investments, of new routes and of different products, pushes airlines to consider carefully the costs of the different services they provide. Whatever pricing strategy they are forced to adopt by the market conditions on each route, the starting point for their pricing procedures should be and normally is an evaluation of the costs of the different services they provide. Even market-related pricing cannot ignore costs. Understanding the relationship between pricing and costs is fundamental to effective airline management. In brief, the key to successful revenue generation is market knowledge, effective revenue management and cost awareness.

11.6   Choice of price and product strategies

The fare charged is only one aspect of the product or service provided by an airline to different classes of passenger. Other product features include frequency, timings, seat comfort, the quality and nature of ground and in-flight services and so on. These have been analysed in Chapter 10, though price is often the most important, particularly for leisure and VFR travel. In planning the supply of services on each route it serves, an airline must also decide on the various price and product mixes which it feels will generate the level of demand it requires. In markets which are less regulated and where there is a high degree of price competition the pricing options available are much wider but the choice between them more difficult to make.

The starting point for deciding on a pricing strategy, that is the structure and level of tariffs and the product features associated with them, must be an assessment of demand and of the airline's pricing objectives. Is an airline setting out to meet a particular profit target, to expand rapidly, to capture market share, or does it have some other objective it wishes to achieve? Given the objectives of its pricing policy, an airline must examine the costs of the different products it can put into the market in relation to its assessment of what potential consumers want and are prepared to pay for. It must also consider its own positioning within each market. Is it setting out to meet the needs of all market segments or is it trying to attract only certain segments? It could concentrate on only the high fare and high product quality end of the market, as Swiss and SAS have done in recent years. In 2007, 20.2 per cent of SAS domestic and intra-European passengers were travelling in business class, whereas the average for all European legacy airlines was 7.7 per cent (AEA, 2008). By going for the top end of the market such airlines aim for high-yield traffic and accept that this may mean lower load factors and a loss of market share.

In those international markets where there is still some government oversight of tariffs, a pricing strategy must also be acceptable to the airline's own government and, on international routes, to the government at the other end of the route. The other government's response will be dependent on the interests of its own airline and in particular on the relationship of the tariffs proposed to its own airline's costs and objectives.

In more price-competitive markets, the pricing strategy may need to be dynamic and changing in response to price or product changes introduced by competing airlines. Airlines have many difficult decisions to make. Should they match a competitor's lower fares when they know the competitor has lower unit costs, or is prepared to face a loss or may be heavily subsidised by his government? What proportion of its capacity should an airline offer at price-competitive fares? Is there any point in undercutting a competitor's tariff if the latter is going to match one's own new, lower tariffs? These and other considerations will affect the pricing strategy and tariff levels that airlines adopt in each of their markets. The ultimate aim must not be forgotten, however: that is to bring supply and demand together in such a way that the airline achieves its corporate objectives.

11.7   Traditional structure of international passenger fares

Progressive liberalisation during the last 30 years has led to the emergence of differing and complex fare structures in various markets or parts of the world. While it is difficult to disentangle precise and consistent patterns in the current fare structures, two broad trends are discernible. First, in many international markets, especially long-haul markets, the traditional structure of fares, with complex rules, based on cabin classes and originally developed through the IATA tariff machinery, prevail in some form or another. (For current role of IATA in tariffs see Chapter 2, Section 2.7.) Second, in liberalised domestic and short-haul international markets more flexible fare structures have emerged, driven, in large part, by the innovatory pricing policies of the low-cost airlines. (These new pricing structures are discussed in the following section (11.8).) Nevertheless, the widespread adoption of IATA tariffs on international air routes in the past means that there is today considerable uniformity in the structure of the air fares of network airlines.

The complexity of traditional international tariffs is of two kinds. First, there is a multiplicity of fare types. These include First, Business and Economy fares as well as preferential fares and a range of promotional fares. Second, there is normally a host of very detailed and complex conditions attached to each one of the individual fares within each fare type. For instance, on many intra-European routes the only fully flexible fare is the normal Business class fare. There may be a fully flexible Economy fare but usually it is not much lower than the Business fare. But many airlines also offer a lower 'restricted' Business fare, which is fully flexible except in one respect: reservations can be changed but only to other flights offered by the airline issuing the ticket. Also, unlike the normal Business fare, one cannot use the 'restricted' ticket to fly with another airline. Traditional airline pricing has been very much rules-based. Conditions attached to the various promotional fares are particularly complicated and increasingly they tend to vary from airline to airline.

11.7.1   *Normal fares: First, Business and Economy*

Partial or total deregulation of airline tariffs on many routes have made it difficult to identify what one might call 'normal' fares. But on most international routes there are three basic fare types corresponding to the separate cabin classes, that is First, Business and Economy. On most European routes and a few long-haul routes there may be a First class fare but no First class services, since many airlines no longer offer First class on such routes. While normally there will only be a single First class or Business fare, or in some cases a couple of such fares, there are frequently several different fares available for the Economy cabin. It is the full Economy fare that is considered as the basic 'normal' fare for the Economy cabin. But there are, in addition, numerous promotional Economy class fares which are discussed below. On long-haul routes a few airlines, such as British Airways and Virgin, have introduced an additional but small improved Economy cabin which is generally referred to as Premium Economy with its own separate fare.

Point-to-point IATA tariffs have an agreed mileage attached to them. This is normally the great circle distance between the two points. In travelling from one point to the other passengers can deviate from the IATA distance by up to 20 per cent in mileage terms (15 per cent on some longer routes) without any increase in the normal fares. This freedom may not apply to some of the promotional fares. The free 20 per cent add-on to the permitted distance allows passengers to take quite circuitous routes to reach their ultimate destination, often with stop-overs en route at no extra cost. This is particularly so on tickets to distant destinations where a 15 or 20 per cent deviation on a distance of several thousand kilometres can give passengers considerable scope for round-about routings. On a few very long-haul routes there may be several sets of normal fares depending on the routing taken. This is done partly to avoid misuse of the 20 per cent add-on. Thus, between London and Sydney there is one set of fares for services via the Eastern hemisphere or the trans-Siberian route, and higher fares for travel via the Atlantic or the polar routes.

11.7.2   *Preferential fares*

Preferential fares are those which are available only to passengers who meet certain requirements in terms of age, family kinship or occupation. They are usually expressed as a percentage discount on the normal fares and are generally applicable over large geographical areas. The most widely accepted and used are the 33 or sometimes 50 per cent discount, on the Economy or more expensive fares, for children under 12 years of age and the 90 per cent discount for infants under two but without the right to a seat. Child discounts on the lower promotional fares, if available, may be similar or less substantial. In particular regions there may be discounts for students travelling to or from their place of study; there may be spouse discounts for husbands and wives accompanying their partners on business trips or publicly available group discounts. There may also be discounts for military personnel or ships' crews. Traditionally, the aim of preferential fares has been partly developmental to encourage demand from particular groups within the community and partly social through the choice of groups to be encouraged, that is families with young children or students. Interestingly, child discounts are not normally available on charter flights or from low-cost airlines.

11.7.3   *Promotional fares*

Promotional fares, sometimes referred to as discount fares, are various low fares, usually with one or more restrictions on their availability, which offer passengers significant savings on the normal economy fares. Such fares are not of general application, as most preferential fares tend to be, but are separately negotiated and agreed for each point-to-point link. Promotional fares have tended to be most widely used on routes where there is charter competition, such as within the Europe-Mediterranean orbit, on routes where there is considerable leisure traffic, and on routes where there is over-capacity arising from the operation of fifth freedom or indirect sixth freedom carriers. They have been least developed on routes where the airlines concerned have wanted to maintain high fares or have believed that demand was likely to be inelastic to fare reductions. The latter is the case on many international routes to and within Africa.

The early development of promotional fares was aimed at stimulating particular market segments, such as off-peak demand or the demand for inclusive tours, while taking advantage of the low marginal cost of scheduled air services once airlines were committed to a published timetable. Off-peak fares, weekend fares, night fares and group (GTX) or individual inclusive tour (ITX) fares have been the most common of a wide range of promotional fares that have been developed. Fundamentally there can be only one justification for them. They must increase an airline's net revenue and hopefully its profits too. They can only do this by increasing traffic by a greater amount than is needed to overcome both the revenue loss arising from the lower fares and the possible diversion of higher fare traffic to these lower fares, and the cost increase caused by the higher volume of traffic. On the other hand, higher traffic volumes may allow the use of larger aircraft and thereby lead to lower unit costs. Promotional fares involve considerable risk. There is the risk that newly generated traffic will not come up to expectations or alternatively that it might be so heavy that it will displace higher-fare traffic. Traditionally tight 'inventory' control, which means control of the number of seats sold at different fares, has been necessary to ensure that this does not happen. The other risk is that too many passengers will be diverted from full fares or other high fares and will travel at the promotional fares, thereby deflating total revenue.

To minimise this risk *fences* or conditions are attached to each promotional fare. A promotional fare tends to have one or more 'fences' built into its conditions. 'Fences' tend to be of three kinds. First, there may be a limit on the *trip duration*. Most promotional fares have a minimum and maximum stay limitation. There is often a requirement that the passenger stay at least one Saturday night at his destination and no more than one month or some other specified period. Inevitably duration limits mean that passengers must buy return tickets. The primary aim of most duration limits is to prevent usage of these fares by normal business travellers who, as previously pointed out (Chapter 8, Section 8.3), prefer short trips and avoid weekends away from home.

Second, there may be *departure time limitations*. It is common to limit the availability of many promotional fares to particular times of the day, or days of the week or seasons. The aim here is to generate off-peak demand or to try to fill up seats that would otherwise be expected to remain empty because of the timing or day of particular flights.

Third, some of the lowest promotional fares entail *purchase time restrictions*. Their aim is to direct demand more effectively than can be done with departure time limitations. Such restrictions require either advance reservation and often simultaneous full payment a minimum number of days before departure or late purchase, normally within 24 hours before the flight or actually at the time of departure. The aim was to use them to push traffic into days where projected demand was expected to be low.

Most promotional fares can only be bought as round-trip fares. In some cases, the return trip must be booked at the time of reservation and neither the outward nor return booking can subsequently be changed except by forfeiting a substantial part of the fare. The aim is to reduce passenger flexibility, thereby making the fares unattractive to business passengers or independent holiday-makers, while at the same time ensuring high load factors by cutting out last-minute changes and no-shows. Higher load factors, by reducing unit costs, justify the lower fares.

A number of additional *routing restrictions* might also be used as a way of reducing the costs of handling low-fare traffic. These include reduced or no stop-overs between the original and ultimate destination; a point-to-point restriction which prevents both stop-overs and use of the 15 per cent distance add-on rule; and a no 'open-jaw' rule to force passengers to start their return trip from the original destination point. Finally, some very low fares may preclude interlining; that is, they cannot be used by the passenger except on the airline which issued the ticket. This prevents any revenue loss by the airline from pro-rating of the ticket with other carriers (see Section 11.10 below).

There is finally a range of *inclusive tour fares* which are not publicly available but which can be purchased by travel agents or tour operators and used to package into inclusive tours. Such package holidays normally include accommodation but might involve some other element such as car hire or tickets for a cultural or sports event instead of or in addition to the accommodation. On some routes there is a single inclusive tour fare while on others there may be a separate IT fare for individuals and a lower fare for groups. IT fares have been aimed at meeting the needs of the independent holiday-maker. At the same time on some routes they may allow scheduled airlines to compete with charters in the package holiday market. As such they are a defensive response.

Most promotional fares whose names tend to differ by region will have conditions attached to them involving several of the above limitations. On certain routes the complexities of the numerous fares available and the conditions attached to them have posed administrative problems for both airline staff and travel agents and have become counter-productive in marketing terms. This is particularly so when passengers become aware of the simplicity of the fares offered by low-cost airlines such as Southwest, Ryanair or easyJet. Airlines are under both internal and external pressure to try to simplify tariffs and the conditions attached to them, some of which are outdated if not absurd. For instance, it has generally been impossible to buy a one-way promotional ticket on a conventional network airline, as one can on a low-cost carrier. All the low promotional tariffs normally require passengers to purchase a round trip.

During the 1990s, progressive liberalisation and increased competition resulted in the widespread introduction of more and more promotional fares. As a result the proportion of passengers travelling on such fares, as opposed to full-fare First, Business or Economy tickets, has steadily increased on most major international routes. In Europe by the late 1990s promotional traffic on scheduled services represented over 75 per cent of the total traffic. Another example is that more than three out of every four passengers on the North Atlantic are travelling on promotional fares of various kinds. In other very competitive markets, such as Asia to Europe, airlines have found themselves selling virtually their entire Economy cabin at promotional fares. This trend is a major factor explaining the long-term decline in average yields. A higher proportion of passengers are travelling on promotional fares than was the case 15 or 20 years ago and at the same time the discounts many are obtaining are much deeper.

The complexity of the traditional fare structures summarised above grew out of two somewhat opposing trends. First, they were the direct result of over 50 years of price regulation, internationally through IATA and domestically through the decisions of governments or government agencies. Regulators tended to believe that the easiest way to protect airlines was to ensure that fares reflected costs. Many airlines supported this view. Cost-based pricing appeared to make sense even though it did not necessarily produce profits. Second, during the 1980s and especially the 1990s, many airline executives began to understand the value of market-related pricing in generating new markets and enhancing revenues. The result was the progressive introduction in many markets of numerous and varied promotional fares. But because of the regulatory environment these were circumscribed by complex rules and restrictions.

Thus the traditional fare structure is a mix of cost-based and market-related pricing. The attempts of regulators to balance the need to protect airlines, many of whom were financially weak, with the interests of consumers, who hungered for easier and cheaper access to air travel, created a pricing framework which was rigid, inflexible and not responsive enough to the changing needs of the market. The fare structure which emerged was extremely complex. On any one flight there would often be a dozen or more separate fares, some publicly available, others only available through agents, each with complicated fare conditions which at times ran to several pages. The longer the routes, the more complex the fares available and the conditions attached to them.

But there was one advantage. Because of IATA, this framework was adopted and understood worldwide, though with regional and local variations. In most medium- and long-haul markets, traditional pricing structures are still used by legacy carriers; also in some short-haul and domestic markets which have not been liberalised. But in the late 1990s and early 2000s the explosive growth of short-haul low-cost carriers, especially in Europe, using a much simpler and lower fare structure forced many legacy network carriers to rethink their own pricing, at least for short-haul routes. Deregulation within the European Union and further liberalisation elsewhere in both domestic and in international markets made this easier. By the mid-2000s, airlines such as Air Canada and Aer Lingus had introduced simpler, more flexible market-oriented pricing.

11.8   New pricing strategies

A key feature of the low-cost model has been the use of very low and simple fares in order to divert passengers from existing carriers, both airlines and ground transporters, and also to generate new traffic from passengers who would not otherwise be travelling. Southwest in the United States, Ryanair and easyJet in Europe, Gol in Brazil and Air Asia in Malaysia have based their rapid growth and success on low, simple fares with the minimum of conditions or constraints. Fares are transparent and easy to understand. The focus is on generating demand by market-related pricing which is flexible and changed frequently in response to changing demand patterns. The fact that LCCs are operating in short-haul primarily point-to-point markets has made it easier to simplify pricing.

All low-cost carriers' fares policies are not identical, but they do exhibit certain features, common to most but not all LCCs, which differentiate their pricing from the traditional fare structures outlined above:

- Passengers can buy a single one-way fare. There is no obligation to buy a return fare. Historically network carriers were unlikely to offer single one-way fares on short-haul routes. If available, single fares were often more than half the return fares. So, there were strong incentives to purchase only return fares. Certainly, the cheaper promotional fares were only available as round-trip fares.
- When booking on a low-cost carrier, there is normally only one, or less frequently, two or three fares available for a particular flight. In 2009 easyJet, Ryanair and Air Asia among others made it very simple. At any one point of time their passengers are

offered only one fare option for each flight. Southwest and Air Berlin in effect offered two fares, though Southwest also had a marginally higher third fare. But fares change over time. The simplicity of the fare structure contrasts with traditional pricing on network carriers where numerous separate fares may be available for any one flight at the same time. The fact that LCCs have only one cabin class has made it easier to simplify pricing.

- While there may be only one (or two) fares available for each LCC flight, different flights on the same route and on the same day may have a different fare on offer. This reflects different demand patterns during the day on each route. Again this contrasts with traditional pricing, where fares generally do not vary between flights on the same route. The numerous fares available are standardised for all flights on the same sector, though there may be some lower fares for flights at unpopular times.

- LCC pricing entails the offer of very low fares well in advance of the departure date. As the departure day approaches or as the number of seats at the low initial fare fill up, the single fare available for each flight moves up in a series of steps. It may also move down if a flight is not selling well. In other words, the fare for each flight is very responsive to the demand for that particular flight. Short-haul fares on network airlines have tended to be much less flexible and less responsive to demand. Yield management was used to open or close different fare or booking classes, but this was cumbersome and unpopular. Passengers could not understand why, when seats were available for a flight, a low published fare could no longer be used but they could travel using one of several higher fares. In some markets fares might be cut at the last minute if a large number of seats was left unsold. This was the opposite of the LCC pricing philosophy, which is to raise last-minute fares.

- Fare conditions on LCCs are few and simple, and uniformly applied to all fares and flights. This is made easier if there is only one fare type available. The fare conditions may be tough, for instance no refund if a ticket is not used, but they tend to be uniform. They are not complex or difficult for passengers to understand, as is often the case with the different fare types offered by network carriers. For example, why did the cheapest economy return fare in 2003 on Air France or British Airways from London to Toulouse, in France, cost 80 per cent less if a passenger stayed in Toulouse for a Saturday night (Doganis, 2006, Table 6.4)?

The key elements of low-cost airlines' pricing strategy outlined above can be seen in the example of easyJet's fares between London Gatwick and Toulouse in France early in 2009 (Table 11.3). The fares, which include a UK government passenger duty as well as airport charges, were for a flight out on Monday 2 March 2009 and back on Sunday 8 March. The fares offered were monitored at two-weekly intervals starting on 15 December 2008, that is, ten weeks before planned departure. In examining Table 11.3 and the development of the fares as the departure date approached, the following features stand out:

- At any one time there is only one basic fare available on each flight.
- Fares vary between flights on the same day despite being on the same route.
- Fares increase as departure-day approaches, especially in the last two weeks or when there is high demand. Even for a booking made on 15 December the evening fare from Toulouse for Sunday, 8 March is already much higher than on the morning flight because Sunday evening flights are popular and sell well early on.

Table 11.3 easyJet fares London Gatwick–Toulouse, 2009: Out Monday 2 March – return Sunday 8 March

	Date of fare quotation on easyJet website					
	Dec. 15 £	Dec. 30 £	Jan. 15 £	Jan. 30 £	Feb. 15 £	Feb. 30 £
Out: Gatwick–Toulouse						
Dep. 07.20	32	33	28	30	33	78
Dep. 18.35	32	33	38	40	58	103
Return: Toulouse–Gatwick						
Dep. 10.35	24	24	24	31	49	69
Dep. 21.50	59	61	69	76	94	144

Note
Fares are one-way inclusive of airport charges and government taxes, but excluded any ancillary charges, such as priority boarding or for baggage, which are at passenger's discretion.

- Fares can be bought as single one-way fares.
- Two days before departure the fares may be very high, depending on the flights chosen. A morning flight out and a morning flight back would have cost £147. BA only offered morning flights with a return fare of £268 (quoted on 28 February).

As the price of fuel escalated, doubling between 2006 and mid-2008 when it reached a peak of nearly $4.00 a gallon, most network airlines added progressively higher fuel charges to all their fares. Low-cost carriers faced the challenge in a different way. Most announced no fuel charges or fare increases, but they began to introduce a whole series of charges for various add-ons or additional services that passengers could choose to pay for or not. The LCCs in Europe were merely following a practice introduced in the late 1990s by many of Europe's charter airlines and tour operators and known as 'dynamic packaging' or pricing.

In the case of the easyJet flights from London to Toulouse in March 2009, passengers paying the fares shown in Table 11.3 would have needed to pay £6.00 each way per bag checked in, since there was no free baggage allowance, and could have opted for priority boarding, that is, boarding the aircraft in the first batch of passengers. With free seating this might have appeared attractive. But the cost would have been £7.50 for priority in London-Gatwick and £6.00 for Toulouse. Thus, if a passenger had one bag to check in and opted for priority boarding on both flights the total cost additional to the round-trip fare would have been £25.50. Golf equipment would have cost a further £16.50 each way. Charges for bags checked in, sports equipment and priority boarding, as in the case of easyJet, are now fairly common. Other charges introduced by various LCCs include a 'service' fee for issuing a ticket, a charge for checking-in at the airport as opposed to online check-in as well as charges which mirror those imposed historically by network carriers, such as fees for changing a flight.

While some US low-cost carriers have followed similar pricing policies to their European counterparts, Southwest has adopted a slightly different approach. Late in 2007 in order to attract more business travellers it introduced a higher more flexible fare. By 2009 it was offering two widely different fares on most routes. A very low 'Wanna Get Away' fare which was non-refundable. A much higher 'Anytime' fare was both changeable and refundable. On many routes, the 'Anytime' fare may be three or four times as high as the 'Wanna Get Away' fare. But instead of offering a series of optional services with add-on charges, Southwest offers a 'Business Select' fare which is essentially the 'Anytime' fare with a small $15 to $25 fare increase, for which passengers get priority boarding, an alcoholic drink and bonus miles. By incorporating its 'add-ons' in this enhanced higher fare, Southwest can then claim and advertise that it has no add-on charges.

The pricing philosophy inherent in the low-cost business model is to offer very low simple fares, with few but easy-to-understand restrictions. Fares vary between flights on the same route and change over time in response to changing levels of demand. Fare yields can be supplemented by 'dynamic' or 'à la carte' pricing, that is, by charging for a variety of service add-ons such as priority booking or checked baggage. There is little attempt to relate fares to the costs imposed by particular users. Even though some of the add-on charges, such as baggage fees, are claimed to be cost-related, any link to additional costs imposed is conceptual rather than real. Low-cost pricing is market-driven. Costs go up, or even down, in response to changing demand as fares change. Costs are not ignored when pricing, but the aim is to ensure that the total costs of a flight or route are covered, not the individual costs of particular passengers. So revenue management is crucial. But, as will be argued later, the simplicity of their fare structure makes revenue management much easier for low-cost carriers.

Traditional network airlines have seen the success of LCCs and have appreciated the marketing advantages which a simpler more flexible pricing structure offers in very competitive environments. In deregulated intra-European and North American markets airlines have had the freedom to adopt new pricing policies. Many, such as British Airways, have adopted some of the LCCs' pricing practices, such as single one-way fares or fares that increase in stages as the departure date approaches. A few have gone all the way and have introduced pricing strategies that are indistinguishable from those of LCCs. Aer Lingus has done this on its intra-European services, even going as far in 2009 as copying its major competitor Ryanair in offering, at certain times on some routes, lead-in fares of zero plus airport taxes. It has also gone further in 'à la carte' pricing by adding numerous add-on charges. For example, Aer Lingus has an extra charge for selecting a seat in the first 5–6 rows and an even higher charge for a seat with more leg-room in an emergency exit row.

In North America it is perhaps Air Canada which, starting in 2006 in response to strong competition from Canadian low-cost carrier Westjet, went further in switching to and adopting the new pricing practices. This is evident from Tables 11.4 and 11.5. The first shows the single one-way fares from Vancouver to Montreal for travel on Sunday 8 March 2009 as posted on the airline's website nearly three months earlier in mid-December 2008. For what is almost a five-hour flight, Air Canada, offered four fare categories or classes. In the Economy cabin fares increased from the lowest Tango fare to Tango Plus and then Latitude. Then there was the executive fare for the Business class cabin. Though the fares shown are all for flights on the same day, the fares in the same category differ between the four flights on that day depending on the level of demand, which varies by time of day. The highest fares are on mid-morning flights, the lowest on the night flight at 23.59 hours. The fares subsequently moved upwards as the departure date approached. This approach is similar to LCC pricing, though Air Canada has kept four fare classes.

Air Canada, like most LCCs, has introduced a wide range of add-on charges, especially for the Tango and Tango Plus fare classes. It also offers discounts if passengers opt out of

Table 11.4 Air Canada's innovative pricing – Vancouver to Montreal one-way fares, March 2009

Fares quoted on 18 Dec 2008	Travel 8 March 2009 (US$)			
Vancouver to Montreal direct (4.75 hrs)	Tango	Tango plus	Latitude	Executive class
AC 150	08.30 hrs	161	198	478	1311
AC 185	10.55 hrs	340	376	656	1311
AC 112	14.40 hrs	275	311	591	1311
AC 182	23.59 hrs	161	198	478	1311

Note

Fares quoted exclude taxes and airport charges = *c.* $80.

Table 11.5 Air Canada's fare add-ons and discounts, 2009 (US$)

	Tango	Tango plus	Latitude	Executive class
Priority check-in			Yes	Yes
Fully refundable			Yes	Yes
Access Maple Leaf lounges		+ $30	+ $25	Yes
Call centre–airport service fee	+ $25	+ $25	No	No
Same day change fee	$150	$50	No	No
On-board food vouchers (value $8)	+ $6	+ $6	Snack	Meal
Seat selection	+$22	Yes	Yes	Yes
Baggage allowance (Number bags)	(2)	(2)	(2)	(3)
No baggage	–$3	–$3	–$3	
Sports equipment, including guns			Free	Free
Aeroplan miles	1 for $3	1 for $2	1 for $1	1 for $1

Tango discounts: if no Aeroplan miles – $3; accept no ticket changes – $5.

certain services. For example, passengers buying Tango or Tango Plus economy fares could save $3 if they had no baggage to check in, and another $5 if they agreed to forgo any right to change their flight. The possible add-ons and discounts available in early 2009 are summarised on Table 11.5. This shows that Air Canada has clearly adopted a strategy of dynamic pricing. The airline's then Chief Executive Montie Brewer summed their pricing strategy as follows:

> *We have been doing à la carte pricing for six years and it is popular with our customers. We offer four basic fare products, the benefits of which are transparent.*

> *About 47 per cent choose a higher fare product for its attributes – even with lower fares available. Then we offer options to either opt out of discounts or to select for purchase – such as checked baggage or lounge access.*

> (*Airlines International,* April–May 2009)

The airline claims that it is this pricing strategy that has enabled its domestic operations to compete effectively and profitably with Westjet, an LCC with low costs and aggressive pricing. Early in 2009 Air Canada was facing problems arising from its earlier financial restructuring. Nevertheless Tables 11.4 and 11.5 do indicate a contradiction.

Is Air Canada in danger of re-introducing complexity while simplifying and making its fares more market-related? Has it gone too far?

The impact of escalating fuel costs in 2007 and especially 2008, on airline profits, forced many network carriers to follow the example of the LCCs and consider the need for ancillary revenues from 'à la carte' pricing. US Airways was planning to raise $400 to $500 million in 2009 from ancillary charges for checked baggage and in-flight catering. After mounting losses in 2008 United Airlines was aiming to raise $1.2 billion from ancillary charges in 2009. It had introduced a $25 fee for the second checked baggage a year earlier. But by early 2009 most US legacy carriers were charging for both the first and second checked bags. This is risky. Passengers may question why they should pay higher fares on network carriers and then be charged add-ons as well. When Swiss introduced charges for in-flight catering in the Economy cabin on their intra-European flights in 2007, the negative reaction was so strong they reversed the policy. United Airlines was similarly forced to withdraw plans to charge for food on international flights from Dulles airport. Nevertheless, à la carte pricing among network carriers for short-haul flights may well become widespread in North America and Europe and possibly in other regions too.

New, simpler and more flexible pricing is progressively being adopted in large domestic markets, as in Canada or the United States, and in international markets where pricing has been fully deregulated as is the case within the European Common Aviation Area. These are generally short- and shorter medium-haul markets in which low-cost airlines have had the greatest impact. In international markets, even those partially liberalised, airlines have been slower to abandon traditional fares structures. The pricing approach is more mixed. This is in part because of the need to maintain clear price differentials between two, three or sometimes four cabin classes.

As airline pricing is deregulated or liberalised in more and more markets, airline planners and pricing strategists will have increasing freedom to decide both the level of fares they want to offer on each route and the conditions attached to those fares. But liberalisation also means more intensive competition, with fare levels and conditions becoming increasingly crucial in attracting or dampening demand. The role of the tariffs manager and his team has become more critical but also more difficult as fares become more volatile and dynamic. Moreover, as fares become increasingly demand or market oriented, tariffs managers become totally dependent on effective revenue management tools to ensure that revenues generated cover costs. This is equally true for network or low-cost carriers.

11.9   The importance of revenue management

Revenue or yield management became an essential marketing tool as a result of US deregulation and the complexity of fares and fare types that emerged within a very competitive and rapidly changing market. It was first effectively used by American Airlines in early 1985 when it introduced a range of very low fares to compete against People Express, a new low-fare entrant in the US market. Using dynamic revenue management on a route-by-route basis it killed off People Express. Today revenue management involves the control of fare access through an airline's reservations control system in order to maximise total passenger revenue per flight. This is not the same as ensuring the highest load factor or the highest average yield. In fact maximising revenue may in many cases mean that neither of these is achieved. Revenue management is equally crucial for both the network and the low-cost business models.

For a long time network airlines thought that the 'fences' or booking conditions attached to different fares were a sufficient safeguard to ensure that yields or revenues were not diluted by high-fare passengers switching to low fares. However, they failed to ensure that revenues on each flight were being maximised. In many cases the opposite happened. The introduction of new low fares as a result of tariff liberalisation in the 1980s and 1990s created a surge of demand at these lower fares. Airlines found themselves putting on extra capacity to meet this demand, but with so much low-yield traffic on each flight they often failed to cover their total flight costs even though load factors increased. An extreme example of this in the early 1990s was Philippine Airlines, whose fares between Manila and the United States were so low that it was capturing around 70 per cent of the market, operating at very high load factors and yet was losing money on the route. Its break-even load factor was over 100 per cent because the yields were so low as a result of its failure to control the number of seats sold at very low fares.

Yield management is based on the simple economic concept of utility as expressed through the demand curve. There is a maximum price which each consumer is willing to pay for a good or service. That price is equivalent to the utility or benefit he gets from consuming it. He will happily pay less for it but will not pay more. Different consumers gain varying levels of utility from a particular good or service and therefore each will only buy it if the price is no greater than that utility or benefit. For air services as for most products the lower the price the greater the demand. By summing up the demand for a service at different price levels we can draw a demand curve. On a simple diagram showing air fare on the vertical axis and seats demanded on the horizontal axis one could draw the demand curve for an air service between two cities. This has been done for a hypothetical short-haul route in Figure 11.2(a). It shows a downward sloping demand curve, indicating the number of seats which would be bought at different fares.

An airline wishing to provide this service with a 100-seater aircraft has estimated a one-way total operating cost of, say, $3,500. It sets a target seat factor of 70 per cent which means carrying 70 passengers. If pricing were purely cost-based then the airline would charge a $50 one-way Economy fare (that is, $3,500 divided by the target of 70 passengers). At that fare the demand curve tells us that the airline would only get 50 passengers, thereby generating an income of only $2,500, which would result in a substantial loss (Figure 11.2, part a). The load factor achieved would be 50 per cent, not 70.

The demand curve also tells us that many passengers who paid $50 would have been willing to pay more. They are getting a good deal. The utility or benefit they get from using the service is greater than the price paid. The difference between the $50 fare and the utility they enjoy is called the 'consumer surplus' and is measured by the shaded area in Figure 11.2(a). One aim of revenue management is to maximise revenue by transferring some of the 'consumer surplus' to producers, that is, the airlines. The demand curve also shows us one more important fact – that half the seats are empty if the fare is $50 but that there are people who would be keen to fly at fares below $50.

The airline, aware both of the 'consumer surplus' issue and the need to fill up empty seats, now decides to introduce a three-part tariff: a full Economy fare of $70, an Excursion fare of $50 and an advance purchase Apex fare of $20. There are various conditions attached, notably that the Apex fare must be bought in advance. In practice, because of the ability to buy cheap seats in advance, many passengers opt for the Apex fare and sales boom. But in the end too many seats (40) are sold at this cheap fare, leaving insufficient seats, only 60,

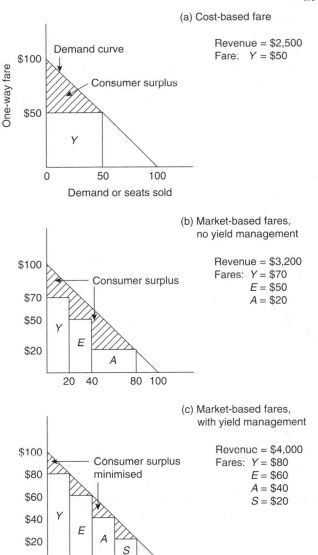

Figure 11.2 Interplay of demand curve and pricing strategies: (a) cost-based fare, (b) market-based fares with no yield management, (c) market-based fares with yield management. Types of fare: *Y* full economy, *E* excursion, *A* APEX, *S* Super–APEX.

for those passengers prepared to pay more but who generally book later. The outcome is shown in part (b) of Figure 11.2. The seat factor has shot up to 80 per cent, but though revenue has also increased to $3,200 it is still inadequate to cover costs. Moreover, since many passengers are still paying less than what they would be prepared to pay, the airline is still failing to capture for itself an adequate share of the 'consumer surplus'.

In theory, to maximise revenues and capture the consumer surplus the airline should sell each seat at the maximum that each passenger is prepared to pay from $100 down to $1 for the hundredth passenger. This is clearly impractical. But to try and maximise revenue more realistically it might introduce four separate fares: a full Economy fare of $80, an Excursion fare of $60, an Apex $40 fare and a Super Apex fare of $20. If it could sell 20 seats at each of these fares its total revenue would be $4,000 per flight, producing a profit of $500 with a seat factor of 80 per cent (Figure 11.2, part c).

The fundamental problem is how to ensure that 20 seats are sold at each fare and more especially how to avoid the earlier situation where too many seats were being sold at the lowest $20 fare. This is the function of revenue management. It is the day-to-day monitoring and control of seat availability in each fare group on each flight to ensure that revenue is maximised. This is done by highly trained staff using the constantly updated information on sales and other key data in the reservations computer. Booking conditions attached to different fares and seat availability are the tools used to channel seats to the passengers paying the higher fares. The tariff conditions or 'fences' should separate the demand for particular fare types into discrete segments which have different booking characteristics. By controlling the seats available for sale one can then direct that segment of demand on to flights where it is needed to maximise revenues. The need for revenue management arises because high-fare passengers tend to book nearer the departure date while many low-fare passengers don't mind booking early, especially if travelling for leisure. The latter must not be allowed to fill up seats that could be sold later for a higher price.

For network carriers, revenue management is especially critical for two reasons. First, because they tend to offer more different point-to-point fares on each sector. Second, because all fare types are being sold simultaneously in many locations at the same time, further diluting the effective yield. The risks can be seen if one examines British Airways' London–Frankfurt service. This has a movable partition between the Business and Economy cabin so seats can be sold at any fare and there may be more than one fare type for each cabin. But the revenue for this sector from promotional tickets in Economy class sold for flights from Canada or New York to Frankfurt via London may be less than 20 per cent of the revenue that could be obtained by selling the same seat for a full Economy or Business class fare to a local passenger between Frankfurt and London. Yet the airline's sales offices in North America are under pressure to generate higher sales revenue. Similarly, even a Business class ticket sold by British Airways in Singapore for Frankfurt via London would generate much less revenue for the London–Frankfurt sector than a ticket sold locally. Thus with tickets for passengers to travel on BA's London–Frankfurt flights, being sold all over the world as part of multi-sector journeys, the danger of airlines, such as BA, losing control of the total sales in each fare group is very real.

To overcome this, fares on each route are allocated to different reservation or booking classes. This is crucial since some routes, such as London–New York, may have up to 60 fare types. Most large airlines will work with 10 to 12 booking classes, and could go up to 20–25. Each booking class may contain several fare types. Thus for the London–Frankfurt sector a BA through ticket sold in New York or Montreal would be put into a low booking class. The lowest booking class is normally for tickets issued in exchange for air miles. Through fares create a major complexity for network airlines, especially those with long-haul routes. While a London–Frankfurt sector on a BA ticket sold in New York may be in a low booking class, the New York–London sector may be in a higher booking class. The airline does not want to lose the revenue from this ticket because its revenue management system will not release a seat for the London–Frankfurt sector. So sophisticated models have been developed to assess through fares on the basis of their total contribution to an airline's revenues as well as their contribution to individual sectors. This then affects the booking class they are put into. The aim of these newer models is to focus revenue maximisation on the end-to-end fare for multi-sector routes rather than optimising the revenue for individual sectors.

Where an airline's flights come onto the reservations system a year before the departure date, 12-month forecasts of demand for different booking classes are used to allocate the number of seats available to each booking class on each flight. When the number of seats allocated to a particular booking class is sold out then that booking class is withdrawn from sale, even though seats may be available in other higher fare classes. If, later on, sales in these other classes fail to come up to forecasts the previously closed, lower booking class may be re-opened for sale.

The forecasts of sales by class are reviewed periodically in the period starting 12 months before departure and booking classes may be closed or opened accordingly. But it is during the last month that most of the critical decisions and changes are made by the yield managers or controllers. A large airline may employ up to 100 of these working in groups controlling particular parts of its network. Using data from the reservations computer on sales by booking class to date and on past booking trends they must make rapid and critical decisions closing, opening or wait-listing particular booking classes on each individual flight scheduled during the coming month. The aim is always to maximise revenue per flight. If sales are going badly as the departure date approaches it may mean allocating more seats to lower fare types. Conversely, if demand is high, low-fare booking classes may be closed very early on and before they are sold out. It is a complex and critical task that could not be done without a sophisticated software programme backing up the reservations system. While some decisions on opening or closing booking classes can be made automatically by the computer system itself, much depends on the revenue manager. In British Airways, the European Revenue Manager will have around 2,500 European flights at any one time on which decisions are pending on whether to change the number of seats allocated to any particular booking class. The task of the revenue controllers working for him is made particularly difficult by a number of factors.

In the first place, accurate forecasting of demand by booking class is the key to success but demand is influenced by many external variables. The closer to the departure date the more accurate forecasting becomes. The yield controller must monitor not only current sales but also external developments which may affect future sales. Second, the same fare type sold in one country may be worth more when sold in another because of fare and currency variations. For instance, as mentioned earlier, seats on British Airways' London to Frankfurt flights are on sale through its offices and agents worldwide at different fares and in different currencies. It becomes particularly difficult trying to control and manage sales in different markets, but it is not impossible. There is a risk, however, of upsetting local sales staff who can sell at the published fares but are stopped from doing so by the yield managers at head office. A third problem area, discussed earlier, is how to deal with interline passengers on multi-sector routes. The pro-ration or allocation of the through fare to the separate sectors flown usually means that an airline may get very low yields from carrying interline passengers, travelling on multi-sector tickets issued by other carriers, on one of its own sectors.

Group traffic provides an important volume of business but poses yet another problem. Group bookings are made long in advance when they are easy to accept, but are usually firmed up only 3–4 weeks before departure and the take-up rate, that is the number of passengers compared to the number of seats originally booked, may be very low. Requests for advance deposits may help to alleviate this problem. In addition agents offering groups may be vetted on the basis of their past performance before bookings are accepted. Then there is the problem of no-shows of passengers with tickets that can be changed or refunded. They may go up to 10 per cent or more of higher-fare passengers. Over-booking can compensate, but one can still end up with off-loading passengers, to whom compensation may have to be paid, or having empty seats. Getting the over-booking right for each flight means more revenue and more satisfied passengers. To do this one must develop models to predict no-show rates, introduce booking conditions which discourage no-shows or even penalise passengers who fail to turn up by cancelling their onward bookings.

Finally, in markets where fares have been deregulated, yield managers must constantly monitor the fares being offered by competitors. While they must maximise revenues they must also have an eye to market share. Losing market share may mean higher unit costs.

Numerous studies have shown that network airlines can increase their revenues by 5 to 10 per cent when they introduce effective yield management on competitive routes. *'The revenue gains come from forcing consumers to pay fares closer to their willingness to pay'* (Belobaba and Wilson, 1997). The impact is greatest if the competitors have not implemented revenue management themselves. Thus, revenue management may be crucial in ensuring profitability.

While revenue management was developed in the mid-1980s by carriers such as American Airlines it has become equally critical for low-cost carriers. But the relative simplicity of the latter's fare structures has made it easier for them to implement effective revenue management. With only one fare available at any one time for each flight it is possible to use simpler algorithms to move that fare up in stages as a certain number of seats are filled and/or as the departure date draws nearer. Or the fare may be moved down, if demand is below expectations. Like network yield managers, low-cost airlines' managers feed into the process past booking patterns, any anticipated external events (such as a sports fixture), seasonal demand variations, their accumulated experience of price elasticity on particular routes and so on. They also monitor competitors' prices. Transit passengers travelling on two sectors are less of a problem too, since many LCCs such as easyJet or Ryanair do not offer through fares. Passengers buy two separate tickets. LCCs that do offer through fares such as Southwest or Air Berlin still have an easier problem to deal with compared to network carriers which must optimise revenue from a variety of fare buckets and with fares in many different currencies.

Revenue management is an essential concomitant of market-related pricing. While some consumers end up paying more than would otherwise be the case or travelling in more congested aircraft, consumers as a whole should be better off. By mixing high- and low-fare passengers to generate higher revenues, flights are operated that would otherwise not be viable. A wider range of fares can be made available while protecting last-minute access to seats for those who must travel at short notice and are prepared to pay more for this.

11.10   Passenger tariffs and costs

The aim of revenue management is to maximise the total revenue per flight and in doing this generate a sufficient profit or, at worst, minimise the loss. For low-cost or network carriers with a single cabin class and similar service standards for all passengers this is a straightforward process. The aim then becomes to maximise the average fare or yield obtained for each passenger carried on each flight, since the average cost per passenger will be the same irrespective of the fare that each one paid. On the other hand, the average cost per passenger will depend on the load factor achieved.

Where airlines offer a two-class cabin or, as in many long-haul routes, a three- or four-class cabin, they may wish to assess and monitor the costs and revenues per passenger in each separate cabin. This is valuable for two reasons. First, it may be helpful in deciding the pricing policy for each cabin class and more especially the fare differentials between them. Second, it would enable airline planners to decide whether maintaining each separate cabin class is financially justified or whether eliminating one or more of the existing cabins would be a more financially attractive option.

To understand the process whereby one arrives at a cost per passenger in each cabin and the contribution of each cabin to the business it is easiest to examine an example. To do this one might consider the case of a wide-bodied Boeing 777–300 ER on a long-haul flight with three cabins each with a different seating configuration and seat pitch producing 8 First, 42 Business and 228 Economy seats. This was Singapore Airlines' configuration for this aircraft in 2009.

If the aircraft was operated with full Economy seating only, it would be possible to arrive at a cost per seat. If the total allocated route costs per Economy seat is then assumed to be 100, it is possible to establish what the cost of providing the First and Business class seats should be after allowing for the extra space they require, both because such seats have a longer seat pitch and because there are fewer seats abreast across the aircraft. Such an analysis (using the actual seat pitches and seating layout in 2009 for an SIA Boeing 777–300 ER) is shown in Table 11.6. This indicates that, purely on the basis of their space needs, the ratio of costs and therefore of fares in the three classes should be 497:351:100, which is roughly 5.0:3.5:1.0 (line 5 of Table 11.6).

In our example, an adjustment might also be made for the greater proportion of space allocated to toilets and galleys, though this has not been done here. What if the planned load factors of the three classes were different too? Airlines often plan to achieve average year-round load factors of no more than 50 per cent on First and 65 per cent on Business class traffic so as not to turn away any high-yielding demand. On the other hand, they will use promotional pricing and their revenue management systems to try and ensure year-round load factors are close to 80 per cent in the Economy cabin. We do not know SIA's planning load factors on its 737–300 ER flights to Europe, but assuming 50, 65 and 80 per cent in the three cabins as the planned load factors, one can convert the cost index per seat into an index of cost per passenger (lines 6 and 7 of Table 11.6).

Lastly, the passenger-specific costs need to be added in to the costing exercise. These include the cost per passenger of the different in-flight services such as meals, drinks, in-flight entertainment, and newspapers or magazines and of any exclusive ground facilities. The higher ratio of cabin staff to passengers in First and Business should also be adjusted for. All this is reflected in the assumed passenger-specific costs (line 8, Table 11.6).

Adding these passenger-specific costs to the passenger cost indices in Table 11.6 produces a final index of relative costs per passenger between the First, Business and Economy cabins of 773:418:100. These suggest that if primarily cost-based, the Business fare in a long-haul Boeing 777–330 ER flight should be four times as high as the normal Economy fare and the First class fare almost eight times as high. In so far as passengers in Economy and, for that matter, in Business or First may be travelling at different market-related fares, this proposed relationship should apply to the average yield per passenger or passenger-km in each class rather than the fare. To what extent do actual long-haul fares and yields for

1.6 Unit costs of different classes on long-haul Boeing 777–300ER

		First (F)	Business (J)	Economy (Y)
1	Cost per seat if all Economy			100
2	Seat pitch (inches)	71	51	32
3	*Seat cost index allowing for seat pitch*	211	159	100
4	Number of seats abreast	4	4	9
5	*Seat cost index allowing for pitch plus seats abreast*	497	351	100
6	Planning load factor	50%	65%	80%
7	*Cost per passenger adjusted for load factor*	994	540	125
8	Passenger-specific costs	50	25	10
9	Cost per passenger including passenger-specific costs	1044	565	135
10	*Index of cost per passenger if Y($135) = 100*	773	418	100

Table 11.7 Singapore Airlines return fares Paris to Singapore, March 2009

Fare type	Ex-Paris (€) 1	Fare index* 2
Economy class		
Sweet deals	869	
Flexi saver	931	
Flexi	1,292	
Average (unweighted)	1,030	100
Business class	4,013	390
First class	7,784	756

Note
* Fare index: average economy fare = 100.

each cabin class reflect a 7.7:4.1:1.0 cost relationship between First, Business and Economy?

In spring 2009 Singapore Airlines was operating a daily flight between Singapore and Paris with Boeing 777–300 ER aircraft with the cabin and seat configuration and density shown in Table 11.6. The fares for a return Paris–Singapore flight, quoted in December 2008, for a flight in March 2009 are shown in Table 11.7. Three different Economy fares were available ranging from €869 to €1,292. The average of the three is €1,030. The actual average yield in this cabin would depend on the way SIA used its revenue management system to maximise the total revenue from the Economy cabin. But it is likely to be somewhere around €1,000 plus or minus €100. If one assumes an average passenger fare in the Economy cabin of, say, €1,030, then the ratio of the fares for the three different cabins is 7.6:3.9:1.0. (column 2 of Table 11.7). This is very close to the cost per passenger relationship indicated by the earlier analysis (line 10, Table 11.6). In practice, while fares show a close relationship with the costs of each cabin, in practice there will be yield dilution (see next section) so the average yield per passenger in each cabin may differ from the published fares. So the fare to cost relationship may be less close than suggested by Tables 11.6 and 11.7. But it will still be there.

While SIA pricing appears fairly traditional in its approach, it too has been affected by the LCC approach to ancillary charges. In December 2008 it introduced Preferred Seat

Selection, which allows Economy passengers booking long-haul flights on its website to pay $50 to pre-book seats with more leg-room in the exit rows.

This simple case study indicates that, while airline pricing has become increasingly market-related, costs still play an important part in the formulation of pricing policy, especially in longer-haul markets involving aircraft with multiple cabins.

Given that the relative level of the First and Business fares compared to the Economy fare reflect cost differences, has Paris–Singapore been a profitable route for SIA in 2009? That, of course, depended on the passenger load factors in each cabin. Fortunately SIA's load factors on long-haul routes to Europe have been high. But IATA studies in the 1990s and early 2000s suggested that in many markets First class load factors for many airlines were not high enough to compensate for the high costs involved. If costed as above, First class for many airlines was consistently unprofitable. Conversely, Business class fares and load factors were high enough in many markets to ensure profitability. In fact, on many long-haul routes, the Business class was the most profitable market segment. The profitability of the Economy cabin varied between routes and airlines. But when it was profitable its contribution in absolute terms was generally less than that of Business. It seems as if the Economy and Business passengers were subsidising the fat cats sitting in the front of the aircraft. Such studies explain why during the 1990s and later many international airlines dropped First class altogether or reduced the number of First-class seats and increased the seating and the quality of service offered for Business class. KLM, SAS, Continental, Air Canada were such airlines. More recently, to bolster Economy yields, several airlines have introduced a premium Economy cabin on longer sectors offering slightly more space but at a high Economy fare.

11.11 Determinants of airline passenger yields

While pricing is an important element in an airline's marketing strategy, from a revenue point of view the level and structure of passenger fares may be less important than the yield that an airline actually obtains. Yield is the average revenue per passenger, per passenger-km or passenger tonne-km performed. These all measure the average revenue per unit of output sold.

For LCCs, offering a single-class cabin the average yield will be close to the average fare charged. On any route, the latter will depend on the mix of different fares and the number of tickets purchased at each of those fares. These will have been determined by the airline's revenue management. The average yield may also be dependent on sales of add-ons, such as priority boarding or checked baggage, the revenues from which might legitimately be considered part of the ticket revenue. Comparisons of average passenger yield (per passenger or passenger-km) between low-cost airlines, operating in the same geographical region, have some validity because generally they will all be short-haul operators offering a single-class cabin with broadly similar stage lengths and operating within a similar market environment.

When it comes to comparisons of average yield of different network airlines, especially if they operate long-haul as well as shorter routes, more serious issues of comparability arise. In Table 1.2, in the opening chapter, one could see that the operating revenue (including cargo revenue) per ATK varies enormously between airlines. For example, several European airlines had unit revenues in 2006 two or three times as high as some Asian carriers. While these yields included cargo, pure passenger yields show equally wide variations.

Why do yields vary so widely between network carriers? The discussion so far has tacitly assumed that an airline can determine its revenue levels and its yields through the pricing strategies it adopts and in particular by the structure and level of passenger tariffs. In practice this is only partly so since the relationship between fares and yields achieved is much more complex and is influenced in varying degrees by a number of factors of which the fare structure itself is only the starting point.

A key factor affecting passenger yields is the geographical areas in which an airline is operating. For a number of reasons, such as past government controls on fares or, more recently, the impact of increased competition, fare levels do vary significantly between different parts of the world. Historically, fares per kilometre have always been high for flights within Europe, whereas in most Asian markets fares on short- to medium-haul routes have been much lower. But even within Europe, fare levels on routes within Northern Europe have tended to be well above those in Southern Europe, reflecting the higher standard and cost of living in the former. This partly explains why Iberia, Air Portugal and Olympic find themselves with the lowest yields among European carriers (Table 11.9 below). In East Asia, because of the long-term appreciation of the Japanese yen and the high cost of living in Japan as well as the traditionally high costs of Japanese airlines, fares per kilometre out of Japan have been extremely high. This explains Japan Airlines' tendency to have high passenger yields, almost double those of other East Asian airlines. Any foreign airlines flying to Japan would also benefit from these high fares.

The geographical spread of an airline's network and the relative mix or importance of different geographical regions in its total revenue will impact on its average revenue or yield. The wide variations in yield by geographical market can be seen in Table 11.8. This shows the average yield generated in different markets by European network airlines in 2007. The markets are ranked by average sector distance flown, with the shortest sector markets at the top. Our earlier analysis of airline operating costs showed that unit costs decline as sector distance increases. It is, therefore, not surprising to find that unit fares in different geographical markets also decline with distance. But some markets appear not to conform. One is the Europe to/from sub-Saharan African market, where yields are very high compared to other route areas with similar average sector lengths. This is because on many routes restrictive air services agreements limit capacity while there is relatively less leisure traffic and much more high-yield business traffic on flights between Europe and Africa. European airlines with a well-developed network to sub-Saharan Africa, such as Air France or British Airways, can benefit from these high yields. Conversely, one would expect yields on mid-Atlantic routes to be higher than on North or South Atlantic markets because of the shorter distances involved. But mid-Atlantic yields are actually lower because a high proportion of the traffic in this market consists of leisure passengers flying to Caribbean holiday destinations. For any European network airline, its mix of traffic between the various geographical markets shown in Table 11.8 will have a major impact on its overall average passenger yield.

Even when operating within the same geographical markets, airlines often find that their average yields may differ widely. Once again, one factor which helps explain such difference is the variation in average sector distances. Since fares per kilometre taper downward with distance, then the yields an airline obtains, compared to others operating in the same region, are much influenced by the sector lengths it operates. This is clearly apparent when looking at the intra-European operations of Europe's major airlines (Table 11.9). Three of the four airlines with the lowest passenger yields in 2005 also had by far the

Table 11.8 Yield variations by region – for European airlines in 2007

Traffic type	Average sector distance (kms)	Passenger yield US cents/RPK
Inter-European	936	17.1
Europe–North Africa	1,707	13.8
Europe–Middle East	2,991	11.9
Mid-Atlantic	4,001	7.5
North Atlantic	6,547	8.9
Europe–sub-Saharan	6,552	11.1
Europe–Far East/Australia	6,898	8.9
South Atlantic	7,308	8.4

Source: Compiled using AEA (2008).

longest average sector distances within Europe. Olympic Airways was the exception. It had very low yields despite operating costly short sectors averaging 712 kms. This partly explains why it has been consistently unprofitable.

Conversely, the highest yields tend to be among those airlines with the shorter sectors. But sector length is not the only variable affecting yield. The yield per passenger-km on any route depends not only on the level of individual fares but also on the traffic mix. There are two aspects to this. First is the overall mix between high-yielding First and Business class passengers and the much lower-yielding passengers in the Economy cabin. Some airlines, as part of their marketing strategy, target the business market and plan their products and in-flight services to try and attract high-fare passengers. The improved services may cost more to provide but can be compensated for by the higher fares that passengers may be prepared to pay. In Europe, while all carriers try to attract business passengers both SAS and Luxair have made a special effort to capture this market segment. As a result, 20 per cent of SAS's intra-European traffic (including domestic) in 2007 was in Business class and 15 per cent of Luxair's. Yet the average for all European carriers was only 8 per cent. This is another reason why SAS achieved relatively high yields in 2005 (Table 11.9). The second aspect of traffic mix relates to the availability and level of discount and promotional fares. This will particularly impact on yields within the Economy cabin. In international markets low promotional fares are more widespread and most used where there is the greatest competition. In Europe, this is usually in the leisure routes between Northern Europe and Mediterranean leisure destinations. In the 1980s and 1990s the competition here came from charter airlines. Since the late 1990s the downward pressure on fares in leisure markets has come from the low-cost sector. Scheduled carriers such as Olympic, Iberia or Air Portugal tend to offer a range of promotional low fares to ensure that they do not lose all their potential to low-cost or charter carriers. The result is that their average yields on intra-European services are relatively low both because their economy yields are sharply depressed and because they carry a higher than average proportion of economy passengers. One sees the same phenomenon on other routes such as those between Europe and Florida or between Canada and the Caribbean where charters pose a major competitive threat to scheduled carriers.

Exchange rates and currency fluctuations also impact on yields. If an airline's home currency is devalued and sales in its home market represent a significant share of its

Table 11.9 Average passenger yield for European carriers on their European services, 2005

	Average yield US cents per passenger-km	Average sector distance (kms)
Lufthansa	20.23	656
Austrian Airlines	18.37	698
Air France	17.14	751
Brussels Airlines	15.99	865
SAS	15.46	649
Alitalia	15.05	713
British Airways	14.68	872
Swiss	14.42	664
European airlines average	14.29	764
Malev	12.09	965
Iberia	11.13	836
Air Portugal	9.22	1,166
Olympic	9.12	712
Turkish	8.96	1,022
Cyprus Airways	5.62	1,922

Source: Compiled by author from annual reports and confidential sources.

revenues, then its average yield when converted to say US dollars will be adversely affected. For large international carriers exchange rate fluctuations in any one of their major markets can push up or depress their average yields. The great volatility of some exchange rates in the mid- and late 2000s has increased the risks of revenue dilution from sudden movements in exchange rates. This happened in the second half of 2008 when the pound sterling lost about 25–30 per cent of its value against the euro and the US dollar.

Another major source of revenue dilution arises from the pro-rating of revenue from passengers on multiple sectors. An interline or online passenger travelling with a single ticket on two or more sectors is charged the end-to-end fare, not the sum of the separate fares on each sector. Because of the taper of fares with distance, the end-to-end fare to be charged is normally less than the sum of the separate fares. Pro-rating is the method used to share the revenue earned between the different sectors flown. The basic principle used is to share the revenue in proportion to the distance of each sector. But shorter distances are given greater weight to allow for the higher costs of operating short sectors. These weighted distances are published each year by IATA and may change as the relative costs of different sectors change. The method of pro-ration using weighted distance is illustrated in Table 11.10. For a Business class ticket used to fly London to Athens in summer 2009 via Hamburg the revenue dilution is considerable. British Airways, carrying the passenger on the London to Hamburg leg, receives 45 per cent less than the full Business fare on that sector for a passenger flying only to Hamburg. On the Hamburg to Athens leg Lufthansa's revenue short-fall is 44 per cent. The same basic method is used to pro-rate cheaper fares as well if such fares allow interlining. Pro-rate calculations based on weighted distance have become increasingly complex in some markets, especially where airlines on the same routes offer different fares. Even in those markets where IATA-agreed fares are not those actually used by the airlines, the value of IATA flex fares is that

Table 11.10 Pro-ration of London–Athens full business ticket (£1,280) used to fly London–Hamburg–Athens (summer 2009)

	Return business fare (a)	Distance (miles)	Pro-rate calculation based on weighted distance factors (b)	Revenue dilution of pro-rate fare
Fare paid to BA: London–Hamburg– Athens	£1,280			
Pro-ration				
London–Hamburg (BA)	£745	450	$£1,280 \times \dfrac{1086}{3421} = £406.34$	−45%
Hamburg–Athens (Lufthansa)	£1,574	1,270	$£1,280 \times \dfrac{2335}{3421} = £873.66$	−44%
Total		1,720(c)	£1,280.00	

Note
(a) Fares quoted March 2009 for July flights.
(b) Weighted distance factors (found in IATA's *2001 ProRate Factor Manual*) are London–Hamburg 1,086 and Hamburg–Athens 2,335. Adding them together gives 3,421.
(c) London–Athens distance is 1,494 miles but permitted mileage is 1,791 or 20% higher. Therefore routing via Hamburg permitted.

they provide the framework and basis permitting worldwide interlining. This is of great benefit for passengers.

Pro-rate dilution is greatest when passengers take advantage of the 20 per cent additional mileage rule to travel on a circuitous routing between their origin and their destination, particularly if travelling long-haul. The end-to-end fare has then to be split over several sectors. Pro-rate dilution will also increase if a domestic sector is included in the ticket and the domestic airline insists on receiving the full fare or a high proportion of it, leaving even less revenue to be shared between the international sectors. Pro-rated interline traffic used to represent as much as a third or more of an airline's total traffic and was particularly prevalent on routes serving geographical gateway airports such as Heathrow, Amsterdam, New York or Singapore which were major interlining centres. However, one consequence of the development of effective hubbing (see Chapter 10, Section 10.6) has been that interlining, the transfer of passengers from one airline to another at a hub, has tended to decline as airlines have focused on transferring passengers to their own flights at their hubs. But whether the passenger switches to another airline at a transfer airport or switches to another aircraft of the same carrier, the revenue dilution as a result of pro-rating the fare still remains.

For both network and low-cost airlines the average yields they achieve will depend both on the prevailing level of fares in the geographical markets they serve but also on the pricing strategies they adopt to generate demand. Fares and therefore yields will also be influenced by the stage lengths being flown. Within that framework of fares it is the traffic mix, that is, the proportion of passengers travelling in each fare class, which ultimately determines the total revenue earned and thereby the unit yield. That is why effective yield management is so important. Network carriers face additional problems. Their revenue will be diluted by pro-ration of interline or online tickets. The proportion of connecting multi-sector interline traffic is for them a further important determinant of the yield. For any airline, the final yield in any market or route will bear little relationship to any single published fare. This further complicates the issue of airline pricing. In deciding on its pricing strategy and in working out the tariffs for different market segments, airlines must balance and juggle with all these factors which transform the various fares into an average yield. It is the yield in conjunction with the achieved load factor and the unit costs which will determine whether an airline's revenue and financial targets can be met.

12 The economics of air freight

> Our customers expect globally functioning logistics and distribution networks.
> (Dr Klaus Zumwinkel, CEO, Deutsche Post WorldNet, October 2001)

12.1   Freight traffic trends

Many of the concepts and principles of airline economics discussed so far apply equally to the cargo side of the industry. At the same time there are particular issues and difficulties which arise in the carriage of air freight which require separate analysis and treatment. The importance of freight is too often under-estimated, yet just over one third of the output of the international airline industry, measured in tonne-kms, is generated by freight rather than passengers and for some airlines it is considerably more than this (Chapter 1, Table 1.6). Though the revenue contribution of freight is much less, at only one eighth of total revenue, it makes a significant contribution to the profitability of many air services. While there are a number of airlines that only carry freight, air cargo is an integral part of most passenger airlines' operations, though not in the case of low-cost airlines.

During the 1990s the annual rate of growth of international air freight, measured in revenue tonne-kms, averaged close to 7.7 per cent, outpacing growth in passenger traffic. During the first eight years of the 2000s growth slowed to an annual rate of around 4 per cent as a result of the economic slowdown in key economies in the early years, and the escalating fuel prices after 2005. Growth rates for air freight swing wildly and are much more volatile and responsive to the economic climate than is the case for passenger traffic. This was very evident in the second half of 2008 and in 2009 as the world economic downturn began to undermine passenger markets and destroy many freight markets. In October, November and December 2008 worldwide passenger traffic (in RPKs) declined by a steady 4.8, 4.6 and 4.6 per cent respectively. Industry-wide freight volumes (in FTKs) for the same three months dropped by 14.4, 13.5 and a staggering 22.6 per cent (IATA Monthly Traffic Analysis). Yet these winter months are normally periods of high demand for air freight, as stocks of many goods are built up prior to the Christmas season. Such volatility plays havoc with the airfreight industry's economic performance.

Until the mid-1970s European and North American airlines were dominant in the carriage of international air freight, attracting between them close to three-quarters of the freight traffic (Table 12.1). Since then their dominant position has been eroded by the exceptionally rapid penetration into the freight markets by East Asian and Pacific region airlines. Based in export-oriented and rapidly growing economies, the latter airlines expanded their international freight traffic particularly rapidly over the 25 years to 2007.

Table 12.1 The changing regional distribution of scheduled international air freight

Region of airline registration	Regional share of international freight tonne/kms	
	1972	*2007*
	%	%
Europe	44.8	27.0
North America	29.0	15.5
Asia and Pacific	12.3	46.0
Latin America/Caribbean	5.8	2.3
Middle East	5.0	8.0
Africa	3.1	1.3
World	100	100

Sources: Compiled by author from ICAO (1990) and IATA (2008a).

Note
If domestic air freight included North American airlines' share jumps to 23.7 per cent.

Airlines such as Korean Air, Cathay Pacific and SIA have grown their freight business at annual rates well above the world average and significantly higher than those being achieved by European or North American airlines. As a result there has been a fundamental restructuring of the international air freight industry with the centre of gravity shifting towards East Asia and the Pacific. As a group the Asian and Pacific carriers overtook North American airlines in the carriage of international freight by the end of the 1970s and they caught up with their European counterparts in the early 1990s. By 2007 the Asian Pacific airlines dominated the international air freight markets carrying nearly half, 46 per cent, of the world's scheduled international freight (Table 12.1). In the year 2007 four of the Asian carriers, Korean Airlines, Cathay Pacific, SIA and China Airlines, ranked among the world's top six freight carriers, with Korean ranked first (Table 12.3).

The vast bulk (88 per cent) of the world's air freight is international and less than one eighth domestic. But much of the domestic freight, in fact most of it, is transported within North America (Table 12.2, column 1) mainly by integrators Federal Express and UPS. When domestic and international freight are combined, these two integrators are the largest freight carriers in the world in 2007 in terms of tonnes-km carried.

Another noticeable characteristic of international air freight is the degree to which it is dominated by three major route groups, namely the Europe to Asia routes (26.0 per cent of international freight tonne-kms in 2007), the North and mid-Pacific routes (23.9 per cent), and the North and mid-Atlantic (15.2 per cent) (Table 12.2). Though the transatlantic market has been declining in importance, these three route groups together generate around two-thirds of the total freight tonne-kms performed on international air services. Interestingly, the very largest international freight carriers, such as Lufthansa, Air France or Federal Express, as well as the Asian carriers previously mentioned, are all heavily engaged in at least two of these three route groups. This seems to be a prerequisite if an airline aims to be really big in international air freight.

While in the early days air freight was considered essentially as a way of filling up spare capacity on passenger aircraft, its very high growth rate in the 1960s induced many airlines to introduce scheduled all-cargo services. Narrow-body aircraft in a passenger configuration had relatively little capacity available for freight and it was in any case unsuitable for large or awkward shipments. All-cargo aircraft, even narrow-body ones, facilitated the carriage of large unit loads and consignments and accelerated the introduction of specialised handling and sorting equipment which speeded up the movement of freight.

Table 12.2 Major scheduled freight markets in 2007

Route area	Share of freight tonne-kms	
	% World total	% International
Europe–Asia	22.9	26.0
Trans-Pacific	21.0	23.9
North and Mid–Atlantic	14.3	15.2
Intra-Asia (International)	9.6	11.1
Europe–Middle East	3.7	4.2
Middle East–Asia	3.0	3.4
Other	13.5	16.2
Total international	83.5	100.0
North America domestic	8.2	
Asia domestic	3.1	
Other domestic	0.7	
World total	100.0	

Source: Compiled by author using IATA (2008a).

Improved handling and the flexibility to ship freight independently of passenger aircraft which, among other things, permitted the use of night hours, allowed airlines flying all-cargo aircraft to reduce freight transit times while offering considerably more capacity. As a result, scheduled all-cargo operations generated new traffic and captured a growing proportion of it. On most major routes the proportion of international freight carried by IATA airlines in scheduled freighter aircraft grew rapidly and peaked at around 43 per cent in the mid-1970s.

After 1973 the market penetration of all-cargo services began to decline. They were hit by two major developments. First, the huge jump in aviation fuel prices in 1974 and again in 1978–9 impacted much more severely on all-freighter than on passenger services. This is because fuel costs represent a much higher proportion of total operating costs for freighter than for passenger aircraft since the latter incur many additional costs such as those of cabin crew, in-flight catering and so on. With fuel prices going up fivefold between 1973 and 1980, freighter operating costs jumped sharply and many such services were no longer viable. Second, the gradual introduction and spread, during the 1970s and 1980s, of wide-bodied aircraft, such as the Boeing 747, on long-haul routes, and the Airbus A310 and Boeing 767 on medium-haul services, produced a huge jump in belly-hold cargo capacity, compared to that of the narrow-bodied aircraft they were replacing. Moreover, these new aircraft carried large containers and other unit load devices (ULD) which facilitated loading and handling of cargo. Airlines discontinued their narrow-bodied and fuel-costly freighters and began switching cargo to the bellies of their new wide-bodied passenger aircraft.

The relative decline of all-cargo scheduled services was reversed in the mid-1990s as a result of the rapid growth in demand for air freight, especially from the export-oriented economies of East Asia. On several trunk routes, belly-hold capacity on passenger aircraft could no longer cope with the demand. In these and other markets airlines began to increase scheduled and charter freighter services. By 2007 the share of international air freight kilometres carried on all-cargo aircraft by IATA member airlines had risen to 53 per cent. On domestic services the share was even higher at 65 per cent. This was because of the dominance of the integrators such as Fedex and UPS operating their own freighters in the large US domestic market. Systemwide, that is international plus domestic, the freighter's share of global tonne-kms was 56 per cent in 2007 (IATA 2008a).

Within Europe, most distances are so short that the economics of all-cargo services have never recovered from the two oil shocks of the 1970s. Today most intra-regional air freight in Europe is trucked by road. In many cases this is done using scheduled lorry services with airline flight numbers. It is cheaper and faster to truck freight in this way, especially as distances are relatively short and most major centres are within an overnight road journey of each other. Even long-haul freight may be trucked by road for the first part of its journey. British Airways, like other major European cargo operators, operates a European freight network. Lorries (generally leased in) collect freight from all over Europe including Scandinavia and Spain and deliver it to BA's cargo centres at Heathrow and Stansted. In this way British Airways can compete with SAS in Scandinavia for freight destined for the United States or Mexico. But SAS also competes for long-haul freight in the UK market by trucking it by road to Copenhagen. Most of Europe's major cargo carriers are heavily involved in trucking. Europe's motorways are criss-crossed nightly by heavy lorries, some with flight numbers, carrying 'air' freight!

International air freight services are regulated by the same bilateral air services agreements as passenger services and broadly speaking in the same way. That is to say that traffic rights and capacity for freight and more especially for freighter services on any international air route will be constrained by the relevant bilateral air services agreement. But in many cases governments have been willing to liberalise and open up cargo rights and capacity more rapidly than for passenger services. Cargo tariffs in regulated markets are agreed through the IATA machinery. Here, too, most governments have appreciated the benefits of freeing up air trade and have been loath to interfere in or attempt to control freight tariffs. Many airlines have ignored the approved tariffs. Tariffs are also difficult to control. But some governments have imposed low tariffs for specific commodities, usually agricultural products such as early vegetables or fruit, in order to stimulate exports from their own countries.

In many key international markets, such as those between Europe and the United States, *de facto* liberalisation of air freight preceded the *de jure* loosening of regulations which occurred as a result of the open skies agreements signed by the United States during the 1990s (see Section 3.4 in Chapter 3). This was partly in response to market pressures and partly because the supply of air freight services became so varied, after the integrators expanded, and the pricing so complex and unstable that economic regulation by governments became difficult if not impossible. Control of capacity or frequencies offered by freighter services still exists in some major markets, for instance between the United States and Japan. But control of cargo tariffs is largely non-existent or ineffectual. The IATA Cargo Tariff Conferences still agree tariffs on close to 200,000 separate routes in regions of the world where governments want regulated tariffs. But these tariffs bear little relevance to what is actually charged in the market place (Section 12.7 below). Their prime purpose is to offer guide-line prices, to facilitate the inter-lining of cargo from one airline to another and as a pricing aid to freight forwarders.

12.2   The key players

Historically, the looser regulation of air freight services compared to that of passenger services has led to the emergence of a fairly heterogeneous industry with several different key players. Clearly the most significant group is that made up of the conventional scheduled airlines who transport both passengers and cargo. These are the so-called *combination carriers* who offer three kinds of cargo service. They carry cargo in the freight holds of their scheduled passenger flights and some also operate a network of scheduled, all-cargo flights. A smaller number operate so-called combi aircraft. These are normally wide-bodied aircraft where part of the main upper deck as well as the belly-hold capacity is used for the carriage of freight. Combi aircraft tended to be used on routes where the demand for air freight was substantial while that for passengers was relatively thin, but their use has declined in recent years.

In addition to the combination carriers there are a few *all-cargo carriers*, who tend to operate both scheduled services and *ad hoc* charters. There used to be many more, some with well-established names such as the US cargo carrier Flying Tigers. But many collapsed following the fuel crises of the 1970s or were taken over by the integrators. The only independent, all-cargo operators of significant size still operating in 2009 were Cargolux, based in Luxembourg, and the Japanese company Nippon Cargo Airlines. Both of these fly primarily scheduled networks, but also offer aircraft for *ad hoc* charters or for leasing. There are in addition a variety of smaller scheduled and charter all-cargo carriers. These include Air Hong Kong (60 per cent owned by Cathay Pacific and 40 per cent by DHL), the Russian airline Air Bridge Cargo and Kalitta Air and Polar Air Cargo in the USA. DHL also has a 49 per cent shareholding in the latter. Some are niche carriers, operating within a particular geographical region as Air Hong Kong does.

The distinction between combination carriers and all-cargo airlines is becoming increasingly blurred as other airlines follow the example of Lufthansa and Singapore Airlines. In the late 1990s, both split off their cargo divisions as separate subsidiary companies with their own accounts, but also with their own staff, pilots and fleets of freighter aircraft. In addition to operating scheduled freighter services, these cargo companies buy and pay for belly-hold capacity on passenger aircraft from the parent airline. They are a new breed of cargo airlines.

The third group of key players are the so-called *integrators*. In recent years this has been the fastest-growing and most dynamic sector of the industry. Unlike combination and all-cargo airlines who traditionally provided an airport-to-airport service with only limited collection and delivery, the integrators provide a door-to-door service. This requires the provision of road trucking for collection and delivery of freight. They were also first in offering guaranteed delivery times and a pricing structure to match. Their success during the last 25 years has been such that integrators are now among the world's largest cargo carriers. Two in particular, Federal Express and United Parcel Service (UPS), are very large. There are, in addition, two medium-sized integrators, DHL and TNT, and a number of smaller regional companies. These four major integrators together control over 80 per cent of the global air package and express market (MergeGlobal, 2008b).

The relevant role in the carriage of international air freight of the three key groups discussed so far can be gauged from Table 12.3. This shows the international traffic in 2007 of the world's 20 largest cargo carriers. The industry appears to be dominated by the combination carriers, especially Asian carriers. Ten of the 20 largest cargo carriers are airlines from East Asia. Only one all-cargo operator and two integrators appear in the top 20. The table is somewhat misleading because domestic air freight services, and in particular the huge United States domestic market, are not included. Within the US market, the large integrators have totally eclipsed the combination carriers. As a result, in terms of total freight, that is scheduled plus domestic, Federal Express is by far the largest cargo

Table 12.3 The world's largest international freight carriers in 2007

Rank	Combination carriers		All-cargo airlines		Integrated carriers	
	International scheduled freight tonne-kms (millions)					
1	Korean	7,498				
2	Lufthansa	8,336				
3	Cathay Pacific	8,225				
4	SIA	7,945				
5					Federal Express	6,470
6	China Airlines	6,301				
7	Air France	6,123				
8	Emirates	5,497				
9			Cargolux	5,482		
10					UPS	5,077
11	EVA Air	4,774				
12	KLM	4,745				
13	British Airways	4,618				
14	JAL	4,269				
15	Asiana	3,094				
16	Air China	2,829				
17	Malaysian	2,581				
18	United	2,452				
19	Thai Airways	2,423				
20	American	2,257				

Source: IATA (2008a).

Note
If domestic freight included, Federal Express becomes by far the largest carrier, followed by UPS.

carrier in the world and UPS is the second largest. This is why the impact of the integrators needs further examination (see Section 12.4 below).

A fourth group of players consists of certain *postal authorities*, especially in Europe. Traditionally letters and small packages have been the domain of government postal offices. Domestically and for short international services they have in the past used their own road vehicles, the railways and in some countries their own small aircraft or aircraft chartered in to operate regular overnight services. For longer international distances they handed their mail to scheduled combination carriers, usually their own country's flag carrier. Post offices continue to play a role in air freight, particularly for small parcels. Thus in 2008 the Royal Mail in the UK chartered in a fleet of 16 jet aircraft (11 Boeing 737–300s and five BAe 146s) for domestic and short-haul international services. However, the loosening of international regulations on air freight, mentioned earlier, allowed the integrators to divert a growing share of the documents and small parcels business away from the national post offices. In the 1990s the post offices began to hit back. One of the first was the Canada Post Corporation which, in 1993, acquired 75 per cent of Purolator Courier Systems, a Canadian integrator. In Europe, the German Deutsche Post bought an initial 25 per cent shareholding in DHL, in which two combination carriers, Lufthansa and Japan Airlines, also held 25 per cent each. By September 2000, Deutsche Post AG had acquired a majority stake in DHL and in March 2001 assumed full control of DHL International, based in Brussels. Launching a strategy of a 'one-stop shop' for freight, Deutsche Post also began acquiring large freight-forwarding companies. In 1999 it bought Danzas and AEI and in 2005 Exel, a British-based forwarder. It rebranded itself as

Deutsche Post World Net (DPWN) and was floated on the stock market. Meanwhile, in 1996 the partially privatised Dutch postal service had purchased TNT, the fourth largest integrator, though two years later TNT was demerged and itself floated on the stock market. Effectively two of the four main integrators are today controlled by or linked to national postal authorities.

Recent years have seen the emergence of a relatively new player in the international air cargo market, the *contract freighter operator*, or *wet-lease provider*. This is the airline which operates all cargo aircraft but primarily on behalf of other airlines, on a wet-lease contract basis. There are 25–30 such operators. In 2007 they carried about 6 per cent, in terms of revenue tonne-kms of the world's air freight. The best-known and most significant example is Atlas Air in the United States, which started flying in 1993. Early in 2009 Atlas had a single-type fleet of 37 Boeing 747–200 and –400 aircraft. These were wet-leased on an ACMI (aircraft, crew, maintenance and insurance) basis to combination carriers, such as British Airways, Emirates, Qantas and Air New Zealand, or less frequently to scheduled all-cargo operators, to meet their freighter requirements. Normally these are three-to five-year contracts with a guaranteed minimum number of block-hours per month. A fixed ACMI hourly charge covers the provision by Atlas, or another wet-lease provider, of the aircraft, flight crew, and all maintenance and insurance costs. All other costs, such as fuel, landing fees or crew hotel costs, are met by the lessee. The ACMI charge is in dollars and insulates Atlas from currency fluctuations. Moreover, the ACMI lessor is not exposed to short-term traffic fluctuations or drops in cargo yield since the hourly ACMI charge is totally independent of traffic or revenue levels. Yet for the airlines ACMI contracts are attractive. Both because they provide great flexibility in adding or reducing cargo capacity and also because the low-cost structure of a specialist such as Atlas means that this capacity can be provided at rates 30 per cent or more below the airlines' own costs of providing such capacity. Several all-cargo operators may also lease out their aircraft on an ACMI basis, but often for shorter periods. For Atlas Air leasing out represents nearly all of their business. In July 2001, Atlas acquired Polar Air. But the intention was that Polar Air would continue as a separate company, a more traditional cargo carrier offering its own scheduled all-cargo services. In 2007, the integrator DHL Express acquired a 49 per cent shareholding and 25 per cent voting rights in Polar Air. This deal guaranteed Polar strong freight flows from DHL on many routes.

Atlas Air, in terms of international freight tonne-kms generated, is among the top five or so airlines in the world. But none of this traffic is carried in its own name. It is all on behalf of other airlines. More significant is the fact that large ACMI cargo operations are among the most profitable sector of the air freight industry. Atlas Air appears to be relatively free of exposure to risk since the short-term risk of a downturn in traffic is largely borne by the airlines that lease in Atlas's aircraft. As a result Atlas Air Worldwide Holdings, the parent company of both Atlas Air and Polar, has generally performed well financially since the mid-2000s and certainly better than many combination carriers. In 2006 its profit margin was 4.2 per cent and in 2007 9.2 per cent. However, when trade flows slow down wet-lease providers are often the first to suffer as lessee airlines cut their cargo capacity. This happened in 2003 and again in 2008. An interesting question is whether the wet-lease business model could also be applied to the passenger side of the airline business.

The final group of key players in air freight are the *freight forwarders and consolidators*. Their role parallels that of the travel agent and tour operator on the passenger's side. They provide the link between the airline operator and the ultimate customer who is the shipper. Their role in this respect is discussed in a later section. But some of the larger forwarders are crossing the line and setting up their own scheduled air services. The pioneer in this trend of vertical integration was Panalpina, a large European forwarder. From the late 1980s it started wet leasing or chartering aircraft from Cargolux and others to operate scheduled services on routes of its choice, particularly on routes where freight capacity was short. Some of these were entirely for its own needs. Other flights were on a shared risk basis with the cargo airline or other forwarders. By the mid-1990s some other large forwarders, such as Danzas, another large European forwarder, began to operate their own flights too, but usually with leased-in aircraft. The German company Schenker leased in Aeroflot freighters from 2003 till 2008 to provide scheduled flights from Hong Kong to Hahn (Frankfurt) four days a week, to carry Schenker's own traffic. The attraction for freight forwarders of operating their own flights is that they can then offer a complete door-to-door service on key routes within a single one-stop company. This has two advantages: they can generate higher yields, but it is also a way of fighting back against the integrators who are trying to cut the forwarders out of the logistic chain.

12.3   The demand for air freight services

Since air freight is much more heterogeneous than passengers there are several ways of categorising it. One may, for instance, consider the commodities being shipped, or one can classify freight by the weight of individual consignments or by the speed of delivery required. As with passenger traffic, it is valuable to try to segment the freight market in terms of the motivation of the shipper rather than in terms of the product, since this has implications for the type of air freight services which need to be provided and for their pricing.

The most obvious role for air transport is the carriage of *emergency freight*. This includes urgently required medicines such as vaccines and spare parts for machinery or for equipment of various kinds, which may be immobilised until the arrival of the replacement parts. Increasingly during the last three decades such emergency freight has also involved documents of various kinds, such as business contracts or other legal papers, medical records, financial papers, articles and reports, as well as films, photographic negatives, artwork and computer tapes or disks. Many such shipments were best handled by the express parcels operators or by the companies providing courier-accompanied services. They provided the basis for the growth of the integrated air carriers discussed below. While the electronic (facsimile) transmission of documents began to undermine the traditional courier services during the 1990s, the further globalisation of trade and commerce has ensured the continued rapid growth of express cargo for the carriage of documents and small parcels.

Air is also used in emergency when surface communications become congested or are disrupted by natural or other causes or when the national postal services are slow or inadequate. In all such circumstances speed is of the essence and cost of shipment is relatively unimportant. Demand to meet emergencies is irregular, intermittent and unpredictable in volume and in the size of individual consignments. It is therefore difficult for airlines to plan for. The need of shippers for high frequencies and good last-minute space availability means that, if adequately catered for, emergency freight demand results in low freight load factors and high unit costs. On the other hand, since the demand is relatively insensitive to price, higher tariffs can be charged.

Goods with an *ultra-high value* in relation to their weight are also normally carried by air primarily because of the much higher security offered. Speed is important not in its own right but because it reduces the time during which the goods are at risk. Gold, jewellery, diamonds, valuable metals and rare furs or works of art fall into this category. Security is of overriding importance, while cost of air freighting, given the value of the goods being shipped, is unimportant.

Both emergency and high-value freight require a high quality of service. Shippers of such consignments normally want to reserve space on specific flights with a guarantee of on-time arrival. They demand preferential handling and clearance through customs and up-to-date information on the progress of their shipments. From this point of view, too, such freight is more costly to handle.

The majority of air freight shipments involve what is called *routine freight*, where the shipper's decision to use air transport is based on an assessment of available transport options and is not a response to a sudden and unexpected problem; nor is it imposed by security considerations. There are many categories of routine air freight. A simple and widely used division is into perishable and non-perishable freight. In the case of *perishables*, the market for the commodities being shipped is dependent on air transport. The commercial life of the products – fish, out-of-season vegetables, newspapers, newsfilm, certain pharmaceutical products, high-fashion textiles, to name but a few – is short and the gap between producer and consumer must be bridged before that commercial life expires. Only freighting by air can do that. The freighting costs are quite high in relation to the price of the product, but they can be justified if the final consumers are prepared to pay a premium because no local substitutes are available. In the case of foodstuffs, the premium consumers are willing to pay for unusual or out-of-season produce is limited. As a result, the demand for air freight is fairly price sensitive. For all foodstuffs being shipped by air there is a tariff level at which the demand virtually dries up because the final market price of the products is no longer attractive to consumers. Since the initial price of many foodstuffs is quite low, that critical tariff level may itself be quite low. Airline pricing strategy then becomes crucial. To develop new flows of perishable freight, airlines may need to offer specific cargo tariffs well below prevailing levels on the routes in question.

The bulk of perishable freight movements are highly seasonal, with very marked and often short-lived demand peaks followed by long periods when demand dries up completely. This happens with the movement of early grapes from Cyprus to the UK, where the period during which air freighting is viable, despite its high costs, may last only two to four weeks. After that, later grapes transported cheaply by road from Italy or France become available. More expensive air-freighted grapes from Cyprus can no longer compete in the shops. The seasonality of much routine perishable freight means that high year-round load factors are difficult to maintain. On the other hand, the demand patterns are known in advance and airlines can try to stimulate demand from other products during the off-peak periods.

Routine non-perishable freight is shipped by air because the higher transport costs are more than offset by savings in other elements of distribution costs. Any one of a variety of costs may be reduced as a result of shipment by air. Documentation and insurance costs will normally be lower, but the biggest direct cost savings are to be found in packaging, ground collection, delivery and handling. These are all transport-related costs. There may also be savings in other areas from reduced stock-holdings and therefore lower warehousing costs and from the lower capital tied up in goods in transit. When interest rates were high in particular countries shippers and manufacturers became very conscious of the high costs of maintaining large inventories. This pushed them to re-examine their logistics chain with the aim of reducing their stock-holding to a minimum. This led to the concept of 'just in time' (JIT). Air freighting is particularly suitable for JIT logistics chains because of its speed and its dependability. These indirect benefits of air freighting tend to be more marked on long-haul routes where a shipment which may take 20–60 days or more by sea and land may reach its destination by air in an elapsed time of two days or less. Taken together, the total distribution costs by air, including costs of warehousing stock or of inventory in transit, should be lower than or close to those of competing modes for air to be competitive.

Routine non-perishable freight consists largely of fragile high-value goods such as delicate optical and electrical goods, clothing and machinery of various kinds, as well as semi-manufactured goods needed in various production processes such as micro-chips. These benefit not only from the higher speed but also from the increased security provided by air transport in terms of reduced damage and loss. This, together with the high value of these commodities, sometimes means air may be preferred even when its total distribution costs are not the lowest. For instance, some shippers or manufacturers may use air freight as a way of breaking into and testing new and distant markets without the need to set up expensive local warehousing and distribution systems. If they are successful, they may then switch to lower-cost surface modes.

Shipments of routine non-perishable freight tend to be regular, known in advance and often of relatively constant size. Although speed is important, small delays of a day or two in collection or delivery can be coped with by the shippers. Non-perishable freight is less price-sensitive than perishable freight because of its higher value, but it is nevertheless responsive to the total distribution costs of air transport, especially in relation to the costs of competing surface modes.

Most goods being shipped by air have a high value to weight ratio. Since cargo rates are generally based on weight, the higher the value of an item in relation to its weight, the smaller will be the transport cost as a proportion of its final market price. Therefore, the greater will be the ability of that good to absorb the higher air transport tariffs. This tendency for high-value goods to switch to air transport is reinforced if they are also fragile and liable to damage or loss if subject to excessive handling, or if the surface journey times are very long, involving the tying up of considerable capital in transit. Consumer demand in many industrialised countries is switching more and more towards goods with high value to weight ratios such as cameras, video machines, home computers, calculators, expensive shoes, and so on. It is goods such as these that lend themselves to shipment by air, so the future prospects for air freight must be good. What is more important from the airline's point of view is that the countries manufacturing such goods will become the largest generators of air freight demand. This is one reason why the growth of freight traffic among East Asian airlines has in recent years far outstripped that of other regions and why Korean, Cathay Pacific, Singapore Airlines and China Airlines are now among the top six airlines in terms of international freight tonne-kilometres (Table 12.3 above).

While freight can be categorised and split into market segments in terms of shippers' motivation, it remains very heterogeneous with a wide range of different manufactured and semi-manufactured goods, raw materials and agricultural products that may have little in common. The commodity mix will vary from route to route, but some broad generalisations can be made. Worldwide, about one third of total international air freight is composed of manufactured goods (Groups 6 and 8 in the Standard International Trade Classification). These include office equipment, computers, electronic goods and components. Another one third is machinery and transport equipment (SITC Group 7), including

Table 12.4 Commodity breakdown of global air freight markets, 2007

	Share of FEU-kms %
High tech products	27
Capital equipment	19
Apparel, textiles, footwear	17
Consumer products	16
Intermediate materials	12
Food: refrigerated/non-refrigerated	6
Primary products	2
All commodities	100

Source: MergeGlobal (2008b).

Note
'FEU-kilometre' is a measure used in cargo logistics. It is one 40-foot container, containing an average 11.7 metric tonnes of goods, tra॒ ॒orted one kilometre.

motor vehicle parts and equipment, construction machinery, industrial machinery, communications equipment and so on. The remaining third or so is made up of a variety of commodities, among which fresh or refrigerated foodstuffs and other agricultural products, medical and pharmaceutical goods and chemicals and clothing and footwear are all relatively important. Another way of breaking down the composition of air-freighted commodities is shown in Table 12.4 for the year 2007. In that year high-tech products accounted for 27 per cent of air freight; capital equipment for 19 per cent; apparel, textiles and footwear for 17 per cent and consumer groups 16 per cent. These four groups generated almost 80 per cent of global air freight.

The heterogeneity of goods going by air poses numerous marketing problems for airlines, particularly when trying to identify and develop new markets. This is aggravated by the fact that not only does the commodity mix vary between different routes but also between each direction on the same route. Thus, while fruit, seafood and vegetables generate over one third of freight from Latin America to North America or Africa to Europe, they are negligible in the return flights.

Another aspect of this heterogeneity is that freight comes in all shapes, sizes, densities and weights. There is no standard unit or size for a freight consignment or any standard unit of space. Freight density is crucial to the economics of air freight. Cargo payload on an aircraft is limited by weight, but also by volumetric capacity. Since generally tariffs are related to weight, an airline can maximise freight revenue on a flight by carrying dense, heavy freight that fully utilises its weight payload. Low-density shipments may fill up the cargo space with a low total weight and a lower total revenue. Surcharges are frequently applied to shipments having a density below a certain level. An airline must try to achieve an average density in its freight carryings which makes maximum use of both the volumetric capacity and the weight payload of its aircraft. Because of the variety of goods being shipped, the risk is that volumetric capacity is used up before the payload weight capacity is fully utilised.

The difficulties of handling large numbers of relatively small individual shipments of different size, shape, weight and density created considerable pressures towards unitisation of air freight, both as a way of speeding up its handling and in order to reduce handling costs. As a result, most air freight now moves in a variety of unit load devices (ULDs), which fall into four major groups. There are various built-up or half-pallets which may be rigid or flexible. Some are no more than a rigid base with netting to cover the goods being shipped. Second, there are IATA-approved lightweight fibreboard or plywood containers or boxes which fit on to full-size or half-pallets. The third group are rigid containers, which come in a number of standard sizes designed to fit into the holds of wide-bodied aircraft. These rigid airline containers now account for the larger proportion of total air freight since much of that freight is being moved on wide-bodied passenger aircraft or freighters. Last, there are ISO inter-modal type containers which can only be used on wide-bodied freighters such as the Boeing 747F. These various unit load devices may be used and filled by the shippers or the forwarders and presented for carriage to the airline. On many routes the lower costs of handling such ULDs may be passed on to them through low tariffs related to particular ULDs. The fact that much of its freight comes forward in ULDs, each perhaps packed with a variety of different goods, perhaps originating from different shippers, is an added complexity in the marketing of air freight services.

12.4   Freight and passenger markets differ

There are a number of significant ways in which the freight and passenger markets differ. These have a major impact on both the economics and the marketing of air freight.

A key characteristic of the demand for air freight is that it is unidirectional. While passengers generally fly round trips or at least return to their origin, freight clearly does not. As a result, considerable imbalances in freight flows can arise. While freight flows on some major international freight routes such as Amsterdam to New York are more evenly balanced in each direction, on most routes there is a marked imbalance. On major freight routes it is common to find that the traffic in the densest direction is twice or more than twice as great as in the reverse direction, as is the case on the Hong Kong to Tokyo or the Bangkok to Hong Kong routes. Between Asia and Europe a similar pattern has emerged on many major routes, with westbound cargo from Asia being often twice as high or more as eastbound. On secondary but still important freight routes, the imbalances may be even more marked, with the dense flows sometimes as much as three or four times greater than the return flows, as happens on the Hong Kong to New York route. Such imbalances create a major problem, especially for all cargo operators, since very low load factors in the low direction inevitably push down the round-trip load factor.

Wide directional imbalances explain why even major cargo carriers with large freighter fleets appear to achieve relatively poor overall load factors in their freight operations. Certainly freight load factors tend to be significantly lower than passenger seat factors. For example, in the financial year 2007–8, SIA Cargo achieved an overall load factor of 62.2 per cent for the carriage of freight, on its cargo flights and in the belly-hold of passenger aircraft, while Singapore Airlines' passenger load factor was 80.3 per cent (SIA, 2008). Cargolux, operating only freighters and with no passenger belly-hold space to fill up, only achieved a 73 per cent load factor in 2007.

On many routes the tonnage imbalance is aggravated by cargo pricing policies that try to stimulate demand on the low-density direction by offering lower tariffs in that direction. The result may well be an even more marked revenue imbalance as the low tonnages in one direction end up paying the lower cargo rates. Where freight is being carried largely on passenger aircraft, weight and revenue imbalances are easier to absorb, though sometimes airlines may find themselves with inadequate belly-hold capacity in one direction. But large imbalances are particularly detrimental for the operation of all-cargo services, since they result in low overall load factors with no possibility of compensating revenue from passenger sales on relatively empty return sectors. The absence of assured return loads creates marketing and pricing problems which are unique to the cargo side of the industry.

A second key differentiator of the air freight market is that whereas the passenger business has tens of millions of individual decision-makers, in freight a few major customers generate the bulk of the traffic. As a result of consolidation among freight forwarders in the last ten years, the top 20 forwarders control about two thirds of intercontinental tonnages for heavier air freight, that is, other than the small packages carried by the integrators. This means that in marketing their services, the major cargo airlines must focus on a small number of key customers, that is the largest freight forwarders in each market. The large volume of business each of these forwarders controls gives them considerable market power. They can play the airlines off against each other to push down cargo rates, especially where there is excess cargo capacity available.

A third difference is that freight decisions are driven by the delivery time at the destination and, unlike passengers, not by the trip duration. The time of a shipment's arrival is the key service requirement of shippers and their forwarders. The total travel time, the routing taken and whether there is a lengthy intermediate stop and trans-shipment are relatively unimportant. This means that competition for freight on any route is intense as even airlines not operating direct point-to-point services on a route can still offer and sell cargo capacity on that route by carrying cargo via their own hubs. They can do this even if this involves a much longer total flight time and a longer elapsed journey time, provided they can deliver to the ultimate destination within the required target arrival time. Freight will put up with journeys that most passengers would find unacceptable. This means that several airlines can enter the airfreight market on any route in addition to the airlines operating direct services. The risk is overcapacity and downward pressure on cargo rates.

The air freight market differs from the passenger market in one further respect. Decisions by shippers or freight forwarders on choice of airline are much more rational. They are very much based on hard facts – freight rates, collection and delivery times, insurance cost and other service elements. They are not based on taste or a subjective assessment of comfort or convenience or personal likes or dislikes. This again influences the way that airlines market their cargo services.

The importance of objective criteria in decision-making was highlighted in 2008 in the IATA Cargo Service Tracker survey, which asked 2,067 freight forwarders to name their two most important criteria in choosing an airline. Though only 44 per cent cited best price as their top priority, in all 82 per cent placed price as one of their top two criteria. After price, service elements were the most critical in choosing between airlines – 27 per cent cited good condition of shipment among their top two factors, 26 per cent cited on time delivery and 17 per cent quoted the schedule (Airlines International, February–March 2009).

12.5   The challenge of the integrated carriers

The biggest change in the air freight industry in the last 25 years or so has been the growth of the express parcels sector spearheaded by Federal Express in the United States. Launched in 1971, this company realised that the traditional airlines were ignoring two key needs of a large segment of the potential freight market. This was for high-speed carriage and rapid handling of small parcels, many of an emergency or crucial nature, such as legal documents. The second requirement was for door-to-door service with no other intermediary. With these two product features in mind, Federal Express set up a parcels 'hub' in Memphis, Tennessee, and in effect introduced hubbing long before the passenger airlines appreciated its benefits (Chapter 10, Section 10.6). Complexes of aircraft arriving in Memphis from all over the United States within an hour or so of each other in the middle of the night were able to swap their parcels and leave to return to their origins within a couple of hours. Operating in this way, Federal Express could guarantee overnight delivery anywhere in the United States and could ensure it by providing its own collection and delivery vans in the cities it served. The freight product was redefined. Instead of weight and price being the key product features, convenience, speed and reliable delivery times became the critical aspects of the product. Services were segmented and priced on the basis of speed of delivery. By 1990, Federal Express had refined its service, offering and marketing different services including 'Overnight Letter', 'Priority One' (delivery within the USA by 10.30 the next business day) and 'Standard Air', which offered delivery no later than the second working day. Flight forwarders and other middlemen were cut out, since bookings and all contacts were made directly with Federal Express (Fedex).

The door-to-door express parcels business in the United States boomed, its growth rate outstripping that of the more traditional air freight sectors. The Fedex model was adopted by others. During the 1980s, courier and parcels companies which had previously used scheduled airlines for their courier services and express deliveries, as well as lorries, followed the Fedex example and set up their own airline operations. A number of such integrated carriers emerged, including Emery Worldwide, Airborne Express, DHL Airways, United Parcel Services (UPS) in the United States, though not all have survived, and DHL International and TNT, which were stronger in Europe. Unlike Federal Express, they did not limit their business to parcels but accepted larger consignments as well. In time, Federal Express began to do so, too. Integrators use their own aircraft but also buy space from the scheduled passenger and freight airlines as appropriate. The essence of such integrated carriers is that they provide a total product, including pick-up and delivery, transportation, customs clearance, paperwork processing, computer tracking of individual consignments and invoicing. A single system can handle all kinds of cargo worldwide and guarantee delivery within specified time periods.

Having captured the major part of the US domestic freight market by the late 1980s, the integrated carriers then turned to developing their international operations, focusing first on European and then on Asian markets. In 1985, Federal Express established a European hub initially at Brussels airport, though it is now based in Paris. DHL also opened its European hub in Brussels in 1985, but moved it to Leipzig in 2008 because of limits on night flights at the former. UPS had earlier based its European operation hub at Cologne/Bonn airport in Germany. This expansion abroad by US companies was accompanied by the rapid purchase of courier and road-based freight companies in many parts of the world. TNT, originally an Australian company, likewise bought up small express parcel and distribution companies as well as small airlines as a way of expanding its European network most rapidly. The integrators also began acquiring freight forwarders in order to attract and handle larger consignments. They too wanted the ability to offer a one-stop shop for shippers, especially for international consignments. Thus in 2001 UPS bought forwarder Fritz and three years later Menlo Worldwide Forwarding. Fedex bought American Freightways. Deutsche Post, which already owned integrator DHL, bought Exel, one of the largest forwarders, in December 2005.

The success of the integrated carriers over the last 30 years or so can be gauged by the fact that in 1977 they had close to 4 per cent of the US domestic air cargo market. But by offering speed, on-time delivery, reliability and responsiveness, the integrators increased their share of the US airfreight market to over 70 per cent. As mentioned earlier, the four major integrators, Fedex, UPS, DHL and TNT, together control around 80 per cent of the global small packages market, which in recent years has been the fastest growing air freight sector.

The size and global impact of the large integrators can be gauged from the example of UPS. In 2008 UPS operated several air hubs in the United States while in Europe its hub was Cologne/Bonn airport. Its Asian links were in Taipei (Taiwan), Pampanga (Philippines), Hong Kong and Singapore. The Latin American market was served from its Miami hub. UPS operated a fleet of 266 jet aircraft and chartered in a further 300 or so aircraft of various sizes. It also used the passenger services of network airlines in particular markets. For surface delivery and collection it operated a worldwide fleet of 30,000 road vehicles. In 2007 it delivered on average 16 million packages or documents each day though most did not use air. Daily deliveries by air averaged 2.3 million in the USA and a further 1.9 million worldwide. In that year, UPS ranked tenth in the world in terms of international freight tonne-kms carried and second, after Fedex, in terms of total freight traffic, that is international plus domestic (Table 12.3).

A major issue facing the traditional passenger-oriented combination airlines is whether they can successfully meet the challenge of the integrated carriers or whether they are doomed to lose much of their freight traffic as the integrators increase the size of shipments they can accept. To survive that challenge they must capitalise on their major assets, which are high-frequency passenger flights to a wide variety of destinations, and combine these with a high-speed door-to-door integrated service. But this would require large investments in road-based collection and delivery systems. Lufthansa, in aiming to be a world leader in air cargo, tried one approach, namely to buy into an integrator. As part of its long-term strategy, in May 1990 Lufthansa, together with JAL, bought a share in DHL's two holding companies but by early 2001 they had both surrendered control of DHL to Deutsche Post. The alternative approach which Lufthansa also adopted later was to try to work more closely with the integrators. In fact all integrators not only use their own aircraft but also send shipments on scheduled passenger flights and may buy space on all-cargo flights, often using block space agreements. Closer co-operation between integrators and combination carriers, especially when the latter are grouped into global alliances, may be a partial answer to the challenge posed by the former.

Lufthansa provides a recent example. Because of its earlier links with DHL, Lufthansa has for long co-operated closely with this integrator. In 2004 Lufthansa started flying five intercontinental routes for DHL using its own freighter. Such co-operation led in early 2009 to the launch by these two partners of a new joint venture cargo carrier, due to be called AeroLogic and having its own dedicated fleet of Boeing 777 freighters. This would enable Lufthansa to participate directly in the high-yielding express parcels business dominated by the integrators.

For freight forwarders the integrators pose a different challenge. By selling direct to customers and shippers, integrators cut out the middle man or the facilitator, namely the freight forwarders. Hitherto, the freight forwarders have taken the view that the challenge to them from the expansion of the integrators was limited to the small parcels end of the market, which in any case was costly for the forwarders to handle. However, in recent years the integrators have started to go for heavier consignments, a market which the forwarders previously thought was their own. They felt that the weight and diversity of many such shipments did not lend themselves to the logistics-oriented approach of the integrators. The reaction of the forwarders has been to consolidate and merge into a smaller number of large companies who can offer a global service and economies of scale as a way of attracting and keeping large shippers.

12.6   Role of freight forwarders or 'global logistic suppliers'

The process of moving freight is considerably more complex than that of moving passengers. It involves packaging, more extensive and complex documentation, arranging insurance, collection from the shipper, customs clearance at origin and destination and final delivery. The complexity involved has encouraged the growth of specialist freight forwarders who carry out some or all of these tasks on behalf of the shipper and provide an interface between shipper and airline. Such firms may be relatively small IATA-approved or non–IATA agents which feed their shipments directly to the airlines or to large freight consolidators. The latter will be handling freight directly for their own customers but may also be collecting and consolidating consignments from smaller agents. There is considerable fragmentation within the industry, with shippers, forwarders, consolidators and airlines all involved to varying degrees with different consignments. Such fragmentation has made the marketing and product planning of freight particularly difficult for the airlines. Any one of the chain of activities necessary to move freight by air may go wrong and undermine the total service being offered, yet the airline may have no control over the activity. The airline is also frequently torn between marketing and selling its service direct to the shipper or concentrating its selling efforts on the forwarders.

Larger forwarders or consolidators have expanded vertically to develop and undertake more and more logistic services, in order to provide shippers with a complete end-to-end service. They can offer supply chain design, documentation, customs clearance, warehousing, inventory control, ground collection and delivery and may even publish their own flight or container ship schedules and tariffs. For customers they take the complexity out of planning their supply chain. They have become supply chain managers. They can provide the best shipping and routing option by shopping around between airlines or even chartering their own aircraft. They can meet the specialised needs of specific industrial sectors such as the oil or automobile industries. They can be flexible in meeting shippers' specific needs and requirements since, unlike the airlines, they are not tied in to specific flight schedules or the need to push up load factors on individual flights. They can also provide better real-time data on the progress of shipments, their individual cost and other transaction data, since their IT systems are customer-oriented, whereas airline systems tend to be geared to meeting internal operational needs. Finally, the large forwarders can offer their services globally, which few airlines can match. As a result of such advantages, freight forwarders have steadily increased their share of freight shipments. It has been estimated that in 2008, freight forwarders' share of heavier air freight shipments (excluding the express packages trade) was around 85 per cent, leaving only 15 per cent of the market to direct sales by the airlines (MergeGlobal, 2008a).

Consolidation within the freight-forwarding industry has been driven by two requirements: first, by the need to obtain economies of scale and the benefits of vertical integration so as to provide customers with a 'one-stop-shop' service; second, by the need to enter new geographical markets so as to provide global coverage. In short, the twin aims have been to provide total logistic support and worldwide reach. As mentioned earlier, Deutsche Post has achieved both these aims through its own acquisition strategy. In the late 1990s it bought the large Swiss forwarder Danzas and in 2000 a major US forwarder, AEI. By early 2001 it had obtained total control of DHL. In 2004 it acquired Exel, the largest UK forwarder with a very strong market presence in Asia, as a result of its own earlier merger with the Ocean Group. By 2009 Deutsche Post World Net operated both DHL Global Forwarding (formed from Danzas) and Exel as major supply chain management subsidiaries. Many other forwarders followed the acquisition trail. For instance, Schenker, a German-based company, in 2006 bought BAX Global which was strong in North America and the Far East. These companies, together with other major forwarders such as Nippon Express and Kuehne and Nagel, began to dominate the air freight market. The largest forwarders to have emerged are really *global logistic suppliers*.

In many individual markets, such as UK–North America, a handful of large consolidators may come to control over half the freight being shipped. This gives them considerable market power. By consolidating numerous small shipments into large consignments they can obtain substantial bulk discounts. In other words, they buy in bulk from the airlines and sell retail to shippers. On certain routes they can go even further. If the tonnage they ship is high, they can play off the airlines against each other and obtain very low contract rates, particularly on routes where there is over-capacity. In this process airline freight yields are pushed down, but the ultimate shipper may not be given the full benefit of the lower rates the consolidators have squeezed out of the airlines.

On markets where there has been over-capacity, airlines have tried to stimulate total demand or to increase their market share by offering special discounted rates to large forwarders or consolidators. Large numbers of small agents have been unable to generate sufficient freight to take advantage of these special low rates. They have also been wary of shipping via large consolidators for fear of losing their customers to them. Economic pressures from smaller agents eventually led to the establishment of a new specialist, the freight wholesaler. They are an important phenomenon. They buy space in bulk at rates comparable to those of the large consolidator and resell to smaller agents. Unlike consolidators, they do not compete directly for the shippers' business and therefore pose no threat to their customers, the smaller forwarders. They are simply brokers of freight capacity.

The growing concentration of freight demand in the hands of small numbers of major global consolidators and wholesalers has created two serious problems for the airlines that supply freight services. First, it cut airlines off from the ultimate customers, with the result that they were possibly less aware of and less responsive to customer needs and new opportunities. Some airlines tried to overcome this by acquiring or establishing their own freight-forwarding subsidiaries. These have generally not been successful. Second, and potentially more damaging, was the downward pressure on cargo yields which, as mentioned earlier, resulted from the activities of large forwarders or wholesalers.

The general impact of consolidators on airline yields can be gauged from the example of a 500 kg consignment on the London to Nairobi route illustrated in Table 12.5. The ready availability of low contract rates on this route in 2009, below the lowest specific commodity rates, encouraged consolidators and wholesalers to buy space from the airlines at these very low rates. They then sold this space to smaller freight forwarders at a higher rate, who in turn sold it on to shippers at an even higher rate. But the shipper was pleased to be paying less than the published tariffs. The result was that the airlines were often receiving

500 kg low-density consignment, London–Nairobi	*£ per kg*
Tariff structure:	
Normal general cargo rate	0.92
Quantity general cargo rate for 100 kg plus	0.56
Lowest specific commodity rate (car parts)	0.56
Contract rates	0.10–0.50
Selling rates:	
Airline's contract rate to consolidator	0.20
Consolidator resale rate to forwarder	0.40
Forwarder's rate to shipper	0.50
Revenues earned:	
Shipper pays forwarder for 700 kg at, say, £0.50/kg	£350
Forwarder 'splits' volumetric weight with consolidator.	
Pays 600 kg at £0.40/kg	£240
Consolidator mixes with dense cargo to lose volumetric weight	
penalty. Pays airline 500 kg at £0.20/kg	£100
Airline revenue (£100) as percentage of shipper's payment (£350)	29%

Note
* Volumetric weight for charging = 700 kg

well below half of the monies paid by the shippers for the transport of their goods; the balance was going to the middlemen. In the case study shown, the airline on the London–Nairobi sector would only receive 29 per cent of what the shipper paid. The dilution of freight revenue in this way clearly undermines the profitability of air freight. The growing power of these middlemen, and in particular their ability to force down cargo tariffs when and where there is space capacity, is a continuing problem for international airlines.

It is of interest to note that in 2001 the general cargo rate on London–Nairobi was £5.32 compared to £0.92 in 2009, a drop of 83 per cent. This is indicative of the long-term decline in cargo rates.

For the airlines, the *global logistics suppliers* which have emerged represent really large customers, but also a threat, since they have the market power to squeeze substantial tariff discounts out of them. This will exacerbate the downward pressure on cargo yields. One response may be for airlines to tie them into joint ventures. But while vertical integration and consolidation is taking place at one end of the market there are still about 4,500 IATA-accredited freight-forwarding agents around the world and several thousand more who are not accredited. In particular markets or countries some of these smaller agents continue to be important.

12.7   The economics of supply

In assessing the economics of carrying air freight and, in particular, the degree to which it is a profitable business, a major dilemma is how combination carriers should allocate costs between passengers and cargo. The problem arises because so many costs are joint costs and are not specific to the carriage of either passengers or freight. For instance, while cabin crew costs are specific to passengers and are only needed if an aircraft is carrying passengers, the costs of the flight crew are joint costs. One needs the pilots to fly the passengers, but, in the process, capacity is also generated for the carriage of freight. Another joint cost is that of the airport landing fees, which are calculated on the basis of an aircraft's maximum take-off weight (MTOW) and are independent of what is actually being transported. The issue of cost allocation arises primarily when freight is carried in passenger aircraft, or in combi aircraft. The latter are aircraft whose main passenger deck is not used only for passengers but part is separated off as a main deck cargo compartment.

12.7.1 Belly-hold capacity

Slightly less than half of international air freight and mail (47 per cent in 2007) which is carried by IATA airlines travels in the belly-holds of the passenger aircraft. If one includes domestic air freight, this market share drops to 45 per cent. Traditionally combination carriers have regarded it as a by-product arising from the supply of passenger services. Provided freight revenues covered those costs, such as ground handling, cargo sales and marketing, or extra fuel burn, which could be directly attributed to carriage of freight, then any revenue in excess of such costs made a contribution towards offsetting the costs of passenger services. The significance of this contribution can be gauged from the fact that British Airways estimates that close to 60 per cent of its freight revenues on passenger flights are sufficient to cover freight-related costs, while the balance of 40 per cent can be used to cover the other costs which would be incurred whether or not freight was carried on the aircraft. Inevitably, on this basis, belly-hold freight appears to British Airways and others to make a valuable contribution to airline profitability. It is for this reason that BA has focused on belly-hold freight and, unlike Lufthansa, SIA or Air France, has not built up its own freighter fleet.

The by-product approach to costing, however, leaves open the question of whether freight should bear its share of other costs. Should the major costs of operating a flight be considered to be joint costs which need to be split and allocated in some way to both passengers and freight? This argument is strengthened by the fact that the lower freight decks of wide-bodied aircraft have possible alternative uses as galleys or lounges. Freight must at least cover the opportunity cost of forgoing these alternative uses. One could also argue that the shape, size and capacity of wide-bodied aircraft has been influenced by the requirement to carry cargo in the belly-hold and that therefore cargo must share all the aircraft-related and direct costs. However, the allocation of joint costs inevitably involves some arbitrariness. The International Air Transport Association's Cost Committee recommended, some years ago, that the profitability of air cargo on passenger and combi aircraft can only be truly assessed after all operating costs have been fully allocated between cargo and passengers. This could be done on the following basis:

(a) The direct operating costs of a passenger aircraft carrying belly-hold freight should be apportioned between passengers and freight on the basis of the usable volume of the aircraft allocated to each. These direct costs include the costs of fuel, flight crews, aircraft maintenance, weight landing fees and aircraft standing charges, that is, depreciation or lease rentals as well as airframe insurance (see Chapter 4, Section 4.3). For example, on an MD-11 aircraft the total volumetric capacity of the two decks is 639.2 cu.m. The main deck's volume as a freighter, that is without overhead lockers, galleys, toilets, and so on, is 445.2 cu.m. The lower deck provides for 194 cu.m. On this basis, the main deck, that is the passengers, should bear 69.7 per cent of the direct operating costs and the belly-hold 30.3 per cent. But it is not so straightforward. One should apportion a part of the belly-hold's volume for passengers' bags. Also, the lower deck's usable volume based on 32 LD3 containers is 157.6 cu.m., not 194 cu.m. Which value should one use to apportion direct operating costs? Key decisions need to be made on how to calculate the volumetric capacity allocated to freight or passengers. Other simpler allocative criteria can also be used. For instance, one could allocate direct operating costs in proportion to the revenue generated by the two traffics. In practice, allocation based on volume is more widely used.

(b) Cargo-specific or passenger-specific costs should be separately identified and allocated as appropriate. These include most, but not all, of the indirect operating costs. On the cargo side, specific costs include those associated with cargo sales and marketing, collection and delivery of shipments, ground handling and warehousing, airport cargo charges and cargo insurance, as well as the administrative costs of the cargo department. On the passenger side one would need to include the costs of ticketing, sales and reservations, of cabin crews, ground handling and ground staff, passenger-related station expenses, passenger insurance, costs of in-flight catering, airport passenger fees, and so on.

(c) Administration and other indirect overhead costs should be split between passengers and cargo in proportion to the sum of all the other costs (i.e. (a) + (b) above).

If joint costs are allocated in this way, then the carriage of belly-hold freight becomes marginal or unprofitable. In most markets belly-hold freight fails to cover its fully allocated costs. Nevertheless, the carriage of such freight on some individual routes, such as Europe to/from East Asia, may still be highly profitable. An increasing number of airlines, Air France among them, do their cargo costing in this way. But many, particularly smaller carriers, still prefer to think of belly-hold cargo as a profitable by-product making a significant contribution to overall revenue, rather than a marginal or loss-making joint product.

From both the suppliers', that is the airlines', and consumers' points of view, belly-hold freight offers numerous advantages. It is certainly low cost if costed on a by-product basis. The higher frequency of passenger services is attractive to shippers, particularly for emergency-type freight, and they are prepared to pay a premium for the better service. This, together with the fact that passenger aircraft tend to carry a higher proportion of small shipments which do not get bulk or quantity discounts, means that average freight yields from belly-hold freight on most routes are generally higher than average yields on freighters.

12.7.2   Combi aircraft

There are routes where the enormous payload of wide-bodied aircraft in all-cargo configuration is too large for the potential freight demand, while belly-hold capacity may be insufficient or unable to cope with bulky consignments. In such circumstances, the wide-bodied combi aircraft, on which both passengers and freight are carried on the main deck, may prove a commercially attractive proposition. By adjusting the main deck space allocated to passengers or freight in response to the demand mix and seasonal variations of each route, total revenue can be maximised. For instance, at times of peak passenger demand the whole cabin may be used for passengers.

In the last 20 years the market share of combi aircraft in global air freight has been declining. In 2007 it was just 2 per cent. It is likely to become insignificant as existing combi aircraft are phased out. This is because larger wide-bodied long-haul aircraft and higher frequencies on many routes ensure sufficient belly-hold freight capacity.

In a combi operation, the allocation of joint costs to the freight side is essential. Freight revenue must be seen to cover its share of capacity costs, since without freight on the main deck the passenger service would use a smaller aircraft or a lower frequency and reduce its total costs. This means that freight pricing must move towards a full cost-recovery basis rather than be based on the by-product pricing strategy that might be adopted for belly-hold freight. Market conditions will determine whether this can be done. The method of allocation varies between airlines, but a small number of airlines – KLM and Air France among them – did the exercise and convinced themselves of the commercial advantages of combi aircraft. During the 1990s, Air France, one of the largest freight operators, was carrying as much as 35 per cent of its total freight traffic in combi aircraft. Another 55 per cent went in freighters and only 10 per cent went on passenger aircraft. However, in recent years combi aircraft have played a diminishing role in the carriage of air freight.

For combi aircraft, allocation of joint costs on the basis of volumetric capacity is relatively simple. On a Boeing 747–300 with space on the main passenger deck for six pallets or containers and with seating reduced from 410 to 360, the volumetric breakdown would be as follows:

Passenger capacity: 360 at 36.1 cu.ft/pass = 12,996 cu.ft, or 65.4%

Cargo capacity: 6 pallets plus belly-hold = 6,867 cu.ft. or 34.6%

Total = 19,863 cu.ft. 100.0%

So cargo would need to cover 34.6 per cent of the joint direct operating costs, plus its own specific costs and a share of the small administrative and indirect overheads.

A few airlines, Lufthansa, SAS and SIA among them, have separated out their cargo operations as stand-alone businesses. Once this is done then the question of joint costs on passenger or combi aircraft has to be resolved head on. Lufthansa Cargo or SIA Cargo, which was launched as SIA's largest subsidiary in July 2001, operate their own freighters with their own flight crew and do all the cargo selling and handling within their own facilities and cargo warehouses. Costing all this is not a problem. But they also need to buy space on their parent companies' passenger flights. This now has to be done on a fully-costed basis. In SIA's case, SIA Cargo buys belly-hold space at a price which reflects joint costs allocated on the basis of the volumetric capacity dedicated to cargo. This space has to be paid for by SIA Cargo. Lufthansa Cargo as a company buys belly-hold space from Lufthansa's passenger business which operates its passenger fleet. With cargo costs made explicit and real, it is easier to assess the true profitability of carrying cargo on passenger flights.

12.7.3   All-cargo aircraft

Freighters or all-cargo aircraft carried 53 per cent of IATA airlines' global freight tonne-kms in 2007 and their share is growing. The major economic advantage of the freighter is that it increases its payload by half or more compared with the same aircraft in a passenger configuration. By stripping out unnecessary and heavy passenger-related facilities such as galleys, toilets, wardrobes or overhead bins, thereby saving weight, a Boeing 747–200 freighter may carry a cargo payload of 100–110 tonnes; the same aircraft with a main passenger deck and belly-hold freight has a typical payload of around 60–67 tonnes. In theory, the greater payload should reduce the direct operating costs per available tonne-kilometre of freighters by up to one-third or more, when compared with the ATK cost on passenger aircraft. In practice, the cost differential between fully allocated costs of cargo on freighters and cargo on passenger aircraft appears to be less.

The full costs of carrying freight on all-cargo aircraft can readily be identified so that, in theory, tariff strategies could be adopted to ensure that revenues exceeded costs. In practice, over-capacity and competition has meant that tariffs are market-based rather than cost-based. Moreover, yields on all-cargo freight, much of it travelling at bulk discount or contract rates, tend to be lower than those from freight on passenger aircraft. As a general rule, airlines have found that yields on scheduled all-cargo services are around 5–10 per cent or so lower than the yields achieved from the carriage of freight on passenger aircraft, though this varies significantly between different markets. Nevertheless, where airlines have managed to sustain high load factors on scheduled freighter services, such services have proved profitable. Yields tend to be higher on freighter flights which are chartered by a specific customer.

The factors which appear to be necessary to ensure continued viability of long-haul freight services are a high level of demand, preferably from both ends of a route, an insufficient volume of cargo space on passenger aircraft and some constraint on the provision of all-cargo services. In some long-haul markets such capacity control is being achieved by the third and fourth freedom carriers operating freighter services jointly rather than in competition. This has been done by Cathay Pacific and British Airways between London and Hong Kong and by SIA and Lufthansa on their Singapore-Germany services. Such joint operations avoid overprovision of freighter capacity, which tends to undermine cargo rates. The North Atlantic is one of the least profitable of the long-haul routes, largely because there is too much capacity available. Conversely, on freighter services between Europe and East Asia the high and rapidly growing demand for westbound freight in the period 2005 to mid-2008, which outstripped the available capacity, ensured reasonable profits for many all-cargo operations in this market. The collapse of Asian exports in late 2008 and in 2009 undermined this profitability.

The danger of over-capacity is present in all markets and as a consequence many airlines are loath to operate freighter aircraft and prefer to concentrate on carrying belly-hold cargo. Yet there is clearly a role for the freighter. Carriers, who feel that freight is important, will continue to operate freighters as a key part of their overall freight operations. They need them to provide a better overall service for their customers by using them in markets of heavy demand, as from China to Europe or the USA, and to transport the 10 per cent or so of freight that is too large or dangerous for belly-holds. All-cargo schedules can also be geared to the delivery time needs of shippers. On some routes, where the demand for passengers is thin, belly-hold capacity may in any case be insufficient to meet cargo needs. This may also be so on routes where payload or range restrictions reduce the effective cargo capacity on passenger flights. The introduction of very long non-stop passenger flights with Boeing 747–400 or other aircraft has resulted in the loss of belly-hold cargo capacity on routes where the extra fuel loads required for non-stop sectors necessitates cutbacks in the freight payload that can be uplifted. When in the mid-1990s airlines began replacing Boeing 747s on some long-haul routes with smaller, twin-engined aircraft, such as the Boeing 767 and later the Boeing 777, there was again a reduction in belly-hold cargo capacity, creating a need in some markets for more freighters. The trend is undoubtedly for the share of freighters in the carriage of cargo to increase.

12.8   The pricing of air freight

12.8.1   *Structure of cargo tariffs*

The structure of cargo tariffs is very complex. This is because there exists a wide range of publicly available tariffs in parallel with a host of confidential tariffs agreed between airlines and their larger individual customers. In many major markets it is the latter which are more widely used rather than the published tariffs. As with passenger fares, the published international cargo tariffs have traditionally been agreed by the airlines through IATA and subsequently approved by governments, though the latter is a formality. With the spread of liberalisation and with over-capacity in many markets, IATA cargo tariffs have tended to become less significant worldwide. Nevertheless they were negotiated by IATA's Tariff Conferences. These IATA tariffs provided the basis for the interlining of freight between carriers, though this was limited, and also acted as the basic rates which the public or an individual shipper saw.

However, during the last decade or so the relevance of the IATA cargo tariff conferences has diminished. First, the United States and then the European Commission argued that fixing cargo tariffs through IATA was anti-competitive and encouraged airlines to discontinue the joint setting of rates by threatening to remove immunity from anti-trust prosecution for IATA tariff agreements. IATA was forced to change and accepted the need to phase out cargo tariff agreements. In 2008, IATA abandoned all cargo tariff agreements on routes between the USA and the European Union countries and on all routes to Australia. On these routes IATA agreed tariffs were replaced by individual airlines' published rates. IATA agreed rates continued to be negotiated through the tariff conferences in other markets, since many governments continued to prefer tariffs to be regulated in this way. But even on routes with IATA tariffs, market conditions frequently push airlines to ignore them. The trend is clear: progressively IATA agreed tariffs will be phased out in more and more markets.

Because of IATA's traditional role in agreeing cargo tariffs, the structure of such tariffs today has a certain uniformity whether they are IATA tariffs or those of individual airlines. The basic rate for any city pair will normally be a *general cargo rate*. Like all air freight rates it is expressed as a rate per kilogram and there may be a minimum charge per consignment. An examination of general cargo rates around the world shows that the rate per kilometre tapers with route distance. But the taper which in theory is cost-related is neither regular nor always evident. In addition there are significant variations in the general cargo rate for opposite directions on the same route. Thus the general rates from African points south of the Sahara to Europe have traditionally been as low as two thirds or less of the rates for cargo originating in Europe. Similar north–south imbalances in rate levels have also existed on air routes between North and South America. For instance, in the mid-2000s the general cargo rate from Buenos Aires to Los Angeles was 40 per cent lower than the return rate from Los Angeles. Such rate variations have clearly been aimed at reducing the imbalances in freight flows and more particularly at generating more northbound traffic. IATA tariffs are expressed in the local currency of the originating point. If this happens to be devalued the rate imbalance in each direction will clearly worsen.

On most routes, tariffs are available which will be lower than the normal general cargo rate. First, there may be *quantity general cargo rates* where the rate per kilogram decreases as the size of the consignment increases beyond certain agreed weight break-points. While most routes may have only one or two quantity rates, 45kgs and 100kgs are common break-points, routes to and from the United States tend to have many more break-points with successively lower rates as consignment weight increases.

While the quantity general cargo rates encourage consolidation into large consignments they fail to stimulate the air freighting of particular goods or commodities. This is done by *specific commodity rates* which are individual low rates for specific and clearly-defined commodities. Some routes may have only one or two commodity rates while others may have 40 or more. Such rates will reflect and encourage the types of goods most likely to be shipped by air on each route and in a particular direction. Many commodity rates also include quantity discounts with lower rates as shipment size increases. The level of the commodity rates varies widely but on occasions they may be as low as 40 per cent or less of the general cargo rate.

The third type of discount rates consists of those related to particular unit load devices, known as *ULD rates*. Such rates are not available in all markets. There is a fixed minimum charge per ULD which declines proportionally as the size of the pallet or container increases. The minimum charge is for a given weight for each type of ULD, known as the pivot weight. If the contents in the ULD weigh more than the pivot weight then there is a charge per kilogram for each kilogram above that weight. The ULD rates are normally lower than the quantity general rates or most of the specific commodity rates. Their aim is to encourage shippers and forwarders to pack as much into the ULDs as possible. Moreover, by mixing shipments of different weight and density in a container, one can reduce the average cargo rate paid to the airline. The aim of ULD rates is also to encourage shippers to use containers or other unit load devices which, from an airline's viewpoint, are easier and cheaper to handle than disparate consignments.

A somewhat different category of cargo tariffs were the so-called *class rates*, which involve a reduction (for unaccompanied baggage or newspapers) or a surcharge (for gold or human remains, for example) on the general commodity rate. They have been applied to certain commodities whose carriage calls for special treatment. Only a very small proportion of freight travels at these class rates.

For major cargo carriers such as British Airways as little as 5 per cent or less of their freight is carried at published IATA rates even in markets where such rates are deemed to apply. This share will be higher for smaller airlines such as Air India or Philippine Airlines, who traditionally have not attached much importance to air freight. Most freight is carried at tariffs which are negotiated directly with the larger freight forwarders and are not publicly available. Many airlines will have a special *account holder tariff* or something similar for their regular customers. These are tariffs with a similar structure to the IATA tariffs, that is, with quantity break-points and ULD rates. They are lower than the published IATA rates but may be higher than the prevailing market rates. They are made available to freight forwarders who generate sufficient business to be regular account holders. Each airline will offer its own rates to these regular account holders. Though not public such account-holder tariffs are known to agents and available to most freight forwarders.

The lowest rates, often reflecting the prevailing market rates on any route, are the *contract rates* negotiated directly between individual airlines and their customers prepared to guarantee a minimum tonnage of shipped freight over a given period. A large cargo airline may find that the 15 to 20 largest global freight forwarders, such as Schenker or Nippon Express, with offices around the world, generate two thirds or more of its business. These, together with very large forwarders in individual countries, can negotiate individual contract rates. The growing market power of freight forwarders and the competitive pressure on airlines to sell excess capacity has created a situation on the North Atlantic, on the North Pacific and some other routes where very low contract rates dominate the market and where freight pricing bears little relevance to published IATA tariffs. Contract rates may fall to 20 per cent or less of the general cargo rate. In addition, to attract and keep business from freight forwarders with offices in many countries, airlines will often offer incentives in the form of rebates payable at the end of each year, if the total business generated exceeds certain agreed levels.

Finally, in order to fill up anticipated spare capacity in certain markets and at particular times, airlines may offer *spot prices*. These are the cheapest rates and are available to all-comers, usually within the last two weeks before the departure dates.

In recent years, as a response to the challenge posed by the integrators with their door-to-door logistic chains and guaranteed delivery times, several airlines have launched time-definite cargo products and *time-definite rates*. The aim is to increase yields and margins both by offering collection and delivery and by guaranteeing delivery within specified elapsed times. Whereas traditional cargo products focus on flight schedules and flight departure times, in marketing time definite (td) services the focus is on minimising the total elapsed journey time, from collection to delivery with a guaranteed delivery time. That is all that concerns the forwarder or the shipper. In Europe time-definite pricing was pioneered by Lufthansa Cargo. In April 1998 it launched three time-definite products: 'td.Flash', which guaranteed delivery within 24 hours, 'td.X' with delivery within 48 hours and 'td.Pro' for delivery within 72–96 hours. The tariffs were obviously higher for the faster services. Within a year of its launch, Lufthansa claimed that around 20 per cent of its standard cargo was travelling on time-definite rates and that the average yield from time-definite freight was 30 per cent higher than other cargo (Kraus, 1999). Subsequently, most of the more important air freight carriers, such as Cathay Pacific and Singapore Airlines, also introduced similar time-definite products and tariffs.

However, increasing competitive pressures during the early and mid-2000s forced the major cargo airlines to develop and further refine their service offering to cater for the specialised requirements of particular product categories. By 2009 Lufthansa Cargo was still offering 'td.Flash' and 'td.Pro' as its two basic products. But in addition it offered specialised services with *specialist product rates*: 'Care/td' for hazardous goods; 'Cool/td' for goods such as pharmaceuticals that need to be transported at constant temperatures; 'Safe/td1' for valuable freight; 'Safe/td2' for goods subject to theft such as luxury consumer goods or electronic devices and Live/td for the carriage of live animals. Using different names, Cathay Pacific and other major cargo carriers offer a similar range of specialist products. Inevitably the tariffs for each product tend to reflect both the costs involved for the airline and also the demand elasticity of the shipment involved for the shipper.

12.8.2   *Pricing is market- not cost-based*

The preceding review of the structure of cargo tariffs suggests that they bear only a tenuous relationship to cargo costs. Different commodities on the same route may be charged at widely different rates with no marked differences apparent in the costs of handling and freighting them. General cargo rates vary markedly between sectors of similar length being operated with similar aircraft. Rates on the same route differ in opposite directions. The taper of rates per kilometre with distance is neither consistent nor closely related to costs. While IATA and some airlines have tried to dress up the cargo tariffs as being somehow cost-related, there can be little doubt that the underlying philosophy, especially for commodity rates, is ultimately one of 'charging what the traffic will bear', that is, market-oriented pricing. Such a pricing strategy was encouraged by the by-product view of air cargo. As a by-product of passenger services the carriage of freight appeared to impose low additional costs and any revenue in excess of these low costs made a contribution to the overall profitability of the services.

It could be argued that market pricing is discriminatory since it entails charging some shipments more than the costs they impose and others less. This is undoubtedly the case, but it is difficult to see how market pricing could be avoided given the nature of the air freight market. It has two distinctive characteristics which bedevil any attempt to establish cost-related tariffs. First, the existence of freight consolidators and wholesalers not only cuts off the airlines from their true customers and distorts the pricing mechanism, but also gives such large freight agents considerable market power. Second, the carriage of freight is inherently more competitive even in regulated markets than is the carriage of passengers. This is because most freight, except for emergency freight, is indifferent to the routing it is offered in order to move from its origin to its destination. A shipper is unconcerned if his shipment goes from New York to Lisbon on a direct flight or via Amsterdam or Frankfurt or Copenhagen, even with a six-hour trans-shipment at one of those airports, provided it gets to Lisbon within the expected time. Few passengers would put up with circuitous and lengthy journeys. Thus in most cases there are numerous routings (and airlines) that freight can use to get to its destination. This ensures a degree of inter-airline competition which may be absent for passengers on the same routes. If one superimposes on these market characteristics the availability on most air services of surplus belly-hold capacity then any attempts to establish cost-related cargo tariffs will inevitably be futile. Airlines have little choice but to pursue a strategy of setting rates aimed at maximising revenue. In prevailing market conditions on most major routes this means charging what the traffic will bear.

In an environment of market-oriented pricing, where consolidators and wholesalers have had a major influence on freight tariffs, and where combination carriers are losing market share to the integrators, it seems inevitable that tariffs will increasingly reflect three variables – the speed of delivery required, whether the shipment is loose or in a unit load device, and whether it requires specialised handling. The level of charges within such a structure will of course reflect market conditions in each market or route. They will be highest where the demand for freight capacity exceeds the supply.

12.8.3   *Freight yields*

As in the passenger market, cargo yields have tended to decline over time. In the 1990s scheduled freight yields fell each year by about 3 per cent after adjusting for inflation. This decline reflected a downward trend in operating costs of both passenger aircraft and freighters, the increased freight capacity on offer and intensified competition. In the early 2000s freight yields began to rise, especially from 2003 onwards, as fuel and security surcharges were introduced. But by 2006 there was renewed downward pressure on yields

Table 12.6 Cargo yields of European airlines in different markets, 2007

Route groups	Average sector distance (km)	Yield – US cents per tonne-km
Short-haul		
Cross-border Europe	940	86.6
Europe–North Africa	1,710	46.3
Europe–Middle East	2,990	29.5
Long-haul		
Europe–Sub-Sahara Africa	5,110	31.8
Mid-Atlantic	6,530	28.3
North Atlantic	6,550	22.2
Europe–Far East/Australasia	6,900	26.6
South Atlantic	7,310	24.8

Source: AEA (2008).

Note
Sector distance refers to passenger and cargo flights.

as access to online booking systems gave shippers and forwarders increased knowledge of competitive market prices. Pricing power shifted from the suppliers, the airlines, to the consumers of their services. So overall, in the 2000s up to 2009, yields declined on average about 1 per cent each year.

For an individual airline, the prevailing cargo tariff levels in its major markets and that airline's traffic mix are clearly the major determinants of its freight yields, that is the average revenues actually received per tonne-km carried. Other factors also impact on yields. Particularly important is the degree to which the general cargo rates have been eroded by the introduction of low specific commodity rates and ultimately by contract or other deep discount rates. This will be determined by market conditions, notably the availability of spare capacity and the degree of inter-airline competition. Consignment mix in terms of the size of various shipments is important in determining the rates paid to the airline since larger consignments will pay less per kilo. The length of haul of those consignments also impacts on yields since cargo rates per kilometre tend to decline with distance. Similar factors will also affect the freight yields achieved in the various parts of an airline's route network.

The wide range of freight yields obtained in different market areas by member airlines of the Association of European Airlines in 2007 is illustrated in Table 12.6. Markets are ranked according to their average sector distance, with the shortest sector markets at the top and the longest at the bottom. Generally speaking cargo yields per RTK go down as sector distances increase. As one would expect, yields are highest on the relatively short European routes where much air freight goes by road. This suggests that much of the international air freight within Europe is composed of relatively small and high-rated consignments, often of an emergency nature. Yields on Europe–Middle East routes appear disproportionately low given that these are medium-haul markets. The average yield obtained in 2007, US cents 29.5, is close to that achieved in long-haul markets with sector distances more than twice as long. This reflects the considerable over-capacity in the Europe–Middle East air freight market in 2007 and also the very marked directional imbalance in this market with much more eastbound cargo than westbound. Conversely, yields on Europe–mid-Atlantic routes appear high compared to other very long-haul markets.

For individual airlines, the average freight yields they achieve will depend on several factors, but three are crucial. First, the degree to which they operate all-cargo aircraft, since yields on them tend to be lower. Second, the markets they are operating in and the degree of competition, but also the sector lengths over which they are flying cargo, since shorter sectors tend to produce higher yields because tariffs per kilometre are higher. Finally, the mix of cargo carried, particularly the balance between smaller, higher yielding shipments and large bulkier consignments normally travelling on the lowest contract rates. If an airline has high time definite rates for cargo requiring rapid delivery and a significant proportion of such freight, then this too will have an impact on its average cargo yields.

As a general rule, yields per freight tonne-km are less than half of the revenues generated from passengers when converted into a yield per passenger tonne-km. In 2007 the average yield per passenger tonne-km on the North Atlantic scheduled services of member airlines of the Association of European Airlines was 91.6 US cents. The average freight yield was 22.2 cents per tonne-km, equivalent to 24 per cent of the passenger yield (AEA, 2008). On services from Europe to East Asia/Australasia in 2007 freight yields per tonne-km were 29 per cent of the yield per passenger tonne-km. The relatively low freight yields explain why freight represents close to one third (29 per cent) of airline production worldwide but generates only one eighth of airline revenues (Chapter 1, Table 1.5). Inevitably the airlines very heavily involved in air cargo and operating freighters, such as Lufthansa or Air France, will have overall yields (for passenger and freight traffic combined) which are lower than those of airlines which focus primarily on passengers and for whom freight is merely a by-product of passenger services.

12.9   Marginal profitability?

Historically, the profitability of air freight has been fairly marginal. Freight is no different from passengers. Its profitability depends on the interplay of the same three variables, namely unit costs, unit revenues or yields and the load factors achieved. This varies between different sectors of the air freight industry.

For those airlines who carry the bulk of their air freight on passenger aircraft, its profitability depends very much on the freight load factors achieved and on the allocation of costs.

In practice, low load factors for freight on passenger aircraft are inevitable. Passenger aircraft generate some cargo capacity on all the routes they operate, irrespective of the level of demand for freight on each route. Most airlines operate many passenger routes where demand for freight is minimal, yet the freight capacity is substantial either because flight frequencies are high or because wide-bodied aircraft are being used. Since such excess or unwanted freight capacity is included when calculating the overall load factor (and total allocated costs) for freight on passenger or combi aircraft it inevitably deflates the load factors to unprofitable levels. Put simply, an airline's cargo manager must try to balance unit costs, yield and load factor, yet has no effective control over capacity so as to push up the load factors. This is an impossible task, since much of his cargo capacity is generated by the demands of the passenger side of the business. As previously discussed, some airlines have overcome this problem by setting up cargo subsidiaries which only buy, and pay for, belly-hold cargo capacity when they need it.

Nevertheless, there are clearly many individual routes, with strong demand for air freight in both directions, where cargo load factors on passengers are sufficiently high to cover fully allocated costs. In the mid-2000s, such routes included many sectors between China and European points and certain trans-Pacific routes.

But ultimately, the profitability of freight on passenger aircraft is also linked to the costing approach adopted. In the past, IATA recommended the full allocation of joint costs between passengers and freight in proportion to the volumetric capacity used by each (Section 12.7 above). If fully costed on this basis, freight on passenger/combi aircraft appears in general to be unprofitable for many airlines. But many others, including British Airways, consider belly-hold freight as a *by-product* of passenger services, rather than as a *joint product*. They then assess freight in terms of its contribution to the total revenues on their passenger services, after deducting from the freight revenue all costs specific to the cargo side. On this basis, belly-hold freight appears to make a valuable contribution to the overall profitability of many routes. Cargo managers, especially those in airlines not operating freighters or heavily involved in freight, tend to prefer this approach.

Scheduled freighter services, whether operated by combination carriers, cargo airlines or integrators, are more likely to be profitable in large part because it becomes easier to match the capacity provided with the demand in particular markets. Load factors can be pushed up since they can be influenced directly by an airline's cargo managers and salesmen. Apart from competition from other carriers, the major difficulty they may face in achieving adequate load factors arises from the imbalance in freight flows in each direction on the same route. Very high loads in one direction may be offset by negligible flows in the return direction. Where loads are good in both directions and there is no oversupply of freighter capacity it should be possible to achieve good load factors and good yields. Demand and supply conditions in individual markets have a major impact on the profitability of all-cargo services. While such operations in general appear to be marginally profitable, results vary considerably both between major markets or routes and between airlines operating freighter services.

Results from the mid- to late 2000s suggest that freighter operations can be reasonably profitable, even when combined with freight on passenger aircraft. Airlines heavily involved in air freight, which have set up cargo subsidiaries or separate cargo business units to operate freighter aircraft and to buy cargo capacity from their parent passenger airlines, did well in that period, though profit margins were low. This is evidenced from the results of Lufthansa Cargo and SIA Cargo in their financial years 2006 and 2007 (Table 12.7). SIA Cargo made a small loss in 2006 but actually contributed nearly $1 billion to its passenger parent for space booked on passenger aircraft (SIA, 2008). Nevertheless, even for separate cargo subsidiaries, freight load factors remain low compared to the passenger seat factors achieved by their parent companies. Thus in the financial year 2007–8 SIA Cargo's load factor was 69.3 per cent compared with 80.3 on the passenger side.

Historically, the profit margins of integrated freight carriers such as UPS or Fedex have tended to be much higher than the margins achieved by the traditional combination carriers or the all-cargo airlines such as Cargolux, though this was not evident in 2006 and 2007, which were generally good years for most major freight operators (Table 12.7). The integrators' business model gives them a major advantage. By offering a door-to-door service, the integrators provide much more added value and can charge substantially more for their services especially those offering guaranteed and fast delivery. This is why the cargo subsidiaries of airlines such as Lufthansa and Singapore Airlines are focusing increasingly on the provision of door-to-door and time-definite services.

e 12.7 Profitability of different types of freighter operators in 2006 and 2007

	Pre-tax profit/loss as % total revenue	
	Financial year 2006	*Financial year 2007*
Integrators:		
Fed Ex	+5.3	+5.5
UPS	+2.9	−1.7
Combination carrier:		
SIA Cargo	−1.1	+3.4
Lufthansa Cargo	+2.9	+5.0
All cargo airline:		
Cargolux	+5.5	−2.9
ACMI operator:		
Atlas Air	+4.1	+8.5

Source: Compiled by author using airline Annual Reports and *Air Transport World*.

12.10 Beyond the crisis – prospects and challenges

The world economic downturn starting in 2000, together with the external shocks such as the attack on the twin towers in New York in September 2001, the SARS epidemic and the Iraq war, undermined the profitability of air freight, which was in any case marginal. However, the rapidly accelerating growth of the Chinese and other Asian economies in the mid-2000s generated an explosion of exports. Many of these exports were goods, such as high-value clothing, electronic and other consumer products, which benefited from carriage by air. On key routes dense air freight flows could only be met by the provision of more freighter capacity. Demand was such that freight load factors went up and profitability improved, but for a short time only. The air freight sector was hit by two new shocks.

First, the explosion in fuel prices, which began in 2004 but reached a peak in July 2008, was particularly bad for freighter economics, since fuel is a much higher proportion of total operating costs on freighters than on passenger aircraft. When the fuel price was around $1.00 per barrel, fuel represented over 40 per cent of the total operating costs of older freighters such as the Boeing 747–200F or the DC10–30F, compared with around 15–20 per cent for more modern wide-body passenger aircraft. The latter were more fuel efficient, but also had high passenger-related costs which made fuel a smaller proportion of total costs. As 2004 fuel prices doubled and then trebled, the impact on freighter costs was dramatic for all aircraft, but especially for older aircraft. For the latter, fuel costs shot up to 70–80 per cent of round-trip costs. Major freight operators such as Air France and Cathay and all-cargo carriers such as Nippon Cargo began to ground and/or retire such aircraft in 2007–8. But for many smaller freighter operators the fuel price escalation was too much and they collapsed. These included the Malaysian carrier Transmile, the United States carriers Kitty Hawk, Kalitta, Tradewinds and Gemini, a substantial ACML lessor, and Variglog in Brazil.

The second shock was the impact of the worldwide financial crisis which began in mid-2007 and gathered pace and severity during 2008. This had a dramatic impact on world trade. From mid-2008 onwards, air freight markets began to collapse at an accelerating rate. IATA's member airlines' freight traffic plummeted by 7.9 per cent in October 2008, compared to a year earlier, by 13.5 per cent in November, with a further year-on-year drop of 22.6 per cent in December 2008. The largest declines in freight traffic were experienced by Asian airlines. This was a real crisis time for freight. For the full year of 2008 freight tonne-kms were down 4.0 per cent. As the economic crisis deepened, the air freight market was expecting an even greater decline in demand in 2009. Many airlines, SIA Cargo and Air France among them, cut back on freight capacity by 5–10 per cent by grounding freighters or reducing frequencies.

On the other hand, long-term prospects for air freight appear to be good. This is precisely because of its dependence on the world's economic climate. All long-term economic forecasts predict that world GDP will grow on average 2.0 to 2.5 per cent each year during the next two decades despite any short-term downturn between 2008 and 2010 or 2011. Given the high GDP elasticity of air freight, this means that air freight should, in time, begin to grow again at a long-term rate of 4 to 5 per cent per annum. In brief, in 2009 the air freight industry was faced with crisis and uncertainty in the short term, but optimism in the longer term.

When growth is re-established, the network airlines will have to adapt and respond to the continued expansion of the integrators and the increased market power of the large forwarders. The traditional view that combination airlines are involved in supplying two joint products, the carriage of passengers and of freight, which are inextricably entwined, will progressively be replaced by the belief that they are two quite distinct products. These two products manifest demand patterns which differ both geographically, in terms of routes, and temporally in terms of seasons and timings. They require airlines to offer different service and product features which are marketed and sold through separate and different distribution channels. They are two quite separate businesses, and as both are developed further the differences between them will become more pronounced and apparent. Certain sectors of the airline industry have known this for a long time. In Europe and elsewhere, the charter airlines have focused almost exclusively on carrying passengers. Though they inevitably generate cargo capacity on their passenger charter flights, they have not entered the freight business. For the low-cost, no-frills airlines carrying freight is also anathema since it would screw up their economics which are dependent on fast turnarounds and minimal ground handling. On the other side of the business, the integrated carriers have also seen the advantages of product specialisation – in their case on freight only.

As a result of both economic and operational pressures to separate the two businesses there is likely to be a growing polarisation among combination carriers in their approach to freight. At one end there will be airlines such as Air India or the Polish airline LOT, who will basically see themselves as primarily passenger carriers. Such airlines will not view freight as a major part of their business, in which they are prepared to invest substantial financial resources or effort. They will carry some belly-hold freight but will treat it as a by-product, one hopefully making a financial contribution to the passenger side, not as a separate business in its own right. Around 20 per cent or less of their revenue tonne-kms will be generated by freight as opposed to passengers and freight will produce well below 10 per cent of total revenues. Moreover, over time both these percentages will be depressed further. Inevitably, these airlines' share of the freight traffic on the routes they operate will also decline.

At the other end of the spectrum will be a few airlines who see freight as a major and potentially profitable business activity with its own needs and requirements; but an activity sufficiently different from the passenger side of their business to merit separate treatment. These airlines will increasingly follow the example of Lufthansa, SAS, SIA, Malaysia Airlines and others and operate their cargo operations as separate and independent subsidiary companies or business units. The latter will operate their own freighter aircraft with their own flight crew and will undertake all their own marketing, selling, ground-handling, warehousing, administration and so on. They will buy and pay for belly-hold capacity as required from their parent passenger airline. Some may be floated on the Stock Exchange, with the parent airline retaining some shares, or they may be sold off entirely.

These large, cargo-oriented airlines or airline subsidiaries will be able to concentrate their business exclusively on freight. More importantly, they will refocus their activities away from the traditional view that air freight is about transporting goods from A to B. Success in the future will depend on understanding that it is much more than that. Air freight is about providing a delivery service and about supply chain management. This is why the integrators have been so successful and why large freight forwarders and even postal authorities have been making incursions into activities and markets previously the preserve of the airlines.

The air freight market has been undergoing many changes and the process of change will accelerate as a result of the industry's downturn in 2008 and 2009. The integrators will continue expanding their business and market, first by going for more non-express traffic and larger shipments; second, by using large forwarders they have purchased to give them greater market spread and facilitate the move into non-core business. This is why DHL, through its parent Deutsche Post World Net, is linked to Danzas and Exel, two of the largest forwarders, while UPS bought Menlo.

The large air freight airlines, in order to meet the long-term threat of the integrated carriers, will need to face up to several operational challenges. First, they must focus on providing customised services and products to meet the very specific needs of large market segments. As Lufthansa Cargo and SIA Cargo already do, anyone wishing to be a significant player in air freight will need to have customised handling equipment for products such as pharmaceuticals, perishable stuffs, hazardous goods or goods requiring high security and so on. Such services may be costly to provide but should generate higher yields.

Second, freighter fleets will need to be modernised. Older aircraft cannot cope with the needs of tomorrow's air freight market. Yield pressure will require airlines to operate the most fuel-efficient freighters. While fuel prices went down in late 2008 and early 2009, they are likely in the longer term to stabilise at levels which are still relatively high. For many older generation freighters, such as MD-11 or Boeing 747–200F aircraft, fuel costs represent close to 50 per cent of round-trip costs when fuel prices are around $1.00 per barrel and over 75 per cent at 2008 fuel prices. Such aircraft are also too noisy in an increasingly environmentally conscious world. They are old and unreliable and subject to delays, with more and longer maintenance down times. Yet time-definite shipments require punctuality and reliability. In short, freighter fleets need to be modernised. While new generation freighters will have much higher capital costs, these will be more than offset by lower fuel costs.

Third, airlines with serious commitment to air freight will need to undertake the substantial investments required to improve their IT systems and to re-orient these systems to providing a time-definite integrator type of service. This means high-speed tracing and tracking of shipments, high technology warehousing, automatic and customer-focused reporting systems and the provision, in-house or through ground handling agents, of time-guaranteed collection and delivery. If the traditional airlines are to succeed in the freight sector, they must appreciate that there has been a logistics revolution. They must invest heavily in distribution networks, in electronic data interchange (EDI) and in other facilities which are needed to meet shippers' requirements. Their aim should be not just to transport freight by air but to add value to the shipper's products. In doing this they may be able to charge more for their services and thereby counteract any downward pressure on rates. Airlines and their governments need to embrace and adopt IATA's e-freight initiative, launched in November 2005, to take paper documentation out of the air cargo by the end of 2010, thereby saving up to $4.9 billion of costs each year. Every air cargo shipment travels with up to 38 documents, wasting time and paper and creating delays. By early 2009 e-freight was operating at 16 locations worldwide, with 13 documents converted to electronic messages. But more needs to be done.

The final challenge which must be met is how to provide a global delivery service. Big users of air freight such as IBM, Nokia, Ford or General Motors manufacture or source their products in many countries, and sell worldwide. They and most of the other big shippers need global scope and coverage from their providers of air delivery services. For the traditional airlines this means creating cargo alliances, to provide a global network. Two major cargo alliances were launched in 2000. In May 2000 an alliance linking the cargo businesses of Lufthansa, SAS and Singapore Airlines was announced. It was renamed WOW in September 2001 when a new harmonised express product was launched. In September 2000 the Sky Team global alliance announced the creation of a cargo alliance focusing on joint selling of their cargo services in the United States and eventually of harmonised products. Added together, the cargo traffic of each of these alliances exceeds that of Fedex or UPS, even when the latter's domestic freight is included.

Despite early optimism, by 2009 it was not evident that these global alliances had had much success. Establishing genuine cooperation between the partners had proved difficult, as each guarded its own customers too jealously. To be more successful in the long run such cargo alliances still have a number of problems to overcome. They must launch a common portfolio of products with common brand names in all markets; they must integrate their IT systems so they can communicate with each other; they must also develop standard handling processes and harmonised service standards and they need to integrate their sales teams and marketing efforts. Such integration will take time. Only if it succeeds will airlines be able to stand up to the challenge and long-term threat of the integrators and the global logistics suppliers.

Future prospects – an unstable industry?

This is an industry that has systemically failed to earn its cost of capital.

(Glen Tilton, CEO, United Airlines,
May 2009)

This book is about airline economics. It is evident from the preceding chapters that at the micro level the airline industry conforms to many of the rules of economic theory – lower fares generate increased sales; fares tend to be higher when there is a monopoly on a route; larger aircraft exhibit economies of size and tend to have lower unit costs, and so on.

But at the macro or industry-wide level, air transport appears to deviate from one of the basic tenets of economics, namely that after periods of instability when weak and/or loss-making companies leave the market, markets tend towards equilibrium. Equilibrium is when supply of a particular good or service matches demand at prices at which suppliers can make an adequate profit or return on their investment. The term is applied mainly to static models in which case equilibrium will be stable. But in many industries equilibrium may be unstable in the sense that there may be fluctuations in supply and demand around the equilibrium point, but prices will still tend towards ensuring that supply matches demand.

The problem with the airline industry is that, rather than being in a state of stable or even unstable equilibrium it appears to be in chronic disequilibrium. This is because the industry seems to be in a permanent state of over-supply; in other words, of over-capacity. The result is constant long-term downward pressure on fares. Unit costs have been declining too because of technological (Chapter 1, Section 1.4) and operational improvements (Chapter 4, Section 4.5) but the endemic over-supply of seats has tended to push yields down faster than costs. In turn this means that, while some better managed airlines continually generate profits, very many airlines are profitable only spasmodically and the industry as a whole fails, and it has always failed, to 'earn its cost of capital' (Figure 1.1, Chapter 1). Yet it still keeps growing! In periods of crisis as in 2009 there are capacity cut-backs but they tend to be too limited and short term.

The industry's chronic disequilibrium is due primarily to the interplay of two factors. The first is a strong, inherent and, it seems, unstoppable tendency for the provision of too much capacity. The second is that ailing and bankrupt airlines, like elephants, take a long time to die. In fact, unlike elephants, some, no matter how ill, never seem to die.

The strong tendency within the airline industry to over-order new capacity is driven by several factors. First, and perhaps most important, is the ease with which airlines can acquire new aircraft. If airlines need debt finance to purchase aircraft directly they can offer the aircraft as security to their lenders. This is attractive to banks and other financial institutions because aircraft are movable assets that can, in most cases, be readily repossessed and placed elsewhere. When a car factory closes its productive capacity is generally lost. If an airline collapses, its productive capacity, namely its aircraft, soon find themselves flying for other airlines or will provide the basis for the creation of a new airline rising like a phoenix from the ashes of the old one. The latter happened when both Swissair and Sabena collapsed in the winter of 2001–2. Their fleets provided the basis for the launch of a new Swiss Airlines and SN Brussels Airlines. Aircraft financiers may have further security in that loans to buy new aircraft may be guaranteed by one of the export guarantee agencies in one of the manufacturing countries such as the Ex-Im Bank in the USA or COFACE in France. These further reduce the risks to lenders, though they pay a premium for this. In addition, the manufacturers themselves may help at the financing stage by offering loans or guarantees to buy back the aircraft at some future date, if they are no longer required. In June 2009, Airbus announced it would double the amount of vendor financing it would offer in 2009 to about US$ 2.7 billion, compared to 2008, to help overcome a shortage of finance in the markets.

As an alternative to buying aircraft, airlines have the option of acquiring capacity either through an operating lease or a finance lease from one of the many aircraft leasing companies. (Morrell, 2007, for leasing) The two largest, GECAS and ILFC, with hundreds of aircraft on their books, control nearly half the lease market. They and several others buy aircraft in bulk and well in advance and so get favourable terms from the manufacturer. They are then keen to place these with airline customers. The lessors make it easy, even for airlines with weak balance sheets or new-entrant start-ups with only projected balance sheets, to acquire additional capacity. Both lessors and financial institutions lending to airlines have been helped and encouraged by the 2001 'Cape Town Convention on International Interests in Mobile Equipment', which has made repossession of aircraft in the event of default on interest or lease payments very much easier.

To further facilitate debt finance or leasing agreements, many governments have been prepared to guarantee the loans raised or the lease payments when the airlines concerned are partially or fully government owned. This is now no longer permitted within the European Union, but does occur elsewhere. A sovereign guarantee offers the further advantage of reducing the interest rate on loans since it provides additional security. But while the EU does not allow governments to guarantee airline debts, the European export credit agencies, as previously mentioned, do provide guarantees for those financing aircraft sales. In effect these appear to amount to sovereign guarantees since the export credit agencies are themselves government backed.

It is indicative of the ease with which airlines can acquire additional capacity that, in the early and mid-2000s, airlines suffering chronic losses each year, such as Alitalia, Olympic or Sky Europe, were still able to obtain new aircraft. In India, in the period after 2005, new-entrant airlines such as Indigo, SpiceJet, Kingfisher and GoAir, had little difficulty in obtaining aircraft to launch their services or being able in 2007 to place substantial new orders despite not posting any profits. Their lack of profitability has been largely due to the fact that these new entrants together with the established carriers, Indian Airlines and Jet Airways, flooded the market with too much capacity. Though traffic boomed, load factors were too low and yields collapsed.

The second driver of over-capacity is the manufacturers themselves. Their teams of sales executives and analysts produce well-documented fleet plans to show how any particular airline can improve its financial results with a different and often larger fleet. They claim that their new aircraft have certain technical improvements – perhaps lower fuel consumption, longer range, higher payload, and so on – which will enhance their operational and financial performance. Many smaller airlines do not have the in-house resources to seriously question the manufacturers' findings. Some of the additional aircraft proposed may indeed be to replace older and less efficient aircraft; but too often there is pressure to add more aircraft to enlarge an existing fleet or to replace smaller aircraft by larger aircraft, thereby offering substantially more capacity. For example, in the early 2000s, Airbus was pressing South African Airways to order giant Airbus A380s to replace its Boeing 747s on its London routes at a time when the airline had lost hundreds of millions of dollars on currency hedges and was losing money on its London flights in part because the 747s were too large.

The pressures from manufacturers to change or increase airlines' fleets is compounded by their willingness, in many cases, to buy back some of the existing aircraft that an airline owns, even if they are aircraft built by a different manufacturer.

The third driver creating over-capacity in some markets is government policies. Airlines in certain parts of the world and at different times have been pressurised by their respective governments to expand their services and widen their networks in support of national policies to develop incoming tourism or local business activity and trade. Such airlines tend to order or operate many more aircraft than are required in the markets they are serving. This inevitably pushes down fares and cargo yields to the detriment of all airlines serving the same markets. The most recent and vivid example of this is that of the Gulf airlines, Etihad Airways of Abu Dhabi and Qatar Airways, which have been tasked by their governments to match the worldwide network and success of their neighbouring carrier, Emirates. Profitability is seen as a long-term, not short-term objective. Both these airlines have placed huge orders for aircraft, which were more than matched by earlier orders by Emirates, which included 45 Airbus A380s. In 2008 alone, in the midst of a worsening industry crisis, Etihad ordered 96 new aircraft, of which 70 were large twin-aisle jets and six were Airbus A380s. It is hardly surprising, then, that in summer 2009, when US, European and Asian airlines were cutting frequencies and capacity in response to falling demand, weekly seats offered in July 2009 on routes between the Gulf and Europe or the Gulf and Asia were some 17 per cent higher than in July 2008 (IATA, 2009)! This additional capacity would destabilise not only these two markets but was also targeting the Europe–Asia through traffic with a stop in one of the Gulf airports. Inevitably yields in all these markets would be driven down.

Over-capacity is endemic in the airline industry not only because airlines find it relatively easy to acquire additional aircraft and are often pressurised to do so but also because loss-making airlines are slow to exit the market, no matter how large or continuous their losses may be.

Economic theory suggests that in any business, firms making losses and unable to cover their cost of capital will collapse and leave the market to those who can operate successfully. In the case of airlines this process has been distorted by the direct and indirect involvement of governments in aviation. Direct involvement has been through majority or minority shareholdings in major national airlines. Indirect involvement has arisen because most governments see their airlines, even if fully or partially privatised, as national assets generating employment and tourism and providing key communication links. As a result, their survival has to be ensured, and governments will do all they can to bring this about. In the mid-1990s European governments provided around $11 billion in so-called 'state aid' to enable their government-owned airlines to survive the economic downturn at the beginning of the decade and to prepare themselves for subsequent privatisation. Though the European Commission in theory did not allow further 'state aid', airlines such as Alitalia or Olympic, despite heavy annual losses, managed to keep flying with 'hidden' government support until both were privatised in 2009. Around the world, many airlines in financial straits, whether government owned or private, have not been allowed to collapse by their governments. Malaysia Airlines, having been privatised in 1994, was then bought back by the government six years later to save it from collapse. In 2001 Air New Zealand previously privatised and on the verge of collapse was rescued by its government which ended up with an 82 per cent shareholding.

As an alternative to saving collapsing or insolvent airlines themselves, governments will often use heavy political pressure to induce reluctant local companies or investors to take over ailing airlines or resurrect airlines that have collapsed. The Belgian government did this in 2001 after the collapse of Sabena, the Swiss government did this to ensure the creation of the new Swiss Airlines in 2002 and the Italian and Greek airlines used such pressure to ensure the privatisation of Alitalia and Olympic in 2009.

Such is the importance of the airline industry that even governments that are traditionally non-interventionist will try to protect and aid their airlines if they perceive a real threat to their survival. Thus, following the total collapse in travel demand in the United States after the 11 September 2001 terror attacks in New York, the Federal Government introduced the Air Transportation Safety and System Stabilisation Act. This set up a Board with funds to compensate airlines for the losses suffered as a result of the drop in demand and the extra security costs subsequently required. Just over $4.6 billion was paid out with some of the largest airlines receiving several hundred million dollars.

The United States, Canada and a few other countries have bankruptcy laws that allow companies on the verge of collapse to seek protection from creditors while they try to restructure their operations and finances. While not specifically aimed at airlines, such laws, particularly in North America, have enabled carriers such as Air Canada to survive. During the 2000s several US airlines filed for protection under Chapter 11 of the US bankruptcy code. US Airways, which went into and out of Chapter 11 twice, United Airlines, which was in protection for three years from December 2002, and Delta and Northwest, who filed for protection later, all survived because they were able under Chapter 11 rules to renegotiate labour agreements, leases, supplier contracts, and so on, while also restructuring their finances. In earlier decades not all airlines that went into Chapter 11 survived. But some of the world's largest airlines in the 2000s managed to keep flying by using Chapter 11 when economic theory would have expected them to exit the market. They did not die.

When the airline industry is doing well, airline executives believing that the good times will continue are desperate to ensure that they do not lose future profits by not having enough aircraft. The manufacturers' long lead times for deliveries create pressure on executives to get their orders in early and to over-order in case future demand is even better than anticipated. They tend to forget that the airline industry like the world economy tends to be cyclical. Repeatedly over the last 40 years, aircraft ordered during the boom years are scheduled for delivery during the following downturn when they are least needed.

The 2000s epitomise this underlying malaise. The early years were characterised by slow growth rates in demand because of the economic downturn which started in 2000 and which was then followed by a number of external shocks such as the attacks on the twin towers in New York in 2001, the Iraq war, SARS and so on. Then in 2004 passenger traffic boomed, growing by 15 per cent worldwide and in the following years to 2007 annual growth averaged almost 8 per cent. But as discussed in the opening chapter rapid growth in demand did not ensure high profits (Figure 1.1, Chapter 1).

High growth rates in the mid-2000s and improving financial returns induced airline executives to place huge orders for new aircraft. After 2004 deliveries accelerated. In 2005, 431 jets were delivered to IATA member airlines. In 2006 deliveries were 525 and the following year 550. In 2008, 683 jet aircraft were due to be delivered (IATA, 2008a). Though some of these would replace aircraft due to be retired, there would be a significant jump in capacity in the four years to 2013.

At the beginning of 2009 the order backlog for all jet aircraft manufacturers was close to 5,000 aircraft. Many of these were due for delivery in 2009 and 2010 at the bottom of the economic cycle. At a time when most airlines were desperately trying to cut flights and capacity, in an effort to hold or push up yields, they were having to accept new aircraft deliveries. Many tried to defer or even cancel deliveries, but with only limited success. They were locked in by their contracts with the manufacturers, which normally included substantial pre-delivery payments which they would lose if orders were cancelled. The only solutions were to ground aircraft or fly them less or terminate lease contracts early, all very costly.

In mid-2009, there was considerable uncertainty about the depth and length of the worldwide economic downturn. Would it be V-shaped with economies, trade and travel recovering almost as quickly as they had declined? Or would the downturn be U-shaped, with a longer delay before recovery commenced? Whatever the outcome, there was an expectation that the airline industry as a whole would return to profit in 2010 or 2011 especially if fuel prices stayed at the manageable levels of early 2009. Those airlines which were most successful in cutting capacity during this period would emerge in the better financial health. But many would continue making losses into 2010 and beyond.

While the industry as a whole might return to profit in 2010 or 2011, profit margins in these and subsequent years were likely to be low and would be insufficient to cover the airlines' cost of capital. Inadequate profitability will continue to be inherent in the airline industry because of the ease with which airlines can continue to add additional capacity and because of the failure of many loss-making airlines to exit the market quickly. The airline industry seems set to continue flying off course.

Appendix
Freedoms of the air

Negotiated in bilateral air services agreements

First freedom   The right to fly over another country without landing.

Second freedom   The right to make a landing for technical reasons (e.g. refuelling) in another country without picking up/setting down revenue traffic.

Third freedom   The right to carry revenue traffic from your own country (A) to the country (B) of your treaty partner.

Fourth freedom   The right to carry traffic from country B back to your own country A.

Fifth freedom   The right of an airline from country A to carry revenue traffic between country B and other countries such as C or D on services starting or ending in its home country A. (This freedom cannot be used unless countries C or D also agree.)

Supplementary rights

Sixth freedom   The use by an airline of country A of two sets of third and fourth freedom rights to carry traffic between two other countries but using its base at A as a transit point.

Seventh freedom   The right of an airline to carry revenue traffic between points in two countries on services which lie entirely outside its own home country.

Eighth freedom (or cabotage rights)   The right for an airline to pick up and set down passengers or freight between two domestic points in another country on a service originating in its own home country.

Sixth freedom rights are rarely dealt with explicitly in air services agreements but may be referred to implicitly in memoranda of understanding attached to the agreement. In the application of many bilaterals there is also de facto acceptance of such rights.

Seventh and eighth freedom rights are only granted in very rare cases. But in the 1991 US–UK bilateral the US granted UK airlines seventh freedom rights from several European states to the USA. They have never been used.

Glossary of common air transport terms

Aircraft kilometres are the distances flown by aircraft. An aircraft's total flying is obtained my multiplying the number of flights performed on each flight stage by the stage distance.

Aircraft productivity is calculated by multiplying an aircraft's average block speed by its maximum payload in tonnes to arrive at the tonne-kms per hour. Or, one multiplies block speed by seat capacity to produce seat-kms per hour.

Aircraft utilisation is the average number of block hours that each aircraft is in use. This is generally measured on a daily or annual basis.

Available seat kilometres (ASKs) are obtained by multiplying the number of seats available for sale on each flight by the stage distance flown.

Available tonne kilometres (ATKs) are obtained by multiplying the number of tonnes of capacity available for carriage of passengers and cargo on each sector of a flight by the stage distance.

Average aircraft capacity is obtained by dividing an airline's total available tonne kilometres (ATKs) by aircraft kilometres flown.

Average stage length is obtained by dividing an airline's total aircraft kilometres flown in a year by number of aircraft departures; it is the weighted average of stage/sector lengths flown by an airline.

Block time (hours) is the time for each flight stage or sector, measured from when the aircraft leaves the airport gate or stand (chocks off) to when it arrives on the gate or stand at the destination airport (chocks on). It can also be calculated from the moment an aircraft moves under its own power until it comes to rest at its destination.

Break-even load factor (per cent) is the load factor required at a given average fare or yield to generate total revenue which equals operating costs. Can be calculated for a flight or a series of flights.

Break of gauge is used in air services agreements to allow an airline, which has traffic rights from its own country (A) to country (B) and then fifth freedom rights onto country C, to operate one type of aircraft from A to B and then a different type (usually smaller) from B to C and beyond. This normally involves basing aircraft and crews in country B. United Airlines and American operated such break of gauge flights from London to European points until the mid-1990s.

Cabin crew refers to stewards and stewardesses.

Code sharing is when two or more airlines each use their own flight codes or share a common code on flights operated by one of them.

Combination carrier is an airline that transports both passengers and cargo, usually on the same aircraft.

Flight or cockpit crew refers to the pilot, co-pilot and flight engineer (if any).

Franchising involves an agreement between a large airline (the franchisor) and a smaller airline (franchisee) under which the latter operates a number of or all its services on behalf of the franchisor, usually with the latter's aircraft colour scheme, uniforms and product features.

Freight tonne kilometres (FTKs) are obtained by multiplying the tonnes of freight uplifted by the sector distances over which they have been flown. They are a measure of an airline's cargo traffic.

Freight yields are obtained by dividing total revenue from scheduled freight by the freight tonne kilometres (FTKs) produced (often expressed in US cents per FTK).

Grandfather rights is the convention by which airlines retain the right to use a particular take-off and landing slot times at an airport because they have done so previously, and continuously.

Integrators are air freight companies offering door-to-door express and small shipment services including surface collection and delivery. Fedex, DHL and UPS are the largest.

Interlining is the acceptance by one airline of travel documents issued by another airline for carriage on the services of the first airline. An interline passenger is one using a through fare for a journey involving two or more separate airlines.

Online passenger is one who transfers from one flight to another but on the same airline.

Operating costs per ATK is a measure obtained by dividing total operating costs by total ATKs. Operating costs exclude interest payments, taxes and extraordinary items. They can also be measured per RTK.

Operating ratio (per cent) is the operating revenue expressed as a percentage of operating costs. Sometimes referred to as the revex ratio.

Passenger kilometres or **Revenue passenger kilometres (RPKs)** are obtained by multiplying the number of fare-paying passengers on each flight stage by flight stage distance. They are a measure of an airline's passenger traffic.

Passenger load factor (per cent) is passenger-kilometres (RPKs) expressed as a percentage of available seat kilometres (ASKs) (on a single sector, this is simplified to the number of passengers carried as a percentage of seats available for sale).

Revenue tonne kilometres (RTKs) measure the output actually sold. They are obtained by multiplying the total number of tonnes of passengers and cargo carried on each flight stage by flight stage distance. (Revenue passenger kms are normally converted to revenue tonne-kms on a standard basis of 90 kg average weight, including free and excess baggage, although this has been increased recently by some airlines, e.g. British Airways have increased the average weight from 90 kg to 95 kg, as a result of a CAA directive.)

Scheduled passenger yields is the average revenue per passenger kilometre and is obtained by dividing the total passenger revenue by the total passenger kilometres. This can be done by flight route or for the network.

Seat factor or passenger load factor on a single sector is obtained by expressing the passengers carried as a percentage of the seats available for sale; on a network of routes it is obtained by expressing the total passenger-kms (RPKs) as a percentage of the total seat-kms available (ASKs).

Seat pitch is the standard way of measuring seat density on an aircraft. It is the distance between the back of one seat and the same point on the back of the seat in front.

Slot at an airport is the right to operate one take-off or landing at that airport within a fixed time period.

Stage or sector distance should be the air route or flying distance between two airports. In practice many airlines use the great circle distance which is shorter.

Transfer passenger is one who changes planes en-route at an intermediate airport.

Transit passenger is one who continues on the same aircraft after an intermediate stop on a multi-sector flight.

Weight load factor measures the proportion of available capacity actually sold. It is the revenue tonne kilometres performed expressed as a percentage of available tonne kilometres (also called overall load factor).

Wet lease usually involves the leasing of aircraft with flight crews, and possibly cabin crews and maintenance support as well. A dry lease involves just the aircraft without any additional support.

Wide-bodied aircraft are civil aircraft which have two passenger aisles (Boeing 767); narrow-bodied aircraft, such as the Airbus A320, have only one aisle.

Yield is the average revenue collected per passenger-kilometre or tonne-km of freight carried. Passenger yield is calculated by dividing the total passenger revenue on a flight by the passenger-kilometres generated by that flight. It is a measure of the weighted average fare paid.

Bibliography

AEA (1996) *Medium-Term Forecast of European Scheduled Passenger Traffic, 1996–2000,* July, Brussels: Association of European Airlines.
—— (2007) *Yearbook 2006,* Brussels: Association of European Airlines.
—— (2008) *Summary of Traffic and Airline Results,* December, Brussels: Association of European Airlines.
Airbus (2008) *Global Market Forecast 2007–2026,* July, Blagnac, France: Airbus Industrie.
Airline Monitor (2008) *Airline Monitor,* August 2008, Ponte Vedra Beach, FL: ESG Aviation Services.
—— (2009) *Airline Monitor,* March–April 2009, Ponte Vedra Beach, FL: ESG Aviation Services.
Arnoult, Sandra (2008) Building a Brand, June, *Air Transport World.*
ATA (1990) *Air Travel Survey 1989,* Washington, DC: Air Transport Association of America.
BAA (1978) *Long Term Airport Traffic Forecasting,* London: British Airports Authority.
Belobaba, P. and Wilson, J. (1997) Impact of yield management in competitive airline markets, *Journal of Air Transport Management,* Vol. 3, No. 1.
Bruggisser, Philippe (1997) Controlling costs, Third International Airline Conference, February, London: UBS.
CAA (1977) *European Air Fares: A Discussion Document,* CAP 409, London: Civil Aviation Authority.
—— (1989) *Traffic Distribution Policy for the London Area and Strategic Options for the Long Term,* CAP 548, London: Civil Aviation Authority.
—— (2000a) *UK Airports. Annual Statements of Movements, Passengers and Cargo, 1999,* CAP 705, May 2000, London: Civil Aviation Authority.
—— (2000b) *The Air Navigation Order, 2000,* London: Civil Aviation Authority.
—— 2000(c) *1999 UK Airport Survey Report, Gatwick–Heathrow–Manchester,* Ref. C-99, London: Civil Aviation Authority.
—— (2005) *Demand for Outbound Leisure Air Travel and its Key Drivers,* December, London: Civil Aviation Authority.
—— (2006) *No-Frills Carriers: Revolution or Evolution,* CAP 770, Annex, November, London: Civil Aviation Authority.
—— (2007) *CAA Passenger Survey Report 2006,* London, Civil Aviation Authority.
—— (2008) *Recent Trends in Growth of UK Air Passenger Demand,* January, London: Civil Aviation Authority.
—— (2009a) *UK Airline Statistics – 2008,* April, London: Civil Aviation Authority.
—— (2009b) *UK Airport Statistics – 2008,* April, London: Civil Aviation Authority.
CAB (1975) *Report of the CAB Special Staff on Regulatory Reform,* Washington, DC: Civil Aeronautics Board.
Carey, H. (1858) *Principles of Social Science,* Vol. 1, pp. 41–3, Philadelphia.
CEC (1983) *Council Directive Concerning the Authorisation of Scheduled Inter-Regional Air Services Between Member States,* Brussels: Commission of the European Communities.

—— (1984) *Civil Aviation Memorandum No. 2 Progress towards the Development of a Community Air Transport Policy*, COM (84) 72 Final, Brussels: Commission of the European Communities.

—— (1987a) Council Directive of 14 December 1987 on Fares for Scheduled Air Services between Member States, 87/601/EEC, Council Decision of 14 December 1987 on the sharing of passenger capacity on scheduled air services between Member States, 87/602/EEC, Brussels: Commission of the European Communities.

—— (1987b) Council Regulations (EEC) No. 3975/87 and No. 3976/87 of 14 December 1987 on the application of rules of competition in the air transport sector, Brussels: Commission of the European Communities.

—— (1988) Commission Regulation (EEC) No. 2671/88 of July 1988, Official Journal, 24 August, Brussels: Commission of the European Communities.

—— (1992a) Commission Regulation (EEC) No. 2407/92, on licensing of air carriers, Official Journal, 24 August, Brussels: Commission of the European Communities.

—— (1992b) Commission Regulation (EEC) No. 2408/92, on access for community air carriers to intra community air routes, Official Journal, 24 August, Brussels: Commission of the European Communities.

—— (1992c) Commission Regulation (EEC) No. 2409/92, on fares and rates for air services, Official Journal, 24 August, Brussels: Commission of the European Communities.

Clark, Paul (2007) *Flying the Big Jets. Fleet Planning for Airlines,* second edition, Aldershot: Ashgate.

D'Arcy Harvey (1951) Airline passenger traffic pattern within the United States, *Journal of Air Law and Commerce.*

Dempsey, Paul S. (1999) Predation in the air. Competition and antitrust law in commercial aviation. First International Air Law and Insurance Forum, London: IIR, December.

Dennis, Nigel (1990) Hubbing as a marketing tool. Air Transport Executive Seminar, November, London: University of Westminster.

—— (2001) The impact of airline industry changes on airports, Airport Economics and Finance Symposium, March 2001, College of Aeronautics, Cranfield University, UK.

Doganis, R. (1966) Traffic forecasting and the gravity model, 29 September, *Flight International.*

—— (1992) *Flying off Course,* second edition, London: Routledge.

—— (1992) *The Airport Business*, London: Routledge.

—— (1999) *The Import and Impact of the Express Industry in Europe* (jointly with Aviation and Travel Consultancy Ltd. and York Consulting Group), Brussels: Association of European Express Carriers and European Express Organisation.

—— (2006) *The Airline Business*, London: Routledge.

DoT (1978) *United Kingdom Air Traffic Forecasting. Research and Revised Forecasts*, London: Department of Trade.

—— (1981) *Report of the Air Traffic Forecasting Working Party 1981*, London: Department of Trade.

—— (1990) *Secretary's Task Force on Competition in the US Domestic Airline Industry,* Washington, DC: Department of Transportation.

—— (1998) *Request for Comments in Docket OST-98-3717*, 6 April, Washington: Department of Transportation.

—— (2000) *Air Traffic Forecasts for the United Kingdom*, London: Department of Transport.

—— (2007) *Final Order: International Air Transport Association Tariff Conference Proceeding*, 30 March, Washington, DC: Department of Transportation, Order 2007.3.23.

Douglas (1989) *World Economic and Traffic Outlook 1989–2010*, Long Beach, CA: Douglas Aircraft Company.

easyJet (2008) *We are turning Europe Orange*, Annual Report and Accounts 2007, February, London.

Eggert, Anselm (1999) Calculating the economic advantages of hubbing, Hub Connection Strategy, IIR Conference, October, London: IIR.

Gallagher, Brendan (2001) BA confidently rides the web wave, Airline E-commerce Supplement, Summer 2001, Air Transport World.

Gemkow, Stephan (2007) Fundamentals matter! September, London: UBS Transport Conference.

Gillen, David, Morrison, William and Stewart, Christopher (2003) *Air Travel Demand Elasticities: Concepts, Issues and Measurement*, Ottawa: Department of Finance, Government of Canada.

Graham, Anne (2000) Demand for leisure air travel and limits to growth, *Journal of Air Transport Management*, Vol, 6, No. 2, April 2000.

Hanlon, P. (2006) *Global Airlines, Competition in a Transnational Industry*, Oxford: Butterworth Heinemann.

HMSO (1956) *Multilateral Agreement on Commercial Rights of Non-Scheduled Air Services in Europe*, Cmnd 1099, London: Her Majesty's Stationery Office.

—— (1969) *British Air Transport in the Seventies,* Report of the Committee of Inquiry into Civil Air Transport, London: Her Majesty's Stationery Office.

IATA (1974) *Agreeing Fares and Rates. A Survey of the Methods and Procedures Used by the Member Airlines of IATA*, Geneva: International Air Transport Association.

—— (2006a) *Profitability: Does Size Matter?* Economics Briefing, June, Geneva: International Air Transport Association.

—— (2006b) *Airline Cost Performance*, Economics Briefing No. 5, July, Geneva: International Air Transport Association.

—— (2007) *Airline Cost Performance*, Economics Briefing, March, Geneva: International Air Transport Association.

—— (2008a) *World Air Transport Statistics*, fifty-second edition, June 2008, Geneva: International Air Transport Association.

—— (2008b) *Air Travel Demand*, Economics Briefing No. 9, April, Geneva: International Air Transport Association.

—— (2008c) *Corporate Air Travel Survey (CATS) 2008*, Geneva: International Air Transport Association.

—— (2009) *Monthly Traffic Analysis*, August, Geneva: International Air Transport Association.

ICAO (1980) *Convention on International Civil Aviation*, sixth edition, Doc. 7300/6, Montreal: International Civil Aviation Organisation.

—— (1988) *Survey of international air transport fares and rates, September 1987*, Circular 208-AT/82, Montreal: International Civil Aviation Organisation.

—— (1990) *The Economic Situation of Air Transport, Review and Outlook, 1978 to 2000*, Circular 222-AT/90, Montreal: International Civil Aviation Organisation.

—— (1997) *Outlook for Air Transport to the Year 2005*, Circular 270, Montreal: International Civil Aviation Organisation.

—— (1999) *Safety Oversight Manual*, Doc. 9734-AN/959, Montreal: International Civil Aviation Organisation.

—— (2009) *Financial Data 2007*, Montreal: International Civil Aviation Organisation.

Johnson, Titus (2007) Air Berlin case study, The Future of Air Transport Conference, December, London: Institute of Economics Affairs.

Jones, Lois (2005) *easyJet: The Story of Britain's Biggest Low-Cost Airline*, London: Aurum Press.

Kellner, Larry (2000) Building a global airline brand, 2000 Transport Conference, London: UBS Warburg.

Kley, Karl-Ludwig (2000) Will quality differentiate in a changing industry? 2000 Transport Conference, London: UBS Warburg.

Kraus, M. (1999) Time definitive services. The shift of paradigm for cargo airlines, *The Tenth World Express and Mail Conference*, May, Brussels.

Lansing, John B. and Blood, Dweight M. (1964) *The Changing Travel Market*, Ann Arbor, MI: Survey Research Center, University of Michigan.

Lill (1889) 'Die Grundgesetze des Personenwerkehrs', *Zeitschrift für Eisenbahnen und Dampfschiffsfahrt der Osterreichischungarischen Monarchie*, Vienna, No. 35–6.

Lobbenberg, A (2001) Strategic Alliances, Air Transport Executive Seminar, Cranfield College of Aeronautics (unpublished).

Maiden, S. (1995) *Heathrow Terminal 5: Proof of Evidence Forecasting*, BAA, 31 April, London: BAA PLC.

Maldutis, J. and Musante, R. M. (1995) *Airline Competition at the 50 largest US airports – update,* New York: May 1995, Salomon Brothers.

MergeGlobal (2008a) Forwarder momentum, March, *American Shipper*.

—— (2008b) End of an era, August, *American Shipper*.

Morrell, Peter (2007) *Airline Finance*, third edition, Aldershot: Ashgate.

Nguyen Dai, Hai (1982) The box Jenkins approach, *ITA Bulletin*, September, Paris: Institut du Transport Aérien.

Nuutinen, Heini (2008) Southwest: Low-cost Pioneer, Aviation Strategy, no. 124, January/February 2008, London.

OAG (2000) *Business Travel Lifestyle Survey 1999,* Dunstable: OAG Worldwide.

OJ (2006) Official Journal of the European Communities No. L272, 3 October.

ONS (2007) *Travel Trends. A Report on the 2006 International Passenger Survey*, Office of National Statistics, London: HMSO.

Parker-Eaton, R (2000) The challenge to charter, ENG Conference. Accelerating Performance Growth of the Low-cost Segment. November, Amsterdam.

Pearson, Roy (1977) Establishing a methodology for measuring airline efficiency, unpublished PhD thesis, University of Westminster, London.

Pilling, Mark (2001) Flights of Fancy, *Airline Business* Presidential Documents (1978) *Weekly Compilation of Presidential Documents*, Vol. 14, No. 34, 2 August, Washington, DC.

Reid, Samuel R. and Mohrfeld, James W. (1973) Airline size, profitability, mergers and regulation, *Journal of Air Law and Commerce*, Vol. 39.

Richmond, S. B. (1971) *Regulation and Competition in Air Transport*, New York: Columbia University Press.

SIA (2007) *Annual Report 2006–7*, May 2007, Singapore: Singapore Airlines.

—— (2008) *Annual Report 2007–8*, May 2008, Singapore: Singapore Airlines.

—— (2009) *Annual Report 2008–9*, May 2009, Singapore: Singapore Airlines.

SITA (2008) *Airline IT Trends Survey*, Sutton, UK: SITA and Airline Business.

Sletmo, G. K. (1972) *Demand for Air Cargo. An Econometric Approach*, Bergen: Institute for Shipping Research. Norwegian School of Economics and Business Administration.

Smyth, Mark (2006) Low cost is necessary; will it be sufficient? Future of Air Transport Conference, November, London.

Solomko, Stanislav (2009) Forecasting demand in underserved markets, Marketing and Market Research in Air Transport, University of Westminster, February, London.

Tae Hoon Oum and Chunyan Yu (1995) A productivity comparison of the world's major airlines, *Journal of Air Transport Management*, Vol. 2 Nos. 3–4, pp. 181–95.

Taneja, N. K. (1978) *Airline Traffic Forecasting*, Lexington, MA: Lexington Books.

UBS (2007) *European Low-cost Airlines*, September, London: UBS Investment Research.

University of Westminster (1989) *Air Transport and the Southern Regions of the Community. Vol. IV. Route Forecasts,* London: Transport Studies Group, University of Westminster.

Vasigh, Bijan, Fleming, Ken and Tacker, Thomas (2008) *Introduction to Air Transport Economics*, Aldershot: Ashgate.

Veldhuis, X. (1988) Forecasting process at Amsterdam Airport Schiphol, IATA Worldwide Forecasting Conference 1988–92, Geneva: International Air Transport Association.

Which (2008) *Best Airline Survey*, June, London: Consumer Association.

Zumwinkel, K. (2001) Challenges for the future of the transportation industry, UBS Warburg Sixth Annual Transportation Conference, October, London.

Index

Note: numbers in **bold** refer to figures (diagrams) and numbers in *italics* refer to tables.